LUTHER'S PROGRESS
to the
DIET OF WORMS
1521

LUTHER'S PROGRESS
to the
DIET OF WORMS
1521

by
GORDON RUPP

SCM PRESS LTD
56 Bloomsbury Street, London WC1

TO
MY WIFE

First published 1951

Printed and bound in Great Britain by
Tonbridge Printers Limited
Peach Hall Works, Tonbridge, Kent

CONTENTS

INTRODUCTION

WHO WAS MARTIN LUTHER? What was he really like? If we had met him, what would have been our personal impression? Should we have said, 'Ah, yes, a very great man! Did you notice those eyes?' Or should we have murmured, 'After all, a very disappointing fellow!'? Not all our historical investigation can bring us there. When the last word has been written, we shall see Luther through a glass darkly, and what we behold will lack something which in the days of his too, too solid flesh was perceptible by some unlettered oaf who gaped at him in the streets of Wittenberg, or by some child who stared back at him along the lanes of Worms. But we cannot summon Luther from the vasty deep (or the Elysian fields) as those other alumni of Wittenberg, Prince Hamlet and Dr. Faustus, were enabled to view the dead. Nevertheless, we need not surrender to scepticism, we may pursue with good heart the search for the historical Luther.

Curiosity seems a vulgar motive for writing history, if not for reading it, yet this essay results from an attempt to find a personally satisfying answer to the question, 'Who was Martin Luther?' I have tried to concentrate on a positive presentation. One learns that the most elderly and grubby libels continue to circulate long after they have been met at the exact level of scholarship, and there is comfort in the knowledge that Luther is beyond gunshot of them all. I have not tried to impress or convert those to whom Luther must always be the Enemy (resembling Mussolini in the famous cartoon, 'The Man who Took the Lid Off!') Sooner or later even polemical publicists will tire of re-hashing Denifle and Grisar, and will turn to the sobrieties of modern Catholic scholars like Kiefl, Joseph Lortz and Dr. Hessen-Köln.

The great discoveries and most exciting monographs of the last thirty years of Luther studies have concentrated on 'The Young Luther', and it is here that for English readers the tale must be told anew. The older English material is still of value: J. A. Froude, T. M. Lindsay, Charles Beard knew how to write and are still to be profitably studied. But much has been written even since the publication of Dr. Mackinnon's four volumes, and we are now better placed to understand Luther's theology, in the context of the ecumenical conversation and of Biblical theology. Whatever the truth about Luther, it will never be found by those who by-pass his theology, though the theologians may deserve also a reminder of the importance of that historical context without which the theological development is but half explained.

The truth about one of the greatest Germans may be of value for the healing of the nations. The truth about the greatest Lutheran must concern the mending of the Church. There is a Luther about whom the Germans and the Lutherans have most right to speak. That does not absolve the rest of us from trying to understand him too. I hope this little book may persuade some to adventure the intricate but richly rewarding field of Luther studies. Getting books from Germany in these post-war days is a highly skilled mystery, and I am grateful to Professors Iwand, Ernst Wolf and H. Bornkamm for the loan of books, to Dr. Wunderlich of the Methodist Seminary in Frankfurt, and to Horst Flachsmeier for seeking volumes otherwise inaccessible. Nearer home, I have to thank Dr. R. N. Flew, Dr. Williams' Library, and the unfailing courtesy and helpfulness of the London Library. A short sketch must beg many questions, but I hope to deal with some of them in more extended studies to be published later.

GORDON RUPP

Richmond College
Surrey
All Saints' Eve, 1949

ABBREVIATIONS

The following abbreviations are used throughout:—

WA	*Works of Luther* (Weimarer Ausgabe).
WA Br	*Letters of Luther* (Weimarer Ausgabe. Briefwechsel).
TR	*Table Talk* (Weimarer Ausgabe. Tischreden).
WML	*Works of Luther* (Philadelphia Edition).

CHAPTER ONE

YOUNG LUTHER

'. . . the man put his fingers in his ears, and ran on crying Life! Life! Eternal Life! So he looked not behind him, but fled towards the middle of the Plain.'

'I WAS BORN at Eisleben, and baptized in St. Peter's there. I do not remember this, but I believe my parents and fellow countrymen.'[1] Thus, with characteristic irony, Luther described his origin. He was born November 10th, 1483, to Hans and Margaret (*née* Lindemann)[2] Luther. If the portraits of Cranach are reliable, Martin grew to resemble his father in frame, his mother in eyes and mouth. His parents came from Mohra, on the edge of the Thuringian forest, and he described himself as a 'tough Saxon' of peasant stock.[3] There was always something of the peasant about him, and the texture of his mind was of a plain, honest grain. He could sum up an Italian diplomat as shrewdly as his kinsmen a huckster at the fair, and he had a peasant mixture of common sense and credulity. If he could be vulgar, he had none of the obscenities of the politely learned. Of avarice, in a venal age, he had not the faintest trace.

Hans Luther had ideas of his own, or maybe he was forced to leave Möhra by the pressure of laws of inheritance which, in that fairytale land of towers and gables, seemed most concerned to reward the youngest son. He moved to Eisleben and thence to Mansfeld, to work in the copper mines where it was hard, but the industry was thriving and there were hopes of getting a degree of independence.[4] He hewed to such effect that he was soon able to rent several furnaces, and in 1491 was numbered among the councillors of the little town. (His brother, also Hans

[1] WA Br.1.610.18 (January 14th, 1520).

[2] Boehmer, *Der Junge Luther* (ed. Bornkamm) 1939, p. 358. We cite from this, and from the American translation, *Road to Reformation*, Philadelphia 1946.

[3] TR 5.255.10. 5.558.13. Other references, WA 58.i.2 ff.

[4] W. Andreas, *Deutschland vor der Reformation*, Stuttgart 1948, p. 322.

Luther, was well known to the Bench in a less reputable connection.)

The whole of Luther's life was spent in Saxony, in the triangle of a few thousand square miles, now within the Russian Zone. Saxony was ruled by the House of Wettin, and at the end of the fifteenth century had been divided into Electoral and Ducal Saxony. It sounds simple, but in fact it is symptomatic of the territorial disintegration into which Germany had fallen and which has bedevilled all its subsequent history, the division of jurisdiction between innumerable authorities, 'all the more bewildering that most of them appeared to be composed of patches lying separate from each other. Almost every ruling prince had to cross some neighbour's land to visit the outlying portions of his dominions'.[1]

There are a few anecdotes about Luther's childhood, and they seem fairly reliable. That Margaret Luther might be seen bowed under the weight of the wood she was dragging home from the forest, no more argues extreme poverty than the similar sights to be seen round Berlin in 1947, though both remind us that life in the sixteenth century was nearer the edge of things, to the elemental facts of hunger, thirst, pain and death, than we can easily imagine.

If Luther's recollections of childhood are sombre, it is perhaps because the young have long memories for injustice: if he never forgot that his mother thrashed him until he bled, for taking a nut, and if at school he got fifteen of the best for muddling a declension he had never been told to learn, there have been overstrained mothers and badly trained teachers in other times, and the sixteenth century had its own stern ideas about discipline. Apart from these, and the glimpse of a very small Martin Luther swaying joyously on the shoulders of his big friend, Nicholas Oemler, as he was carried to school, we have to imagine the world of sunshine and shrill laughter and shouting companionship which, we must believe, existed also.[2]

At seven he was sent to the Latin school at Mansfeld, and at fourteen to the city of Magdeburg, perhaps to the Choir School, certainly to receive instruction from the famous fraternity of the

[1] A. D. Lindsay, *History of the Reformation*, 1906, p. 35.

[2] O. Scheel, *M. Luther*, Tübingen 1921, i, p. 32.

Common Life.[1] He made his first acquaintance with the bustle of an ecclesiastical city, and an indelible impression was made upon him by the sight of Prince William of Anhalt-Zerbst, who had turned Franciscan and could be seen with his sack, gaunt, intense, emaciated, 'so that he looked like a dead man, sheer skin and bone',[2] as he begged through the streets. After a year, Luther went to Eisenach where he had kin and where he made new friends, including Johann Braun, Vicar of St. Mary's. At Eisenach and Magdeburg he went on frequent carol-singing expeditions, one of the milder forms of adolescent intimidation, and long afterwards he loved to tell how he and his friends ran as a door opened and a loud voice roared gruffly, 'Where are you, you young ruffians?'—to return shamefaced when it became plain that the owner of the voice was offering them some sausage! The terrifying figure, half seen against the surrounding dark, whose voice of wrath was a mask for kindness, became for Luther a parable which summed up a deal of his theology.[3]

Hans Luther and his wife must have pondered the problem of what to do with their gifted son, and the direction of their thought can be inferred from the fact that in April, 1501, 'Martinus Ludher ex Mansfeld' matriculated in the faculty of Arts, at the University of Erfurt. Erfurt was a renowned university, one of the oldest (1397) and best attended in Germany, and early known as a centre of international study (*studium generale*).[4] At this time its faculty of Law was notable, and Martin may have gone there rather than to Leipzig because he was destined for the Law. Though in Saxony, Erfurt came under the jurisdiction of the Archbishop of Mainz. A fair city, of perhaps 30,000 inhabitants, well known for its gardens and gardeners,[5] if its morals left a good deal to be desired, and if relations between town and gown were in constant tension, the same could be said of a good many other university towns.

Luther had bed and board at the student hostel of St. George, and he made friends, talked a good deal (they nicknamed him 'the philosopher') and learned to play the lute. He took the usual

[1] Scheel, i, p. 67; Mackinnon, *Luther*, 1925, i, p. 14; W. J. Kooiman, *Maarten Luther*, Amsterdam 1948, p. 11 ff.

[2] WA 38.105.

[3] WA 58.i.3 for many references.

[4] Rashdall, *Mediæval Universities*, 1936, i, p. 7; iii, p. 334.

[5] Andreas, *Deutschland vor der Reformation*, p. 342.

Arts course and proceeded to the Bachelor's degree in 1502.[1] The so-called *trivium* (grammar, logic and rhetoric) may have become arid, but to learn that words have precise meanings, that their right assembly is important and that clear expression determines intelligibility, these 'lost tools of learning' would seem a basis for liberal education for lack of which a good many modern substitutes have gone awry.[2]

Erfurt was a citadel of the latest form of mediæval philosophy, that of the 'modern way' (*via moderna*), the Nominalists. In its late mediæval form it had been launched by William of Occam (1300?–1349) as a rigorous critical antidote to the age of synthesis which had found its thirteenth-century norm in St. Thomas Aquinas.[3] The Nominalist teachers at Erfurt were Jodocus Trutvetter and Bartholomew Arnoldi of Usingen, and under them Luther studied the *quadrivium* (geometry, mathematics, music, astronomy) and the natural, metaphysical and moral philosophy of Aristotle. At the age of twenty-two Luther took his M.A., placed second among seventeen candidates. In an age when only a small proportion of those who went up proceeded as far as the Master's degree, Luther had done all that his parents could have hoped.

For a youth in his position, having respect to the resources and station of his parents, there were two possibilities—lawyer or parson? It may be that the sturdy anti-clericalism which Hans Luther shared with many of his class and age was decisive. Hans Luther paid for a new copy of the *Corpus Juris* and Martin was entered in the faculty of Law. He might one day make a name for himself in Saxony as public notary of Eisleben or Eisenach, or he might achieve the dignity of an official at the court of the Elector Frederick. Then, to crown all, he might win the hand of a mayor's daughter, or the young widow of a merchant of standing![4] Such elevated hopes, we may suppose, were in his father's heart. It might very easily have fallen out

[1] Scheel, i, pp. 170–215; Mackinnon, i, pp. 17–27.

[2] D. L. Sayers, *The Lost Tools of Learning*, 1948.

[3] Nominalism began in the age of Abelard (twelfth century). The *via moderna* was concerned with more than the problem of the nature of Universals. M. H. Carré. Realists and Nominalists. *Dict. Théol. Cath.*, xi, articles 'Nominalisme', 'Occam' (P. Vignaux).

[4] WA 8 (*De Votis Monasticis*, 1521) 573.24. 'You planned for me a respectable and wealthy marriage.'

that way, and if it had, the name of Martin Luther might have been known to history from the recondite archives of a little German town. Suddenly all these thoughts were thrown into confusion. To his dismay, mortification and rage, Hans Luther learned that the son for whom he hoped so much, who had but recently been home, talking eagerly about his music and his literary friends, had decided to enter religion and was seeking admission to the monastery of the Austin Friars in Erfurt.

What underlay this fateful decision, so sudden and unexpected that Luther did not inform his father until it had been made?[1]

The evidence is confused, and when we consider that Luther's close friends, Melanchthon and Justas Jonas gave different and irreconcilable versions of the story,[2] we may suspect a reticence on Luther's part which does not exactly tally with the stories in the *Table Talk*.

There are two pieces of primary and authentic evidence. The first is a letter to Luther (October 31st, 1519) from his former fellow student Crotus Rubeanus, now a humanist of high repute, a letter written in the flowery rhetoric of the humanist circle:

> Go on, as you have begun! Leave an example to posterity. For you do this not without the divine power. For divine providence had an eye to this when, returning from your parents, celestial lightning flung you to the ground, like another Paul, before the town of Erfurt, and compelled your most doleful severance from our company, within the Augustinian walls.[3]

The other statement is from Luther, in the open letter to his father which prefaced the tract *Concerning Monastic Vows* (1521):

> I remember, when you had calmed down, and were talking with me, that I asserted that I had been called by heavenly terrors [*de coelo terroribus*], for not freely or desirously did I become a monk, much less to gratify my belly, but walled around with the terror and agony of sudden death [*terrore et agone mortis subitæ circumvallatus*] I vowed a constrained and necessary vow.[4]

[1] 'I did it without telling you, and against your will.' WA 8.573.19.

[2] Melanchthon mentions the death of a friend, and Jonas a vague story of how Luther was on his way home from Gotha when 'there came to him a terrifying apparition from heaven which he at that time interpreted to mean that he should become a monk'. Mackinnon, i, pp. 33 f.; Scheel, i, pp. 321 ff.

[3] WA Br. 1.543.105.

[4] WA 8.573.30.

The two passages are generally regarded as confirming the story in the *Table Talk*[1] according to which, on July 2nd, 1505, Luther was returning from a visit to his parents when he was overtaken by a thunderstorm near the village of Stotternheim, not far from Erfurt. In terror, Luther cried, 'Help, St. Anne, and I'll become a monk!' It may be true. St. Anne's was the popular cult, not least among the miners, and she was patroness of a Brotherhood closely connected with the Austin Friars of Erfurt. If Luther considered himself pursued by the thunderbolts of an angry God, the story is possible.

When we ask what did happen, there is confusion, and later versions of the story have been affected by the account given in Luther's *Monastic Vows*, and no doubt, too, by the edifying parallel of the sudden conversion of St. Paul.[2] But how did it happen? Luther might have been severely shaken by a near miss. But it would be all over in a moment, and by the time he could think clearly and had felt himself all over, the natural reaction would surely be relief and not panic-stricken fear of another stroke of lightning such as to evoke this drastic vow? If he was not stricken, we must suppose he felt himself pursued by the anger of God. But we cannot press the point,[3] though another incident in the *Table Talk* deserves to be remembered.

In this, Luther was on a journey home, when he fell and the short dagger which he wore struck deep into his leg, severing an artery. His companion set off to Erfurt for help, and while he was gone Luther tried to staunch the swift bleeding. In peril of death he cried 'Help, Mary!' A surgeon came and Luther was carried to Erfurt.[4] In the night the wound broke open afresh and he again called out to the Virgin. The date assigned in the *Table Talk* is April 16th, 1503, and the place a different road.[4] But there are some striking similarities between the stories, bearing in mind the vagueness of the thunderstorm account, and allowing for the influence of the story of St. Paul. Certainly,

[1] TR 4.4707.

[2] Dr. Nathin said (according to report) that Luther had been 'wonderfully converted through Christ, like another Paul'. Scheel, ii, p. 10.

[3] In favour of the thunderstorm story is WA 44.598.39: 'If a man were struck by divine lightning he would feel his conscience labour vehemently, stripped of all consolation, nor would it easily be assuaged.'

[4] TR 1.119. Scheel, i.320.20. According to Scheel, Biereye in a special study of the problem suggests March 25th, 1505, for this, along the same road as the thunderstorm.

Luther alone, bleeding to death, would be 'walled around by the agony and fear of sudden death' and surrounded by 'heavenly terrors' in such a way as to make a desperate vow intelligible.

If both stories are true, then the crisis of a serious accident may have suggested reflections to Luther which recurred sharply when, a little later, he again faced the imminence of death. The death of a friend, which Melanchthon reports, and which finds some confirmation in the Wittenberg archives, may have deepened such serious consideration. But about the inward state of his mind, there is no real evidence.[1] So Martin Luther sold his books, keeping back his Virgil and his Plautus, and on July 16th, 1505, he had a farewell meal with his friends. The following day he greeted them with, 'To-day you see me, and then, never again', and the sober little group approached the Augustinian monastery.[2] Clutching his bundle, he turned away from them as the gates closed behind him. Within, he was embraced, and entered a new world.

In turning Austin Friar, or, more properly, becoming a member of the Reformed Congregation of the Eremetical Order of St. Augustine, Luther had joined an order of considerable importance, not only in Erfurt. Incorporated by Innocent IV in 1243, confirmed by Alexander IV in 1256, the mendicant order of Augustinian Friars had over two thousand chapters by the middle of the fifteenth century. In 1473 Andreas Proles carried through a reform of the order, and the house at Erfurt was numbered among those Observant houses which accepted a strict interpretation of their Rule, with Proles as Vicar-General. Under his successor, Johannes Staupitz, a revised constitution was made in 1504.[3]

About Luther's monastic career as a whole we have his own abundant testimony in after years. True, the integrity and accuracy of this has often been called in question, notably by Denifle, who declared it to be a deliberate and lying invention which Luther only dared ventilate when those who could contradict him had passed from the scene. But the modern

[1] WA Br.2.384.80 (September 9th, 1521) to Melanchthon: 'I was more snatched than drawn towards it' (*magis fui raptus quam tractus*).

[2] 'Then they led me with tears,' TR 4.4707. Scheel, i, p. 257. For a full discussion of Luther's vocation, see Scheel, i, chap. 5, and notes *ad loc.*

[3] Preserved Smith, *Luther*, London 1911, p. 8; Scheel, i, p. 256.

Catholic historian, Joseph Lortz, declared this 'moral depravity' theory to be a complete failure.[1]

In fact there is independent testimony to Luther's integrity at a much later date than the theory of Denifle could sustain. In 1543 Matthew Flaccius Illyricus reported a conversation with a former companion of the Reformer who had remained a Catholic and who 'declared that Martin Luther lived a holy life among them, kept the Rule most exactly, and studied diligently'.[2]

It may be, as Scheel suggests, that traces of the later 'Luther legend' can be found in stories in the *Table Talk* of the jealousy of other monks, which led them to give Luther menial tasks and sent him out ('Sack on your back, you!') on begging expeditions.[3] On the other hand Luther was greatly gifted, he was zealous, and the prodigious mental activity of his later life must have had some anticipation. But during the period of his novitiate Luther must have been fully occupied learning the etiquette of conventual discipline, the duties of prayer and choir. Of the Master of the Novices he spoke with great affection in later years.

Luther made his profession, with its serious and irrevocable vows, in September, 1506, and was then prepared for ordination (about half the seventy members of the house were priests). He was ordained Sub-Deacon, December, 1506; Deacon, February, 1507; Priest, April, 1507.[4] The first Mass, a great occasion, took place at the beginning of May, and to it Luther invited friends, including his old friend Johann Braun from Eisenach. Second only to the solemnity itself, however, was the reunion with his father. Hans Luther had at first addressed his son with cold and formal displeasure, but others in the home had given softening counsel, and then two sons died of the plague and perhaps it did not take so much after all to reconcile Hans Luther to the boy of whom he must always be proud, however distasteful the thought of his unwelcome calling. Having decided to go, Father Luther

[1] H. Strohl, *L'Evolution religieuse de Luther*, Strasbourg, pp. 12 ff.; E. G. Rupp, *Luther: the Catholic Caricature;* Theology, Oct., 1942, references *ad loc.;* J. Lortz, *Reformation in Deutschland*, 1947; G. Miegge, *Lutero*, Torre Pellice 1946, pp. 71 ff.

[2] Scheel, ii, p. 10 *n.*

[3] 'They were jealous of me on account of my study, saying "What's good enough for me is good enough for you. Sack on your back, you"' (*saccum per naccum*). TR 5.452.34; TR 3.580.5; TR 5.99.24; Scheel, pp. 599 ff.

[4] Following Scheel, Boehmer, Miegge.

did the thing handsomely, sent a generous sum towards the celebration, and rode up with a cavalcade of twenty. Martin took the first opportunity to explain the imperious nature of his vocation, to which his father, with great effort to keep his temper, grunted, 'Let's hope it wasn't all imagination'.[1] But the undercurrent was there, and his indignation exploded on the company when across the table and amid an embarrassed silence he asked loudly, 'Have you not read in Scripture that one shall honour one's father and mother?' To Martin Luther the words struck deeply home.

In reading for ordination, Luther studied the treatise on the Canon of the Mass by the famous Tübingen preacher and Nominalist theologian, Gabriel Biel (d. 1495). Thus he approached the sacred rite with an overwhelming sense of the Divine Majesty, and of the dreadful prerogative vouchsafed to one who was commissioned to intercede with the Living God.[2]

The Augustinians at Erfurt had close association with the University, and Luther was selected as apt for advanced theological study. Under Johann Paltz (who left in 1507) and Johann Nathin (a former student under Biel) Luther imbibed the doctrines of the *via moderna* as refracted through Biel and his own preceptors.

The nature and extent of Luther's debt to Occamism cannot be clarified in the present state of studies of late scholasticism.[3] Many of Luther's apparently deferential remarks about Occam prove to be ironical.[4] Luther's first onslaught on tradition was directed against an Aristotelianism as marked in Occam as in Scotus or Aquinas. When the theological controversy opened, it was the Nominalist doctrine of human nature which was the centre of Luther's attack. There is no evidence that Luther was influenced by Occam's anti-papal writings, and Biel, the more immediate influence upon him, is hailed by Catholic scholars as impeccable in his attitude to Rome.[5]

[1] WA 8.574.2: 'Would (you said) that it may not have been an illusion or phantasy.' Cf. K. Holl, *Gesammelte Aufsätze. Luther*, Tübingen 1927, p. 15, *n*. 1.

[2] The stories of Luther's attempt to flee from the altar are so riddled with confusion that in the light of Scheel's discussion (ii, pp. 97–109), accepted by Mackinnon (i.46) and Miegge (47) they can be dismissed.

[3] See the remarks of P. Vignaux (*Dict. Théol. Cath.*, xi, pp. 717, 876). Since then (1931) there has been some improvement.

[4] K. Holl, *Ges. Aufs. Luther*, p. 49, *n*. 2; TR 2.516.6; WA 30.ii.300.9.

[5] C. Rich, *Dict. Théol. Cath.*, ii, pp. 814–25.

This is not at all to deny the influence of the *via moderna* upon Luther. It was the one form of scholasticism which he knew intimately, for we misunderstand entirely if we suppose late mediæval German Catholic theology to be dominated by Thomism: in many places the struggle for the future must have seemed to lie between Scotus and Occam. Never before or since have Germans been so preoccupied with, or so respectful to, British theology![1]

Occam bequeathed his followers a tradition of logical, critical enquiry which was bound to influence those who used the dialectical weapon. To the end of his life, Luther kept a partiality for the syllogism, and for illustrations drawn from logic and from grammar. As regards the problem of Universals, Luther repeatedly affirmed himself a Nominalist.[2] There is continuity as well as discontinuity in Luther's thought. P. Vignaux has suggested that in his disputations on the Trinity (1543–5) Luther used arguments already to be found in his marginal notes of 1509.[3] The rigorous and sustained argument of his 'Bondage of the Will' (1525) against Erasmus, and 'Of the Lord's Supper' (1528) against Zwingli, are not, as his opponents gibed, an inconsistent relapse into scholasticism, but are rather the full deployment of theological resources which he never repudiated, for despite his attack upon it, Luther had more respect for scholastic theology than Erasmus or Zwingli.

Recent studies upon Occam[4] have counselled caution about the generalizations of the older historians of dogma, in regard to the alleged Occamist 'Voluntarism', the stress on the Divine Will, the sharp division which, it is claimed, the Occamists interposed between reason and revelation.

[1] It is refreshing to find that Luther thinks of the English rather than the French as the logical people. TR 5.649.26: 'Scotus, Occam, were English. The French could never produce people like that!'

[2] TR 5.653. WA 39.ii.11.36.

[3] P. Vignaux, *Luther. Commentateur des Sentences*, Paris 1935, pp. 25, 29; WA 39.ii.253, WA ix.31.31.

[4] E. A. Moody, *Logic of William of Ockham*, London 1935; E. Guelluy, *Philosophie et Theologie chez Ockham*, Paris 1947; *The Tractatus de Predestinatione . . . of Wm. of Ockham* (Ph. Boehner) New York 1945; E. Gilson, *La Philosophie au Moyen Age*, Paris 1930, chap. xi; G. De Lagarde, *Naissance de l'esprit laïque au déclin du Moyen Age*, Paris 1942–46, iv–vi; *Wm. of Ockham. Dict. Théol. Cath.* articles, 'Nominalisme', 'Occam' (P. Vignaux); P. Vignaux, *Justification et Predestination au XIV siecle*, Paris 1934, *Luther, Commentateur des Sentences*, Paris 1935.

We are better placed in the light of recent detailed study to see the positive Occamist concern for the Liberty of God (against the doctrines of necessity in Pelagius, and Peter of Auriol, and, in the case of Biel, as against a fellow Nominalist, Gregory of Rimini), the refusal to entangle God in his own systems, and the stress on the Divine mercy. We have learned not to make Occam too modern, for he worked with the mediæval ingredients, Scripture and Fathers as focussed in Peter Lombard, Augustine and Aristotle, and he puts his most daring expositions forward as an interpretation of the authentic Augustine or Aristotle.[1] The Occamist stress on the immediacy of the Divine knowledge and action, and the refusal (as against Scotus) to construct a divine psychology, may also have had some effect on Luther. These influences, however, are of a kind to be reflected in subtle undertones, to be detected by deep and sympathetic study. They are in no wise, as in some recent polemic, to be apprized on the strength of superficial verbal similarities, or on what Milton called 'the ferrets and mouse-hunts of an index'.

Late in 1508 Luther was transferred to Wittenberg, to lecture in the Arts Faculty on the Nichomachean Ethics of Aristotle. It was to be a fateful association, this of Luther's with Wittenberg, but at the time it was drastic and depressing. Wittenberg, with its sandy, inhospitable soil, 'on the edge of beyond', presented a dismal contrast to the gardens of 'many-towered Erfurt', and seemed to struggle to support its two thousand inhabitants without the supererogatory burden of a new university.[2]

But over Wittenberg the Elector Frederick brooded with loving care. To it he was as generous as he could afford to be, though his good intentions did not always filter through the thrifty care of his treasurers, and in the matter of rebuilding, promises tended to fall short of performance. Still, one way and another a good deal of building went on between the Castle, the Castle Church, the monasteries and the town, in a descending order of priorities. Frederick contrived that the Chapter of the Schlosskirche and the two monasteries should bear as much as possible of the charge of the University professorships. Within the Schlosskirche itself he housed an impressive and growing

[1] M. H. Carré, *Phases of Thought in England*, 1949, pp. 88–178.
[2] TR 3.2871, TR 4.681.

collection of sacred relics, to which were attached privileges nicely calculated to provide edification to visitors and profit to the citizens. But his special interest was the University, since Leipzig and Erfurt fell within the jurisdiction of his neighbours. The foundation was approved by the Emperor in 1502, and confirmed by the Pope in 1503. Dr. Martin Pollich was appointed the first Rector, and the Dean was to be the Vicar-General of the Saxon Province of the Augustinians, Dr. Johann von Staupitz. The Augustinians provided two teaching Chairs, one in Biblical Theology which was held by Staupitz, the other in Moral Philosophy, to which Luther was now suddenly called. In Wittenberg, Luther had to combine his teaching duties with his own studies, and he found the programme strenuous, the enforced preoccupation with Aristotle increasingly uncongenial. 'The study takes it out of me,' he sighed to Johann Braun, 'especially in philosophy which from the beginning I would gladly have exchanged for theology, I mean that theology which searches out the nut from the shell, the kernel from the grain, and the marrow from the bones.'[1]

Johann von Staupitz was of moment in Luther's life, and their friendship was to endure more than common discouragement, and to persist across a growing divide until the death of the older man. Staupitz (b. 1460?) came of noble family and studied at several universities, all associated with the *via antiqua*. He was at Cologne (1483), Leipzig (1485) and Tubingen (1497), taking his doctorate in 1500. It has been plausibly conjectured that his theological affinities lay between the Thomists and the school of Aegidius Romanus, one of the great doctors of his own order. It would be strongly Augustinian.[2] As Vicar-General of the Saxon Province, Staupitz revised the constitutions of the order as prelude to a programme of reform, supporting the Observant Austin Friars who stood for the primitive integrity of the Rule, as against the more relaxed discipline of the Conventuals, who adhered to the accommodations by which the Rule had been adapted to later circumstances. This business of the Order involved long and frequent journeys, and Staupitz

[1] WA Br.1.17.4: 'Violentum est studium.' 'Violentum' appears to be used in the active sense. I think Boehmer is wrong in referring Luther's desire for the really discriminating theology to his zeal for Occamism.

[2] Scheel, ii, pp. 364 ff.; E. Wolf, *Staupitz und Luther*, Leipzig 1927, pp. 30–35.

must have found it difficult to discharge his University responsibilities. He may have had early thoughts about looking for an eventual successor among the young men. Although most recent historians are against the view, the possibility exists that he had made earlier acquaintance with Luther, had been directly responsible for calling him to further studies and to Wittenberg.

In the following March Luther took the degree of 'Baccalaureus Biblicus' at Wittenberg. He returned to Erfurt for the next rank of Sententiarius and became entangled in a sufficiently modern difficulty of university red tape. Wittenberg was very young, and Erfurt very conscious of its seniority, and so there was an Oxbridge *v.* Redbrick affair of ruffled academic dignity. The thing was to flare up again when Luther would take his doctorate at Wittenberg. Then he recalled how, on this earlier occasion, the Dean, Sigismund Thomae of Stockheim, had been droning drowsily away with lengthy extracts from the University regulations when Dr. Nathin exploded impatiently, waved the Dean aside, and read simply the list of required text-books from a chit of paper in his hand. A lively scene, the point of which is that in the fuss nobody asked Luther to make the regulation promise to take his further degrees and duties at Erfurt![1] As Sententiarius, Luther was required to lecture on the Sentences of Peter Lombard, the great theological text-book of the Middle Ages. We have Luther's notes on them, and on the collection of works of St. Augustine which he read at this time.[2] Hitherto he had not been drawn to St. Augustine,[3] but now he really devoured him with the rapture of a younger theologian for his first theological love, as the enthusiastic marginal comments ('Beautiful! Beautiful!', in striking contrast to the 'Completely mad!' of his later marginal comments on Biel) eloquently witness. This new and headlong enthusiasm for Augustine may account for the ferocity of his note against the Alsatian humanist Wimpfeling, who (in his 'De Integritate' (1505)) had roused

[1] WA Br.1.30 (December 21st, 1514), 15–25.

[2] WA ix, pp. 1–94; P. A. Vignaux, *Luther. Commentateur des Sentences;* Holl, *Luther*, pp. 187 ff.

[3] WA Br.1.70.20 (October 19th, 1516): 'Before I fell in with his books, I had very little room for him.' TR 1.140.5: 'In the beginning I devoured Augustine.' Luther had not yet come to know the anti-Pelagian works of Augustine.

the embattled fury of the Augustinians by denying that St. Augustine had ever been a monk.[1]

Though we cannot agree with those who find in these notes the beginning of Luther's doctrine of grace and justification, or the evidence of the theological influence of Staupitz, there is a boldness of judgment and a discrimination between authorities which is remarkable. For the Master of the Sentences, Luther maintained lifelong respect, and it is significant that Peter Lombard represents the twelfth-century combination of Scripture and Fathers on the eve of the great thirteenth-century invasion of Aristotle. In Luther's acid comments in the notes upon Aristotle, there is a discrimination between traditional theology and what P. Vignaux has called the philosophic 'envelope' of Aristotelian scholasticism.[2] Luther's attack on indulgences in 1517 was to be preceded by a public attack on the Aristotelian domination of theology, but here are its beginnings in a positive programme of simplification, the return to what Luther was later (1516) to call 'our theology . . . the Bible, St. Augustine and the old Fathers'. The great humanist attack on scholasticism did not get fully under way until the Reuchlin affair of the next decade, but here in 1509–10 is another programme, different from that which Erasmus was to adumbrate in the return to the 'philosophy of Christ' in the Gospels.

Meanwhile, Staupitz had conjured up a quarrel which cut dangerously across the party line. Seven Observant houses (including Erfurt and Nuremberg) withstood a project to unite all the German congregations, and Luther was told off to assist Dr. Nathin in concerting the opposition. An attempt to win support from the Archbishop of Magdeburg failed, and it was decided that two brothers should take the case to Rome. The senior was probably selected at Nuremberg, and his 'socius itinerarius' was to be Martin Luther. It was to be the longest journey of his life, and since the Eternal City was the goal, he looked forward to it with eager and filial expectancy. It was late in the year 1510 that they set out for the arduous crossing of the Alps and the descent into the Lombard plain. We have only a few anecdotes in later years about the journey. There is the vivid story of how the two brethren slept on one occasion with

[1] WA ix.12.7.

[2] See P. Vignaux, *Luther, Commentateur*, p. 24.

their windows open to the Italian mists, with dire results, so that for one day they could only crawl miserably along, parched with thirst for water too dirty to drink, and nauseated by the sickly wine, until the gift of two pomegranates relieved them, and as they munched noisily, cheerfulness broke in.[1] When Luther came in sight of Rome, he dropped to the ground with a pious 'Hail, holy Rome!'[2] Their business broached to the authorities, the two travellers made the customary tour of churches and of catacombs, drinking in the manifold and edifying marvels. The Italian cities must have been intriguing, and Rome, twice the size of Erfurt and, despite the absence of Pope and court, an emotional climax of bustle, swagger and Italian panache, great buildings, churches innumerable, and acres and acres of unintelligible and reverend ruins. Luther was disgusted by the Roman clergy with their slick and cynical professionalism, as they murmured their devotions at high speed, nudging him angrily with '*Passa, Passa!* Get a move on, you!' The story that on the stairs of the Scala Sancta Luther heard a premonition of his later gospel is a fable,[3] though there may be the germ of truth in the story that at this point he wondered 'Who knows whether all this is true?' Luther was simple enough, and good enough, to be deeply shocked by some of the things he saw, by the living proof of the tales of vice and luxury, covetousness and degradation in high places. 'I would never have believed that the Papacy was such an abomination, if I had not myself seen the Roman court.'[4]

Homesick, the two travellers found friends among the members of the German Church in Rome, and they patriotically agreed that this was the best of all the Roman churches.[5] The appeal to Rome was a failure, and perhaps Luther himself became convinced of the weakness of the cause, for on his return to Germany he no longer supported the opposition to Staupitz and he and his friend John Lang won a good deal of unpopularity from their Erfurt brethren. Staupitz was impressed by Luther, and, as we shall see, not a little concerned about

[1] TR 4.4104.
[2] TR 5.467.13.
[3] It is a pity that it was accepted by Dr. N. P. Williams (*Ideas of the Fall and Original Sin*, London 1927, p. 426).
[4] WA 47.432.28.
[5] WA 47.425.5.

him. He decided that Luther must proceed to the doctorate and succeed him in the Chair of Biblical Theology at Wittenberg.

Although this was the logical climax of his academic training, Luther shrank from it. He told later how under a pear tree in the garden he discussed the matter with Staupitz, pleading (perhaps only half seriously) his own expectancy of an early death, until Staupitz joked his objections aside and commanded him to the new step as a matter of obedience. To become a Doctor in Theology meant much more than to take a higher degree: it committed the graduate to a life of public teaching, and to a life of preaching, from which also Luther may have drawn back. The minor question arose, whence would come the not inconsiderable expenses for the occasion, and this was solved, on the petition of Staupitz, by the thrifty generosity of the Elector. It seems likely that it was contrived that the Elector should hear Luther preach, but what settled the matter was the assurance that Luther would succeed Staupitz in the Chair of Theology. On October 19th, 1512, with the rich, solemn proprieties which inaugurated a Doctor in Theology, Luther was invested with his new calling. 'Calling' it was for him, not only in the mediæval sense of an *officium*, but in the important sense of his own later doctrine of the Christian life. In this moment, Luther became a public as well as a private person, solemnly called upon to defend the Word of God and to drive away all erroneous and strange doctrines, and the compulsion of this calling was to sustain his courage in many difficult hours.

So once again it seemed that the lines of Luther's career were settled. At the age of twenty-eight he was a Doctor of Divinity and a Professor of Sacred Theology, with some sort of understanding made over his head[1] that he would spend the rest of his days in Wittenberg. It all seems rather final for a young man, this settled prospect of a long succession of interesting but uneventful years, a narrow horizon bounded by disputations, lectures, and academic gossip. In one sense it was just that. We shall never understand Luther unless we remember that he was by trade a Theological Professor, that year in, year out (the exceptions can be counted on the fingers), twice a week at the

[1] 'Martin should discharge for the rest of his life the lectureship at Wittenberg pertaining to him' (Staupitz). Scheel, ii, p. 556.

appointed hour, he walked into the lecture-room and addressed successive generations of students, and this for thirty years until he was old and feeble and could only croak his last lecture.[1] This was the career which opened for Martin Luther in 1512. In between lectures, so to speak, he attended the deathbed of a world and assisted the birth of a new age.

[1] H. Boehmer, *Luther's Erste Vorlesung*, Leipzig 1924; H. Bornkamm, *Luther und das Alte Testament*, Tübingen 1948, p. 6.

CHAPTER TWO

MR. FEARING

'When we came at the Hill Difficulty, he made no stick at that, nor did he much fear the lions: for you must know that his trouble was not about such things as those: his fear was about his acceptance at last.'

WHETHER LUTHER'S ENTRY into the monastery was as abrupt as it seems, or as Holl suggested, 'the fulfilment of a secret wish',[1] has been much debated. Luther's own words, 'Walled around with the terror and agony of sudden death', remind us that it was the prospect of death, and death not so much as physical dissolution but as the door to judgment, which moved him. In the cover of his copy of Augustine's *City of God* there is written, in Luther's hand, the quotation from the *Phædo* of Plato, '*Divinus Plato: Philosophia esti melete thanatos*' ('Philosophy is the study of death'), and as P. Vignaux comments, sometimes a very personal experience may underly a classical quotation.[2] There are very few periods in Luther's life when he did not feel death to be an imminent possibility, and it may have been more in earnest than in jest that he put this to Staupitz as a reason why he should not proceed to his doctorate.

In contrast was the assurance given Luther at his profession: 'Keep this Rule, and I promise you eternal life.'[3]

He sought evangelical perfection with earnest and strenuous zeal, and with that wholeheartedness which was the quality of all his undertakings: 'I had no other thoughts, but to keep my Rule.'[4] In 1533 he could say, 'I was a good monk, and kept strictly to my order, so that I could say that if the monastic life could get a man to heaven, I should have entered: all my companions who knew me would bear witness to that.'[5] The Master of the Novices gave him the *Lives of the Fathers*, and for a time

[1] K. Holl, *Luther*, p. 15.
[2] P. Vignaux, *Luther, Commentateur*, p. 13.
[3] WA 51.83.8, 40.i.244.7.
[4] WA 47.92.10, 40.ii.15.15, 43.255.9.
[5] WA 38.143.25.

his head was stuffed full of devout fancies about the desert hermits. 'I used to imagine such a saint, who would live in the desert, and abstain from food and drink, and live on a few vegetables and roots and cold water.'[1] He exercised himself in austerities to the point of danger. 'I vexed myself with fasts and prayers beyond what was common,[2] and he said later, 'If I could have got to heaven by fasting, I should have merited that twenty years ago.'[3]

At first things went well: 'I know from my own experience, and that of many others, how peaceful and quiet Satan is accustomed to be in one's first years as a priest or monk.'[4] Then, trouble began. They were not 'carnal temptations' of a physical kind, for Luther, though not wood or stone, did not find them cause of racking torment, and he marvelled that St. Jerome should have been thus harassed, while he himself was vexed, 'not about women, but about the really knotty problems.'[5] Even as an adolescent, Luther had made his confession with more than common exactitude,[6] and now, confronted with the goal of perfection, the divine imperative became something which withered all joy, and brought him a torment of doubt and uncertainty and guilt, an inner scepticism which ate corrosively through all the offices of consolation which were offered him. 'When I was a monk, I tried with all diligence to live according to the Rule, and I used to be contrite, to confess and number off my sins, and often repeated my confession, and sedulously performed my allotted penance. And yet my conscience could never give me certainty, but I always doubted and said, "You did not perform that correctly. You were not contrite enough. You left that out of your confession." The more I tried to remedy an uncertain, weak and afflicted conscience with the traditions of men, the more each day found it more uncertain, weaker, more troubled.'[7] 'After watchings, studies, fastings, prayers and other most severe exercises with which as a monk I afflicted myself almost to death, yet that doubt was left in the soul, and I thought "Who knows whether such things are pleasing to God?" '[8]

He tried mental prayer and contemplation, and fancied himself

[1] WA 40.ii.103.12. [2] WA 40.ii.574.8. [3] WA 40.ii.453.8.
[4] WA 8.660.31. [5] TR 1.240.12, TR 1.47.15. [6] TR 1.200.26.
[7] WA 40.ii.15.15, WA 40.i.615.6, WA 26.12.12. [8] WA 40.ii.414.15.

among choirs of angels, drove himself nearly daft, as he said, trying to follow the mystic counsels of St. Bonaventura, until his own common sense bade him desist,[1] leaving him permanently suspicious of all who relied on visions and on ecstasies. His spiritual directors were wise and kindly, though even they found their patience[2] tried with what seemed to them just a rather extreme case of 'scruples'.

'Scruples' were a well-known morbid condition of the anxious soul, discussed in a whole literature of moral theology, including treatises by Cassian, William of Paris, Gerson, John Nider and Gabriel Biel, and the symptoms could be recognized as easily as a modern physician can diagnose measles.[3] One method of treating anxious souls was to put their offences in more cheering proportion, and some of the advice given by Gerson is along those lines. There is a type of vanity which loves to parade its own shortcomings, and for such the old rhyme is salutary:

Once in a saintly passion
I cried with desperate grief
'O Lord, my heart is black with guilt,
Of Sinners I am chief.'

Then stooped my guardian angel
And whispered from behind,
'Vanity, my little man!
You're nothing of the kind!'

But Luther was not to be jokingly fobbed off into a false security which he judged to be one of the dreadful vices of the age:

'Ah!' they say, 'what are you so careful about? It isn't necessary. Just be humble and patient. Do you think God requires such strictness from you? He knows what you are thinking, and He is good. One groan will please him. You imagine that nobody can be saved

[1] TR 1.302.30; WA 26.55.17.

[2] TR 1.201.1.

[3] D. Carey, S.J., *The Nature and Treatment of Scruples*, Dublin 1948. There would seem to be specifically Catholic forms of scruples surrounding the sacraments. The Protestant form of the disease was to evoke a casuistry of faith in the seventeenth century, though here there is continuity as well as discontinuity, for we find William Ames transcribing whole passages from William of Paris!

unless he acts so rigidly . . . it really is necessary to observe discretion.' And so gradually the unhappy soul forgets the fear of the Lord, and that the Kingdom of Heaven suffers violence.[1]

But Luther (it is the measure of his torment) could not forget the fear of the Lord, and it was his own soul which suffered violence. That is why he came to choose the word *Anfechtung* for 'temptation', as a description of his spiritual conflict.[2] The full significance of this word for him can only be discussed in terms of his developed theology, and he was only to feel the full force of it in the lonely decisions of what Miegge has called 'his terrible vocation as a revolutionary'. Yet the spiritual struggles of his monastic career belong to the same story. They, too, are *Anfechtung*.

In the monastery, I did not think about women, or gold, or goods, but my heart trembled, and doubted how God could be gracious to me. Then I fell away from faith, and let myself think nothing less than that I had come under the Wrath of God, whom I must reconcile with my good works.[3]

What it means to feel oneself under the Wrath of God is something that modern man can hardly understand. Luther described the experience in many passages of sombre and compelling beauty, of which the most moving is his exposition of the flight of Jonah (1526). But in 1518 he describes it in terms which, if not directly autobiographical, derive power from his own experience:

I knew a man, who said, that he had often suffered these pains [infernal torments] in the shortest possible compass of time, so great and infernal that 'nor tongue nor pen can show' nor can those believe who have not experienced, so that if they were completed, or lasted half an hour, or even the tenth part of an hour, he would utterly perish, and his bones be reduced to ashes. Then God appears horrifyingly angry and with him, the whole creation. There can be no flight, no consolation, neither within or without, but all is

[1] WA 3.447.21 ff.

[2] Some fine essays have been concerned with this problem, notably G. Jacob, *Der Gewissensbegriff in der Theologie Luthers*, Tübingen 1929; E. Vogelsang, *Der Angefochtene Christus bei Luther*, Berlin 1932; Y. J. E. Alanen, *Das Gewissen bei Luther*, Helsinki 1934; L. Pinomaa, *Der Zorn Gottes in der Theologie Luthers*, Helsinki 1938; P. Buhler, *Die Anfechtung bei Martin Luther*, Zurich, 1942.

[3] WA 47.590.6.

accusation. Then he laments, 'I am cast away from thy face: Lord accuse me not in thy Wrath.' In this moment, marvellous to relate, the soul cannot believe it can ever be redeemed, but that it is suffering a punishment not yet complete, . . . and left only with the naked longing for help, and terrifying trembling, but it knows not whence help can come. This is the soul stretched out with Christ, so that all his bones can be numbered, nor is there any corner not filled with the most bitter bitterness, horror, fear, dolour, but all these things seem eternal. And to use an illustration, it is as though a sphere should pass over a straight line, so that the point of the line which is touched supports the whole sphere, yet does not embrace the whole sphere. So the soul at this point, when it is touched with this passing eternal inundation, feels and drinks nothing less than eternal punishment, but it does not last, for it passes on.[1]

The projection of a wounded conscience on the world outside, with the sense of claustrophobia and agoraphobia, resembles Pip's experiences in *Great Expectations*. 'Instead of my running at everything, everything seemed to run at me. This was very disagreeable to my guilty mind. The gates and dykes and banks came bursting at me through the mist, as if they cried as plainly as could be, "A boy with somebody else's pork pie! Stop him!" '

Here it is, in Luther's recurrent illustration of a 'driven leaf':

Then the conscience feels that all the ill fortune which overtakes it is the Wrath of God, and it thinks that all the creatures are simply God and the Wrath of God, even if it is just a rustling leaf . . . for there is nothing more trivial and insignificant than a dry leaf, which lies on the earth, so that the very insects crawl over it . . . yet when its 'hour' comes, at its rustling shall steed, man, spear, armour, King, Prince, the whole might of an army, and all such proud, bloodthirsty and angry tyrants which otherwise no hell nor yet any Wrath of God, nor judgment can terrify, but only makes them harder and prouder. What fine fellows we are! We are not afraid for any Wrath of God, and we stand upright, and yet we panic and run away from a powerless dry leaf! At such a rustling a leaf becomes the Wrath of God, and the whole world too narrow upon which a little before we strutted upon in our pride.[2]

And, in another place:

Then comes remorse and terrifies the conscience. Then all's right with the world, and he alone is a sinner. God is gracious to all the world save to him alone. Nobody else has to meet God's Wrath save

[1] WA 1.558. [2] WA 19.226.12.

he alone, and he feels there is no wrath anywhere than he feels and he finds himself the most miserable of men. So it was with Adam and Eve when they sinned: had God not come when the cool of the day arrived, they would never have noticed their sin. But when He came, they crept away . . .'[1]

There are those who see in such descriptions only a morbid sensitivity. Yet it is to be noted that those who have attempted a psychological description of Luther's troubles, not only disagree but cancel one another out, while the most impressive of such attempts can only make its diagnosis by abusing evidence in a manner which no historian could countenance, and by making nonsense of Luther's theology.[2]

Luther, says Boehmer, was grateful by temperament, and in later life he again and again recalled the comfort he had received from Staupitz. 'If I didn't praise Staupitz, I should be a damnable, ungrateful, papistical ass . . . for he was my first father in this teaching, and he bore me in Christ. If Staupitz had not helped me out, I should have been swallowed up and left in hell.'[3] To the Nominalist philosophy with its recurring 'perhaps' and its emphasis on the power of the human will, Staupitz brought the wholesome corrective of the *via antiqua*, with its emphasis on the design of God, and the work of grace within the human soul. He brought the mystical emphasis of the 'modern devotion' which found temptation and tribulation to be a sign of grace, a mark of conformity with Christ.

Luther's most illuminating testimony to this help was written in 1518:

> I remember, dear Father, that once, among those most pleasant and wholesome talks of thine, with which the Lord Jesus often gives me wondrous consolation, this word 'penitence' [*poenitentia*] was mentioned. We were moved with pity for many consciences, and for those tormentors who teach with rules innumerable and unbearable what they call a 'method of confession'. Then we heard you say, as with a voice from heaven, that there is no true penitence which does not begin with a love of righteousness and of God, and that this love

[1] WA 19.210.14.

[2] Dr. Med. P. J. Reiter, *Martin Luthers Umwelt, Charakter und Psychose*, vol. i, Die Umwelt 1937; vol. ii, *Luther's Persönlichkeit, Seelenleben und Krankheiten*, Copenhagen 1941. The second volume has a useful assembly of evidence.

[3] WA 58.i.27 ff.

which others think to be the completion of penitence is rather its beginning.

This word of yours stuck in me like a 'sharp arrow of the mighty' (Ps. 120, v. 4) and I began from that time onward to compare it with the texts of Scripture which teach penitence. And then began a most joyful game. The words played up to me, smiling agreement and jostling one another on all sides. So that whereas before there was no word more bitter to me than 'penitence' which I feigned sedulously in the presence of God, and sought to express in a forced and fictitious love, now none has to me a more sweet and pleasant sound. For thus the precepts of God grow sweet when we seek not so much to understand them in books, but in the wounds of the most sweet saviour.[1]

Luther goes on to tell how, when he came to study Greek, he found that the authentic meaning of 'penitence' as 'repent' rather than 'do penance', confirmed what Staupitz had told him.

It is possible that Luther's doubts had taken a more desperate turn. The doctrine of Predestination he could not ignore, for it was treated in all the text-books. The torment of his conscience, the anguish which seemed to anticipate infernal pain, was bound to suggest the possibility that he might be numbered among the reprobate. In this problem lay an almost final anguish. As he wrote in 1525:

I myself have more than once been offended [by this doctrine] almost to the very depth and abyss of despair, so that I wished I had never been created a man, until I realized how salutary was this despair and how near to grace.[2]

And when, sometimes, the skies cleared and he had good days, there came the thought that this might be yet a further sign of divine displeasure: 'the greatest temptation is to have no temptation.'[3] We can see how such thoughts choked every attempt of Luther, following scholastic teaching, to make acts of Love to God, and resulted in a constrained and hypocritical devotion, while deep down he felt a murmuring against a God who weighted everything against the sinner, driving him almost to the point of explicit and open blasphemy. But we cannot say when Luther's thoughts about Predestination began to trouble him, or when they reached their most acute tension.

[1] WA 1.525. [2] WA 18.719.7 ff. [3] WA 3.420.16 ff.

There remains the most important piece of evidence, the autobiographical fragment embedded in Luther's preface to his *Works* (1545). There, after rehearsing his career until the year 1519, he pauses and adds:

Meanwhile, in that year [1519] I turned once more to interpret the Psalms, relying on the fact that I was the more expert after I had handled in the schools the letters of St. Paul to the Romans and Galatians, and that which is to the Hebrews. I had indeed been seized with a great eagerness to understand Paul in the Epistle to the Romans, and, as Virgil says, 'It was not coldness of blood' which held me up, but this one word, that is, in Chap. I. The Justice [*Justitia*] of God is revealed in [the gospel]. For I hated this word 'Justice of God', which by the use and custom of all doctors I had been taught to understand philosophically as they say, as that formal and active justice whereby God is just and punishes unjust sinners.

For, however irreproachable my life as a monk, I felt myself, in the presence of God, to be a sinner with a most unquiet conscience, nor would I believe him to be pleased with my satisfaction. I did not love, indeed I hated this just God who punished sinners, and if not with silent blasphemy, at least with huge murmuring I was indignant against God, as if it were really not enough that miserable sinners, eternally ruined by original sin, should be crushed with every kind of calamity by the law of the Ten Commandments, but God through the Gospel must add sorrow on sorrow, and through the Gospel bring his wrath and justice to bear on us. I raged with a fierce and disturbed conscience in this way, and yet I knocked with importunity at Paul in this place, with a burning desire to know what St. Paul could intend.

At last, God being merciful, as I meditated day and night, pondering the connection of the words, namely, 'The Justice of God is revealed, as it is written, the Just shall live by faith', there I began to understand that Justice of God in which the just man lives by the gift of God, i.e. by faith, and this sentence, 'the Justice of God is revealed in the Gospel' to be understood passively as that whereby the merciful God justifies us by faith, as it is written, 'the just shall live by faith'. At this I felt myself to be born anew, and to enter through open gates into paradise itself. From here, the whole face of the Scriptures was altered. I ran through the Scriptures as memory served, and collected the same analogy in other words as *opus dei*, that which God works in us; *virtus dei*, that in which God makes us strong; *sapientia dei*, in which he makes us wise; *fortitudo dei*, *salus dei*, *gloria dei*.

And now, as much as I formerly hated that word 'Justice of God' [*Justitia Dei*] so now did I love and extol it as the sweetest of all words and then this place was to me as the gates of paradise. Afterwards I read St. Augustine, 'Of the Spirit and the Letter', and beyond all hope, found that he also similarly interpreted the Justice of God as that with which God clothes us and by which we are justified . . . armed with these cogitations I began the second course on the Psalms.[1]

The document involves complicated historical questions which cannot detain us here.[2] But the whole autobiographical fragment has been critically examined by Stracke, and Luther comes out of it surprisingly well.[3]

A long catena of passages can confirm that, in fact, the thought of the 'Justice of God' as retributive punishing justice lay at the heart of Luther's troubles. Thus, in 1515:

If I may speak personally, the word 'justice' nauseated me to hear, so that I should not have been sorry if somebody had made away with me.

And in 1531:

For this the holy fathers who wrote about the Psalms were wont to expound as the 'Just God' as that in which he vindicates and punishes not as that which justifies. So it happened to me as a young man, that I hated this term for God, and even to-day I am as though terrified when I hear God called 'Just'.

Here, Luther's fears congealed. The thought of the severity of God, of Christ as a judge, he had learned from his childhood, and perhaps the sombre mood was reinforced by the strictness of the home.[4] Next, the inexorable demand of the monastic discipline, the goal of evangelical perfection. Then, the Nominalist

[1] WA 54.179–87.

[2] I hope to deal elsewhere with the questions raised by Denifle in his famous 'Die Abendländischen Schriftausleger bis Luther, über Justitia Dei', *Luther und Luthertum*, 2. Aufl. Bd. 1, 2 Abt. Mainz 1905. See the two replies: K. Holl, *Ges. Aufs.* iii, Westen, *Die Justitia Dei in der vorlutherischen Bibelauslegung des Abendlandes;* E. Hirsch, *Initium Theologiæ Lutheri, Festschrift für J. Kaftan* 1920.

[3] Stracke, *Luther's Grosse Selbstzeugnis*, Leipzig 1926.

[4] In a sermon Luther says: 'When such a fear is inbred in a man as a child, it will only with great difficulty be uprooted as long as he lives, for he who trembled at every word of his father or mother, for the rest of his life is afraid of a rustling leaf.' L. Pinomaa, *Zorn Gottes*, p. 153, *n.*

theology with its jargon of merit, the apparently easy-going demand that a man should do 'what within him lies' which led instead to preoccupation with self, to uncertainty and despair, and the increasing tendency to think of salvation in quantitative rather than qualitative terms. So Luther's religious problem strikes into the wider pattern of popular piety, the 'religious' life, and late scholasticism.

That the word *Justitia* contained Luther's religious problem is important. It is even more momentous that within this word lay the tension between two mighty vocabularies, the Hellenic conception of Justice and the Biblical theme of the Righteousness of God. But for Luther *Justitia* was the problem, not to be softened by putting alongside it other ideas, such as the mercy (*misercordia*) or the goodness (*bonitas*) of God. Luther did not need to be told that all mediæval theologians had a doctrine of Grace and of Justification. The illumination came when, through this very conception 'Justice', there burst the saving intervention of a merciful God, displayed in Jesus Christ and freely bestowed on sinners. As Karl Holl has it, 'God does not send His Grace alongside His Righteousness, but He sends it through His Righteousness . . . this was more than a new exposition of Romans, I. 17 . . . it was the fountain spring of a new doctrine of God.'[1]

[1] K. Holl, vol. iii, *Westen*, p. 188.

CHAPTER THREE

'IN EXITU ISRAEL'

'Then was Christian glad and lightsome and he said with a merry heart, "He hath given me rest by his sorrow and life by his death." Then he stood still awhile to look and wonder, for it was very surprising to him, that the sight of the Cross should thus ease him of his burden.'

WHEN LUTHER'S MONASTIC PRECEPTOR handed him a copy of the Bible, bound in red, he read it avidly, and we may suspect that, following the advice he later gave to Spalatin, he began at the beginning and read it through, not once or twice, but until his mind was drenched through and through with the Biblical material, and he could handle his Bible with a facility which was the marvel of his friends and the envy of his enemies.

It was natural that, for the matter of his first exegetical lectures, he should turn to the Psalms, for it would be difficult to exaggerate what the Psalter—'the Bible in miniature'—meant to him. The Psalms were the first considerable part of the Bible which he got by heart for use in cell and choir. Month by month the Divine offices moved through the Psalter with stately measure, touching the height and depth of every emotion, every mood and almost every human crisis. Now it was the poignant cry of Israel, ravished and discomforted, in exile among her foes; next the exultant joy that God's right arm had swept giant foes into oblivion; the long, backward glances down the corridor of the past, with their reminders against the folly and faithlessness of Israel, of the enduring faithfulness of God. The piteous complaint of the poor man, betrayed, defenceless, while the ungodly struts before him in insolence and pride; the shout of crowds at some high festival; the impatience of the saints, beset by temptation and anguish; music and dancing, the noisy clamour of the temple courts, the silent eloquence of the little hills, the valleys thick with corn, the great sea, the sun and the stars, the ancient offering of a contrite heart, and through them all the solemn testimony to the transitory glory of this world, against the abiding Word of God. No wonder Luther cried:

> In short, would you see the Holy Christian Church painted with living colour and form, fastened together in one picture, take your Psalter, and you have a fine, clear, pure mirror which will show you what Christianity is.[1]

To it he returned again and again, and when he would console his Prince in sickness, or instruct a young man in the art of politics, or send a word of comfort to his own dying father, it was to expound the Psalms that he turned. 'The Psalter,' says Heinrich Bornkamm, 'linked him with his own world by a thousand ties.'[2]

For to Luther and to his contemporaries, as we can hardly understand, the Psalter was a Christian book. It was not simply a manual illustrating the Religion of the Hebrews, from which, as from an embarrassingly narrow ethical and historical context, the scholar might withdraw some edifying platitudes. It was well that Luther came to break with the traditional fourfold method of scriptural exegesis he inherited, but there is reason to be glad he began with it. According to this, the Psalms could be interpreted, in the literal-prophetic sense, with reference to Christ; tropologically they related to the individual soul; allegorically to the Church; anagogically, to the eschatological end of all things.[3]

Used in a wooden way, the fourfold exegesis could excite the most fantastic, arid and unedifying speculations. But we may consider that, as applied to the Psalms and as first one and then another interpretation became paramount, it might yield rich meaning. To begin with, God's mighty acts in His Son, the groundwork of the historical revelation; then, the counterpart of these objectivities within the experience of each human soul; next, the reminder that the great biblical 'Thou' confronts the believer only within the Israel of God; finally, the knowledge that here all our solutions are broken, pertaining to man as stranger and pilgrim (*homo viator*) and beckoning beyond history

[1] *Preface to the Psalter* (1534).

[2] H. Bornkamm, *Luther und das Alte Testament*, Tübingen 1948, p. 8.

[3] E. Vogelsang, *Die Anfänge von Luthers Christologie nach der ersten Vorlesung*, Berlin 1929, pp. 19–21.

to the final consummation. As a framework of devotion, there is a good deal to be said for it, and it is a good deal richer than that of many modern Christians.

In an important essay, Vogelsang suggested the importance of this method for Luther. In the combination of the Christological and tropological interpretation of the 'Justice of God' in the Psalms, we find the clue to Luther's solution.

Thus he came to see the 'Justice of God' as a righteousness revealed in Jesus Christ and bestowed to man on the ground of faith. Without committing ourselves to the details of Vogelsang's further hypothesis that we can trace the exact point of impact of the discovery on Luther's lectures on the Psalms, viz. Ps. 70–71, we may believe that Luther did in fact make his discovery during the lectures on the Psalms, i.e. 1513–4.[1]

Perhaps too much has been read into Luther's so-called 'Tower Experience' (*Turmerlebnis*—from the room in the monastery at Wittenberg in which, according to the *Table Talk*, Luther came to a new understanding of Rom. 1. 17). We must not read into it any preconceived pattern on the lines of an evangelical 'conversion'. The attempt, on the other hand, to divorce Luther's religious problem from his theological research, seems still more unsatisfactory.[2]

Bornkamm's words are salutary: 'One thing is more and more clear from recent research: the inmost, most personal experience of Luther, and his scholarly, theological, above all exegetical discoveries cannot be separated . . . the secret lies . . . in the indissoluble unity of personal experience and theological and exegetical research.'[3] We might remember Luther's own words: 'I did not learn my theology all at once, but I had to search deeper for it, where my temptations took me.'[4]

The facts, then, may have been more humdrum than legend

[1] E. Vogelsang, *Anfänge*, p. 50. The difficult problems of the MSS. of these lectures have been sifted further by H. Wenndorf, *Der Durchbruch der neuen Erkenntnis Luthers im Lichte der handschriftlichen Uberlieferungen, Hist. Vierteljahr schrift*, 1932, pp. 124, 285. Wenndorf's strictures on Vogelsang's handling of the MSS. may be justified, but they do not shake the theological value of his essay. We shall not perhaps get much nearer than the general date 1513–14. See L. Pinomaa, *Der Existentielle Charakter der Theologie Luthers*, Helsinki 1940, pp. 130–7.

[2] As with U. Saarnivaara, *Luther's Path to Evangelical Faith*, Helsinki 1947.

[3] Boehmer, *Junge Luther* (ed. Bornkamm), pp. 362–3.

[4] TR 1.146.12.

suggests, less than that dramatic intervention in which, we conceive, God is wont to deal with His servants the prophets. But it is perhaps the way in which in His inscrutable wisdom He addresses His theological professors. And we, who are considering Martin Luther, shall not have much to complain about in the way of lack of excitement in what follows.

The discovery and publication of the material from which Luther delivered his great courses of lectures in these years (Psalms, 1513–4; Romans, 1515–6; Galatians, 1516–7; Hebrews, 1517–8) has been a great achievement of the last thirty years of Luther studies, and it has revolutionized the conception of his development. It is clear that, in all essentials, his theology was in existence before the opening of the Church struggle in 1517. The old polemical assertion that Luther lacked all originality is untenable: no more than the paintings of Rembrandt, or the music of Bach, can he be explained in terms of the past alone. The Catholic Lortz says: 'Luther did not express many ideas to which we can find no parallels from earlier theologians and reformers. Nevertheless, Luther is new.'[1]

It has been said, with but slight exaggeration, that the whole of the later Luther may be found in the lectures on the Psalms.[2] Luther can still use the jargon of the schools, the distinctions of Peter Lombard,[3] and Augustine is still a dominant theological influence.[4]

He retains the doctrine of the *Syntheresis*—the inextinguishable spark of the divine in man, which desires the good.[5] His (and St. Paul's) great distinction between Law and Gospel has yet to be developed.[6] But here, proof that it is no later improvisation, are the outlines of his doctrine of the Church, the theme of the Word of God, and the assertion that the Church is intelligible to faith alone (*intelligibilis per fidem est ecclesia*). Here is the demonstration that Luther no more thinks in terms of a purely invisible Church than such modern Catholic writers as

[1] J. Lortz, *Reformation*, i, p. 147.
[2] K. Holl, *Luther*, p. 155.
[3] *ibid.* p. 156.
[4] A. Hamel, *Der Junge Luther und Augustin*, 2 vols. 1934–5.
[5] WA 3.535.36, 603.33; WA 4.255.24; Pinomaa, *Existentielle Charakter*, p. 41; W. Loewenich, *Luthers Theologia Crucis*, Munich 1933, p. 56.
[6] Runestam, *Den kristliga Friheten hos Luther och Melanchthon*, Stockholm 1917, p. 44.

E. Mersch and H. de Lubac in their expositions of the doctrine of the Church as the Mystical Body.[1]

To turn from the lectures on the Psalms to those on Romans (1515–6) is to recall G. K. Chesterton's remark about H. G. Wells that you could almost hear him growing in the night, so plain is the growth in maturity, independence and coherence in a few months. There is still much of traditional orthodoxy, and of St. Augustine. But there is now a more radical diagnosis of the sin of man, the seat of which, under all disguises and idolatries, is his egoism, lifting itself in rebellion against God.[2] The repudiation of self (*accusatio sui*) is something a man cannot achieve without the inspiration of the Holy Spirit. Concupiscence is no longer for Luther the desire of the flesh, and inbred sin is more than a mere material, a tinder (*fomes peccati*); it is a restless egotism which is active and working even in our dreams.[3] Luther has discarded the psychological teaching of Aristotle of a *habitus* within the soul, and in its place is a new anthropology of the person, the whole man. It breaks with the Platonic and neo-Platonic division between soul and body and returns to the biblical division between 'flesh' and 'spirit', the conception of man as a sinner confronted in all his personal existence by the person of the living God.[4]

More clearly expressed than ever before, is the assertion that sinful man must find a righteousness which comes from without himself. 'For God wills to save us, not by a righteousness and wisdom from within [*per domesticam*] but from without [*per extraneam*] Not that which comes and is born from ourselves. But which comes from without into us. Not which rises from the earth, but that which comes down from heaven.'[5] 'For not because he is Just is a man reckoned to be so by God, but because he is reckoned to be just by God, therefore is he just.'

[1] WA 3.259.18, 139.19, 347.25 ff.; WA 4.183.17 ff., 189.17; Holl, *Luther*, pp. 288 ff.; H. Stomps, *Die Anthropologie Martin Luthers*, 1935.

[2] WA 56.356.4. 'And this agrees with Scripture, which describes man as turned in upon himself (*incurvatum in se*) so that not only in bodily but also in spiritual goods he turns to himself and seeks himself in all things.' 357.4, 357.11.

[3] See Holl, *Luther*, pp. 62 ff. and quotations.

[4] WA 56.343.16, 343.24. 'The whole man is "flesh" because the Spirit of God abide not in it.' Regin Prenter, *Spiritus Creator*, Copenhagen, 1946, 26.

[5] WA 56.158.10, 169.29, 172.3.

It is important to guard against misunderstanding at this point, for some of the wisest scholars have warned us against supposing we are here confronted with some abstract doctrine of the imputation of the merits of Christ like that of some forms of later Lutheran orthodoxy. The righteousness of God which is given to us is, as Prenter says, 'the living Christ in his own person'.[1] Faith is much more than an intellectual acceptance of new truth, 'that is why it would be impious just to doubt or think that a man is justified by faith, but it is necessary most certainly and firmly to believe it and to know it'.[2] Peter Lombard had suggested the identity of the Holy Spirit with the charity infused into the redeemed soul, but in Luther, as his discussion of Rom. 8. 26 shows, the Spirit is no longer a transcendant cause of salvation, but the living personal presence of God, at work, and interceding for us with groans that cannot be uttered.[3] There is a characteristically Lutheran stress on the gladness, willingness and spontaneity with which the Christian man obeys and loves the will of God.[4]

The unrighteous sinner may stand in the presence of God because his unrighteousness is lost 'in the infinite abyss of the righteousness of God'.[5] We cannot linger over the doctrine of sanctification in these lectures, or compare Karl Holl's discussion of it in the light of the formidable criticism his treatment has received from Scandinavian scholars in recent years.[6] Yet all are agreed that Luther's doctrine of justification in no wise contemplates a man remaining in his sins, with no prospect of ever leaving them. On the contrary, Luther returns again and again to the thought of movement and growth in the Christian life. 'Now they begin to be Christians whose life is not in rest, but in movement, from good to better, as a sick man moves from sickness to health.'[7] The threefold formula is important: 'Always a sinner, always a penitent, always right with God.'[8] Luther goes on to speak of the renewal of our minds day by day, and how the Spirit transforms our feelings and enables us to recognize the will of God.[9] Two illustrations recur in these

[1] Prenter, p. 67 ff. [2] WA 56.39.18. [3] WA 56.378.

[4] WA 56.366.14. 'To be led by the Spirit of God is freely, promptly, cheerfully to mortify the flesh, i.e. the old man.'

[5] WA 56.204.23.

[6] K. Holl, *Luther*, pp. 115–54; Prenter, *Spiritus Creator*, p. 60.

[7] WA 56.441.14. [8] WA 56.442.17. [9] WA 56.443.5, 446.5.

lectures. The first, taken from St. Augustine, the thought of Our Lord as the Good Samaritan who finds the sinner half dead, but who takes him in his care until he is cured. The second is the thought of God as some skilled master craftsman who can demonstrate his skill in three ways: first, when he corrects the mistakes and bad workmanship of his apprentices; second, when the excellence of his own work is shown by comparison of his work with theirs; but third, when he gives away his own skill, by teaching others the secrets of his own mystery, for the third, says Luther, shows his own 'benevolence' and *humanitas*, and so the 'just God is laudable in us, because he makes us like himself'.[1]

Whatever the date when Luther first began to be exercised about predestination, his notes on Rom. 8. 28 contain a poignant discussion of the problem, which anticipates his discussion in the *De Servo Arbitrio* (1525). Luther ends with a remarkable note. 'Here I must enter a warning, lest any whose minds have not been purged rush into these speculations and fall into an abyss of horror and despair: let him first purge the eyes of his heart in meditating the wounds of Jesus Christ. Nor would I talk about this, did not the order of the lectures and necessity compel me to do so. For this is the very strongest wine and the most perfect and solid food for the perfect. The most advanced theology! But I am as a child who needs milk, not food. Let those who are as I am, do likewise. The wounds of Jesus are safe enough for us.'[2]

It is a matter for discussion how far Staupitz helped Luther to come to this conclusion.[3] One other influence must be remarked. It has been suggested that Luther turned away from the traditional theology, and from the influence of St. Augustine, because at this time he came under the influence of the mystics.[4] We need to distinguish. The word 'mysticism' is often vaguely used to cover any kind of 'inward religion'. We ought, as Vogelsang suggests, to distinguish between the mysticism of the Victorines (and of the writings of Pseudo-Dionysius), which is to be discounted in Luther's case, and that of the Roman type of St.

[1] WA 56.221–2.

[2] WA 56.400.1.

[3] E. Wolf, *Staupitz und Luther*, pp. 169–222.

[4] Miegge, *Lutero*, p. 118 *n.*; H. Bornkamm, *Eckhart und Luther*, Stuttgart 1936, *Luther und Böhme*, 1925; J. M. Clark, *The Great German Mystics*, Oxford 1949.

Bernard which but slightly influenced him, and third, the mysticism of the *devotio moderna* in the German form in which it reached him in the writings of Tauler, and the little book known to us as the *Theologia Germanica*.

Luther became acquainted with Tauler's writings through his friend John Lang, in 1516, and in the next months spoke enthusiastically about his sermons and even more warmly about the little *Theologia Germanica*. Luther may have taken some of his terminology from these writings, but their value to him seems to be that they confirmed rather than inaugurated any doctrines, by their emphasis on 'inward religion' and on the wholly personal character of sin. We may compare the similarly real but peripheral influence of William Law upon the brothers Wesley at an early stage in their theological and religious development. But as Luther's own notes on Tauler show, he did not read him uncritically, and maintained a stern sense of the superiority of theology over mystical literature. Had he been under deep influence of the mystical writings, he could never, as he did at this time, have broken with the doctrine of the *Syntheresis*, the divine spark in man, a conception especially sympathetic to mystic thought.

In any case, Luther had come to a way through his temptations about predestination apart from them. The doctrine of resignation (*resignatio ad infernum*) in Luther is different from that of the mystics. Luther believed at this time that the soul might come to the point when it joyfully agreed to the will of God, even though that will might consign it to hell, and that such a resignation must, paradoxically, be a sign of grace and a hope of predestination! But it has been powerfully shown that Luther's thought is Christological: here is no abandonment (*Gelassenheit*) of the creature before the infinite God. Instead, Luther stresses the grim reality of the humiliation of Jesus Christ, in Gethsemane and on the Cross, and in the supreme cry of dereliction, and affirms that for us men and for our salvation Christ underwent the most hideous of temptations and trod the way of horror and despair.[1] Luther does not speak of the 'imitation of Christ' as conceived by the 'modern devotion' but of the conformity of the Christian with Christ, in death and resurrection and in living

[1] Vogelsang, *Angefochtene Christus*, pp. 81 ff.

faith. Anguish, tribulation, temptation (*Anfechtung*) are signs that the Christian really is in the hands of God, and is sharing the Cross of Christ. Salvation is appropriated not through abstract consideration of a doctrine of atonement, but through the recognition of the Living God whose strange work (*opus alienum*) it is to bring us through the Law and the Wrath to knowledge of divine and infinite mercy (*opus proprium*). Law is not for Luther an abstract principle of the universe. As Macbeth saw with horror Birnam Wood, which he had thought immovable, closing in on him since behind natural phenomena was personal direction, so for Luther the Law is the personal, saving activity of God himself, and the Wrath of God (which is no fiction) becomes the engine of salvation.

One of Luther's students (1518–22) has left us a vivid picture of him at his lectures:

> He was a man of middle stature, with a voice which combined sharpness and softness: it was soft in tone, sharp in the enunciation of syllables, words and sentences. He spoke neither too quickly nor too slowly, but at an even pace, without hesitation, and very clearly, and in such fitting order that each part flowed naturally out of what went before. He did not expound each part in long labyrinths of words, but first the individual words, then the sentences, so that one could see how the content of the exposition arose, and flowed out of the text itself. For it all hung together in order, word, matter, natural and moral philosophy as the Dialectic of Philip [Melanchthon] teaches. For this was how he took it from a book of the essential matter, which he had himself prepared, so that he had his lecture material always ready to hand, conclusions, digressions, moral philosophy and also antitheses: and so his lectures never contained anything that was not pithy and relevant. And, to say something about the spirit of the man: if even the fiercest enemies of the Gospel had been among his hearers, they would have confessed from the force of what they heard, that they had witnessed, not a man, but a spirit, for he could not teach such amazing things from himself, but only from the influence of some good or evil spirit.[1]

Luther's other duties had grown formidably. Since 1511 he had been preaching in the monastery, and from 1514 in the parish church. In May, 1512, he became sub-prior and regent of the monastery school. In May, 1515, he was made

[1] *Der Junge Luther* (ed. Bornkamm), p. 367.

district overseer of eleven monasteries. He wrote wryly, complaining:

I do almost nothing but write letters all day long . . . I am conventual preacher, reader at meals, sought for to preach daily in the parish church, am regent of studies, district Vicar (i.e. eleven times Prior), inspect the fish ponds at Leitzkau, act in the Herzberg affair at Torgau, lecture on St. Paul, revising my Psalms, . . . I seldom have time to go through my canonical hours properly, or to celebrate, to say nothing of my own temptations from the world, the flesh and the devil. You see what a lazy fellow I am.[1]

Meanwhile, Luther's teaching had excited more and more bitter opposition from the Gabrielists at Erfurt, and there was rising tension at Wittenberg itself. It came to a head at a public disputation on September 25th, 1516, when Luther, for this special occasion, presided while his pupil Bartholomew Bernhardi defended a series of theses about grace and the human will, which directly attacked the Nominalist teaching.[2] But the sensation of the day came when Luther himself caused an uproar among his own colleagues by denying the authenticity of Augustine's *True and False Penitence*,[3] a writing often quoted in the *Sentences of Peter Lombard* (Bk. IV, Dist. 14–17) and which Luther asserted had been used to torture the consciences of simple folk. Andreas Karlstadt fumed, and went off to Leipzig as soon as he could to get the book. He returned, not only converted to Luther's opinion, but more enthusiastically Lutheran than Luther. The disputation had certainly cleared the air.

With the autumn mists, the plague came to Wittenberg, but Luther wrote to Lang:

Where should I fly? The world won't come to an end when brother Martin does [he was to write the same sentiment to his wife in almost the last letter of his life]. I shall send the brothers away, if the plague gets worse. I am stationed here and may not run away because of my vow of obedience, until the same authority which bids me stay, commands me to depart. Not that I do not fear the plague (I am not the Apostle Paul, but only a lecturer on him) but I hope the Lord will deliver me from my fear.[4]

[1] WA Br.1 (October 26th, 1516), p. 72.
[2] WA 1.145.1 ff.
[3] WA Br.1 (October, 1516) p. 65, 1.25.
[4] WA Br.1.73.34.

He was now quite clear in his mind about the Nominalists. 'I am not going to dispute whether Gabriel said this, or Raphael that, or Michael the other thing. I know what Gabriel says, and he says everything well—except when he talks about grace, charity, hope, faith, the virtues, about which he Pelagianizes as much as his Scotus.'[1] In February, 1517, he felt constrained to carry the war into the opposite camp, and he sent a series of propositions against Aristotelian theology to Trutvetter, via Lang, in which he poured out his deep indignation. 'The greatest part of my cross is to see brothers, with brilliant gifts, born for good studies, and yet compelled to spend their life and waste their achievement in these follies.'[2]

But in Wittenberg, the battle had been won. In May, he could write:

> Our theology and St. Augustine are going ahead, and reign in our University, and it is God's work. Aristotle is gradually going down, perhaps into eternal ruin. It is wonderful how the lectures on the *Sentences* are out of favour. Nobody can hope for an audience unless he professes this theology, i.e. the Bible or St. Augustine, or some doctor of real authority in the Church.[3]

He could not let matters rest there, without a sense of responsibility for the other teaching centres of his order, and in the autumn he decided on a bold step. At the promotion of Franz Gunther to the degree of Bachelor, he put forward a series of ninety-seven Theses: they were a careful and direct attack on the whole Nominalist position, Gabriel Biel, William of Occam, Peter D'Ailly, with a few spare shots at Scotus and 'many other doctors'.[4] It seems probable that Luther had them printed and sent to Erfurt and to Nuremberg. He wanted them publicly debated, and offered to go to Erfurt himself to defend his propositions in the university or in the monastery. His letter to Lang shows how anxiously he awaited the outcome, and with what long deliberation he had taken this step. 'They need not think I have done this thing in a corner, if indeed our University is so mean that it seems like a corner.'[5] It may have been the most carefully planned act of public defiance of Luther's career, and it seems completely to have misfired. Here, surely, might have been the opening broadside of a great controversy to shake

[1] WA Br.1.66.3. [2] WA Br.1.88.24. [3] WA Br.1.99.8.
[4] WA 1.224 ff. [5] WA Br.1.103.14.

Germany in a way second only to the Reuchlin affair. But nothing happened, and it seemed that Luther was not destined to live in history as a reformer of university studies. Not for the first, or the last, time did Luther find his best plans came to nothing, while immense and unintended consequences came when least expected.

By the autumn of 1517 Luther had come a long way. We misunderstand entirely if we think of him as a restless innovator, or, in Gerhard Ritter's fine phrase, as a kind of academic bully. When Holl calls Luther's religion the religion of conscience, it is not due to Holl's Kantianism, or Luther's subjectivism. But Luther's fight was within his conscience, and it was in the City of Mansoul he learned the art of the warfare he would one day carry to the gates of Gath, and into the streets of Askelon. His anger against the Nominalist teaching, and the Aristotelian domination of the schools, was that they were leading souls astray, fobbing men off with a false security, which failed them, as Luther had seen again and again, when they stood terrified by the fact of death. But conscience for Luther meant facing the Wrath of God, rather than preoccupation with his own emotions, and so led directly to the great saving objectivities of his *Theology of the Cross*.

He had learned that the Christian warfare is the fight of faith, faith which may run counter to all human thoughts, feelings and experiences, since it is by faith that our lives are hid with Christ in God. There is no finer or more illuminating saying of Luther's in these years than that uttered during his lectures on the Epistle to the Hebrews:

> It is a great matter, to be a Christian man, and to have a hidden life, hidden away, not in some place like a hermit, nor in his own heart, though that is an unsearchable depth, but in the invisible God himself, and to live thus in the world, but to feed on that which is never seen, except by way of the Word and only through the medium of hearing.[1]

[1] *Hebrews* (ed. Hirsch), Ruckert, Berlin 1929, p. 235.

CHAPTER FOUR

THE HUBBUB

> *'One chanced mockingly, beholding the carriage of the men, to say unto them, "What will you buy?" But they, looking gravely upon them, said, "We buy the Truth." At that there was occasion taken to despise the men the more, some taunting, some speaking reproachfully, and some calling on others to smite them. At last things came to a hubbub, insomuch that all order was confounded.'*

The Wrath of God, as a clue to the interpretation of history, is out of fashion, relegated among those categories characterized by the Master of Trinity as 'pietistic flapdoodle'. The moralizing of Carlyle or Froude has given place to the doctrinaire antinomianism of the modern historian who listens to the past as a psychiatrist to a patient, determined at all costs never at any point in the story to be shocked. Yet what men have believed about history is itself part of the story. When Michelangelo scrawled over the Pope's private chapel the vision of Judgment, and of a Christ risen in wrath, his arm forked like the lightning, a Christ, as J. A. Symonds has it, who is 'what the sins of Italy and the Church have made him', he tells us something about the sixteenth century which is important for our understanding of that age. And something apart from which we cannot understand Martin Luther.

The Church is the New Israel, the People of God. The history of the Hebrew people tells us that when the heirs of the divine promises rebel, deny, forsake their pastoral and evangelical vocation, there follows, in real history, inexorable and grim disaster. 'For every false word or unrighteousness, for cruelty and oppression, for lust or vanity, the price has to be paid at last: not always by the chief offenders, but paid by somebody—Doomsday comes at last.' But Froude's moralizing is, as he acknowledged, only an echo of the Book of Amos.

What, then, is the application to Church history? What are the inexorable consequences of the sins of the New Israel? What is the historical entail of the misdeeds, not of Political or Economic Man, but of Ecclesiastical Man, who has done so much to bedevil European history, and who reached his apogee in the late Middle Ages? What happens when the successors of the Apostles betray, deny, forsake their evangelical vocation? And what shall be done in the end thereof? It is a question which the Church has never willingly faced, but always deferred until Doomsday, for great masses of men have rarely been moved to drastic reform save under the impulse of grave disaster. But Doomsday has come, when the Church has had to face in history itself the consequences of its unassoiled sins. The Reformation is—ordeal by History. We shall see how when the Pope tried to deal with Martin Luther, the history of a thousand years intervened, with its political intrigue, juridical chicanery, moral laxity, and in the Curia itself a levity and indifference on the part of many high ecclesiastics, in sad contrast to the deep earnestness of the man they arraigned.

M. Gilson made a penetrating criticism of the Reformers when he accused them, in philosophy and theology, of failure to appreciate the importance of secondary causes. There is a worse fault, to have allowed the prime vocation, the pastoral care, to sink to the bottom of an agenda which became more and more elaborate as the whole machinery of the Church became entangled in social, political, juridical pressures. These things are freely granted by Catholic historians. But we must ask what could be the result in history of the fact that almost all the defects of the late mediæval Church touched this supreme issue. 'The hungry sheep look up and are not fed.' When the Shepherds of Israel evoked the prophetic indictment of Ezekiel, the Wrath of God was seen to be at work in inexorable historical tragedy, involving innocent and guilty. That the Shepherds of the New Israel should bring doom upon their age is a judgment which, no doubt, begs a number of important questions, though in the end the conception of the Wrath of God as an ingredient of history gives more scope for righteousness and mercy than the current popular theme of history as the dialectic of the wrath of man.

Protestants have often overdarkened the shadows. We need

not fear to acknowledge that, as the Conciliar movement had shown, the Church could produce men of learning, piety, genius, at least in as high a proportion as the modern ecumenical movement. The fifteenth century could produce a Savonarola, Geiler of Keysersberg, Thomas à Kempis, Nicholas of Cusa, Gabriel Biel. Indeed, when we consider the early sixteenth century, we may wonder if the worst had not already passed. Were these men sinners above all others? Here some suggestive words of Kingsley may be remembered: 'It is not the worst, but often the best specimens of a class or of a system who are swallowed up by the moral earthquake, which has been accumulating its forces, perhaps for centuries . . . so far from being sinners above all around them, they are often better people than those around them. It is as if they were punished, not for being who they were, but for being what they were.'[1]

It is true that a culture was dying, and that much of the life of the Church was entangled with it. If there are revivals of religion, there are revivals also of superstition, though these are less often chronicled, and the paintings of Jerome Bosch remind us of the diablerie, the revival of Gnostic cults, of astrology, the dark background of a 'failure of nerve' against which the growth of witchcraft and witch hunting have to be observed. But what was dying, like the Holy Roman Empire, and what had the secret of inner renewal, like the Papacy, was not easy to discern. A strange world was being born, its birth pangs a series of political and social tensions which baffled statesmen to comprehend, let alone resolve, while for one new world across the Atlantic to attract the bodies of men, a dozen new horizons of the mind were opening, offering the Church that challenge to baptize a culture which in the first, the fifth, the ninth centuries she had marvellously accepted, but which now, sick, enfeebled and in sin, she was unable to comprehend.

Nine out of ten men did not ponder such high themes. They worked hard, produced children and watched too many of them die, they drank beer and grumbled, and reckoned with the Church when and where it touched their own souls, in their prayers and in their pockets; and in one matter, the Indulgence affair, in a combination of both.

Over the whole doctrine of the Church, of the papal authority,

[1] C. Kingsley, 'The Judgments of God', *Westminster Sermons*, p. 237.

the doctrine of merit, the doctrine of indulgences, there reigned an uncertainty and vagueness which Lortz regards as a prime cause of the Reformation, and not least of the hesitant attitude of the orthodox with regard to Luther's teachings. The Indulgence was primarily the commutation of the act of satisfaction which was one of the three parts of the Sacrament of Penance (contrition; confession; satisfaction). In 1300 Boniface VIII issued a Jubilee Indulgence to all who visited the tombs of the Apostles on fifteen successive days: originally limited to one-hundred-year intervals, the Jubilees became more and more frequent as papal financial difficulties deepened. The practice found theoretical justification in the doctrine of the Treasure of Merits of Christ and the Saints, expounded by Alexander of Hales (*Summa*, IV, qu. 83) and confirmed in the Bull *Unigenitus* of Clement VI, 1343, which includes the statement that Christ 'acquired a treasure for the Church militant'. In 1476 Pope Sixtus IV extended the scope of an Indulgence to the souls in purgatory. By the beginning of the sixteenth century, Indulgences had become a holy business (*sacrum negotium*) so complex as to demand the superintendence of the Banking House of Fugger.

In 1513 the young Hohenzollern Prince Albert of Brandenburg (aged twenty-three) became Archbishop of Magdeburg and administrator of the diocese of Halberstadt. In 1514 there fell to him a more glittering prize, the Archbishopric of Mainz and the Primacy of Germany. Enormous fees were due to the Pope for this accumulation of benefices, and Albert was soon heavily in debt to the accommodating but watchful Fuggers. It was finally decided that when the Indulgence should be promulgated on behalf of rebuilding St. Peter's, Rome, half the proceeds should, by private agreement, go to Albert and the Fuggers. To this indulgence were attached four privileges: 'The first, the plenary remission of all sins; the second, a confessional letter allowing the penitent to choose his confessor; the third is the participation in the merits of the saints; the fourth is for the souls in purgatory.' Albert's own instructions to his sub-commissary are carefully worded to include the phrase *corde contritus et ore confessus*, i.e. they presuppose contrition and confession. But the pardoners went less discreetly to work. The literature of ecclesiastical rebuilding schemes rarely attains the higher levels of edification, but the sermons of John Tetzel (1470–1519), the Dominican charged to dispose of Indulgences in Saxony and Brandenburg, touched new depths.

The indulgence procession moved from town to town with the devout furore of a modern ecclesiastical exhibition. 'The Bull was borne on a satin, or gold-embroidered cushion, and all the priests and monks, the town council, schoolmaster, scholars, men, women, maidens and children went out to meet him with banners and tapers, with songs and processions. Then all the bells were rung, all the organs played . . . a red Cross was erected in the midst of the church, and the Pope's banner displayed.'[1]

Financial embarrassment was not confined to the Pope, or to Albert of Mainz. Shortage of coin led most German rulers to be chary of letting currency leave their territories. Frederick the Wise had little love for the new Archbishop, and the Indulgence was prohibited in Electoral Saxony. This did not greatly inconvenience the Wittenbergers, who could go off to Zerbst and Juterbogk, a few miles off, to return with extravagant stories about the sermons they had heard, and with pardons which some of them flourished in the presence of Luther.

For Luther it was no new concern, for he had already spoken publicly on the subject. True, it was a delicate matter to raise in Wittenberg, for within the Castle Church reposed Frederick the Wise's rapidly expanding collection of relics. From 5005 in 1509, they had grown in 1518 to 17,443 particles (including 204 portions and one whole corpse of the Holy Innocents!) and to them was now attached an indulgence of 127,799 years and 116 days.[2] On the other hand, for Luther to protest against Albert of Mainz was to invite the public suspicion that he was but the tool of the jealous interests of the House of Wettin. But the Indulgence caused a good deal of comment, and in public and in private Luther had been asked for his advice.

Once again, he sat down and wrote a series of Theses. He wrote fluently, for he had a gift for this kind of pithy, aphoristic paradox, and if there were some points on which he was un-

[1] B. J. Kidd, *Documents of the Continental Reformation*, Oxford 1911, v, pp. 6, 8, 9; H. Boehmer, *Road to Reformation*, pp. 167 ff.; Mackinnon, ii, pp. 290–305; H. E. Jacobs, *Martin Luther*, New York 1898, pp. 59 ff.; Preserved Smith, *Life and Letters of M. Luther*, p. 36.

[2] Scheel, *Luther*, ii, pp. 333–4.

certain, and which went beyond his own definite conviction, these were, after all, Latin theses for disputations which traditionally had a good deal of licence.

He took them over, it seems, to his printer, John Grunenberg, and asked him to run off a few copies for his own private use. One he despatched with a covering letter to Albert of Mainz, and the other to his ordinary, the Bishop of Brandenburg. But he consulted nobody, and let nobody at the court know of his intentions. About midday, on the Eve of All Saints', he strolled with Agricola the length of the little town, along the streets which to-morrow would be thronged with the faithful. He mounted the steps of the Schlosskirche and affixed his placard, as he had a right to do, and in the normal way: 'In the desire and with the purpose of elucidating the truth, a disputation will be held . . .'; at first sight no more exciting than most notices on most university boards. He turned away and went home, and no doubt ate a hearty meal. Yet this was far from casual: 'I had first prostrated myself in prayer that God would be with me.'[1] There was the ominous fact that nobody attended the disputation.

It might seem as though the operative text of the Reformation was not 'The just shall live by faith', but 'Concerning the collection'. Yet, although the ninety-five Theses on the 'Power and efficacy of Indulgences' do not mention 'Faith' or 'Justification', to read them is to be reminded again and again of the road along which Luther's thought had moved.[2] The last two Theses, and the last three words of all are revealing: 'Christians should be exhorted that they study to follow Christ, their head, through the pains of death and hell [94] and let them rather hope to enter heaven through much tribulation than to confide in the security of peace' [*Per securitatem pacis confidant*]. For it was this same 'security' which Luther had again and again attacked, the terrible false security which could delude simple men into believing that the Wrath of God could be appeased by a money payment to God's commissaries, what a modern Lutheran martyr (Dietrich Bonhoeffer) has called the doctrine of 'cheap grace' against the doctrine of 'costly grace'. In Luther's great

[1] TR 5.658.1.

[2] Wace and Bucheim, *Luther's Primary Works*, pp. 414 ff.; *Works of Martin Luther* (A. J. Holman, Philadelphia), vol. i, 13 ff.; *M. Luther's 95 Theses* (Kleine Texte 142); H. Bornkamm, *Luther's Geistige Welt*, Luneburg 1947, pp. 39 ff.

conviction (62) 'the true treasure of the Church is the Holy Gospel of the Glory and the Grace of God'. Or turn to the first Thesis: 'When Our Lord and Master Jesus Christ said *Poenitentiam Agite* . . . he wished the entire life of believers to be one of penitence . . .' with the reminiscence of his own discovery of the inwardness of repentance through the offices of Staupitz, the echo of his own aphorism in his 'Romans'—'*semper peccator, semper PENITENS, semper Justus.*'

For the rest, they are no revolutionary manifesto. The authority of the Pope is affirmed. The existence of Purgatory is taken for granted. Thesis 71 says: 'Let him who speaks against the truth of apostolic pardons be accursed and anathema.' It is true that there is an edge to these admissions, and a sharp comparison with the true Christian priorities, the duty to preach the Word of God, and to perform works of charitable service.

We hear much nowadays of the importance of 'technics' in society. Rarely has one invention had more decisive influence than that of printing on the Reformation. Luther's Theses were printed and translated into German, reprinted and posting through Germany in a fortnight, and circulating everywhere within a few weeks. In March, 1518, Luther was annoyed to get printed and translated copies of his Theses from his Nuremberg friend, Cristopher Scheuerl.: 'For I have certain doubts about them myself, and should have spoken differently and more distinctly, had I known what was going to happen.'[1] He had invited a public disputation, and nobody had come to dispute. Now, by a stroke of magic, he found himself addressing the world. All he could do was write a long and careful exposition of his Theses, and send these 'Resolutions' to the Bishop of Brandenburg. To him he explained his original intention, to provoke a learned and public discussion, and how his plans had gone astray, from their publication in the vulgar tongue. He persisted, however, in his plea for full discussion. But he made plain he had not intended to act impertinently. 'I submit all things to the judgment of holy Church,' and he begged the Bishop to take pen in hand and strike through anything amiss.[2] We are not to suppose that Luther was dissembling. At the end of his life he could affirm (1545): 'When I took up this matter

[1] WA Br.1.152.13. [2] WA Br.1.139.

against Indulgences, I was so full and drunken, yea, so besotted in papal doctrines, that out of my great zeal I would have been ready to murder—at least I would have been glad to see and help that murder should be done—on all who would not be obedient and subject to the Pope, even to his smallest word.'[1] Luther also published in German some notes of a sermon on the subject of Indulgences, at the end of which the first glow of his future polemical power may be discerned.

Authority had taken action. Albert of Mainz had forwarded the documents to Rome, with the request that Luther be inhibited. In February, 1518, orders to this effect were handed to Gabriel della Volta, pro-magistrate of the Augustinian Order, and the command was transmitted to Staupitz.

The serious danger came from the Dominicans. At their Saxon Chapter in January, 1518, Wimpina and Tetzel propounded a series of counter-Theses, and formally charged Luther at Rome on suspicion of heresy. The German Dominicans were soon boasting that Luther would be burned, and there must have been many at the time who saw in the controversy just one more squabble among the always quarrelling religious. Tetzel sent eight hundred copies of his Theses to Wittenberg, where the adventurous colporteur was roughly manhandled by the students who made a bonfire of the documents, winning a reprimand from the authorities, since the tumult could hardly have helped Luther at this delicate juncture. Luther's greatest ally was his friend and admirer Spalatin (1484–1548), librarian, secretary and chaplain to the Elector Frederick, and throughout these critical months it would be hard to exaggerate the debt he owed him. Alarmed though Luther's fellow Augustinians might be (they begged him not to bring the Order into discredit),[2] they had no intention of throwing him to the Dominicans. So Luther set out in April, 1518, for the Chapter at Heidelberg, despite alarming rumours, and provided with letters of credence of such high testimony that one official exclaimed, 'By God, that's a fine passport they've given you!'[3]

Luther did the long journey on foot, and not all the soft beauties of the Neckar in spring could assuage his physical

[1] WML 1.10. [2] WA 31.i.111.34, 40.iii.620.32. [3] WA Br.1.173.21.

exhaustion. When the Chapter opened, far from being in disgrace, the occasion became an unexpected and personal triumph. He was relieved of the post of District Vicar, which was given to his friend Lang, but this was a wise tactical move, and it must in the circumstances have been a welcome relief. Luther himself presided at a full-dress theological disputation where the Indulgences were forgotten, and once more the battle raged around the Aristotelian Nominalism and the new antidote proffered by Wittenberg. Luther's Heidelberg Theses rank high among his theological writings, and in recent years Walther von Loewenich has made them the starting point for an illuminating exposition of Luther's *Theology of the Cross*.[1] Luther sharply distinguishes between the 'Theology of the Cross'—'thus the true theology is in Christ crucified, and there is the true knowledge of God'—and the 'Theology of Glory', a theology of speculation on the attributes of deity which is ignorant that 'God is not found save in sufferings and in the Cross'.[2]

It may be that Luther has not yet emerged from his Augustinian tendency to put 'humility' in the place of 'faith', but here, clearly established, is his now normative division between the ministry of the Law and of the Gospel, the first as God's Strange Work (*opus alienum*), and the second, God's own work (*opus proprium*) by which he makes sinners righteous.[3]

The debate was lively and there was some opposition, but when the junior Heidelberg divine shouted angrily, 'If the peasants heard that, they would stone you!' his voice was drowned in general laughter.[4] But it was among the younger men that Luther made his conquests that day. One of them, the young Alsatian Dominican, Martin Bucer, was overwhelmed, and wrote home in high glee because he managed to have lunch with Staupitz and Luther:

> Their wiles were not able to move him an inch . . . his sweetness in answering is remarkable [Bucer was not always to find it so remarkable in respect of himself!], his patience in listening is incomparable, in his explanations you would recognize the acumen of Paul, not

[1] W. von Loewenich, *Luther's Theologia Crucis*, Munich 1933.
[2] WA 1.362. [3] WA Br.1.173. [4] WA 1.361.

Scotus: his answers, so brief, so wise and drawn from the Scriptures, easily made all hearers his admirers.[1]

Two other notable converts among the young men were John Brenz and Theodore Billicanus. The Reformation, like every other movement, cut through the generations, and the older men were not much impressed.

Luther got a lift back, and travelled part of the way with his old teacher, Usingen. As the wagon jolted and rumbled along, Luther poured out his soul with eager fire, but the time and the place were not propitious for a seminar, and he left the old man glum and silent, and a little dazed. To be cooped up with Martin Luther at close quarters, in this exuberant stage of his career, was apt to be a wearing experience. On his way through Erfurt, Luther tried to see his other old teacher, Trutvetter, but the old man was too ill to receive him, though Luther sent him an affectionate note disclaiming any intention of making a personal attack on Trutvetter 'to whom I owe everything', but explaining his own position: 'I am of the plain conviction that it is impossible to reform the Church, unless the Canon Laws, the decretals, the scholastic theology, philosophy, logic as they now are, are uprooted from the foundations, and other studies put in their place. To you I may not seem much of a logician, and perhaps I am not: but I do know this, that I fear nobody's logic in defending this thesis.'[2]

In May, Luther sent a copy of his *Resolutions*, with a letter of humble appeal, to Pope Leo X. The contrast between Luther's first draft and the fair copy reminds us that it was probably overseen by Spalatin and Staupitz, the first of many curious examples of what happened when Luther tried to temper his own forthright vehemence to the diplomacy of more tactful friends. In the same month, the Dominican Chapter met in Rome, and Tetzel was awarded a doctorate (a year later, discredited and disgraced, he was to die in Leipzig). Matters now took a more serious turn in Luther's case. In March (14th) he had preached a fiery sermon about the notorious abuse of the power of excommunication for trivial offences. Two Dominicans, who probably attended for the purpose, extracted articles from their notes, exaggerated them, and despatched them with some

[1] P. Smith, *Luther's Correspondence*, Philadelphia 1915, p. 82.
[2] WA Br.1.169–70.

even more dubious gossip to Rome, but not before they had enlisted the interest of the Emperor, through the Cardinal Cajetan. On the ground of this spurious information, Luther was declared to be a notorious heretic, and the formal sixty days' citation to Rome interrupted by a new order to Cajetan to arrest Luther, to demand that the Elector surrender him, and to order the Augustinian authorities in Germany to carry out the arrest.

CHAPTER FIVE

GREAT ARGUMENT

'The Judge directed his speech to the prisoner at the bar, saying, "Thou runagate, heretic, and traitor, hast thou heard what these honest gentlemen have witnessed against thee?"

FAITHFUL: *May I speak a few words in my own defence?*

JUDGE: *Sirrah! Sirrah! Thou deservest to live no longer, but to be slain immediately, yet that all men may see our gentleness towards thee, let us hear what thou, vile runagate, hast to say.'*

THE LUTHER MEMORIAL in the City of Worms is what we might expect of a near contemporary of the Albert Memorial in London. Even the egregious Baedeker who, like charity in St. Paul, is always eager to believe the best, can only say about it that it looks well enough in the early morning (*Morgenbeleuchtung günstig*). In the centre, an enormous Luther (3.2 metres high) gazes skyward with fixed intensity (heroic faith!), cuddling an enormous Bible. And there, among a number of lesser worthies, stands the figure (2.8 metres high) of the Elector Frederick the Wise.

The Elector Frederick earned his place on the memorial. He could have had little sympathy with Luther's theological protest against Indulgences. But he had a lively concern for his University and respect for all he had heard of Martin Luther. He had enough patriotism, not least where the Italians were concerned, to be unwilling to sacrifice Luther as a gambit to the cruel mercies of the Curia. But it is well to remember that at almost any time, had he so willed, the Elector could have ended the career of Martin Luther, and that it was due to him that Wittenberg remained for Luther the strangely calm centre of the cyclonic storm which raged all around.

When one considers the short shrift given to the Cambridge Reformers in England in the next two decades, one can only marvel at the fatal delays, hesitations, and patience of the

Roman authorities, and seek the reason in the realm of politics. For, just now, the Pope needed Frederick's goodwill. The arrangements for the succession in the Empire were under consideration, and the Pope was most unwilling that the House of Habsburg should find further aggrandizement. An order was sent to Cajetan that he should interview Luther at Augsburg, and that though there could be no question of argument with Luther, all possible deference must be shown towards the Elector. The Pope also intended the signal compliment of the Golden Rose.

Luther was now in deadly danger, uncertain from day to day that he might not be the price of some diplomatic deal in high places. Staupitz, whose heart made up in warmth what it lacked in stoutness, could only write gloomy encouragement—'You have only the Cross to expect. Leave Wittenberg while there is still time, and come to me, so that we might live and die together.' Luther went to Weimar, however, to receive his expenses and letters of recommendation through Spalatin (he never spoke more than a dozen words to the Elector in his life). At length he arrived in Augsburg, *pauper et pedester*, afraid and sick at heart. Now, one individual, he must meet the angry engine of the mightiest institution in the world, the accumulated majesty of centuries, speaking with the authority of God himself. His fears were not lessened when the two Saxon councillors in the city warned him, in view of rumours, not to go near the Cardinal without a safe conduct.

Even a modern schoolboy knows of Luther's defiance at Worms, though the traditional utterance may be apocryphal. But in 1521 it was plain that half Germany was at Luther's side. If we look for a moment and a saying to admire, then we must turn to this moment in Augsburg, with Luther alone indeed (his friend had gone off to look for Staupitz) when the Italian diplomat Urban de Serralonga visited him, putting into words Luther's own secret doubts and fears, and ending with the capital taunt, 'Do you really think the Elector is going to war on your account?' Luther: 'By no means.' Urban: 'And where will you go then?' Luther: '*Sub Coelo*' (Under heaven). We do Luther less than justice if we underrate the earnestness of his words, of his naïve confidence that a man might go out, like Abraham, knowing not whither, and find his God a sufficient guard against a world in arms.

Perhaps because he had faced his own fears openly, the interview cheered him. Then came the four momentous interviews with Cajetan himself, a theologian of parts. If Luther had been so simple as to suppose authority would bandy words with him, he was soon speedily disillusioned. The Cardinal told him he was to do three things: repent and revoke his errors, promise not to teach them again, and refrain from all future mischievous activities. The veneer of etiquette soon wore thin and the Cardinal found, willy-nilly, that he was entangled in a wrangle about the meaning of the word 'Treasure' in the Bull *Unigenitus*. The Bull, Cajetan condescended to explain, means that 'Christ acquired a treasure', and this treasure consists of the merits of Christ and His saints. He was flabbergasted when Luther denied this. In fact, whatever the Bull might imply, it did not explicitly state the connection between the 'treasure' and the merits of Christ and the saints. For Luther this was more than a verbal quibble, for it was this very ambiguity which underlay his Theses 56–62, which culminated in the affirmation: 'The real treasure of the Church is the Holy Gospel of the Glory and the Grace of God' (Cajetan's haste, in the following days, to get some clear confirmation of his own exposition from Rome, is a sign that Luther had found a real loophole). Other interviews were not more successful, and the Cardinal haughtily denied 'bandying' words with Luther. When, on October 14th, Luther produced a written statement, Cajetan spoke of it so contemptuously that Luther's pent-up emotions burst out: voices were raised on both sides, and the Cardinal cut short the interview, telling Luther not to come near him again unless he were ready to recant. He saw Staupitz and Link privately, however, with a view to using their influence upon the obstinate monk. Affairs reached an impasse which only action could break. On October 16th Staupitz and Link judged matters to be so dangerous as to demand their own hasty withdrawal from the city. Luther wrote a formal appeal to the Pope and a long letter to Cajetan. As hours and days slipped away in ominous silence, Luther's friends became alarmed, and finally, in view of a persistent rumour that he was to be seized and sent in chains to Rome, they panicked. Luther was suddenly bundled out through a postern gate, ill clad and ill mounted, and he rode until forced to stop from exhaustion. A letter from Spalatin a few days later told him he had got away just in time.[1]

The Cardinal was furious at the defection, and wrote a stern letter to the Elector complaining of Luther's insolence. He had given Luther a hearing, and Luther had made plain the depth of his errors, 'part of them contrary to the teaching of the Apostolic See, and part of them damnable errors—and believe me, Your Grace, I know what I am talking about'. The letter ended with a contemptuous reference to Luther (*fraterculus*). Frederick passed it to Luther, who wrote a long and careful reply (his life might depend on it). He charged Cajetan with breaking his promises to the Elector, since all along there had been no discussion such as he had demanded, and since judgment had been passed on him before he had been heard. But Luther ended, 'I am willing to leave your territory and go wherever the merciful God would have me go.'

It seemed that go Luther must, though the Elector did not relish losing his pet theological professor to the King of France. At the end of November Luther said farewell to the Wittenbergers. On December 1st he gave a farewell supper, in the course of which two letters dramatically arrived, the first, expressing through Spalatin the Elector's surprise that Luther was not already gone, the second saying that if he had not departed he was to remain, in view of new and urgent matters which must be discussed. It seems probable that the change of plan was due to the appearance of the Papal emissary, Charles von Miltitz. On December 18th the Elector made up his mind. He would not send Luther to Rome, or into exile, unless he were first duly heard and properly convicted.

In the interval, happier events had occurred. The Elector was concerned that humanist studies at Wittenberg should not lag behind those at other universities, and had been prevailed upon to instal a Professor of Greek (to be followed by a Professor of Hebrew). In Germany there were more impecunious humanist scholars than pensions and professorial stipends, so that there was the usual polite jostling and touting. It looked as though the prize must go to the tedious Mosellanus from Leipzig, when it was suddenly announced that the post would be

[1] Mackinnon, ii, pp. 72–92; Boehmer, *Road to Reformation*, pp. 230, 244; Bainton, *Church History* (September, 1947), p. 174.

filled by a young prodigy, a beardless boy, nephew of the great Hebraist Reuchlin, Philip Melanchthon (1497–1560). He was small, thin, with an enormous brow, looking so absurdly youthful that one would have liked to hear Luther's comment when the new professor (aged twenty-one) announced as the subject of his Inaugural 'On the Reform of Adolescent Studies'! But the address itself, a mature and scholarly programme of humanist reform, was swift to win hushed respect and, at the end, wondering applause. Soon the new professor was lecturing to crowded audiences of several hundreds of students, where dons and undergraduates jogged one another's elbows in a zest for note taking. Luther wrote to his friends with huge glee, and with characteristic generosity declared that this young colleague surpassed himself, not only in polite letters, but in theological exposition. It was the beginning of an historic friendship. Luther's was the stronger character, but in some measure each supplied the defects of the other, while both owed more than they knew to this enduring bond which at times became sadly strained, but which never broke.

On January 12th, 1519, the old Emperor Maximilian died. 'Kaiser Max' as warrior, hunter and mountaineer, had greatly appealed to German sentiment, but his mixture of family and imperial ambition had fatally weakened his achievement, and he had opposed the constitutional reforms within Germany proposed by the 'Peace and Order' movement of Archbishop Berthold of Mainz (1484–1504)[1]. His nephew Charles came from the Netherlands, and brought a fateful association with Spain: he would represent such an accumulation of Imperial power as had never been wielded since the days of the Emperor Charles the Great. The Pope exerted full pressure to prevent the Empire passing to the formidably encircling sovereignty of Charles, and he was willing rather to favour the claims of Francis I of France or even of the Elector Frederick. The result was that in the matter of Luther the delaying tactics of the Saxon court found full scope. On March 29th the Pope wrote Luther a note gentler in tone than any previous communication. In June the word was passed to Frederick that if all went well in the election there

[1] V. Ranke, *Deutsche Geschichte im Zeitalter der Reformation*, pp. 167 ff.; W. Andreas, *Deutschland vor der Reformation*, pp. 244–55; H. Holborn, *Ulrich von Hutten*, Yale 1937, pp. 10–12.

might be a Cardinal's hat available for one of the Elector's friends! This was the peak of papal accommodation, however, and a new situation was to arise with the formal election of the new Emperor. What with one thing and another, the action against Luther hung fire during the critical spring and summer of 1519. From the Catholic view, it was a fatal delay, and the historian J. Lortz quotes with approval the judgment that nothing could go so far to justify Luther's protest as this subordination of the peril of heresy to the momentary interests of papal and Italian politics.[1]

Two important figures emerge in 1519, the Papal Agent, Charles von Miltitz, and Doctor John Eck, the theologian from Ingolstadt.[2]

Miltitz was that florid sixteenth-century type, an Italianate German with enormous self-confidence, always planning diplomatic gestures on the grand scale which deceived nobody more than himself, a kind of ecclesiastical Von Ribbentrop. Eck was a theologian with a prodigious memory, steeped in scholasticism, skilled in disputations (people did not forget his energetic *Distinguo*). He was also vain, loud-mouthed, violent, a heavy drinker, who according to an unamiable account looked like a butcher—for all the world like the caricature of Luther imagined by some people. Between them their intrigues add a streak of fantasy to the papal strategy in these months: on the one hand, the 'Walrus and Carpenter' tactic of Miltitz (' "I weep for you," the Walrus said, "I deeply sympathize" '); and on the other, the summary 'Off with his head!' of Eck, as the Queen in *Alice*.

Miltitz came over the mountains replenished with polite bribes which ranged from dispensations for Frederick's illegitimate children to the great compliment of the Golden Rose for their devout parent. He brought enough reassuring gossip about the Curia to make Frederick more hopeful about Luther, since the Cardinal Accolti and the Holy Father himself had expressed some trenchant opinions about Tetzel and Prierias, Luther's chief enemies.[3] Miltitz was ready to do all he could to make an

[1] J. Lortz, *Reformation in Deutschland*, Freiburg 1948, p. 217.

[2] John Maier of Eck (1486–1543) of the Universities of Heidelberg, Tübingen, Freiburg im Breisgau (D.D. 1510).

[3] Despite R. Bainton (*Church History*, 1947, p. 176) I think Boehmer has the right interpretation of a most confusing passage.

accommodation. He would attend to Tetzel personally, if that would be appreciated. Luther had a series of interviews with Miltitz at Altenburg: he was not at all deceived by the nuncio's slobbering and lachrymose benevolence, but he was willing to refrain from controversy if his opponents would likewise observe an armistice. Miltitz promised to arrange for a more impartial arbitrator—the Archbishop of Salzburg, perhaps, or His Grace of Trier. Luther published a short statement intended to clear away popular misunderstanding of his teaching, and it included two notable paragraphs. The first, 'I have not forbidden good works. I have simply declared that, just as a tree must be good before it can bring forth good fruit, so man must be made good by God's grace before he can do good.'[1]

The other, *On the Roman Church*, must be set within its context. Eck had struck up a friendship with Luther in 1517, and Luther was deeply hurt and angered when Eck circulated among his friends a slashing attack on Luther's Theses. Into this situation leaped the impulsive Karlstadt, and the result was that Eck challenged Karlstadt to a public disputation, though his real objective was Luther. Negotiations for the disputation dragged on for months, and involved a small pamphlet war by way of preliminary. From these preliminary skirmishes a matter arose which was for Luther of catastrophic importance.

In an almost casual aside, in the course of his *Resolutions*, Luther had suggested that, in the time of Gregory I, the Roman Church was not over all other churches (*non erat super alias ecclesias*)[2]. Eck fastened on this in the twelfth of a series of Theses which he published against Karlstadt and Luther. 'We deny that the Roman Church was not superior to other Churches in the time of Sylvester, but we recognize that he who had the seat and faith of blessed Peter has always been the successor of Peter and the Vicar of Christ.'[3]

This was the provocation which turned Luther towards an intensive study of Church History (in the *Historia Tripartita*) and of the Canon Law. In the 'Articles' published after the agreement with Miltitz, the extreme tension of loyalty is apparent. 'The Roman Church,' says Luther, 'is honoured by God above

[1] *Unterricht auf etlich Articckel*. WA 2.69 ff.
[2] WA 1.571.
[3] WA 9.209.40.

all others, by the undoubted fact that SS. Peter and Paul, 46 Popes and many hundreds of thousands of martyrs have shed their blood there . . . if unfortunately there are such things in Rome as might be improved, there neither is, nor can be any reason that one should tear oneself away from the Church in schism. Rather, the worse things become, the more a man should help and cling to her, for by schism and contempt nothing can be mended.'[1]

On March 5th he wrote to Spalatin, 'I was never of a mind to desert the Apostolic See . . . I am quite content that he should be called, and in fact be "Lord". What is that to me? I know that the Grand Turk should be honoured and that he wields his authority by the grace of God, because it is certain that he could have no power unless God willed it.'[2] Here Luther reckons the Papacy as among the 'powers that be' (Rom. 13. 1).

But Eck was a genuine *advocatus diaboli* where Luther was concerned. Luther could not resist capping Eck's twelfth Thesis with his own thirteenth: 'That the Roman Church is superior to all Churches is indeed proved by the far-fetched decrees put out by the Roman pontiffs in the last 400 years. But this ecclesiastical dogma is contrary to the approved histories of 1100 years, the plain teaching of Divine Scripture, and the decree of the Council of Nicea, the most sacred of all councils.' Whatever the effect of this startling view on Luther's enemies, it badly scared all his friends, and Karlstadt and Spalatin, hastily conferring, groaned in apprehension to Luther. He wrote back in vehement annoyance at their temerity: 'Your letter almost made me sick [*ego prope fuissem stomachus motus*—it was probably the truth!], you press me to tell you my plan of campaign . . .'[3] Unwillingly, as though the advertisement of his tactics were tempting Providence, Luther explained that it was really a trap for Eck, that it would certainly entice him into some yet more extravagant thesis, and force him to take up positions from which he could not retract. Subtlety in conflict was not Luther's strong point, and this dangerous game, he was to learn, could be played by others. Meanwhile Luther's appeal to history proceeded, and on March 13th, immersed in study of the Decretals, he wrote: 'And (a word in your ear) I don't know whether the

[1] WA 2.72. [2] WA Br.1.356.8. [3] WA Br.1.353.1.

Pope is Antichrist himself, or only his apostle, so grievously is Christ, i.e. Truth, manhandled and crucified by him in these decretals.'[1]

The Disputation took place at Leipzig at the beginning of July, 1519 (a day or so before, a fanfare of trumpets had announced in Frankfurt the election of Charles V as Emperor).[2] Duke George had put the Pleissenburg Castle at the disposal of Leipzig University. The Duke was a blunt, honest, rather obtuse prince, something of a Colonel Blimp (witness his remark to Luther—'God's law, or man's law, what's it matter? The Pope's the Pope!') He had been reluctant to allow the intrusion of Luther into what had been arranged as a disputation between Eck and Karlstadt. There was some irritating haggling about this, and about what judges should be appointed, until Luther consented to name the Universities of Erfurt (where he had friends) and Paris (the citadel of the Conciliar view that the Papacy existed 'by human law'). On July 1st Eck, grumbling loudly at the poor quality of the local beer, announced to a friend that the Wittenbergers had arrived. They had come in such numbers (two hundred, to say nothing of dons) that the town hastily armed its Home Guard. The Wittenberg procession was headed by two wagons. The first bore Karlstadt, hugging his beloved text-books, while the second bore the Rector of Wittenberg (Duke Barnim of Pomerania), Luther and Melanchthon. As they entered the gate, the first wagon broke down, depositing Karlstadt heavily in the mud, to the delight of lewd fellows of the baser (Leipzig) sort. But it was a nasty fall, and he hurt his hand and had to be bled, so that what with the injury and the medical treatment he was not in his best form in the succeeding days.

Preliminaries were exhausting. They began at 7 a.m. with a Mass of the Holy Ghost, a new work in twelve parts (and a first performance) by the local musician, George Rhau. There followed a tedious harangue in Latin by Mosellanus on the procedure of debate, and at the end of two long hours the packed audience watched hopefully as the Professor of Poetry subsided, bowing repeatedly, through a back door, only to re-emerge smiling an instant later to introduce more musicians, so

[1] WA Br.1.359.29.
[2] K. Brandi, *Kaiser Karl V*, Munich 1941, vol. i, p. 96.

that the hot audience was fain to kneel during a hymn to the Holy Ghost. At long last, came lunch. Later, with the flourishing of trumpets, the disputation began, in courteous, leisurely, mediæval fashion. The first week was spent by Eck and Karlstadt in a debate on the subject of grace and free will. The most lively moment was when an exasperated Eck appealed to the regent whether it was absolutely necessary for Karlstadt to bring all his books with him, and to look up every reference; and, to the relief of most, the decision was in favour of Eck. The debate occupied but part of the day, and there was time for sightseeing. The only positive achievement of Miltitz had been to secure the disgrace of Tetzel, and as he lay dying in Leipzig at this time, Luther sent his enemy a warm and generous word of comfort. By night, a score of heated unofficial disputations waged among the students, under the bright, smoking lights of the taverns and the hostility of the armed watch posted thick about Eck's lodgings.[1]

As the debate continued, the laity found that the entertainment value of a theological disputation on correct and formal lines was soon exhausted. Even some of the theologians preferred to follow the debate with closed eyes, and needed a sad amount of prodding in the intervals. Then, on July 4th, Luther came into the debate and the crowd surged back:

> Martin [wrote Mosellanus] is of middle height, of spare body, spent alike with care and study, so that you can almost count his bones: still in the prime of life, with strength undiminished, and a high clear voice.[2]

He began carefully, safeguarding his thirteenth Thesis with the assertion that the Papacy existed by human right (a widespread opinion since the Conciliar movement, and one held by Sir Thomas More in his youth). Danger came, as so often, from the unexpected quarter. In the preliminary correspondence, Eck had flung the epithets 'Hussite' and 'Bohemian' at Luther. But the University of Leipzig had its own historical reasons, and Duke George his own family motives, for being sensitive about Bohemia. Luther had grown up with the normal horror for the

[1] P. Smith, *Luther's Correspondence*, p. 195.
[2] P. Smith, *Luther's Correspondence*, p. 261.

notorious heretic who had been burned at Constance. The pride of the Erfurt Augustinians was John Zachariae, the so-called 'Scourge of Huss', and Luther had often seen the proud tomb on which was carved the Golden Rose awarded to the Augustinian for his zeal.[1] Luther protested vehemently at the charge, but at last his opponent's taunts and this flagrant playing to the gallery got under his guard, and he affirmed that 'among the articles of John Huss and the Hussites which were condemned, are many which are truly Christian and evangelical, and which the Church Universal cannot condemn!' This was sensational! There was a moment of shocked silence, and then an uproar above which could be heard Duke George's disgusted, 'Gad, Sir, that's the Plague!' For Luther had, in fact, moved beyond discussion of the papal power: he had called in question the authority of the great German Council which had so proudly achieved a reunion of the broken Christian world. Eck pressed his advantage home, and Luther, trapped, admitted that since their decrees are also of human law, Councils may err. The rest was anti-climax. Eck could afford to make concessions about Indulgences now that Luther had made this huge admission. Somehow Karlstadt got back into the debate on July 14th, and Duke George hastily closed the proceedings (the Elector of Brandenburg was coming on a hunting visit, and the Saxon Duke must have looked forward to the baying of hounds as a refreshing change from the bellowing of theologians). Once again George Rhau appeared, 'with a hundred pipers and a' and a' ', the Town Musicians, and with an elaborate *Te Deum* the debate concluded. Both sides naturally claimed the victory. It was a tactical success of momentary value for Eck. But the strategic victory was Luther's. Lortz has seen the fatal weakness of the Catholic party in the fact that in the next weeks Eck was entirely preoccupied with his personal success, sunning himself in his new glory, swaggering about the city, culpably heedless of the deep and tragic issues now revealed. Lortz also sees in the refusal of the universities to pronounce judgment against Luther, and the silence of most of them, yet another proof of the genuine theological confusion prevalent in Christendom.[2]

For Luther the debate had been important, for it made him face the implications of his protest. The whole momentum of the

[1] Scheel, ii, p. 64. [2] J. Lortz, *Reformation*, i, pp. 222–4.

Church struggle was increased by this public attention and by the pamphlet war which flared anew. It gave the final impetus to the hostility of Eck which would lead to Luther's impeachment at Rome. Yet though Eck had secured a triumph, the Leipzig disputation set new forces in motion throughout the German nation. A year hence Eck would be horrified, on returning to Leipzig, at the swift movement of national opinion to Luther's side.[1]

[1] Mackinnon, ii, chap. 5; Charles Beard, *Martin Luther and the Reformation*, London 1896, pp. 289 ff.

CHAPTER SIX

THE REFORMER

'Hear of him! Ay, and I also heard of the molestations, troubles, wars, captivities, cries, groans, frights and fears that he met with, and had in his journey: besides, I must tell you all our country rings with him. There are but few houses that have heard of him and his doings but have sought after and got the records of his pilgrimage.'

THE YEARS 1519–21 saw a prodigious mental activity which drew from Luther a vast, tumultuous flood of ideas, as tracts, treatises, commentaries, polemic, trod on the heels of one another, too fast for three printing presses to keep pace. 'I hold the sword with one hand . . . and with the other build the wall, lest, should I give my whole attention to either pursuit, I should accomplish neither.'[1] In fact, each negative criticism is matched by some positive edification. It is as though the distinction between Wrath and Mercy were reflected in his mind, since his writings fall roughly into those two categories.

He had to meet a vociferous band of polemical opponents, Prierias, Alveldus, Eck, Emser, Catherinus, Cochlaeus, not a man among them of first quality of mind or character. They remind us of Belloc's gibe at Extension Lecturers:

We circulate throughout the Land,
The second rate, and second hand.

But this could not compete with the first-rate and first-hand as it came pouring out of the mind of one of the greatest controversialists of all time. Often he ignored them, and Luther has never received sufficient credit for the books he never wrote. Like Milton, he had a terrible polemical talent, and both enraged their opponents because they could outpace them in vocabulary and verve, and could invariably contrive that last

[1] P. Smith, *Luther's Correspondence*, p. 479.

and rudest word which would be repeated chuckling even among their enemies. For Luther was touched with the comic spirit. His *Answer to the Note of the Stolpen Official*[1] made Miltitz writhe with laughter, and drove Duke George to a series of bellowing guffaws.

He found he could write for common people in the language which they could understand. 'Many people . . . say I write only little pamphlets and German sermons for the unlearned laity. . . . Would to God I had in all my life . . . helped one layman to be better.'[2] It was notoriously a coarsely-spoken age when an English Queen might use language to make the traditional fishwife blush. Anybody who will study Pieter Breughel's conglomeration of Dutch proverbs will realize that a high proportion of the commonplaces of peasant speech would be unmentionable and unprintable in modern polite society. The problem of Luther's language about the Papacy is not of this class, however, and needs more careful treatment than we can give it here, save for the reminder that a similar imagery is to be found in Ezekiel with something of the same psychological motive.[3] By and large, to concentrate, as Grisar had done, all the dirt within a few pages, is to give a completely false impression of Luther as a writer, and even as a polemic divine. And Luther is far removed from the 'Dirt for Dirt's sake' attitude of many of the humanists, and even from the *Merry Tales* which deface the writings of St. Thomas More. This is not at all to deny that Luther's popular polemics reveal him at his worst. Again and again Luther returns to the theme of the Church. It is a misconception to suppose that he fled from reality towards an 'invisible' spiritual Church, or that he preached only an individualist doctrine of Justification. Paul Althaus has suggested that the phrase *communio sanctorum* is one of the keys to his writings in these fateful months, and he loves to expound the solidarity of believers.

Among the heavenly hierarchy, none were object of such popular superstition as the so-called fourteen Auxiliary Saints (SS. Acacius–Vitus) whose combined intercessions covered a grotesque variety of bodily afflictions, and who huddle together on the paintings of a Matthias Grunewald or Lukas Cranach

[1] February, 1520. WA 6.135 ff. [2] WML 1.185.

[3] See the essay 'Dirt' by E. Bevan in *Hellenism and Christianity*.

with moody benevolence. Luther turned instead to the Psalms, to the beautiful *Fourteen of Consolation*, a series of meditations on divine help and spiritual conflict written to comfort Frederick in the illness which overtook him in the late summer of 1519. It is a meditation on the comfort of Christian solidarity—'When we feel pain, suffer, die, let us firmly believe that it is not we, or we alone, but Christ and His Church are in pain, suffering, dying with us. We can apply to ourselves the words of Elisha—"and the Lord opened the eyes of the young man, and he saw: and behold the mountains were full of horses and chariots round about Elisha." This remains for us, too: that is, to pray that our eyes may be opened (the eyes of faith, I mean) that we may see the Church round about us. Then there will be nothing for us to fear.'[1]

Luther wrote his classic tract, *Of Good Works* (1520), at the request of Spalatin. It disproves two common misconceptions, that Luther was not really concerned for morality, and that his doctrine of justification leaves Christian ethics hanging in the air. Luther demonstrates how Christian behaviour derives from the fact that 'the first, the highest and most precious of all good works is faith in Christ'.[2] Faith for Luther is, as in the New Testament, not one of a long agenda of virtues, but a whole dimension of Christian existence, with hope and love the fountain from which the Christian life must spring. The Christian man moves in two worlds: a world which is hid with Christ in God, and the visible, fallen, tangible world where also God has called and placed him. Faith is the point where the Christian unites both worlds,[3] and Luther's doctrine of Temptation (*Anfechtung*) is seen to be the affirmation that the ultimate, unremitting Christian warfare is this good fight of faith, which comes home to the Christian in the real decision of everyday life. Luther wrote it too quickly, and the tract tails off badly, but the first half is fully occupied with what we have called the dimension of faith. He explains how, from the Christian point of view, it makes all the difference whether good works are done in faith, or apart from it. He uses the effective illustration of a young couple very much in love. 'They make no difference in

[1] WML 1.167. [2] WML 1.187.

[3] See Luther's startling references to faith as a 'mathematical point', WA 40.3.572.23.

works: they do the great, the long, the much: as gladly as the small, the short, the little, and vice versa: and that too, with joyful, peaceful, confident hearts, and each is a free companion of the other'. The important fact is that they are in love with one another, and whether the young man says it with flowers, with a box of chocolates, with a bus ride, a walk, or a trip to the theatre is a secondary thing. But, adds Luther, 'where there is a doubt, search is made for what is best: then, a distinction of works is imagined, whereby a man may win favour: and yet he goes about with a heavy heart, he is . . . as it were taken captive, more than half in despair, and often makes a fool of himself'.[1] It is when a man is not sure whether his love is returned, that he begins to think quantitively, in terms of bigger and better boxes of chocolates, brighter and more expensive bouquets of flowers, and these assume an altogether different meaning because of the uneasy, unadjusted personal relationship from which they spring. So, says Luther, the Christian does good works 'because it is a pleasure to please God thereby, and he serves God purely and for nothing, content that his service pleases God. On the other hand, he who is not at one with God, or who is in a state of doubts, hunts and worries in what he may do enough, and with many works, to move God'.[2] So, 'Faith must be in all works the master workman, or captain, or they are nothing at all.'[3] And faith is evoked when we turn to Christ. 'Lo, thou must form Christ within thyself, and see how in Him God holds before thee and offers thee His mercy . . . faith therefore does not begin with works, neither do they create it, but it must spring up and flow from the blood, wounds and death of Christ.'[4]

In the second part, Luther expounds the Ten Commandments, beginning with the three Commandments of Love to God. 'See then what a fine golden ring these commandments and their works naturally form, and how from the first commandment and Faith, the second flows into the third, and the third in turn derives from the second into the first. For the first work is to believe, to have a good heart and confidence towards God, the second is to praise God's name, to confess His grace, to give all honour to Him alone. Then follows the third, to worship by praying, hearing God's Word, considering God's benefits,

[1] WML I.191. [2] WML I.191. [3] WML I.199. [4] WML I.204.

and in addition, chastising oneself and keeping the body under.'[1]

On the fourth Commandment, Luther preaches a homily on obedience in the home, which speaks to the condition of sixteenth- and twentieth-century indiscipline, and he expands it to cover obedience to 'the spiritual mother, the Holy Christian Church', and the temporal rulers. There are two memorable sentences. The first, Luther's conviction that 'there is not such great danger in the Temporal power as in the Spiritual when it does wrong . . . for the temporal power has nothing to do with preaching and with faith and with the first three commandments. But the spiritual power does harm, not only when it does wrong, but also when it neglects its own duty and engages in other things, even if they were better than the very best works of the temporal power. Therefore we must resist it when it does not do right, and not resist the temporal power although it does wrong'.[2]

The second is the famous picture of the Ruler as the 'Mad Coachman', a stern warning to all rulers, courts and courtiers, 'for when a Prince rules after his own mad will and follows his own opinion, he is like a mad coachman who rushes straight ahead with horse and wagon, through bushes, briars, ditches, water, up hill and down dale, regardless of roads or bridges: he will not drive long, for all will crash in ruin'.[3]

Luther expounds the other Commandments in company with most sixteenth-century moralists, deploring luxury, gluttony, litigiousness, chicanery and brawling, and he adds a sufficiently modern comment: 'The trouble is, there is no real government in the world. No one wants to work, and therefore the mechanics must give their workers holidays: then they are free, and nobody can tame them.'[4] Those who have accused Luther of writing down the Sermon on the Mount in terms of the Ten Commandments will find that the reverse is the case, and that here there is a powerful presentation of the Commandments in terms of the magisterial command of love, which springs from faith in Christ.

[1] WML 1.249. [2] WML 1.263.

[3] WML 1.265. For a fine modern Lutheran exposition see Eivvind Berggrav's address *Wenn der Kutscher Trunken ist* (illegally circulated in 1941); E. Berggrav, *Der Staat und Der Mensch*, Stockholm 1946, pp. 365 ff.

[4] WML 1.267.

'Again you see that faith must be the master workman . . . so entirely are all works comprised in faith.'[1]

Luther's relations with the humanists are complex. In Erfurt, their circle was formed after his profession, but its members included some of his former undergraduate friends, and when he took his Plautus and Virgil with him into the monastery he must have had some thought of continuing classical studies. He shared the humanist concern for 'good letters' (*bonæ litteræ*) and also their second objective 'sacred letters' (*sacræ litteræ*) in the more restricted sense of the search for more accurate texts and editions of the Bible and of the Fathers. We know how eagerly he turned to the latest critical tools, to Le Fevre's edition of the Psalms, to Reuchlin's Hebrew Dictionary, to the New Testament of Erasmus, and how he used them for the basis of his own lectures. He worked hard at Greek in the next years and acquired a working knowledge of Hebrew. In yet a third direction, he was at one with the humanists, in their opposition to late scholasticism and the demand for simplification of studies in the schools, a demand such as, in the sixteenth century, joined Sir Thomas More and William Tyndale, Stephen Gardiner and Robert Barnes, Erasmus, Luther, Hutten. In the Reuchlin controversy, in which the great Hebraist was attacked by the Dominicans, and a combined menace of anti-Semitism and obscurantism brought a distinguished career to misery and ruin, Luther was unreservedly on the side of Reuchlin. Yet there is a difference. The humanists were greatly given to anonymous writing, and to satire, to a gifted mockery which acted as a dangerously negative corrosive to popular opinion. Luther distrusted the brilliant obscenities of the *Letters of the Obscure Men* which set the world laughing at Reuchlin's enemies, and later, the *Antibarbari* and the *Praise of Folly* of Erasmus, not least because he felt the times demanded tears rather than laughter.

Luther was primarily a theologian and preacher, not an academic. Europe owes an enormous debt to the humanist bookworms who loved the very feel of a book, who tracked down manuscripts across the continent, who appreciated the differences of type and who set a high value (witness the lovely handwriting of Erasmus and Sir John Cheke) on fine penman-

[1] WML 1.284.

ship. Luther had no time for such preoccupations. He was early sensible of a difference between his theological beliefs and theirs. Their catchword, the 'renaissance of Christ', was alien to his way of thinking. In a letter about Erasmus in 1516,[1] and again in 1518, he put the difference between them in shrewd and penetrating criticism: it was, in effect, the same contrast as between Jerome and Augustine. It was a pity that Spalatin passed on the criticism without softening it at all, for Erasmus was thin-skinned. But with the opening of the Church conflict, Luther found he needed all the support he could get, and he corresponded with almost all the leading members of the humanist circles in the great universities and cities, Erfurt, Heidelberg, Nuremberg, Strassburg, Basel. This need for support, and the softening influence of Melanchthon (the lifelong friend and correspondent of Erasmus) may account for the warmth of Luther's letter to the humanist in March, 1519:[2] 'Who is there whose inmost being Erasmus has not penetrated, whom Erasmus does not reach, in whom Erasmus does not reign? . . . wherefore, dear Erasmus, learn to love this insignificant brother also [*Fraterculus*—the rankling epithet of Cajetan]: he is assuredly your most zealous friend.'

Erasmus sent a polite reply, not too cordial, for this kind of semi-private correspondence was bound to get printed sooner or later after it had gone the rounds. That criss-cross of correspondence provided this intelligentsia with the faint premonition of the modern quarterly review, so that the sixteenth century is littered with tiffs and broken friendships over real or imaginary breaches of confidence. As Luther moved out into public controversy, the admiration of the humanists deepened, the more so as they found it difficult to get full information about his doctrines. 'About Luther there is no really certain news,' wrote Beatus Rhenanus to the eager enquiry of his Swiss friend, Ulrich Zwingli, in 1518. And among this circle it was agreed that Luther was the embodiment of their ideal of a Christian (*homo vere Christi imaginem referens*), a mixture of Hercules and David! As Luther's troubles deepened, and public condemnation became imminent, they grew more wary. Zwingli had his own troubles to get along with, but his biographers have had to note the striking fact that,

[1] WA Br.1.70. [2] WA Br.1.361.

though he bought most of Luther's tracts in 1519, none of them bears a single comment in Zwingli's own hand, who was otherwise wont to cover his margins with his jottings. And in July, 1520, Zwingli could write pointedly: 'I read almost nothing of Luther nowadays.'[1]

Erasmus, writing to Albert of Mainz (November, 1519) said: 'Luther is as unknown to me as anybody, nor have I yet had time to read his works, except that I have glanced at them hastily.'[2] In September, 1520, he wrote even more circumspectly to the Pope: 'I do not know Luther, nor have I read his books, except ten or twelve pages, and those hastily.'[3]

In the pamphlet war which broke out in 1519, the humanists took a manful share, and produced the famous *Eccius Dedolatus* (Mr. Corner Polished Off!) which set Germany laughing at Luther's most formidable opponent. But Erasmus did Luther better service than the Reformer knew. In part, this was a struggle between generations, and Erasmus now belonged to an older period of humanism, and had now to watch the young men turn more and more away from his spiritual leadership—Zwingli, Bucer, Melanchthon, Oecolampadius were all Erasmians turned Reformer. If Erasmus could have understood Luther's doctrines he would have preferred his smooth and rounded 'philosophy of Christ'. He was not by temperament a fighter, and he found himself in a moving situation not at all to his liking where the things he cared most for were placed in jeopardy.[4]

Though there was much about Luther he disliked and deplored, he would never condemn him outright and altogether, and he hated with all his heart the blind obscurantism which had dogged him from his youth, had ruined Reuchlin, and now closed on Luther. 'The chiefs of the Dominican monastery have acted in . . . a disgraceful way. One of their number said in the hearing of some laymen, 'Would that I could fasten my teeth in

[1] A. Rich, *Die Anfänge der Theologie Huldrych Zwingli*, Zurich 1949, pp. 73 ff.; O. Farner, *H. Zwingli*, Zurich 1946, pp. 334 ff.

[2] P. Smith, *Luther's Correspondence*, p. 238 (No. 192).

[3] P. Smith, *Luther's Correspondence*, p. 355 (No. 297).

[4] K. A. Meissinger, *Erasmus*, 1948; M. M. Philipps, *Erasmus and the Northern Renaissance*, London 1950; Renaudet, *Études Erasmiennes*, Paris 1939; R. Stupperich, *Der Humanismus und die Wiedervereinigung der Konfessionen* (Ver. Ref. Ges.), Leipzig 1936; Huizinga, *Erasmus;* P. S. Allen, *Age of Erasmus;* P. Smith, *Erasmus.*

Luther's throat: I should not fear to go to the Lord's Supper with his blood on my mouth.'[1]

At a time when the theologians of Louvain and Cologne were enraged against him, when the Papal Nuncio was reporting that Erasmus was worse than Luther, Erasmus had an important interview with the Elector Frederick at Cologne (November, 1520). The scholar's well-planted anti-clerical epigrams were too subtle for the Saxon, and he was annoyed by his evasiveness. But if Erasmus had thrown the weight of his reputation against Luther then it might have been serious. As it was, the Elector persisted until he obtained the promise from the young Emperor that Luther should not be condemned unheard (*nisi auditus*).

Erasmus was the patriarch of cosmopolitan humanism: Ulrich von Hutten of the ardent nationalism of the German scholars. Like Erasmus, the flitting Dutchman, Hutten was a wandering scholar (he abandoned the monastery in the year in which Luther made his profession) darting from university to university like a restless dragonfly, penning poems and satires, plotting politics and brawling with Italians in their taverns, truculently mingling braggadocio with sentimentalism—a recognizable type and uncomfortably modern. He was a mixture of academic, politician and fanatic (the Sir Harry Vane of the German Reformation?). In Hutten we link Luther not only with humanism, but with the political fate of Germany. Constitutionally, Germany was to defy all amendment: the entail of centuries of division and conflict, exacerbated by the tension of Pope and Emperor, was too intricate, and the divisions between Emperor (imperial and dynastic interests) and Princes, the Knights, the cities and the towns, and the tradesmen and peasants, were deep clefts.[2] There could be no such alliance between royalty and gentry as in England would produce a Reformation Parliament, or between the gentry and the boroughs as could achieve the Elizabethan House of Commons. Amid a tangle of jurisdictions and sovereignties, the knights of Germany lived in a brutal world, on the fringe of the economic and social revolution, the veneer of chivalry worn thin, the prey to family feuds and mutual brigandage. Yet there was

[1] P. Smith, *Luther's Correspondence*, p. 376 (from Erasmus).

[2] Gerhard Ritter, *Luther: Gestalt und Tat*, Munich 1949, p. 70 ff.

indubitably a surging life and a great weight of frustrated aspiration. For a moment it seemed that the knights might have found leaders in Hutten and his politically-minded chief, Von Sickingen, for a fleeting interval as though the young Emperor might achieve the unity of the German nation. For a few months it seemed that Martin Luther himself, 'the hero of the German nation', might fuse the whole people in a national revival out of which it might find independence and equilibrium of soul. Luther's writings of 1520, with their appeal to national feeling, may be playing to the gallery (it was more than this, for it was his own deep German emotion), but at least the gallery was there, crowded, excited, vociferous.

The attempts of Miltitz (continued throughout 1519) to quench the conflagration only created, from the Saxon point of view, a useful amount of smoke. But at the end of the year Eck sent a formidable, documented indictment to Rome. Early in 1520 the Universities of Louvain and Cologne prepared a detailed condemnation of Luther's doctrines and forwarded their report to the Curia. The Pope appointed a formal commission. The first (February 1st) was soon dissolved, since even the Cardinals Cajetan (theologian) and Accolti (canonist) could not ensure a judicious report. The second (February 11th) made a wise attempt to discriminate between Luther's heretical articles and those 'scandalous and offensive to pious ears'. Then Eck arrived, and the upshot was a third commission and the Papal Bull (signed June 15th) *Exsurge Domine*—'Arise, O God and judge Thine own cause . . . the wild boar has broken into the vineyard . . .' It condemned forty-one articles, but did not name Luther, and was content to append an evangelical 'Monition' to him, giving him time to recant. Eck and Aleander were appointed to bring the Bull to the cities of South and North Germany. They were horrified to find how swiftly public opinion was moving to the side of Luther. In the scene of former triumph, Leipzig, Eck was openly menaced in the streets, and had to take refuge with the Dominicans, while he had the indignity of knowing that his servants were manhandled severely, soon after their master had scampered to a safer place.

Miltitz made a last attempt to retrieve the situation and his waning reputation, and he saw Luther who agreed to write a last letter to the Pope, and, even now, to make an armistice with his opponents. Luther wrote the letter and despatched it with a copy of his little book, *The Liberty of a Christian Man*. But in the last weeks his own mind had fatefully and decisively hardened.

The letters between Luther and Spalatin reveal the stress within the Reformer's mind and the attempt of the latter to act as a brake upon his leader's impetuosity. 'Let there be a new and great conflagration,' answered Luther, 'who can resist the counsel of God? Who knows whether these insensate men are not predestined by Him as the means of revealing the truth? . . . God alone is in this business. We are carried away by Him. We are led rather than lead.'[1]

'I beg of you, if you have a right feeling for the Gospel, do not think this matter can be carried through without tumult, scandal, or sedition . . . this is God's war, who did not come to bring peace . . . you ought to beware of thinking that Christ will achieve things in the earth quietly and softly, when you see that he fought with his own blood, and afterwards all the martyrs.'[2] Since the Leipzig disputation he had been in touch with some Bohemian humanists and he now read the Huss-Wycliffite *De Ecclesia*. He told Spalatin, 'I have been teaching all that John Huss taught unawares, and so has Staupitz. In short, we are all Hussites, though we have not known it, even Paul and Augustine.'[3]

He firmly opposed Spalatin's temerity. 'Good God . . . I wrote you before not to presume that this matter has been begun or wrought in your, my, or anybody's decision and action; if it is of God, its bounds are far against, beyond, above, below, your and my comprehension.'[4] But he admits his own weakness. 'I cannot deny that I am more violent than is befitting,' and then he growls, 'those who know this ought to beware of baiting the dog!'[5] He read Hutten's edition and exposure of the *Donation of Constantine*, and in his present mood the effect was devastating. 'Good God, how great is the darkness and iniquity of these Romans . . . I am so horrified that I have hardly any doubt left (*prope non dubitem*) that the Pope is that very Antichrist himself which the common report expects, so well do all the things he lives, does, speaks, ordains, fit the picture.'[6]

[1] WA Br.2.39.9–12.21. [2] WA Br.2.41–3. [3] WA Br.2.42.2.22
[4] WA Br.2.43. [5] WA Br.2, *ibid.* 1.65. [6] WA Br.2.48.22.

In May, the Franciscan, Alveldus, published a trenchant writing asserting the divine origin of the Papal Primacy, and Luther wrote rapidly a tract which was in print by June. He does not deny the reality of the visible Church, but he finds its essence in an assembly of persons, the external marks of the Church being 'Baptism, the Sacrament, and the Gospel: not Rome, or this place, or that'.[1] Over this Church Jesus Christ Himself rules actively, and presently 'Christ is the Head and He ruleth alone'.[2]

During these weeks Luther reached a turning point in this thought about the Roman Church. He wrote these final words: 'Farewell, unhappy, hopeless, blasphemous Rome! The Wrath of God hath come upon thee, as thou deservest. We have cared for Babylon, and she is not healed: let us then, leave her, that she may be the habitation of dragons, spectres and witches, and true to her name of Babel, an everlasting confusion, a new pantheon of wickedness.'[3] The result was the writing of the three revolutionary manifestos of the summer of 1520. It is a clue to Luther's character that in these very weeks, when serious student riots broke out in Wittenberg over internal matters between town and gown, Luther himself was on the side of authority, and preached publicly to the students on the duty of obedience, thereby winning a good deal of unpopularity, and the threat of physical violence from the ringleaders.

Luther was fortunate in finding superb titles for his tracts. The first, *An Open Letter to the Christian Nobility of the German Nation concerning the reform of the Christian Estate*, is the real manifesto. It is an appeal to the leaders of Germany, to the young Emperor, to the Princes and the Knights, and to the great Imperial Cities. It begins with a solemn warning to the leaders of the people that they must never imagine they can achieve the amendment of Christendom by might of arms. 'We must go to work despairing of physical force, and humbly trusting God,' for 'we are not dealing with men, but with the princes of hell, who can fill the world with war and bloodshed, but whom war and bloodshed do not overcome.'[4] Luther begins by describing the three walls of the Romanists: their claim to possess jurisdiction superior to that of the temporal power, their claim to

[1] WML 1.361. [2] WML 1.357. [3] WA 6.329. [4] WML 2.64.

have the sole power to interpret Scripture, and the papal claim to have sole authority to call a general council.[1]

Much of the pamphlet is not original, for it consists of widely aired grievances of the German people, the kind of abuses and exactions about which Duke George was as vehement as his brother ruler, the Elector. More striking is the theological ground of Luther's appeal. He enunciates the doctrine that fundamentally there is only one Christian estate (*Stand*) though Christians may be called to fulfil a different office (*Amt*). That estate is that ultimate situation in which as sinners we are accepted by God for Christ's sake, and in consequence there is a priesthood common to all believers, in virtue of their baptism and their Christian faith. In spiritual things this fundamental priesthood involves equality, so that when a bishop is chosen, it is as though 'ten brothers, all kings' sons and equal heirs, were to choose one of themselves to rule the inheritance for them all . . . they would all be kings and equal in power, though one of them would be charged with the duty of ruling'.[2]

Nevertheless, Luther establishes an important principle when he continues: 'No one must put himself forward, and undertake, without our consent and election, to do what is in the power of all of us. For what is common to all, no one dare take upon himself without the will and the command of the community.'[3] This raises the important question of the ground on which Luther asks the secular authorities to intervene in the desperate state of Christendom and to take the initiative in calling a free, Christian council. Luther had no naïve and exaggerated optimism about the rulers of Germany: that 'a prince is a rare bird in heaven', and that power corrupts, are affirmations we can find at all levels and all periods of Luther's writings, from his *Romans* (1515) to *Genesis* (1540). But, as we have already seen, Luther regarded the abuse of spiritual power as far more deadly than that of the temporal power. He is writing, moreover, in an emergency situation, in which the Church has failed to obtain reform from the spiritual authorities who have become themselves an obstacle to amendment.

In this case, reform becomes the common concern of the whole Christian estate. In this emergency, the persons most fit to intervene on behalf of all are the secular authorities, since it

[1] WML 2.65. [2] *ibid.* 67. [3] *ibid.* 68.

is their God-entrusted office (*Amt*) to wield the sword of government and administration, and to protect the whole community.[1] 'Therefore when necessity demands, the first man who is able should as a faithful member of the whole body, do what he can to bring about a truly free council.' 'No one can do this as well as the temporal authorities, especially since they also are fellow Christians, fellow priests.'[2] If a fire breaks out in a city, it is the duty of each citizen to act in the emergency, '. . . how much more in the spiritual city of Christ, if a fire of offence breaks out'.

Here again is Luther's insistence on the active, present rule of Christ. 'For Christ in heaven . . . needs no Vicar, but He sits and sees, does and knows all things, and has all authority.'[3] In one sense the tract belongs to a vast literature concerning the spiritual and temporal powers: in another it is symptomatic of the sixteenth-century emphasis on the 'godly Prince'; yet Luther's appeal is grounded in his theology, and again and again includes stern warnings of the perils and limitations of all earthly power. 'Ah! well, for the Lord God it is a small thing to toss empires and principalities to and fro! He is so generous with them, that once in a while he gives a kingdom to a knave, and takes it from a good man.'[4] 'All do as they please . . . and the government is of as much use as if it did not exist . . . O what a rare bird will a lord or ruler be in heaven.'[5] Luther concludes: 'I think I have pitched my song in too high a key, and have made too many proposals . . . have attacked too many things sharply . . . but what am I to do? I am in duty bound to speak . . . I prefer the wrath of the world to the Wrath of God: they can do no more than take my life.'[6] By the end of August, copies were circulating in thousands all over Germany. 'Few writings of Luther have had comparable effect upon German public opinion.'[7]

'I know another little song about Rome . . . I will sing that, too, and pitch the notes to the top of the scale.'[8] Luther fulfilled the threat in his Latin treatise, intended for the humanists and

[1] K. Holl, 'Luther und das Landesherrliche Kirchenregiment', *Ges. Aufs., Luther*, p. 326 ff.
[2] WML 2.78. [3] WML 2.109. [4] WML 2.155. [5] WML 2.163.
[6] WML 2.164.
[7] 'Martin Luther', *Werke*, Munich 1948, vol. ii, pp. 391–2.
[8] WML 2.164.

for the clergy, *A Prelude on the Babylonian Captivity of the Church.* It had grown immediately under the impulse of a series of fierce attacks upon him ('they cling to me like mud to a wheel'), but it also embodies the full implications of his decision against Rome, and he announced its publication to Spalatin at the same time as he reports the arrival of Eck with the Papal Bull.[1] Luther declares, 'I must deny that there are seven sacraments and hold for the present to but three—baptism, penance, and the bread.'[2] Much of the treatise is a compilation from other writings of the last months. The writing was bound to shock clerical opinion, if only for its revolutionary attack on the doctrine of transubstantiation and upon the sacrifice of the Mass. More positively there is a development of his doctrine of the Word, and a full position of the Sacrament of Baptism, which restores the eschatological significance of its symbolism. 'Just as the truth of this divine promise, pronounced over us, continues until death, so our faith in the same ought never to cease, but be nourished and strengthened until death, by the continual remembrance of this promise made to us in our baptism.'[3]

'When we rise from sins or repent, we do but return to the power and faith of the baptism from whence we fell, and find our way back to the promise then made to us.'[4] 'Baptism signifies two things—death and resurrection: that is, full and complete justification.'[5] 'Therefore, whether by penance or by any other way, you can only return to the power of your baptism.' 'We therefore are never without the sign of baptism, nor yet without the thing it signifies: nay, we must be baptized more and more completely until we perfectly fulfil the sign, at the last day.'[6] 'For we are indeed, little children, continually baptized anew in Christ.'[7] That Christianity is no legalism is affirmed: 'Neither Pope nor Bishop nor any other man has a right to impose a syllable of law upon a Christian man without his consent,[8] although 'I admit that Christians ought to bear this accursed tyranny as they would bear any other violence.'[9] Underlying the exposition of the Sacraments is Luther's theme of the Word: 'The Church owes its life to the Word of promise,

[1] WA Br.2.191 (October 30th, 1520). [2] WML 2.177. [3] *ibid.* 221.
[4] WML 2.221. [5] *ibid.* 230. [6] *ibid.* 232. [7] *ibid.* 236.
[8] WML 2.233. [9] *ibid.* 234.

and is nourished and preserved by this same Word—the promises of God make the Church, not the Church the promises of God.'[1]

The Priesthood of All Believers again appears, but this time to make plain that there must be a regular ministry: 'We are all priests . . . we have the same power in respect of the Word and all the Sacraments. However, no one may make use of this power, except by the consent of the community, or by the call of a superior.'[2] Luther concludes that, properly speaking, there are two sacraments (promises of God, with signs attached to them) 'Baptism and Bread, for only in these two do we find both the divinely instituted sign and the promise of the forgiveness of sins'.[3] Luther emphasizes, in the case of the Sacrament of the Altar, as in the case of Baptism, the eschatological character of the sacrament: 'For the bread is truly the sacrament of dying: for in it we commemorate the passing of Christ out of this world, that we may imitate Him.'[4]

Luther's *Of the Liberty of a Christian Man*[5] belongs to the writings of Mercy rather than of Wrath, yet there is an inner connection, in doctrine with the other two tracts, and though it treats the relation between God and the individual soul it is plain that Luther thinks of this within the solidarity of the Church. The little book continues the theme of the sermon *Of Good Works* in expounding the life of faith. The opening words strike the theme: 'What great virtue there is in Faith.'[6] Luther enunciates the famous paradox:

> A Christian Man is a free lord over all things, and subject to none.
> A Christian Man is a bounden servant of all things, and servant of all.

He explains that man has a 'twofold nature, a spiritual and bodily' (II Cor. 4. 16). But this dualism is explained in biblical, not Platonic, terms, as the antagonism of 'flesh 'and 'spirit'

[1] WML 2.273. [2] *ibid.* 283. [3] *ibid.* 291–2. [4] *ibid.* 292.
[5] Luther, *Werke*, Munich ed. 1948, 2.269 ff; R. Will, *La Liberté Chrétienne*, Strasbourg, 1922; Runestam, *Den Kristliga Friheten*, p. 11 ff.
[6] WML 2.312.

(Gal. 5. 17).[1] No external righteousness whatever can 'produce Christian righteousness or liberty' for the Christian: but on the other hand, no affliction or persecution or outward peril can hurt the 'clear conscience'.[2]

For this, one thing, and one thing alone, is needful—the Word of God. 'The soul can do without all things except the Word of God . . . if it has the Word it is rich and lacks nothing, since this Word is the Word of life, of truth, of light, of peace, of righteousness, of salvation, of joy, of liberty.'[3] This was the supreme ministry for which Christ was sent. 'The Word is the Gospel of God concerning His Son . . . for to preach Christ means to feed the soul, to make it righteous, to set it free and to save it, if it believe the preaching.' Through this faith 'you may become a new man, in that all your sins are forgiven, and are justified by the merits of another, namely, of Christ alone'.[4] Scripture is divided into Law and Promise, and the law teaches a man his own weakness . . . then being truly humbled and reduced to nothing in his own eyes, he finds in himself no means of justification and salvation.'[5] But when he turns to the promises of God he finds 'that the soul which clings to them with a firm faith, is so united with them, nay, altogether taken up into them, that it not only shares in all their power, but is saturated and made drunk with it . . . if a touch of Christ healed . . . how much more will this most tender touch of the Spirit, this absorbing of the Word, communicate to the soul all things that are the Word's'.[6] For 'in the soul, faith alone and the Word hold sway. As the Word is, so it makes the soul, as heated iron glows like fire because of the union of the fire with it'.[7] 'This is that Christian liberty which does not indeed cause us to live in idleness or in wickedness, but makes the law and works unnecessary for any man's righteousness and salvation.'[8]

This faith is 'in all things most obedient to God'. 'It unites the soul with Christ as a bride united with her bridegroom . . . nay, human marriages are but frail types of this one true marriage.'[9] Thus the believing soul can claim 'whatever Christ has as if it

[1] Runestam, 11. [2] WML 2.313. [3] *ibid.* 314. [4] *ibid.* 315.
[5] *ibid.* 317. [6] *ibid.* 318.
[7] *ibid.* 318; Runestam, 12: 'Word and faith, these constitute Christian liberty.'
[8] WML 2.319. [9] *ibid.* 320.

were her own, and whatever the soul has, Christ claims as His own'. In an important sentence, Luther shows that this is no mystic quietism, for it is union with Christ in death and resurrection 'not only of communion, but of a blessed strife and victory, salvation and redemption'.[1] Christ 'by the wedding-ring of faith shares in the sins, death and pains of hell which are His bride's, nay, makes them His own, and acts as if they were His own, and as if He himself had sinned: He suffered, died and descended into Hell that He might overcome them all'.[2] Faith, then, is no mystic 'abandonment' (*Gelassenheit*) but the appropriation of this 'mighty duel' in which Jesus Christ has conquered sin, death and the devil. Luther goes straight from this thought to that of the Priesthood of All Believers, and it is plain that the heart of the doctrine for him lies in no individualist conception of private judgment, or the denial of priesthood altogether, but rather that solidarity of Christian communion expressed in the ministry of intercession: 'As priests we are worthy to appear before God to pray for others, and to teach one another the things of God.'[3]

The believing Christian has an immovable source of peace and joy. 'Who would have power to harm such a heart, or make it afraid?'[4] In the second part of his treatise, Luther turns to the outward man, and begins by denouncing those who misunderstand the teaching of the New Testament or abuse it by crying: ' "We will take our ease and do no works, and be content with faith." I answer: "Not so, ye wicked men, not so. As long as we live in the flesh we only begin and make some progress in that which shall be perfected in the future life." '[5] But in this life, the justified man 'must needs govern his own body and have dealings with men', even though 'it is his own occupation to serve God joyfully and for naught, in a love that is unconstrained'. His works do not justify him, 'but he does them out of spon-

[1] WML 2.321.

[2] *ibid.* 321.

[3] It is noteworthy that Dr. Asmussen's profound exposition of the theological grounds for the famous 'Guilt Declaration' of the German Evangelical Church (October, 1945) with its conception of Christian solidarity, is grounded in this doctrine of the Priesthood of Believers. WML 2.325.

[4] WML 2.327.

[5] *ibid.* 328.

taneous[1] love in obedience to God and considers nothing save the approval of God, whom he would in all things most scrupulously obey'. The Christian man 'does all that he does out of pure liberty and freely'. 'We should devote all our works to the welfare of others, since each has such abundant riches in his faith, that all his other works, and his whole life, are a surplus with which he can by voluntary benevolence serve and do good to his neighbour.'[2] 'Why should I not then freely, joyfully, with all my heart and an eager will do all things which I know are pleasing and acceptable to such a Father . . . I will therefore give myself as a Christ to my neighbour, just as Christ offered Himself to me.'[3] Thus love flows from the relationship with God through faith, and from the love of God to us flows our love for our fellows. 'From faith flow love and joy in the Lord, and from love a joyful, willing and free mind that serves one's neighbour willingly and takes no account of gratitude or ingratitude, praise or blame, of gain or loss.'[4] This love makes us 'free, joyful, almighty workers and conquerors over all tribulations, servants of our neighbours, and yet lords of all'. For this is the ground of the Christian ethic, 'as our Heavenly Father has in Christ freely come to our help, so we ought freely to help our neighbour through the body and its works, and each should become as it were a Christ to the other, that we may be Christs to one another, and Christ may be the same in all, that we may be truly Christians'.[5] For this it is to be a Christian man: 'We are so named after Christ not because He is absent from us, but because He dwells in us, that is because we believe in Him and are Christs to one another, and do to our neighbours as Christ does to us.'[6]

'We conclude, therefore, that a Christian man lives not in himself, but in Christ and his neighbour. Otherwise he is not a Christian. He lives in Christ by faith, and in his neighbour through love. By faith he is caught up beyond himself into God,

[1] Luther's stress on the spontaneity of Christian obedience is important for the understanding of his ethic (and to be remembered against his doctrine of the 'Bondage of the Will' of the unredeemed). 'This doctrine of the freedom of real moral action is the central thought in Luther's ethic' (E. Sormunen, *Die Eigenart der Lutherischen Ethik*, Helsinki 1938, p. 36; see also G. Wingren, *Luthers lära om Kallelsen*, Lund 1948, pp. 105 ff.)

[2] WML 2.336. [3] *ibid.* 337. [4] *ibid.* 338. [5] *ibid.* 338.

[6] *ibid.* 339.

by love he sinks down beneath himself into his neighbour: yet he always remains in God, and in His love.'[1]

Its fine title has perhaps caused its exaltation above the *Of Good Works* in repute, but taken together the two tracts form a coherent exposition of the ethic of faith and hope and love, which, as in the New Testament, links the whole Christian life with the drama of salvation, with the death and resurrection of Christ's 'mighty duel', and with a perfect and sufficient righteousness freely available in Him apprehended here and now through faith, hope and love. When the burning fire of the *Christian Nobility* had gone, and the earthquake of the *Babylonian Captivity* had ceased to quiver, there succeeded this still, small voice, more gentle than the dark apocalyptic background could presage, the sweet reasonableness (*epieikia*) not of Aristotle, but of Christ.

Rumours reached Luther of the progress of the papal nuncios, of the burning of his books in one city after another (but always with some counter-demonstration, and often with the secret substitution of other books!). Then, on December 10th, was enacted the solemn scene which Lord Acton saw as the true inauguration of the Reformation. Near the Elster Gate in Wittenberg, a fire was kindled by Agricola, and into the smoke were cast the volumes of the Canon Law, the Papal Decretals, and the *Summa Angelica* of Angelo of Chiavasso. That Luther should single out the Canon Law is significant, and is a comment not so much on the gallant attempt of the great lawyer popes of the fourteenth and fifteenth centuries to spin a legal way out of the web in which they were involved, as on Luther's mental pilgrimage. He saw in these books, says Boehmer, 'the confusion of law with religion, of the kingdom of the world with the Kingdom of God, of politics with the cure of souls, of legalism with piety, and the secularization which is the necessary consequence of such confusion . . . the *Summa Angelica* served as a typical example of how far the cure of souls had been led astray by this profane botching of religion'.[2]

Suddenly, Luther himself stepped out from among the doctors and, deeply agitated, consigned a small volume to the rising

[1] WML 2.342.

[2] Boehmer, *Road to Reformation*, p. 376.

flames. His words of imprecation were but faintly heard, and many could hardly have known that he had burned the Papal Bull against himself. The group stared at the red flames, burning brightly in the winter air. Then, somebody broke the tense silence, and the professors and doctors edged and elbowed their serious way out of the crowd. The undergraduates remained for rough sport and foolery, at an occasion which gave them more than usual scope for noisy demonstration.

CHAPTER SEVEN

THE KNIGHT OF FAITH

'GREATHEART: *And did none of these things discourage you?*
VALIANT FOR TRUTH: *No, they seemed as so many nothings to me.*
GREATHEART: *Then this was your victory, even your faith.*
VALIANT FOR TRUTH: *It was so. I believed, and therefore came out, got into the way, fought all that set themselves against me, and by believing am come to this place.*'

THE LUTHERAN AFFAIR was a graver danger than the Curia could be made to realize, and this accounts for the hysterical intensity of Aleander's despatches to Rome, in which he tried vainly to shock the authorities beyond the Alps into apprehension of the ferment moving distant Germany. For the Church was fighting a new war with the weapons of a bygone age. As the papal nuncios had moved from town to town with their stock of Bulls (Eck had the levity to employ them for purposes of personal vendetta, adding his own enemies' names to that of Luther), they might wrangle, browbeat, plead with the authorities to post the Bull. But if they succeeded, like as not it was torn down overnight, to be replaced with some insolent scurrility against the Pope. The pamphlets of Hutten and Luther, and broadsheets bearing their pictures side by side, streamed out in their thousands, and, despite all the papal controversialists, kept the firm initiative. Papal diplomacy vainly hoped that the old diplomatic tricks could succeed against the deep earnestness of men who cared only to buy truth. The letters of Aleander openly confess the failure of his attempt to win allies by bribery and lying, but for every man amenable to papal intrigue, there was a dozen, even among the worldly nobles, who caught the heady infection of national indignation and pent-up anti-clerical resentment. Aleander complained bitterly to his masters. He who liked to do himself well (a popular academic turned diplomat liked his little comforts) found to his chagrin that, wherever he went, hotels became mysteriously full, rooms engaged, and that his money was refused with contempt, until in mid-winter he had to shiver without a fire in the dingiest room, overlooking the dank mists of Father Rhine. He tried to warm himself with epithets against Luther, 'this Mohammed', 'this Arius', this 'Son of Satan', but he had to confess: 'The whole of Germany is in full revolt: nine-tenths raise the war cry "Luther!", while the watchword of the other tenth who are indifferent to Luther is "Death to the Roman Curia".'[1]

On the one hand the indifference and ignorance at the Curia: on the other, political intrigue about the Emperor. Of the orthodox intentions of Charles V there was never any doubt. He deliberately and publicly tore up Luther's *Appeal*, and ventured to rebuke the powerful Von Sickingen for speaking well of Luther in his presence. But between the person of the Emperor and the Imperial Mandate stood formidable vested interests, including his own advisers, Chièvres and Gattinara, and his wily confessor, Glapion. The forthcoming Diet would be a delicate matter, and the Emperor could ill afford to antagonize any powerful party. He promised the Elector Frederick that Luther should come under a safe conduct. But the publication (January 3rd, 1521) of a Papal Bull of excommunication against Luther strengthened Aleander's attempt to upset the project, for in his despatch he put a firm finger on the disadvantage from the papal standpoint of a public hearing for Luther at Worms. 'If he did not recant, and on account of his safe conduct could not be punished, the moral judgment of the world would be confused, and everyone led to the opinion that he had justified his godless doctrine.'[2]

Von Sickingen and Hutten tried to get Luther to join them, for they meditated open war. In those notes on Prierias, which mark his decisive break with Rome, Luther had indeed laid himself open to misrepresentation by quoting Psalm 58, 10: 'If we punish thieves with the gallows, robbers with the sword and heretics with fire, why do we not turn with force of arms against these teachers of iniquity . . . why do we not "wash our hands in their blood"?' Yet a few weeks later Luther made his

[1] P. Smith, *Luther's Correspondence*, p. 455.
[2] P. Smith, *Luther's Correspondence*, p. 419.

meaning plain when he described Hutten's anti-clerical plans as 'to make war on women and children'.[1] 'What Hutten is looking for, you see. I refuse to fight for the Gospel with force and slaughter. With the Word, the world was won, and by it the Church is preserved, and by it the Church will be restored. For as Antichrist arose without arms, so without arms will it be confounded.'[2] And in a phrase which he repeated in other letters: 'If the Gospel were of such a nature that it could be propagated or preserved by the powers of this world, God would not have entrusted it to fishermen.'[3] When the journey to Worms was determined, he wrote: 'If he [the Emperor] calls me to Worms in order to kill me, or because of my answer, to make me an enemy of the Empire, I shall offer to come. For I shall not run away (Christ helping me) nor shall I abandon the Word in this contest.'[4]

Not only Charles, but Frederick also, was uncertain whether it was wise to bring Luther to Worms. As the Diet drew near, the politicians liked the prospect less and less, and Glapion even persuaded Von Sickingen and Hutten that it would be better if Luther did not appear.[5] Even when the Imperial summons had gone out, the authorities hoped he would not obey. There was only one man to whom it had become increasingly simple and clear that he must go, and he was Martin Luther.

It was the climax of months of inner struggle. For Luther was no loud-mouthed fanatic with a hide like a rhinoceros. The taunts flung at him by his enemies found an echo in his own tormented self-questioning. 'How often has my trembling heart palpitated—are you alone the wise one? Are all the others in error? Have so many centuries walked in ignorance? What if it should be you who err, and drag so many with you into error, to be eternally damned?'[6] It was out of the darkness of such temptation (*Anfechtung*) that Luther found fortitude and calm, which shines out of his writings in these weeks, in the white heat of faith which the New Testament calls 'boldness' (*Parresia*), something we find reflected in the pages of the Acts of the

[1] WA Br.2.271.35.
[2] WA Br.2.249.13 (January 16th, 1521).
[3] WA Br.2.210.10 (November 4th, 1520).
[4] WA Br.2.289.11 (March 19th, 1521).
[5] K. Brandi, *Kaiser Karl V*, i, pp. 106 ff; ii, pp. 112 ff.
[6] WA 8.412.1; TR 1.51.4.

Apostles, in the Journals of John Wesley, and in not very many other places in Christian literature besides. There was no stopping him now. 'I shall enter Worms under my Captain, Christ, despite the gates of Hell,'[1] he told Philip, and 'I come, my Spalatin, and we shall enter Worms despite the gates of Hell, and the powers of the air.'[2] Months later he declared: 'When I came into Worms, had I known there were as many devils ready to spring upon me as there were tiles on the roofs, I would joyfully have sprung into the midst of them.'[3]

The Imperial Herald, Sturm, reached Wittenberg on March 26th. The politicians had outwitted Aleander who raged when he heard the name of the herald ('an impudent fool . . . clown . . . world-famous liar'). In fact, so far from being hushed up, the affair became a progress out of which the herald extracted full publicity value, as in village after village the people turned out to see, and sometimes to cheer. Luther himself was unwell, for great nervous strain always went to his stomach, if not to his heart. Two temptations to turn aside intervened with apocalyptic suddenness. News reached the party of an Imperial mandate against Luther's books, and the herald asked Luther if, in the circumstances, he would rather go back. 'I trembled,' said Luther, 'but said, "I'll go through with it".'[4] Finally (Satan disguised as an angel of light) Martin Bucer appeared to plead that Luther should take refuge with Hutten and Von Sickingen in the castle of the Ebernburg. He rode on.

On the morning of April 16th, a trumpet sounded and the crowd pressed towards the gates (Aleander's agent elbowing his way among them), as a proud cavalcade of nobles and knights clattered by; at the end the little covered wagon swaying round the bend. The crowd stared and murmured their fill at the Black monk who stared back with quick, shining eyes. At the Hospital of the Knights of St. John, Luther alighted, and 'looking about him with his demonic eyes, he exclaimed "God will be with me".'[5]

The next afternoon, he was escorted privately to the assembled Diet. He had to wait outside for two interminable hours, and

[1] WA Br.2.296.7 (April 7th). [2] WA Br.2.298.5 (April 14th).
[3] WA Br.2.455.52 (March 5th, 1522). [4] TR 3.282.8.
[5] P. Smith, *Luther's Correspondence*, p. 522.

then entered the crowded, tense assembly. It is no wonder that he turned nervously and a little jerkily from side to side, and greeted an old friend with excited and exaggerated cordiality. Before him, piled high, were the collected works of Martin Luther—so formidable that Charles V and Aleander refused to believe that one man, in a few months, could have composed them all. The official put the formal query whether Luther acknowledged the books to be his own, and Luther was about to reply, when the warning shout of his lawyer friend, Schurpf, rang out—'Let the titles be read!'

Luther turned, his body bent in the presence of Majesty, to confront the might of the Christian Empire, embodied in the pale, forbidding countenance of Charles, by God's Grace, Augmentor of the Realm of Germany; of Spain, the Two Sicilies, Jerusalem, Hungary, Dalmatia, Croatia, etc., King; Archduke of Austria, and Duke of Burgundy, etc., etc., and as the audience chamber focused on him in a moment of hushed silence, Luther's voice sounded faint and abashed. He did acknowledge his writings, he said, but since they involved faith, salvation and the Word of God, he asked time to consider. It was a good tactical move, though he disappointed the crowd. That evening he prepared a few notes (they have survived) which betray little agitation.

The next audience was in a more crowded and larger room. In the darkening hall, amid the smoking flares, Luther made his statement. He must discriminate between his writings: those of edification he could not retract; for too much violence in personal controversy he would gladly and humbly apologize; but about the reality of the Papal tyranny he must be adamant. He repeated his statement in Latin, and, the question being put whether he would recant, answered firmly: 'Unless I am proved wrong by the testimony of Scriptures or by evident reason [those who consider Luther the supreme irrationalist, should note!] I am bound in conscience and held fast to the Word of God . . . therefore I cannot and will not retract anything, for it is neither safe nor salutary to act against one's conscience. God help me. Amen.'[1]

It was not his greatest oration, lacking the famous apocryphal 'Here stand I. I can do no other. God help me. Amen'. Yet, as

[1] Boehmer, *Road to Reformation*, p. 415.

so often, a fine myth embodies the deeper truth. When we read J. A. Froude's comment, 'One of the finest—perhaps the finest scene in human history,'[1] the tendency to debunk is irresistible, for it could be suggested that Froude admired Luther for all the wrong reasons, that at this moment Luther had more in common with Hurrell, Froude and the men of the Oxford Movement than with the moralism of a liberal historian who cared little for theology but admired human heroism and the premonition of nineteenth-century liberty of thought. Not that the scene belies the great Protestant platitudes either, of liberty of conscience and obedience to the Word of God, though if this were the whole story we might have to find St. Thomas More a more perfect example of the former, and William Tyndale of the latter, since they resisted unto blood.

Nevertheless, had Luther succumbed to the enormous pressures put upon him to recant, whole ranges of European and Church history must have been different. Looking back, we realize the great forces on his side. When Kierkegaard reproached Luther for not having achieved martyrdom, it was hardly fair to Luther. That Luther did not suffer the fate of Huss was not due to lack of courageous witness or Luther's fault, but to the change in the climate of opinion after a century. But that this change was as great as it was, did not immediately appear. It has been said of the great strokes of the military art that they seem simple —afterwards! But place ourselves at the moment of uncertainty, weighed down with the possible consequences of inexorable decision—so it had been with Luther in these days when he accepted his revolutionary vocation with fear and trembling, amid a strain on body and nerve that left him a spent old man before his time. We can sympathize with Catholic historians who emphasize the appalling tragedy now enacted. Luther felt it to be appalling. Yet he made sure that if warfare had to come in Christendom, it should be the right war at the right place. But for him, the Reformation movement must have centred in those secondary issues which had preoccupied the Hussites and the later Lollards, and were to obsess the *Schwarmerei*, if, indeed, the whole matter of the Reformation had not been engulfed in a dark tide of greed and pride, or smothered among the fierce, secular energies of a new age.

[1] J. A. Froude, *Luther*, p. 33.

The Emperor cut short the audience with a quick, imperious gesture, and there was an ugly moment of confusion when some imagined Luther was put under arrest. But he reached safely the friendly faces, and as they pressed out into the hall Luther stretched out his arm like a victorious warrior, and his voice sounded clear above the din—'I am through! I am through!' The problem what to do next was a dilemma for Frederick as well as for the Emperor. They had demanded a hearing. Had not Luther been heard? Must he not come under the ban of the Empire? This was the view of the majority of the Electors, but the situation in the city was electric. In the night a placard was posted on the Town Hall of Worms, threatening violence on behalf of four hundred knights, and ending with the yet more alarming *Bundschuh! Bundschuh! Bundschuh!*—the peasant war cry which sent shivers down the not very firm spine of Albert of Mainz. Despite the speech of Charles V next day, affirming his own orthodoxy and repudiating Luther, the heretic was granted what he had asked vainly for three years, a hearing before learned and reasonably impartial judges. It was too late: in this topsy-turvy world, sentence had come first, then the judge's summing up, and now at long last the hearing. The debates were keen and courteous, but Luther had now committed his mind well beyond the limits even of the Conciliar theologians, and the discussions broke down, not over Papal authority, but on the subject of the fallibility of councils. They ended with Luther's final refusal: 'Even if I were to lose my body and my life on account of it, I cannot depart from the true Word of God.'

The latest Romanist apologist, Cochlaeus, impudently suggested that Luther might be prepared to surrender his safe-conduct for the pleasure of a debate with himself. This very silly suggestion nearly cost him his life, for on hearing it there were drawn swords among the German knights, who saw in it a transparent wile of Aleander (there they over-estimated his intelligence, not his morals). Amid a garbled and indignant report sent from Cochlaeus to Aleander there is one incident which may contain truth. Cochlaeus appealed to the witness of the Counts of Mansfeld 'whether they did not hear Luther say he would like the judge to be a boy of eight or nine years, or one of the pages whom he pointed out?'[1] Is it fanciful to think of

[1] P. Smith, *Luther's Correspondence*, p. 563.

Luther tousling the fair hair of a pageboy, and with august precedent setting him in the midst of the learned and noble, in anticipation of one of his own greatest sayings—'Thank God, a child of seven years old knows what the Church is, namely, the Holy believers and the Lambs who hear the Shepherd's Voice.'?

Throughout, Luther had shown a simplicity which is a mark of greatness. Had he been a man of guile, or even had he consented to play the politician, or even to be guided by the politicians, the Wars of Religion might have begun in the streets of Worms in April, 1521. We should treat seriously Luther's later statement:

'I simply taught, preached, wrote God's Word: otherwise I did nothing. And then, while I slept, or drank Wittenberg beer with my Philip and my Amsdorf, the Word so greatly weakened the Papacy that never a Prince or Emperor inflicted such damage upon it. I did nothing. The Word did it all. Had I desired to foment trouble, I could have brought great bloodshed upon Germany. Yea, I could have started such a little game at Worms, that the Emperor would not have been safe. But what would it have been? A mug's game. I left it to the Word.'[1] The Imperial Ban would follow (it was not signed until May 26th, with the assent of a rump Diet, and the edict was no theological masterpiece). Meanwhile Luther had departed, and bidding farewell to the escorting knights and the Imperial Herald, he moved slowly homeward towards Wittenberg on a journey which, for a public enemy, seemed likely to be calm and uneventful.

If any justification were needed for calling Luther by Kierkegaard's fine phrase, 'the Knight of Faith', it is to be found in the remarkable book the writing of which was actually interrupted by the journey to Worms. There were not many who, in such circumstances, could have concentrated upon an exposition of the *Magnificat*. Luther wrote it for the young Prince, John Frederick of Saxony, and it contains material for a philosophy of the place of power in history. There are passages of almost womanish tenderness (a side of Luther's character not to be confused with Teutonic sentimentalism) and beauty. 'She does not proclaim with a loud voice that she is the Mother of God—but goes about her wonted household duties, milking the cows,

[1] WML 2.399 (1522).

cooking the meals, washing pots and kettles, sweeping out the rooms, and performing the work of maidservant or housewife in lowly and despised tasks as though she cared nothing for such exceeding great gifts and graces.'[1] That loving insight into nature which Heinrich Bornkamm suggests to be a side of Luther which later Protestantism neglected to its cost, appears here, as Luther considers the ingratitude of man: 'If they looked beneath them, they would find many that have not half of what they have and yet are content in God, and sing His praises. A bird pipes his song and is happy in its gifts: nor does it murmur because it has not the gift of speech; a dog frisks gaily about and is content . . . all animals live in contentment and serve God loving and praising Him. Only the grudging, evil eye of man is never satisfied.'[2]

Most striking of all, the tract contains material for a philosophy of history, a profound diagnosis of the might and vulnerability of human pride, that 'bubble'-like quality by which arrogance resting on violence has been able, again and again, to stretch and swell into vast and terrifying systems of empire, battening upon great historical forces, until it seems to be invincible, until, with breathtaking suddenness, its hour comes (what Luther called a *stundlein*, and the Bible *kairos*) when God stretches forth His finger and the vast balloon collapses, and the once paralysing and terrifying painted face upon it sags into sudden ruin, like Egypt, Babylon, the Third Reich.

'God lets them puff themselves up in their own power alone. For where man's strength begins, God's strength ends. When their bubble is full blown, and everyone supposes them to have won and overcome, and they feel themselves safe and secure, then God pricks the bubble—and it is all over . . . therefore their prosperity has its day, disappears like a bubble, and is as if it had never been.'[3] 'For God does not destroy the mighty as suddenly as they deserve, but lets them go for a season until their might has reached its highest point. When it has done this, God does not support it, neither can it support itself: it breaks

[1] WML 3.164.
[2] WML 3.153. H. Bornkamm, *Luther's Geistige Welt* (*Das Bild der Natur*), pp. 172 ff.
[3] WML 3.179.

down of its own weight without any crash or sound . . . for while the earth remains, authority, rule, power . . . must needs remain. But God will not suffer men to abuse them. He puts down one kingdom and exalts another; increases one people and destroys another: as He did with Assyria, Babylon, Persia, Greece and Rome, though they thought they should sit in their seats for ever.'[1]

The critical date of these utterances suggests a striking hypothesis. In the Latin, the word for 'bubble' (*bulla*) is the same as the word used for a Papal Bull, and in other writings Luther often puns upon the double meaning. One is bound to ask whether Luther's profound meditation on the character of earthly tyranny was not evoked by the fact of the Papal Bull, that symbol of what he had come to see as a great earthly tyranny resting upon pride and violence? It explains a good deal, if it is so. For Luther saw a deep truth. In fact Ecclesiastical Man, no less than Political and Economic Man, has to reckon with power, is tempted by it, and had come in the Middle Ages to build up a mighty system which had seemed to men to be invincible, but which the events of 1521 had shown to have decayed within, and to be more vulnerable than any had dreamed. For Luther the Papacy could not merely be a system of earthly sovereignty like other empires: it was the degradation of spiritual power, and so invited a more dreadful judgment than any earthly tyranny. We can see how Luther came to see the Papacy as Antichrist, even though Luther himself did not see all the truth. But we have to set over and against this the triumphant confidence of Luther's comfort to the meek and oppressed in this exposition of 'the *Marseillaise* of all poor devils.' 'We too shall see the mercy of God together with all His might . . . we suppose our cause to have lost and our enemies to have won . . . because we do not know His proper works, and therefore do not know Him, neither His mercy, nor His arm. For He must and will be known by Faith.'[2] So once again it is faith which gives unity to the writing—'Such a faith has life and being: it pervades and changes the whole man—to this faith all things are possible.'[3]

Luther reached Eisenach, and preached there on May 3rd. Then he visited his kinsmen at Möhra. As they rode away

[1] WML 3.183. [2] WML 3.179. [3] WML 3.136.

through the woods, a band of horsemen swept round them, throwing the little party into confusion and flight, but carrying off Luther, clinging to his books, into the darkening forest glades; nor did they pause until, late that night, the dark shadow of the Wartburg loomed black against the stars. They rattled over the drawbridge, into the lights and bustle of the castle yard. The great moment was over. Luther had proved the power of faith to overcome the world. There remained the flesh—and the Devil.

EPILOGUE

THE OLDER HISTORIANS were not wrong in singling out the Diet of Worms as marking a landmark in the story of the Reformation, though it is of the order of events which reveal, rather than inaugurate, historical forces. We have seen that the theological development of Luther is an integral part of its context. To trace that development in detail (beginning with Luther's marginal notes of 1509 and finding a halting place in his fine *Contra Latomus* (1521)) demands skill and care. It is not immediately evident, since Luther uses scholastic jargon and Augustinian categories long after the direction of his thought has changed. The full extent of continuity and discontinuity in Luther's thought will not be clarified until studies of late scholasticism are further advanced.

May we speak, after the *motif* research[1] of the Scandinavians, of a coherent centre of Luther's theology, or is it, as Lortz supposes, a tumultuous, genial, inchoate flood? May we speak with the Swedish theologian, Anders Nygren, of Luther's *Copernican Revolution*, his substitution of a God-centred doctrine of redemption for the man-centred theology of the late Middle Ages?[2] Or, with the Danish theologian, Regin Prenter, of Luther's return to the biblical realism, of personal encounter with God, in contrast to the mediæval and Augustinian doctrines of 'infused charity'?[3] Or, with the Finnish scholar, Lennart Pinomaa, of the break-through of Luther from formal and academic notions to a genuinely 'existential' theology relating thought and life?[4] To this last, the Catholic Lortz makes large and unconscious concessions when he recognizes the failure of even Thomism, in sixteenth-century Germany, to do more than provide a cold and 'correct' intellectual answer to the poignant questions raised by Luther.

[1] E. M. Carlson, *The Re-interpretation of Luther*, Philadelphia 1948, pp. 36–44.

[2] A. Nygren, *Eros and Agape*, Pt. II, vol. i, 1938, pp. 463 ff; P. S. Watson, *Let God be God*, 1947, pp. 33 ff.

[3] R. Prenter, *Spiritus Creator*, Copenhagen 1946, pp. 80 ff.

[4] L. Pinomaa, *Der Existentielle Charakter der Theologie Luthers*, Helsinki 1940.

Positively these fine expositions are based on deep research. How far, negatively, and with one deadly phrase, mediæval theology can be written off, is another question. The expositions of MM. Gilson and P. Vignaux would seem to demand a re-examination of that side of the question. Luther, says J. Lortz, 'constructed a new world'.[1] He carried through a drastic simplification of late mediæval theology, rejecting its philosophic envelope, and returning to 'the Bible and the old Fathers'.[2]

The word 'restatement' has been so grossly abused that it is probably unwise to use it, but something like it does occur when new categories of thought with new relations to one another, and with a new technical vocabulary, are erected (in Luther's case, on the fundament of the Bible). The controversy between Catholic and Protestant is more than the Great Misunderstanding, but since the ecumenical conversations ceased (about 1541) there has been a persistent element of genuine misunderstanding, due to the insistence of both orthodoxies in interpreting the other's words in terms of their own defined meaning.

But when allowance has been made for criticism of him, and when it is recognized that an infallible Luther is no part of any Protestant confession, when it is allowed that much of Protestant life and thought has another origin than in Luther, the Protestant churches have mainly persisted throughout four centuries upon the theological foundation of justification by faith, Luther's assessment of the biblical gospel, in a way inconceivable had it been the mere concatenation of errors of older Catholic description, or the hodge-podge of incoherences and subjectivism of recent Catholic comment. Chesterton's great saying that Newman, apart from his Catholicism, would not have been Newman, but something quite different, must be applied to Luther and his influence (the old assertion that all that is good in Luther is Catholic, is a naïve begging of the question). The music of J. S. Bach, the hymns of Paul Gerhardt, the philanthropy of Francke, the passion with which Heinrich Wichern launched the great 'Innere Mission', the witness of Dietrich Bonhoeffer, Martin Niemöller and Eivvind Berggrav

[1] J. Lortz, *Die Reformation in Deutschland*, 1.201.

[2] Luther's appeal to history and tradition was far more earnest than the rhetorical flourish Newman supposed it to be.

are rich diversities of Christian character and expression which owe something characteristic to Luther's teaching. They provide a *prima facie* case for the sympathetic reconsideration of his theology.

We have halted on the verge of Luther's creative achievement. Those grievously err who see a merely negative and destructive meaning in the Protestant Reformation. Who in 1510 could have imagined that within a generation there would exist new forms of Christian language and worship, clothed in new forms of Christian institutions and discipline, new pieties, capable of growth, of transmutation and development, of nourishing innumerable holy souls? Consider Luther's literary work: the vast correspondence in that neat, small, scholarly hand, which overflows many folio volumes, and dealt with practical and spiritual problems across half Europe, and for half a century. And the serried ranks, volume upon volume, of his other writings testify to the prodigious energy which could produce something like a writing a fortnight over twenty-five years. Much of it is second-rate and of ephemeral value, but much also of imperishable worth. He was a fine pamphleteer and wrote scores of pamphlets, every one of them what Humpty Dumpty would call 'a nice, knock-down argument for you'. And he wrote from his heart, and out it came, tumbling hot and choking with anger, or shaking with laughter, but always lucid, always able to be understanded of the people.

For the rest, compare the list of those who in England must do a work comparable with his. He gave his people their open Bible, was to them what Tyndale, Coverdale and Rogers were to us; if anything, his German Bible was more important. He could shape a liturgy as well as Thomas Cranmer, though he did not fall into our error of abolishing that variety on which the continuing life of liturgy depends. Luther wrote a classical catechism which has really no parallel in English (for even the Shorter Catechism hardly survives its magnificent opening lines). He was as great a preacher as Hugh Latimer, and his sermons had effect comparable with the Book of Homilies. For a collection of hymns like his, England had to wait until Isaac Watts. His commentaries and theological works have never been fully explored, let alone exhausted. We remember how John Bunyan got hold of Luther's *Galatians* and said, 'I found my condition in his experience so largely and profoundly handled as if the book had been written out of my heart', and how the reading of Luther's preface to the Romans was the occasion of the evangelical conversion of John Wesley. Luther did in twenty years almost single-handed what it took six notable Englishmen the span of two centuries to accomplish: beside that which came upon him daily, the care of the churches, the fighting against Popery and the fanatics, the forming a communion world wide and recognizably his debtor. This is to say nothing of his great services to education, and church music, and a dozen other weighty matters.

The man counts, too. To our six Englishmen we might add a seventh. In the Strand, in London, stands a figure, burly and blunt, reading from a book. It might almost—*mutatis mutandis*—be Luther, but it is Samuel Johnson. The two men had much of their greatness in common, in their plain common sense, their humour and their melancholy, their delight at shocking their friends, the pathos of their inner struggles, and the loyalty and love they contrived to keep among their friends. Perhaps Luther was less fortunate in the dozen or so inferior Boswells who were permitted to frequent his table and whose garbled and sometimes fuddled remembrances, recorded in the *Table Talk*, are not always faithful and true. But at least we can see Luther and Johnson at home. Nobody ever wore his heart more on his sleeve than Luther, and there for all to see are his fun and tenderness, his deep love of his family and his home, his mighty prayers, and the vulgarity which prevents us thinking of him as some stained-glass figure, or cloying his memory with sickly romanticism. For there are shadows as well as lights.

Luther lived to see the Reformation become a great movement, under the most diverse leadership. It can be confessed that there is more to be said for Karlstadt, Münzer and the Peasants, for Zwingli and the Zwinglians, than Luther ever saw or believed. He lived on the edge of time, and believed that the Papacy was just another human institution swollen in arrogance and power, and now toppling to its doom, the engine of Antichrist. This was worse than a crime: it was a mistake. That Luther could be brutal and violent, that the physical impact of a dozen ailments affected his temper and his manners, cannot be gainsaid. But he had great virtues too, including the two indispensable characteristics of moral greatness, simplicity and magnanimity.

We cannot even broach the subject of the influence of Luther upon the subsequent course of German history. The studies of Törnvall and Wingren[1] in recent years have shown how profound and subtle is Luther's teaching of the two realms of spiritual and temporal authority, how remote from the ethical dualism of modern German political development. On the whole, perhaps the chief villain of German history is—History: the vast complexity of social, economic, political pressures, the long entail of the past as it touches the future. Decisive differences appear when we compare the German and English political scene on the verge of the Reformation, and the Thirty Years' War was to influence and deepen them far more radically than any misunderstanding and misappropriation of the meaning of Luther.

Now, Luther has more to tell us than almost any of the sixteenth-century Reformers. His doctrine of Justification by Faith, his conception of history, recover that eschatological context which modern biblical theology is interpreting anew. The revival of Continental theology associated with Karl Barth has behind it the 'Luther renaissance' of the last thirty years. Luther himself did not take kindly to the idea that men might at some distant date study his writings, when they would be better employed studying the Word of God. Now, Protestants must be occupied with nothing less than the Reformation of Reformation itself. The characteristic language, forms, institutions, disciplines, which began four hundred years ago, have come to the end of their journey, as evangelical and pastoral vehicles, however imperishable their value to the trained and instructed within the household of faith. If our gospel is to come home to lost, secular, revolutionary man, the Churches of East and West, Catholic and Protestant, must face the need for creative and drastic change. Within our lifetime new forms of Christian existence may need to arise as different from those of the past, as the world of modern Protestantism differs from that of the later Middle Ages. Here Luther would encourage us. 'For what, I ask,' he said, 'is not new that faith does? Was it not a new

[1] G. Törnvall, *Andligt och världsligt regemente hos Luther*, Stockholm 1940; G. Wingren, *Luthers Lara om Kallelsen*, Lund 1948.

thing when the Apostles instituted their ministry? Was it not a new thing, when Abraham offered his son? Was it not new when Israel crossed the sea? Will it not be a new thing when I shall pass from death to life?' Luther bids us look beyond Ecclesiastical Man, even in the guise of prophet and Reformer, to the inspiring prospect of history as the royal progress of the Word of God, going forth conquering and to conquer.

INDEX

CHAPTER I

AN AIRLINE IN MODERN SOCIETY

A SURVEY of an airline such as B.O.A.C. inevitably becomes a study of individuals. No individual hero, no single Titan from whom the whole thing stems. No master-mind or visionary genius. The British Merchant Air Service, of which B.O.A.C. is one of the substantial components, has no Nelson to raise upon a column of individual achievement, nor even a figure to match what Trenchard has been to the Royal Air Force.

This airline which had become a household word by mid-century, linking the Commonwealth and circling the globe, carrying the Queen on her duty and schoolchildren eight thousand miles home for the holidays, has yielded its heroes and men of ideas. Yet its achievement, its flexibility and its goodwill rely upon an almost fortuitous pattern of people of diverse talent, character and training. It is the pattern rather than the individual which has created an air service which can be reckoned as a force in the contemporary world, a force that is so much more than a mere assembly of efficient aeroplanes.

No airline is old in years. Though B.O.A.C., as this book will show, derives its pedigree from the first daily international scheduled air service ever to be flown, it is still young. For all its tradition and character, it is young enough still to be employing men who flew, serviced and operated the first airliners which set forth hazardously to cross the English Channel in 1919. Scattered throughout the world are people of all ranks who have participated in its beginnings or in its years of growth. Younger men, and those who are recruited year by year, become aware of a tradition which cannot easily be put into words. One of its characteristics indeed is a determination not to be tied by the past. The timetable can never be bound in leather and put on the shelf. However well or ill a day's job may be done, there can be no settling down to satisfaction or remorse. Another day will put a new complexion upon existing routines, will bring new problems, perhaps new opportunities—and a new timetable.

An airline such as B.O.A.C. may be equipped with the best staff, bases and machines that money and good judgement can acquire. Yet it must still be sensitive to weather, the climate of men's minds, social change, political conditions, scientific invention and the hand of God. A monsoon, a fallen Government, a city fogbound, a currency frozen may have their instant effects. An airline, or rather those who serve it, must be conditioned and skilled to meet the diverse emergencies, tremendous and trivial, which this century so lavishly provides. The tradition of the airline and its present sense of responsibility requires that it shall operate, adapting itself to all circumstances short of war, political black-out or physical disaster.

The antecedents of B.O.A.C. had their small beginnings at the end of the First World War. Itself only just incorporated, B.O.A.C. flew on to play a not inconsiderable part in the Second World War. Imperial Airways, an immediate predecessor of B.O.A.C., opened up the communications of the British Commonwealth between the wars: and British Airways helped to consolidate a European network. In the post-war years, B.O.A.C. has furthered those lines of communication across the face of a map which is rarely static, registering year by year the courses of political change and human upheaval.

The onus of combining flexibility and regularity with an eye to the future and a thought for tradition lies squarely upon thousands of individuals in Britain and abroad who fly the aircraft and run the day-to-day business of the airline. That is not to deny that responsibility also has always rested with the Government of the day, which changes often, and with the Board of the airline, which has changed a good deal. At the top there have been, and are still, names which leave their mark upon the story of British civil aviation. More widely acknowledged and justly honoured, too, are the pioneers such as Alcock and Brown, Kingsford-Smith, Cobham, Ross and Keith Smith, to mention only a few, who flew ahead of civil aviation and proved the possibilities of a world airline. Nevertheless, it is the rank and file, on the ground and in the air, who, over the years, individually and collectively, have forged this new element in twentieth century society—an airline carrying the British flag through the seven skies as resolutely as it formerly went across the seven seas.

These are men of many talents and unusual degrees of responsibility who have lent themselves to an idea at once practical and realistic, imaginative and idealistic. There are pilots and aircrew who must be dedicated to their tasks but who must also acquire an international outlook. Equally specialized are the engineers and technical staffs who work on the ground in all the six continents, assimilating local conditions and applying them to the pattern of the airline. Those who handle the traffic, deal with the passengers and sell the seats, furnish the visible façade of which the public is conscious—a calling in which diplomacy mingles with salesmanship.

All such people may be aware of an established tradition, but they cannot fail to recognize that theirs is a service young enough to be healthily repugnant to a set pattern. Though regularity and safety are among its essential elements, it must forever eschew the *status quo*. Every twenty-four hours will differ slightly from the one before; and it is the human element that compensates.

It is too soon for men and women to be born to this. Though the world traveller may encounter many B.O.A.C. staff who have spent their working lives in service with the airline and its predecessors, they will also find many who have joined from other professions and a younger intake of recruits since the last war who have come in as trainees to start a career. Whatever their background, they soon acquire an air of ubiquity which has a special magic for the stay-at-home. A duty officer in the midnight snows of Gander, Newfoundland, mentions that his last posting was for three years in Rome. A Hammersmith lad in Istanbul speaks of moving shortly to Ceylon. A captain retired from flying casually recalls the year in which he gave up his flat in Hong Kong to move to Cairo for a few months before taking up a posting in the West Indies for a term of years.

There seems to be little standardization in qualification, character or attainment, though there are severe tests in training, personality and efficiency. B.O.A.C., to this writer at least, has failed to furnish any set 'type' in the sense that there seem to be recognizable B.B.C. 'types' which, for some reason, lend themselves to burlesque. That is explained easily enough by the fact that the personalities of the B.B.C. have invaded the nation's firesides while those of B.O.A.C. and its forerunners were speeding to the ends of the earth with a good deal of emphasis on anonymity.

Absence of 'type-casting' and personality-appeal does not mean lack of public interest. Even if national indifference came near to killing British civil aviation at birth in the twenties, the public and the politicians have more than made up for their early lapses. As a national institution, B.O.A.C. stands uncompromisingly in the limelight. In the course of its devious development, it has undoubtedly claimed many more thousands of lines of Hansard than the B.B.C.

But then, unlike the B.B.C., it is expected first of all to perform as a commercial undertaking, in keen competition with international rivals and, to some extent, with interests within the United Kingdom. Yet its status is also that of a public enterprise—the first industry, in fact, to be nationalized by a Conservative Government. Public ownership has not imposed the rigid departmentalism of the Civil Service nor the disciplinary pattern of the Armed Forces. There is a measure of the authority and responsibility of both in the present make-up of the Corporation which also admits trade union representation on all appropriate levels within its structure.

B.O.A.C. and its predecessors from 1919 to the present day have always been a ministerial responsibility in Parliament. Britain is the only country in which there has been such continuing and direct Government tutelage. As the nature of the airline has developed from a private operation through State-subsidized enterprise to public ownership, Parliamentary and public scrutiny has been constant. At times, it has reached a degree that would have withered the very bones of many a commercial venture in competition with international rivals.

For the year 1946/47, B.O.A.C. received a Deficiency Grant of just over nine million pounds. In 1951/52, it had an Exchequer Grant of a million and a half. In subsequent years, the airline was entitled to grants, but did not take them up. Indeed it may be said to have moved towards a degree of commercial success as solid if less colourful than that prophesied by Alfred, Lord Tennyson, who, with a Victorian eye to business:

'Saw the heavens filled with commerce,
Argosies of magic sails.
Pilots of the purple twilight,
Dropping down with costly bales.'

Commercial solvency, however, is not an end in itself. The obligations of an airline extend to national and political solvency also: and they are much concerned with prestige. Possession of a commercial air service has become, since the Second World War, a symbol of sovereignty and independence, and its operation internationally a cherished gesture of self-assertion and propaganda. At the time of writing, more than thirty nations run scheduled services into London Airport. These operators include many nations which have acquired a new status since the last war ended. There are many more, new and old, with unfulfilled ambitions to fly their flags into the greater capital cities of the world. Few indeed of these aircraft would fly without the financial support of their respective governments in the form of direct or concealed subsidy during a part or the whole of their operational life.

Government support is widely and openly acknowledged to be necessary in the interests not only of commerce but of prestige and long-term strategy. The attitude of the United States was summarized in 1954 in a speech by Mr. H. D. Denny of the Civil Aeronautics Board which controls American civil aviation:

> 'It should be obvious to all of us that we must keep our American air carriers in top condition with the best equipment, for they not only provide our commerce and our people with healthy, efficient and economic high speed transportation but at the same time back up our military power with an unequalled logistic force in the event of any national emergency.'

Not least of the birth pangs of British civil aviation at the outset was a Government that declared that air transport would have to 'fly by itself'. This attitude did not last, though it remained long enough to cause a near-paralysis of the infant air services. Then, none too soon, it was recognized that the early airlines, and subsequently Imperial Airways into which they merged, were likely to undertake a world-wide commitment and to become a vital element in the integration of the British Commonwealth, as, in fact, is B.O.A.C. today.

Emanating from a small country such as Britain, in which there is hardly space for internal air services, an airline with a world commitment is a proposition too big, too strategically and politically important, to be sponsored by private finance. Its operation is too closely linked with Government needs and national prestige for it to stand outside Parliamentary control. Realization of this gives B.O.A.C. its singular status as a public service and a vehicle for national self-expression. The achievement of this status, over the period of forty years covered in these pages, has not been without controversy, hesitance and compromise—and has also inspired much individual courage, resilience and far-sightedness.

Britain was never without men of vision who foresaw something of B.O.A.C.'s present scope even before the first civil aeroplanes had left the ground. In the midst of the First World War, in October 1916, George Holt Thomas, a son of the founder of Britain's first picture newspaper, registered the international airline company which was to be the first in the field three years later. His declared intention was to establish lines and to 'enter into contract for the carriage of mails, passengers, goods and cattle'.

A more renowned student of the future whose active participation in aviation affairs, is now almost forgotten in favour of his fiction, was H. G. Wells. He served as member of Lord Northcliffe's Civil Aerial Transport Committee appointed in 1917 to study 'the development and regulation, after the war, of aviation for civil and commercial purposes from a domestic, and imperial, and an international standpoint'. He was chairman of a sub-committee dealing with problems of labour and technical education: characteristically, he submitted a minority report. These least remembered of his literary activities show him as a man of determined and impatient vision.

> 'An excess of tenderness for the no doubt deserving private groups that may wish to undertake "air" transport at the end of the war, and an excess of financial timidity, seem to have blinded the Special Committee to the supreme importance to the Empire of the immediate establishment of Imperial Air Services at the Peace. . . .
>
> 'The British Islands are small islands and our people numerically a little people; their only claim to world importance depends on their courage and enterprise, and a people who will not stand up to the necessity of Air Service planned on a

world scale and taking over thousands of aeroplanes and thousands of men from the very onset of peace, has no business to pretend to anything more than second-rate position in the world. We cannot be both Imperial and mean . . .

'Assuming, as he does, that boldly conceived air service is essential to our Imperial pretensions, the Chairman deplores the narrowness of outlook that has debarred the Special Committee from seizing its opportunity to plan an Air Service not only great in scale but great in spirit. . . .'

Those words were printed in 1918, the year before the start of the first air service, small in scale, great in courage, without Government support and with no great stirring of the spirit of the nation. It was all too many years before the author of *The Shape of Things to Come* could have felt that the plea in his minority report had not been altogether in vain.

He was not, of course, alone in his vision. A strangely assorted company of prophets, practical men, technicians and dreamers, some already engaged in flying, some, like Northcliffe, who never flew, saw aviation in the sweeping global terms which we have learned to accept today. While Britain was still fighting for her life in the First World War, Lord Northcliffe renewed his pre-war offer of the £10,000 prize for an Atlantic flight—eventually won by Alcock and Brown.

When that war ended, there was another man of vision, one too impatient to wait on events. Already a professional airman, Sir William Sefton Brancker, Air Vice-Marshal and Master-General of Personnel, Royal Air Force, resigned his exalted position and left the Service in order to throw his energies into the organization of a then non-existent air service. His energies were dynamic, his foresight formidable.

In January 1919, not so many months after H. G. Wells had his say, and still months before there was any sign of the first airline in Britain, Brancker was preaching a global concept.

'I feel that our future is in the air. In the last four years we have made the most astonishing developments in aviation. We have greater advantages than any other nation in the world, and with an Empire that spreads all over the world we have a wonderful incentive to throw ourselves into the work. . . . In my belief, aviation will be the greatest factor in linking up our world-wide Empire.'

When Brancker lost his life eleven years later, his concept was still far from fulfilment. The very manner of his death, in the disastrous attempt to fly the airship R.101 to India, was an indication in itself of the hazards of years of trial and error, before the air links of the Commonwealth, today taken for granted, were tempered and proved.

Another World War stressed the strategic value which these men rightly foresaw as the essential partner of trade. At its birth B.O.A.C. was embodied as an element in the strategy of war. Once again warfare forced the pace of aeronautical development and made men think ahead to an era of increased speed and movement, expanded trade and global strategic conceptions. The airline had to be not only rebuilt after the war, but reorientated. It was not just a matter of equipment and logistics, but of policy and ideas. In the post-war years, Britain's long-range airline would be more than ever an expression of national character.

Could it have been even more than that? During 1944, while the Commonwealth was still at war, attempts were made to form a Commonwealth Air Service. This idea was not entirely new. Lord Reith, last Chairman of Imperial Airways and first Chairman of B.O.A.C., had made some moves in that direction. He had envisaged '. . . A Commonwealth or Empire Corporation flying all the main routes of the world, owned and managed by all the partners in the British Commonwealth, a representative of each on the board—the first of its kind.' At that time Reith had been engaged in the amalgamation of Imperial Airways and British Airways to form B.O.A.C., to the title of which, incidentally, he claims authorship—'the name was my suggestion and no one thought of anything better . . .' He achieved some measure of agreement between the proposed partners and even managed to secure the interest of the Republic of Eire. But that was in 1939; and with the outbreak of war the whole thing was immediately forgotten.

The new project of 1944 was to be called The British and Commonwealth Empire Air Corporation, nicknamed the All Red Route. Its purpose was to operate 'through services' connecting all communities within the Commonwealth in a single round-the-world joint undertaking. Each country concerned would continue to run what was sometimes described as its own 'local bus services'. Beaverbrook was attracted to the venture. The British Cabinet had approved it in principle.

But Mr. C. D. Howe, the Minister responsible in Canada, who had listened with some interest to Beaverbrook, turned down this new single-corporation proposal. It was argued that Canadian participation in a Commonwealth Corporation would deprive her of the right to develop her own airline and would jeopardize the Dominion's close friendship with the United States. South Africa, similarly, saw no advantage in participation in the development of routes in which she could have no direct interest. No more was heard of the scheme during the post-war years, though B.O.A.C. developed and maintained valuable partnerships within the Commonwealth, to which we shall refer later.

An airline depends ultimately upon friendly association, partnership and goodwill—with a measure of shrewd international bargaining as an ever-present ingredient. Though its purpose is essentially to act as a carrier, our way of life as a nation and as a Commonwealth is forever moulding the carrier's task to new purposes and wider responsibilities. Its one constant and steady characteristic now is that it is never at rest, not for a moment at any hour of the day or night.

Before the Speedbird emblem of B.O.A.C. became a reassuring, punctual presence in remote places, the first airliners to come lumbering down to alight in Africa frequently caused awe and consternation to the tribal peoples who gathered from great distances to witness the wonder of these gigantic man-made birds. On one of these occasions, an elderly chieftain, impressed but shrewdly thoughtful of the future, sought an audience with a member of Imperial Airways staff and asked if he might acquire one of the eggs of the great bird for propagation in his territory.

At the time the old man was dismayed by a polite refusal. It is on record, however, that he lived to acknowledge that a far greater boon than a mere egg was his own passage, years later, to a conference in London. This he accomplished, to the wonder and benefit of his people, borne by one of the Speedbird services which to his sons are as familiar as any bird of the forest. Thus the words of H. G. Wells 'not only great in scale, but great in spirit', in these people at least found a realistic echo.

CHAPTER II

AT THE FORTIETH YEAR

Less than a dozen miles west of Piccadilly Circus you come to the area once celebrated as Hounslow Heath, now known to the world as London Airport. On the London side of the perimeter, almost within sight of the field from which Britain's first airliner took off in 1919, lie the headquarters buildings of the British Overseas Airways Corporation.

The surrounding dead-flat alluvial acres were once imaginatively described by an eighteenth century writer to be 'as little improved by the labours of man as if they had belonged to the Cherokees or another tribe of American savages'. The only folk who laboured in those parts to improve themselves were highwaymen. In all the British Isles there was no more dangerous place. A century and a half ago, anyone going that way may well have found themselves face to face with the notorious Claude Duval. There was plenty of trade for such people. When Queen Victoria came to the throne in 1837, five hundred stage coaches and carriages passed that way in a day. There are sometimes more than that number of aircraft movements nowadays in this no longer dangerous place and it is appropriate that the Corporation has set its headquarters building of 17 acres floor space within sight of the runways where all the B.O.A.C. trunk services start and finish their journeys.

A functional building, this headquarters, which controls a staff of over eighteen thousand people employed by B.O.A.C. in the United Kingdom and overseas. The sight and sound of aircraft are never absent from the four thousand who work in headquarters building. The higher command of the Corporation meets literally over the shop. Parallel with the boardroom table is a range of sound-proof interior windows forming part of a gallery overlooking the huge engineering halls where maintenance, repairs and manufacture are going on. Members of Board and Executive Management meetings upstairs, dealing with a route network of some 73,000 miles, can never fail to be aware of the practical side of the business, the men in overalls or the airliner fleets they service.

This and the consciousness of one of the world's most active international airports outside, gives a wholesome sense of proportion to a headquarters which is the springboard of world-wide operations. If it were housed in the centre of the capital something of its virtue would be lost. Being where it is, and what it is —a curious mingling of industrial plant with executive offices and operational aviation—it seems in all its sparseness to stand as a physical embodiment of a new element in society. It belongs at once to London and to Government, to the Commonwealth and international aviation, to commerce and industry. It stands on its own ground, geographically appropriate, in an area where nothing is stereotyped, everything is of this century, except perhaps for the cut-purse ghosts of old Hounslow Heath who must curse the lights that never go out, the runways that are never still. Nevertheless, there is nothing makeshift or transitory about the place. If it were not so determinately functional, it might seem to lack character. In other surroundings, it might be considered plain to a point of ugliness. Its merit, to one who begins to know it, is a not-over-dramatized atmosphere of living in the present and being committed to the future.

That is not to say that any undertaking of this size will not have its post-mortem discussions. In an airline, these are often far-reaching. A single chain of events, such as the early Comet misfortunes, may alter the whole face of the business. Yet in its day-to-day thought, an airline such as B.O.A.C. is concerned more than most undertakings with tomorrow and the day after. Expenditure is an affair of today: yet it is always made with reference to the future. Sales and revenue belong also to today, but the services which are paid for are tomorrow's. Today's policies are never static. They must not be judged only in the light of the present, but applied to tomorrow, next week, next season, next year.

The basic service which is offered may be scheduled, but it must be sensitive to conditions—political, social, physical and seasonal. It must be ever open to improvement and development, in the face of international competition. The airliner fleets of B.O.A.C. have relatively short operational lives: but every hour in the air and on the ground is worked out in the terms of usefulness. Those who operate them must think and plan not only in the terms of Britain and British industry, though the airline be wholly British. The commitment is not only Commonwealth-wide but world-wide. B.O.A.C. accountants have day-to-day dealings with fifty-five different currencies. The Corporation holds 111 bank accounts with 41 different banks in various parts of the world.

The non-committal, painstakingly discreet, interior décor of the Hounslow headquarters conceals a rare diversity of activity and human interests. People behind these numbered doors may be dealing with the airliners of the future, vintage wine for the transatlantic service, motor coaches for Hong Kong, tropical and Arctic clothing, toys for younger passengers, Middle Eastern politics, aviation medicine, freight charges for a consignment of monkeys or bullion, seat upholstery for a royal flight, an engine change in Bahrein, an aircraft in flight over the Timor Sea, the recruitment of ground staff in Labrador, or the text of announcements to be made by stewardesses over aircraft loud-speakers. Such a list, culled at random, could be as easily compiled by monitoring the telephone calls passing through the headquarters switchboard at any given moment. If an element of triviality sticks in the mind of the eavesdropper, it does not mean that the sum total of activity is trivial. Each item has some relevance to the impressive curved horizontal map of the world in the centre of the circular Movement Control Room where aircraft models show the geographical position of every B.O.A.C. airliner in flight at that given moment.

Control Rooms are never easy to describe in print, though they look well on film. That is surely because the atmosphere of use is arresting while the 'machinery' is deceptively simple. Maps, situation boards, aircraft models, coloured symbols and lights make up this machinery. Immense technical accomplishments in equipment, not visible to the casual eye, lie behind these apparently uncomplicated systems that offer information about the B.O.A.C. fleets. Their movements are plotted on the ground and in the air, spread over fifty different countries, in parts of

Europe and the Middle East, North and South America and the Caribbean, Africa, the Persian Gulf area, India and Pakistan, the Far East and Australasia. The Movement Control Duty Officer and his staff can tell at a glance when aircraft are airborne, their last ports of call, when they are due to arrive at their destinations. Signals and information pour in by radio, teleprinter and telephone. By pressing a button, the Duty Staff can speak direct through a multi-broadcasting system to any or all departments at headquarters or on the airport.

Such a system cannot, of course, claim to be unique. It has grown up with aviation in war and peace. It is the best of its kind, like so many other intricate innovations of contemporary life. Nevertheless, it suggests to this writer, at least, a unique atmosphere, dramatic in its calmness, subdued yet potent, an affair of routine yet one demanding constant decision and resource.

It is reproduced on various lesser levels, with always a Watch on duty on all the six continents served by B.O.A.C. In New York and Newfoundland, in Beirut and Bangkok, there are similar systems on different scales. Each contributes the vital watchfulness to B.O.A.C. aircraft movements covering more than forty-two million miles a year.

'The Corporation's policy for the future is one of expansion.' This uncompromising statement was made recently in an annual report presented by the Corporation as a State-owned enterprise to the Minister of Transport and Civil Aviation. Who is responsible for this expansion and in what field?

To take the field first. It must be explained that B.O.A.C. divides this with its sister State-owned service, British European Airways Corporation. As its title implies, B.E.A. is responsible for short-haul services in Europe. B.O.A.C. makes calls at stations in Europe such as Frankfurt, Zürich, Barcelona, Rome and Istanbul, but its job is an inter-continental, long-haul one. B.E.A. was established as a separate entity under the Civil Aviation Act in 1946. The two Corporations have early history in common. There are many close current ties such as the sharing and interchanging of staff on stations overseas. In operations, policy, management and general pattern, each has its own identity, equal in status, in its individual field. Certain of their services are interchangeable or complementary.

B.E.A. has a story of its own to tell. These pages are concerned only with B.O.A.C. though there are so many incidents and personalities in the days before 1946 which are matters of common ground. There are such personal links, for instance, as Lord Douglas of Kirtleside, Chairman of B.E.A. and formerly a Director of B.O.A.C. who, as Lieutenant-Colonel Sholto Douglas was a pioneer civil aviation pilot on the first flight on September 2, 1919, of the second air line, Handley Page Transport Ltd., to run a regular cross-channel service.

With the division of the field between the two Corporations defined in the White Paper that preceded the Civil Aviation Act 1946, the future expansion of B.O.A.C. lies in greater speed over greater distances. But that is not all. More people will travel: and this means rapid development of tourist- and economy-class traffic. For it is a feature of the late nineteen-fifties that air travel can no longer be envisaged by any nation as a perquisite only of the wealthy and privileged but as part of the heritage of the common man.

There is keen international competition from airlines backed by other Governments. There are also partnerships within the Commonwealth and with foreign nations. 'The promotion of closer co-operation in air transport development within the Commonwealth continues to be a major objective of the Corporation' says this annual report: but adds a word of warning: '. . . constitutional changes within the Empire may create for the Corporation a new situation of increasing competition on routes which provide communications with British territories overseas. As former Colonies attain independent status, they cease to form part of the United Kingdom cabotage area, within which traffic is reserved exclusively to United Kingdom airlines. Traffic to and from the new States becomes international and traffic rights may be granted which will introduce foreign competition with the Corporation.' While topical issues are not within our terms of reference here, such problems are relevant because they are typical of those confronting the men at the top.

It must be admitted that in the relatively short lifetime of civil aviation, B.O.A.C. and its forerunners have been subjected to many changes at the top. The present chain of command and division of responsibility are the results of evolution. Not evolution in the sense of smooth progression but rather of expediency and some measure of trial and error. That is not unexpected in an age of invention, research, war and social change. Ministers responsible have naturally changed with switches of Government. Between 1919, when Mr. Winston Churchill was the first Air Minister to be responsible for civil aviation, and 1945, when Air Minister Sir Archibald Sinclair handed over to the newly formed Ministry of Civil Aviation, there were twelve changes. From 1945 to 1951 there were five Ministers of Civil Aviation, all of them in the House of Lords. Since the creation of a joint Ministry of Transport and Civil Aviation, there have been, at the time of writing, (1958) four Ministers, all of them in the House of Commons. Change has not been confined to ministerial level. Since the formation of B.O.A.C. in 1940, there have been seven Chairmen of the Board: Lord Reith, the Hon. Clive Pearson, Sir Harold G. Howitt, Lord Knollys, Sir Harold Hartley, Sir Miles Thomas and Sir Gerard d'Erlanger.

The authority of Ministers, and their delegation of it, has varied and evolved a great deal in the course of nearly forty years. The status, power and responsibility of the top management has changed even more frequently.

A notable critic of this process, the late Mr. John Longhurst, stated: 'The original structure has, as it were, been coated with successive applications of new paint in the form of new layers of managers at the top level with the arrival of each new Chairman and chief executive.'

Those words were written in 1949 while the Corporation still suffered from the hangover of the Second World War and accepted a grant of over six million pounds from the Exchequer in a single year. But even against a more favourable financial background there has been little continuity at the top compared with that, say, at Pan-American Airways or K.L.M.

With the appointment of Sir Gerard d'Erlanger as part-time Chairman in 1956, there was a reversion of the pattern of management to that of Imperial Airways days. His predecessor, Sir Miles Thomas, had been Chairman of the Board which, under the Government, is the policy-forming element in the Corporation, at the same time as being Chief Executive and thus chairing the Executive Management, which executes the policy dictated by the Board. Without reflecting unfavourably upon the renowned abilities of Sir Miles Thomas, who is one of the great names in post-war civil aviation, this duality of function seemed in some ways unfortunate. With the resignation of Sir Miles, therefore, the next Chairman, a merchant banker of great experience in aviation, was appointed to the Board in a non-executive capacity. At the same time, a whole-time Deputy Chairman—Sir George Cribbett—was appointed, who had special responsibilities, to which reference is made later. Mr. Basil Smallpeice, already a Member of the Board and Sir Miles Thomas's Deputy Chief Executive, became Managing Director.

It is the Executive Management which provides the basic managerial structure of B.O.A.C. The Managing Director, assisted by a Deputy Managing Director, administers the business of the Corporation through the heads of the operating departments—Chief Engineer, Chief of Flight Operations and the General Managers of the Corporation's Western, Eastern and Southern Routes whose activities are co-ordinated by the Chief Commercial Manager. In addition the Managing Director is assisted by a number of staff officers—Financial Comptroller, Secretary and Legal Adviser, Director of Personnel and Medical Services, Chief Press and Information Officer and Central Planning Manager.

The Managing Director is responsible to the Chairman and the Board for the administration and management of the Corporation's own affairs within the general lines of policy laid down by the Board. The Chairman and the Board are responsible to the Minister, who in turn is answerable to Parliament.

This sounds rigid in its conception, but in practice Parliamentary intervention in the day-to-day running of the airline is wisely restricted. Questioned on this in 1950, Mr. Herbert Morrison, then Lord President of the Council, stated that the admission of questions in Parliament on day-to-day administration would be inconsistent in principle, and that the Board should be free from detailed Ministerial or Parliamentary supervision of their commercial operation. He was not referring specifically to B.O.A.C. but to nationalized industries in general, of which B.O.A.C. was the first. This statement, which is regarded as having set a precedent, went on to add that Ministers would answer questions on general policy and on a wide range of other matters such as 'the appointment, salaries and conditions of service of board members; programmes of research and development; programmes of education and training; borrowing by the boards; form of accounts and audits; annual reports; pensions schemes and compensation for displacement; the appointment of consumers' councils and other matters connected with their organization and operation'.

Thus the Speaker's Table in the House of Commons diverts the possibility of frivolous intervention with what might be called 'the running of the business'. The very nature of the business, however, is in constant need of Government co-operation and support, for an airline depends upon its traffic rights—governing passage over and landing facilities in countries outside Britain. These are fundamentally controlled by international and national law, but they are negotiated by bilateral agreements. It is the Government, not the airline, which has to negotiate. Hard bargaining is frequent, with foreign countries and within the compass of the Commonwealth. In all such matters affecting its own networks, B.O.A.C. works closely in an advisory capacity with the Ministries concerned.

From its beginning, civil aviation has depended upon such bargaining and B.O.A.C. and its forerunners, operating from a small country across the seven seas, have depended more than most upon international agreement. At the outset when the air route to India and the Far East was surveyed by Imperial Airways, problems of national sovereignty became manifest. For many years Persia would not let the British airliners through, and the early routes had to be 'bent' to comply with Persian sovereignty. 'We were blackmailed by every country between Britain and India for five years,' writes a former member of the top management. Since then, political changes, war and minor conflicts in the whole Middle Eastern area have continued to raise such problems. The operational resources of the airline must be kept flexible to meet them. A recent example of this was the Suez crisis of 1957, when all movements through Cairo were rerouted at short notice.

There is, alas, no free trade in the air. For years the nations have been engaged in a game of put-and-take. 'If I let you fly a service across my territory from x to y, then you must let my weekly service operate through your capital.' At its crudest, this is the sort of bargaining in which B.O.A.C. and its predecessors, through the British Government, have been frequently involved.

Though it would be absurd to suggest that a state of hostility exists with any other airline, it is fortunate that B.O.A.C. has friends and allies who support and amplify the pattern of the Corporation's world-wide commitments. To visualize this, the end-paper map is more potent than words.

Before the Second World War, the route mileage of Imperial Airways was just over 21,000. Since the war, B.O.A.C. has increased this from 56,615 to 65,918. The number of passengers carried by Imperial Airways in 1938 was just over 68,000; twenty years later B.O.A.C. were carrying over 480,000. Since the war B.O.A.C. routes have been greatly extended, providing services to Canada and the U.S.A. with an extension to South America. There is a multiplicity of services to West, Central, East and South Africa, to the Near East countries, to Pakistan, India and Ceylon, to the Far East—Singapore, Hong Kong and Japan—and to Australia. A new round-the-world service is being brought into operation at the time of going to press.

Characteristically, ordinary B.O.A.C. inter-office memoranda are couched in the sort of terms that make the addressee reach for an atlas. 'We made a start last year at breaking the world down,' wrote the Managing Director in a circular letter addressed to all staff in October 1957, 'by dividing responsibility for selling and for management of ground services into regions. . . . In our case the best way of sub-dividing the world is by the main groups of routes we operate. These are:

(a) the Western Routes—to Canada, U.S.A., the Caribbean and South America
(b) the Eastern Routes—to Australia, Asia and the Far East
(c) the Southern Routes—to East, South and West Africa.'

This unintentionally grandiose memo is an indication of the scale of things which the staff normally is expected to appreciate. To give any detailed account of these routes might be tedious. They reach out over land and ocean, like the main limbs of a tree. Towards their extremities they develop a kind of foliage of partnership and associated companies. This 'foliage' has proliferated during the last decade to become of great significance to B.O.A.C. in particular and to British prestige in general. The associated companies not only benefit the Corporation as feeder airlines but they also constitute areas of pro-B.O.A.C. influence throughout the world. To use the words of the Managing

Director—and change our metaphor—these are now regarded as 'flying buttresses to the main walls of our world-wide trunk route system'.

The Air Corporations' Act 1949 authorized the Corporation to acquire or hold shares in any air transport undertaking, to promote such concerns, or invest money in them.

After the Second World War, it was apparent that some areas of the Commonwealth were in need of local air services and that these would reinforce the commercial position of B.O.A.C. Assistance in various forms was therefore provided in the West Indies, the Bahamas, Aden, the Persian Gulf, Malaya, Hong Kong, East and West Africa. In addition, B.O.A.C. became associated with a number of foreign airlines—for example, Middle East Airlines in the Lebanon, Turkish Airlines (T.H.Y.) and Kuwait Airways. The Corporation was also able to invest money in concerns which are not airlines but are vitally connected with the business, such as Mideast Aircraft Service Company, a maintenance and engineering organization in Beirut and in Airways Aero Association, a flying club in London which undertakes contracts for training.

The actual form of association varies widely, from total ownership to technical agreements. As the number of associates increased, the B.O.A.C. organization for supervising such investments has had to develop rapidly during the 'fifties, and in 1957 a Company was formed to control and administer these very varied interests. The growing importance of the Companies, the size of the investment in them and the problems created by difficulties of a changing world made it necessary to focus the concentrated attention of a separate Board on their affairs. B.O.A.C. Associated Companies Limited, as it is called, has the Deputy Chairman of B.O.A.C., Sir George Cribbett, as Chairman, with three B.O.A.C. Board Members, and five other Members with specialized knowledge or experience of the areas in which the associated companies operate. B.O.A.C.'s capital commitment in this undertaking now exceeds twelve million pounds—and the advantages of this are evident.

Many places now enjoying regular air transport facilities could not have acquired them but for this arrangement. Apart from the financial support from B.O.A.C. they have had seconded to them Management Staff and Flying Crews, and have received training, technical services, expert advice and representation in London.

For the Corporation, the associates offer many indirect benefits besides their feeder line value. From being operators of the smallest kind of aircraft, many of these companies have now entered the field with modern aircraft equipment with which they are able to take part in international services on an increasing scale.

Some idea of the scope of the work of B.O.A.C. Associated Companies Limited may be gathered from the following list of companies in which at the time of writing, investments are held by it:

(i) Aden Airways Limited
(ii) Arab Airways (Jerusalem) Ltd.
(iii) British International Air Lines Ltd.
(iv) Gulf Aviation Company Ltd. (which holds an investment in Aircraft Services (Gulf) Ltd.)
(v) Middle East Airlines Co. S.A.
(vi) Bahamas Airways Ltd.
(vii) Borneo Airways Ltd.
(viii) British West Indian Airways Ltd. (which holds investments in Leeward Island Air Transport Services and British Honduras Airways)
(ix) Hong Kong Airways Ltd.
(x) Malayan Airways Ltd.
(xi) Mideast Aircraft Service Co. S.A.
(xii) Turkish Airlines (T.H.Y.)
(xiii) Ghana Airways Ltd.
(xiv) W.A.A.C. (Nigeria) Ltd.

The main branches of the parent tree, the pattern of B.O.A.C. itself, can best be expressed in the three points of the compass into which it is naturally divided.

The Western routes across the Atlantic take in stations in Iceland and Newfoundland. The main points of destination on the North American continent are Montreal, Detroit, Chicago, Boston and New York, continuing with the long haul across the United States to San Francisco. This in turn connects with a Trans-Pacific flight in partnership with Qantas to Australia. Another of the Atlantic routes runs from the United Kingdom to Bermuda, and thence to the West Indies, which are also served by a branch line from New York and Miami. Within the Caribbean area, B.O.A.C. branches out, through the medium of British West India Airways and Bahamas Airways. Through that area a route was opened up in 1958, serving South America.

The Eastern routes throw out a heavy limb of traffic across Europe to the Middle East. There is a profitable branching out of partnership and associated companies covering the Levant, Arabia and the Persian Gulf. At Istanbul there is an association with the Turkish Airlines. At Beirut and Baghdad, there are headquarters of associated companies. With its allies, B.O.A.C. is a potent force in the Middle East.

Karachi is the busiest junction on the route to the East. Branches spread again from there. One goes south through Ceylon to Singapore and beyond. Another serves India. Another reaches out to Rangoon and Bangkok, and thence spreads north-east again to Hong Kong and Tokyo. From Singapore, services carry on south to Jakarta and Australasia. The famous Kangaroo route, covering 12,000 miles from London to Sydney, is shared in the long-standing partnership with the great Australian national airline, Qantas.

The third system of airways, the Southern routes, serves Africa. The B.O.A.C. route runs down through Khartoum and East Africa, terminating in Johannesburg. Partnership with South African Airways and association agreements with the separate Central African and East African Corporations, W.A.A.C. (Nigeria) Ltd. and Ghana Airways Ltd. provide an immense network of feeder services throughout the continent.

With these three limbs, together with the burgeoning of many branches throughout six continents, and a round-the-world service, the early dreams of the pioneers may be said to have been realized indeed. Yet there is nobody in the business who regards these accomplished facts as the end of accomplishment. Theirs is a practical world, and they are specially trained people. The majority of them are far from Parliamentary questions and Ministerial decisions. Many of them have never even seen that policy-forming board room or the executive nerve centres at Headquarters. Nevertheless, they are in constant touch with London by signal, by the aircraft they serve and by personal contact with a management which is always on the move. They are probably more closely integrated with the home country than the employees of any other British undertaking overseas. Yet, unlike members of the diplomatic or consular service or of the armed forces, they cannot entirely identify themselves with their own national interests. Their customers are people of all nations. They provide services for the country where they are stationed. There must be contacts at all levels with local people and affairs. They employ and work with the people of the country, conform to local airport regulations and to the law of the land. In a foreign country they are responsible not only for the welfare of their own nationals, and foreigners who happen to be passengers, but also for a multitude of engineering services and for the commercial salesmanship which is vital to the airline. B.O.A.C. maintains fifty-six stations overseas. After visiting many of these, it becomes impossible to generalize about them. Each is so attuned to local conditions that the wave-lengths are always slightly different even if the B.O.A.C. regulations and standards are always the same.

The New York Office, elegantly laid out in a new building in Fifth Avenue, has a character of its own. So has the charming eighteenth century pillared façade of the Bermuda office. The manager's secretary in the effulgent pink sari in Calcutta is no less striking for some than the taciturn Sikh who drives the manager in Singapore. In Ceylon, the station manager may accompany you only a few miles up country for a close view of a kabogoya, which is a prehistoric lizard, nearly five feet long, whose favourite meal is cobra. In Istanbul the local representative may show you the fabulous Seraglio of the Sultan. Many of the men encountered along the B.O.A.C. routes have served overseas for most of their lives. They have curious stories to tell, and many have contributed to the chapters which follow. Theirs is an unusual status, midway between commerce and diplomacy, closely associated with engineering, catering, the tourist trade, mail, and even the children's holidays. Senior men overseas are quite properly provided with houses in keeping with their local status. Their social contacts must be wide and judicious. Their casual contacts with travelling celebrities are frequent and sometimes stimulating.

A multitude of departments at the London Headquarters serves the needs of these men in the outstations. They in their turn have to cope with a multitude of unexpected subjects. They must be armed with a good measure of self-sufficiency and independence. Their support is the B.O.A.C. tradition backed by the forces and the potency of a great international organization. Just as necessary to the airline and to themselves are what they jocularly call 'the visiting firemen'. These may be emissaries from London or from some other station. B.O.A.C. has a sound tradition about consulting the men on the spot and 'seeing for yourself'. That may mean that it is difficult to get in touch in London with Board Directors, senior executives of the airline or specialists working for B.O.A.C., because such men are frequently abroad. The mileage they log every year is impressive. The 'visiting firemen' who drop in to outstations keep the man on the spot in personal contact with higher authority, and with such matters as accounts, catering, public relations, sales, engineering, servicing and projected plans for the future.

The tradition of the 'visiting firemen', which has existed since the pioneer days of Imperial Airways, is not by any means confined to business between members of the staff. Officials of the airline in the course of their journeys have recorded many strange encounters and curious episodes. A personal diary of one such traveller, Major J. R. McCrindle, written more than a decade ago, offers an example of unpremeditated public relations. It was the month of December when the diarist was travelling westward from Karachi to carry out an inspection of airline stations in the Arab world. He had been told there was a truce among the Sheikhs in a certain district and that the Political Officer, wishing to keep them together, had suddenly suggested that they should be invited to meet the diarist on his way through their territory.

On arrival, McCrindle was met by the Political Officer and by the airline's local representative—called for the sake of this narrative Smith—and by Sheikhs with bodyguards, armed with knives, rifles, swords and daggers.

> 'I was introduced and made to lead the way into the marquee which had been erected for the occasion. The etiquette and ceremonial is complicated and I was instructed in quick asides by the Political Officer.
>
> 'The Sheikhs sat down to eat with their rifles between their knees and their bodyguards squatting around the marquee. X.

however, was in his own territory and only carried a ceremonial dagger.

'One eats with one's fingers, never using the left hand. The most difficult feat was fishing slippery tinned peaches out of a communal bowl. I had X., the most important Sheikh, on one hand and Y. on the other. I nearly slipped up once. X. and I were passing the small cup of villainous coffee from one to another, protesting that the other should have it first when I, thinking Y. was out in the cold, started to pass it to him. Suddenly I remembered that they merely have a temporary truce and that neither had spoken to the other. To hand him a cup from X. would have insulted them both. Y. had a magnificent sword with a gold hilt and scabbard which had been presented to him by Queen Victoria. I wonder what H.M.G. got in return?

'X. is a most benevolent and venerable looking old gentleman. When we left I tried to make him go first but he gently took my hand and led me out with him and, hand in hand, we started the procession back. I was reminded afterwards that this benevolent old man a short time ago had the eyes of some of his subjects put out as he doubted their loyalty to him, but one—a rich merchant—had bribed the executioner to be left with one eye.'

The diarist was not too overwhelmed by the occasion to forget to take a quizzical glance at his own staff.

'Smith has been here a month and appears to be settling down well; the change from fleshpots appears to have been a good thing. He told me that he had spent a week-end shooting with Y. who incidentally pressed me to do the same.'

In spite of such personal contacts which are frequent if not always so colourful, a supposed over-centralization of the business of the airline in London has been criticized from time to time. Managerial mobility goes towards meeting that complaint. Nevertheless, an airline engaged in annihilating time and space and promoting mass movement must clearly have one central brain.

It is indeed difficult to see how the executive management could be otherwise than centralized. The planning and purchase of aircraft alone are matters of high importance not only to the Board in London, but to the British Government. B.O.A.C., moreover, has the disadvantage compared with many of its competitors, of carrying an exceptionally large burden of expense and responsibility whenever it is called upon to introduce a new British type of aircraft into service. No other country in the world expects its airlines to carry the additional expense entailed in developing a new airliner to make it fit for competitive service and for export.

The financial commitment for a single machine has increased prodigiously during the years reviewed in these pages. In the early days of Imperial Airways, for instance, a Hannibal airliner—the best of its kind in the contemporary world—cost about £20,000. A DH 86 cost only £9,000. The purchase price of a B.O.A.C. airliner today may be in the region of £1¾ million pounds. This, many times multiplied to arrive at the cost of an operational fleet, becomes an expenditure not merely of commercial but of national significance. It can have an immense impact on the industry of Britain.

In the opinion of Mr. A. C. Campbell Orde, himself one of the pioneer pilots in 1919 and a former Development Director of B.O.A.C., it takes seven or more years to produce a large main line aircraft. The twentieth century airliner is not born overnight. The planning of its power, its range, its capacity, moreover, must be related not only to passenger needs but to airport facilities along the trunk routes. The tendency for aircraft is to become bigger and heavier, with higher tyre pressures leading to greater wheel loading. This, of course, calls for increased runway bearing strength and sometimes for longer runways. Not every nation can hold its place in providing suitable airports.

On such problems of integration, a dozen or so B.O.A.C. Departments may be working to form a single policy in the central brain. When decisions are made, their effects may be profound within the Corporation and controversial outside it. Instances of these were the decision to switch from flying-boats to landplanes on the main trunk routes, or, later, the purchase of American aircraft when no British aircraft were immediately available.

Then there are such questions as the opening of new routes or the extension or closure of existing ones. These are subjects for a system of market research, but not an entirely conventional one. British prestige and the prestige of the airline itself are imponderables. B.O.A.C. is not obliged to undertake an unprofitable service, but there have been occasions when the national interest has outweighed commercial consideration.

Hand in hand with the planning of the machines and the routes over which they fly goes the study of the customer for air travel, who in the course of forty years of civil aviation has changed as well as multiplied. The whole of the Civil Service overseas now relies upon air travel for communication and for many of the amenities of life.

Domestic life on foreign service for commercial as well as official employees throughout the Commonwealth has been revolutionized by air travel during the middle years of this century. There are much more immediate contacts with the Home Country; and educational facilities for children which were inconceivable a few decades ago. For the British residents abroad wherever they may be, B.O.A.C. services have provided new dimensions in social, business and domestic life.

An airline, whether it happens to be owned by the State or by private enterprise, must foster a relationship with its customers which is at once commercial and intimate. Air travel operators are particularly sensitive to passenger reaction. Nearly everyone who has travelled on B.O.A.C. services is familiar with the 'Comment Card', usually handed round to passengers just before reaching their destinations, on which they are invited to make, confidentially, specific and general comments on the journey. At one time these cards were regarded with a certain amount of good-humoured suspicion by the flying and cabin staff of B.O.A.C. as having been designed as a sort of spying system on their activities. Nothing could be further from the truth. The Corporation obtains most valuable information from the jottings of the public. The decision in the 'fifties, for instance, to put back the Stratocruiser into luxury service on the North Atlantic was the result of comments of first-class passengers who said they preferred to take a little longer for the journey if they could enjoy the cosiness of a downstairs bar which this aircraft offers.

Some passengers have been overheard to wonder a little cynically what happens to the cards after they have been collected. They are, in fact, shipped on the first available service to the Passenger Relations Officer in London, Mrs. Sheila Portch, who has had well over twenty-five years' experience in B.O.A.C. and its predecessor. With a specially trained staff, Mrs. Portch analyses the comments and answers them. In cases of praise and humorous complaint, the correspondence sometimes becomes personal. On occasions when passengers have indulged themselves with verse, the Passenger Relations Officer has replied in good measure. Where a passenger protests about some specific incident in the air or on the ground, an acknowledgement, explanation or apology is mailed right away. In some circumstances, a representative may even call on the passenger. More serious complaints of this kind are at once brought to the attention of those who should know about them.

Every letter is answered. The Passenger Relations Office has built up a great structure of goodwill. To assist in furthering this, B.O.A.C. Sales Offices in Britain, North America, Canada, India and Hong Kong are supplied with a list of passengers in their areas who have made comments—to be followed up if necessary.

Within the departments of the B.O.A.C., appreciations of good service are passed on. Later they are included in a summary of comments which goes out to all departmental heads. These contribute to the basis for meeting the demands of the future—whether they be to travel fast regardless of expense or to go for greater comfort and a more leisurely pace at a more modest price.

It is already evident that there are those who will welcome supersonic flight when it comes. But there is still the more sedate type, who, even in the 'jet-age', wrote in to suggest a glass floor for the airliner to permit travellers to enjoy the view.

CHAPTER III

HOUNSLOW BEGINNINGS

THE first airline passenger of all was not concerned about a glass floor. He was enchanted with the view. 'As we climbed in a fairly rapid spiral up to 1,000 feet, London appeared almost invisible to the east within our radius of vision of the order of four to five miles. Soon the altitude was 2,000 feet and through a rift in the cloud, the Crystal Palace showed like a child's toy. For a moment the Thames appeared like a varnished zinc strip and unexpectedly close.'

His name was George Stevenson-Reece. He was travelling on the morning of Monday, August 25, 1919. This was the inauguration of a civil aviation service in Great Britain. It was also the first scheduled flight commercially operated from one country to another.

Huddled in First World War flying kit in a makeshift cabin, he went on record with a first account by an airline passenger of the ecstasy of arrival: 'With almost a start, suddenly the mist clears and houses begin to thicken. The aerodrome of Le Bourget stretches in front and we begin to descend. Yes, Paris was away on the right but even now it is scarcely visible as a whole owing to the fog. I search in vain for the Eiffel Tower and Sacré Coeur and try to persuade myself that I like "banking" as we curl downwards to arrive just two hours twenty minutes after leaving Hounslow.' Mr. Stevenson-Reece telephoned this account to the London *Evening Standard* and made history.

His return journey, recalled thirty years later, was more mundane in its details. He did not feel too good. 'I have painfully vivid memories of being sick without stopping throughout the return journey to London after gobbling a half-cooked lunch at Le

Bourget before starting back within the hour. Just as we were landing at 2.45 p.m. at Hounslow, a last-minute zoom added the final touch and made me grab my hat for a purpose for which in modern air-travel paper-bags are thoughtfully provided.'

The pilot on this historic occasion was a genial, burly fellow called Bill Lawford, who died in 1955. He was very fond of the music of Wagner and never at all happy about the vagaries of the weather in the English Channel. He recollected his inaugural flight some years later in a broadcast: 'We had *no* wireless to help us, *no* blind flying instruments, *no* flight engineers, *no* parachutes or brollies and only one engine that had had a lot of war use. Anyway, hedgehopping over the old familiar route, I soon picked up the coast. Then came some wave-skimming which wasn't so funny in the sea mist. Crikey! What's that ahead—pull the old bus up sharp, that's the Varne lightship, that was—missed it by a few feet, and the sea doesn't look at all matey!'

He was not without friends, however, when he touched down at Le Bourget: 'I was soon taxi-ing happily across the aerodrome, where a very enthusiastic welcome awaited us from a gathering of distinguished people—but what amused me most was the dear robust old gendarme, who rushed up and embraced me with "'Allo!! Mon vieux, 'Allo—if I do not see you again, 'Allo, 'Allo; Passports s'il vous plait!" Good heavens, I thought—I'd been flying to France for years in the Royal Flying Corps and the Royal Air Force without a passport—what a comedown—I'm just a mere civilian now.'

Of that company of pioneer pilots who were still surprised to find themselves civilians when they started the airline which is B.O.A.C.'s first ancestor, Lawford, who had begun his flying career in 1911, said: '. . . they flew by instinct and literally sensed their way through in all sorts of weather. They flew old aeroplanes with single engines of doubtful reliability. Yet they established a record of regularity which has scarcely been beaten with all our vastly improved multi-engine aircraft.'

The year 1919 was indeed *annus mirabilis* for civil aviation. Behind the exploit shared by Lawford and Stevenson-Reece on that forbidding August day, lay a turmoil of dreams, good intentions and ambitions which suddenly seemed within reach of their fulfilment. It was only ten years since Blériot crossed the English Channel. Yet already, that June, Alcock and Brown had crossed the Atlantic in about sixteen hours in a converted Vimy bomber. Less than five months later, Ross and Keith Smith flew from Britain to Australia. In February a Department of Civil Aviation had been formed within the Air Ministry. Winston Churchill was Air Minister with Trenchard as Chief of Staff.

The first progress report issued by the new Department gave the official date of the opening of civil flying as the 1st May. From February 12 till that date 'a small staff began to attack the multiplicity of problems and difficulties . . . attending on the commencement of civil aviation.' The starting signal came on July 14, when Air Ministry announced that on the following day aircraft would be allowed to ply to destinations outside the United Kingdom. Prior to departure, aeroplanes and crew were required to report at the Customs Station which was to be established at Hounslow Aerodrome. The announcement, though eagerly awaited, had no immediate significance, for it took at least a month to organize regular services and advertise them properly to the hoped-for fare-paying public. There was, however, one business man who read the notice and decided to take immediate action. Colonel W. N. Pilkington of the St. Helens glass firm, picked up the telephone and asked for a quotation for a flight to Paris the following morning—July 15, the first day of the new freedom.

Terms were arranged. Captain Jerry Shaw, chief pilot of Aircraft Transport & Travel Ltd., who was assigned the job, met his passenger at 7 a.m. at Hendon Aerodrome. It was a depressing morning, with torrents of rain and low cloud. Jerry Shaw watched his passenger being fitted out with flying coat, helmet, goggles, gloves and life belt, 'then bundled into the back seat—umbrella and all.' There was no crowd to wave them off on this rather special occasion in the history of British Civil Aviation. 'We took off at precisely 7.30 a.m.,' writes Shaw, 'and made for Hounslow where, viewed from 300 feet, there was not a sign of life. Figuring that nobody had remembered to tell the Customs man he was supposed to be there to receive visitors, I decided to push on as we had no time to waste, and fix my outward and inward clearance on the way back.

'Apart from a few tricky minutes in low clouds near the North Downs, the journey over Folkestone and Boulogne down to Beauvais was uneventful but wet, and hardly ever over 200 feet above ground. With the advantages of a following wind, we had made very good time, but then lost half-an-hour trying to find a gap in the clouds to get over the hills which form a barrier south of Beauvais. We eventually landed at Le Bourget at 10.15 a.m. after being in the air for 2¾ hours.

'Le Bourget in those days consisted of several canvas hangars, some wooden sheds and a lot of mud. Of course, nobody took the slightest interest in our arrival, so I taxied over to the French Air Force Officers' Mess, where I had many friends, for coffee and some advice on procedure—seeing that I had not yet acquired a passport. That deficiency was easily overcome by the simple expedient of boarding a tramcar in the village and alighting once we were through the barrier at the Octroi, where we picked up a taxi into Paris—invariably the most dangerous part of this trip.'

There is no record to tell us whether Colonel Pilkington enjoyed himself or had a successful meeting. He was back at Le Bourget the next day at two o'clock and set off with Captain Shaw duly armed with the necessary Customs clearance for the return flight to Hounslow, which took 2 hours and 55 minutes, where they were confronted with an indignant Customs official. 'After a fatherly lecture on the number of laws I had broken and the penalties I was liable to suffer, I was allowed in with a caution.' Such was the first commercial return flight from the United Kingdom. It was, of course, an individual charter flight and not the beginning of the scheduled service, which came later, in August.

Under Service conditions, there had already been many Channel crossings. In the very month when the R.A.F. itself was formed, April 1918, a couple of twin-engined Handley Page bombers were gutted to be turned over to transport work. These aeroplanes, carrying a total of sixteen persons, including crew, were used between Boulogne and Lympne to return pilots who were flying reinforcements of warplanes from Britain for service on the Western Front.

After that war, when the Army of Occupation took up its position along the Rhine, a number of Royal Air Force Squadrons were used for the conveyance of troop mail. There had been considerable speculation among the men of the R.A.F. during the last year of the war about the future commercial prospect of aviation. Most of them then discovered the term 'civil aviation' for the first time. With the flying of this mail from England to Cologne, it was felt that a real beginning had been made. Those in authority, however, took the view that passengers should not be carried until the unknown dangers of flying had been overcome. This was logical. Despite all the Service flying which had been accomplished, aviation was still very much in its infancy. Because of the war, it had become associated in many minds with danger. No attempt in fact had been made to operate aircraft from place to place on a regular schedule.

In any event, the troops on the Rhine and their mail from home seemed to offer a wonderful opportunity for experiment, particularly of flying 'in the weather'. Regular daily 'services' were arranged. No. 122 Squadron from Hawkinge, near Folkestone, flew, in their DH 9 aircraft, the large sacks of mail across the Channel. There, at their aerodrome at Maisoncelle, 110 Squadron took it over and flew it to Cologne in their superior DH 9A aircraft.

During 1918, the R.A.F. also had an aircraft set aside for communications. Winston Churchill had a machine on call during that year for his journey between London and headquarters in France. David Lloyd George was the first Prime Minister to use air communication for official business. A communication flight of the R.A.F. stationed at Hendon was expanded to form No. 1 (Communication) Squadron at the end of 1918, to meet the increased passenger traffic in politicians and what we now call V.I.P.s arising from the Armistice. This was followed within a few months by the formation of No. 2 (Communication) Squadron, under the command of Major J. R. McCrindle, who later became a member of the Board of B.O.A.C. McCrindle recalls that Bonar Law in the early days asked for a covered-in cockpit, for his secretary and himself, in order that the Minister could work, talk and not be blown about. 'To our surprise the machine went much faster when this was done——' and Bonar Law's modification was generally adopted.

No. 1 Squadron, which was the first to operate a regular London–Paris service, was commanded by Major Cyril Patterson, who later, as a civilian pilot, made the first scheduled flight from Paris to London. Its equipment included two Handley Page saloon aircraft, each accommodating six passengers, the *Silver*

Star and the *Great Britain* officially described as *H.M. Air Liners*. Among their achievements was the first night passenger flight across the Channel. When these two Communication Squadrons were disbanded in October 1919, they had made 749 flights, carrying 934 passengers, despatches and mail. Ninety per cent of their flights had been made over the London–Paris route and there was only one accident in which a passenger was killed.

During this R.A.F. pioneering period, the 'Met-Man' spoke for the first time when Air Ministry issued its first public aviation weather reports. The second of these, published on February 1, 1919, sounded a slightly ominous note for the airmen of the period. 'Low clouds, poor visibility and snow showers are likely to continue today over the British Isles. Cross-country flying will be dangerous on these accounts.' Such a met. report might not daunt the captains and crews who fly in and out of London Airport at the present day: but civil aviation in general, and B.O.A.C. in particular, owe everything to the men who were not daunted by such warnings during the fledgling years. When demobilization came, and men cast off their uniforms to start the civil air services they had dreamed of, few of them had any idea that they were assisting, however humbly, in starting up an industry which was to become a major factor in the life of every nation within a relatively few years.

A man who was waiting to offer such pilots a career in civil aviation was George Holt Thomas. He was imaginative, cautious, commercially experienced in aviation and had already registered his airline, Aircraft Transport and Travel Ltd. He had become interested in aviation when Blériot flew the Channel in 1909. Before the First World War he held licences for the manufacture and sale of Farman aircraft in Britain. He had financed Paulhan's London to Manchester flight in 1910, which won the *Daily Mail* £10,000 prize in a Farman machine.

By the end of the war, he was the head of the Aircraft Manufacturing Company Ltd. with Geoffrey de Havilland as his Chief Designer, and thus was a founder of the de Havilland Aircraft Company. He had other subsidiary interests in aviation, and was in fact one of the few to be commercially committed to the new element of the air long before the war ended. He succeeded in realizing the dreams of generations of prophets—but in a matter-of-fact and businesslike manner, making ample preparations for every step he took. As early as May 1917 when he read a paper on commercial aeronautics before a huge audience he supported his arguments by showing a film—then something of a sensation in itself. In the text of the lecture subsequently printed, appeared two illustrations—a de Havilland single-engined aeroplane in flight with the words 'LONDON–BIRMINGHAM' painted in large letters on the side of the fuselage, and a Handley Page with the legend 'LONDON–MANCHESTER–LIVERPOOL'. The titles given to these illustrations were 'Future Aerial Mail' and 'The Parcel Post'. There is, of course, no evidence of such flights having been made before the lecture was given. It must be assumed that the aircraft were specially painted and posed for the propaganda value of their pictures.

Holt Thomas was an able propagandist—but never cared to step far out of his self-cast role of shrewd business man. When in 1920 he published a fat volume called *Aerial Transport*, his foreword stated: 'What I desire particularly is not to appear as a fanatic. I am just as aware of the limitations of an aircraft as I am of its powers. . . .' Nevertheless, his end-paper map showed the London–Australia route of the Smith brothers triumphantly plotted in red.

Such was the man who announced—prematurely as it turned out—to the world four days after the signing of the Armistice in November 1918 that 'arrangements were in hand with Aircraft Transport and Travel Ltd. to operate as soon as possible an air service between London and Paris.'

He had to wait for official sanction. Meanwhile he went about his preparations with characteristic thoroughness. He had a flair for people. He appointed one of the key men of the R.A.F., Sir Sefton Brancker, as Managing Director, with General Sir Francis Festing as General Manager of his new concern. He remained aloof from the pilots but through Brancker he obtained the services of experienced men. Though he had clear-cut ideas of his own, he was prepared to let the experts run his airline. In spite of his own affiliations with the manufacturing side of the business, he held that no transport concern should be bound to any single constructional company either for aircraft or for equipment.

A somewhat Edwardian figure, with a neat beard and stiff winged collar, his feet were always on the ground even if his head was sometimes realistically among the clouds. 'One would be guilty of a very foolish action if one held out hopes of hundred-miles-an-hour travel throughout the world unless there was a very strong probability of this becoming possible. It ought, indeed, to be something more than a probability. It should be a certainty and that, in effect, it now is. But it is perfectly true it cannot be done at once. When it takes months to prepare a short 250 miles stage like that between London and Paris, it is obvious that these huge, long-distance journeys overseas will not only be a matter of time in their organization but also of very large sums of money. The whole question, as I have indicated, becomes so gigantic and so universally important that it is not a matter for private enterprise alone but for private enterprise going hand-in-hand with the Governments of the world.'

He did not confine himself to the universal. He was much exercised by the problems of what he called 'an involuntary descent'. His remedy was a 'Ten Mile Chain' of emergency alighting grounds all along the route. Though no such 'chain' was ever laid out, emergency landings were frequent enough. There was no radio communication from air to ground; nor between London and Paris. Weather information and arrival and departure messages were passed by telephone. There were various visual aids for pilots such as 'aerial lighthouses' at the terminal points, and even the painting of the names of places such as Redhill, Tonbridge and Ashford in white capital letters on the roofs of railway stations. Nature assisted art at Edenbridge, Kent, where the name was cut in chalk close to the station.

On the London–Paris route, emergency landing grounds were, in fact, provided at Penshurst, Marden, Lympne and Littlestone in the south of England and at St. Inglevert, Berck Plage, Abbeville, Poix and Beauvais in the north of France. But these were not enough. 'Often pilots driven down by cloud and rain would land in fields and push on again with the slightest improvement in the weather,' recalls Jerry Shaw.

This pioneer pilot, who is now in the service of the de Havilland Company, has himself put on record the opening of Holt Thomas's first airline.

'The first week of our operation was critical, with a very sceptical public, the G.P.O. and business-houses watching points, budding competitors checking our results from the fence and, of course, the news-hawks panting for a nice juicy headline story. On the first Thursday gales and storms caused cancellation of the London to Paris service, but ignorant of these conditions I left Paris with two passengers in a DH 4A, and with a fine following wind made a swift if somewhat turbulent passage up to Boulogne, where, turning to cross the Channel, we were buffeted about the sky, with cloud down to 400 feet and a 40 degrees drift. When the English coast came into sight, I had had quite enough and decided to land at Lympne to put the passengers on the train, but as I struggled to put the machine into the wind with literally no forward ground-speed I was amazed to see one of the Bessoneaux hangars careering across the aerodrome and fetch up in the next field. The Air Ministry recorded winds up to 110 m.p.h. at that time. Anyhow, the idea of trying to make a landing was quickly abandoned and we swung off for Hounslow. That journey across Kent was one I would not wish on anybody; heavy rain squalls and drifting low cloud accompanied the full gale. Once or twice I gave a passing thought to what was going on in the cabin behind me, for there was no means of communication, and after doing half a turn of a spin over Westerham I wondered if it mattered anyway.

'At long last the closed sheds of Hounslow loomed through the rain. The wind indicator was in shreds, but the way trees were lying over left no doubt of the wind's direction. Out in the middle of the aerodrome could be seen two huddled groups each of three men, with a distance of some 50 feet between the groups. With the engine practically full-out, I flew the machine close to the ground and, when positioned between the groups, eased back the throttle and they grabbed the wings and held the machine securely on the ground. Fortunately the duty-officer at Lympne had 'phoned Hounslow, advising our passage, and those six soaked volunteers had worked out the landing scheme. With further willing assistance we managed to taxi straight into the hangar. The sight of my passengers as they emerged will never be forgotten. Beaming all over their faces, although all that remained of the bowler belonging to one, was the rim round his neck—he had hit a hole in the roof of the cabin—and the other an Irish padre, still clutching a brandy bottle in which they had saved a modicum for the driver. Handing it over, they thanked me for what they had thought was a wonderful display of stunting!'

After this satisfactory disposal of his passengers, there was the General Manager's office to be faced:

'That journey was accomplished in 1 hour 55 minutes and every moment of agony was turned into joy as sitting in General Festing's office, a few minutes later, a G.P.O. official called him up and jeeringly inquired which train he thought the Paris mail would arrive by, only to be staggered by Festing's reply that they could expect it at Mount Pleasant twenty minutes ahead of schedule.'

Jerry Shaw's passengers, the man in the bowler hat and the Irish padre, paid £21 apiece for their trip (no reduction on return tickets). This fare charged by Aircraft Transport and Travel Ltd. included road transport to Hounslow Aerodrome from any point within a mile of Piccadilly Circus and road transport from Le Bourget to Paris.

After ten weeks of operations, Holt Thomas's airline on November 1, 1919, had flown 37,750 miles on its London–Paris route, completing 147 flights out of its scheduled 154.

He was not alone in the field. There was Frederick Handley Page whose span more than covers the whole of this story, then, in 1919, a tall broadly built man of thirty-three whose early baldness gave an impression of maturer years. Before the war he had been a respected but not eminently successful pioneer of flying: at the end of it his name was already renowned in connection with big aeroplanes. These, he intended to use for civil aviation. Indeed he saw it as a necessity. The year 1919 marked not only the birth of civil aviation but the wholesale dropping of war contracts and large-scale dismissals. Frederick Handley Page spent little time at his glass-topped, scrupulously tidy desk during that period. He was out and about the almost deserted shops of the Cricklewood aerodrome superintending the reconditioning of warplanes for civil use, and working with his test pilot and research engineer. His organization, which had been founded in 1908, began unscheduled flights between London and Paris on August 25, 1919. Handley Page Transport Ltd., based on Cricklewood, inaugurated regular operations on the route in September 1919, when seven passengers and goods were carried on the first of the Company's thrice-weekly services. The pilot of the inaugural service on September 2 was Lieutenant-Colonel W. Sholto Douglas, holder of commercial pilot's licence No. 4, now Lord Douglas of Kirtleside, who remembers that 'he went to Handley Page and asked for a job and was given £500 a year as chief pilot'. He also piloted Handley Page o/400's on the first demonstration commercial flights between London and Brussels. The Handley Page Transport people were the first to begin regular operations on that route in September 1919. They were also one of the pioneers in air catering. On October 11, 1919, they introduced lunch baskets on their services; a modest but sustaining luncheon consisting of six sandwiches, fruit and chocolate was offered to the less queasy passengers for 3s.

A railway strike in Britain in the autumn of 1919 put unexpected pressure upon the newly-fledged air services. Handley Page airline carried a quarter of a million letters between London and Paris during this period, and the frequency of all services was stepped up. The strike also brought into operation a third service, by the Marine Aviation Works Ltd., between Southampton and Le Havre in single-engined flying-boats. This was, in fact, the first international flying-boat passenger service, but apart from that it has no particular relevance to this story as it was short-lived.

The third British cross-Channel service of importance was started in 1919 by the Instone brothers, who were coal exporters, shipowners and ship brokers with headquarters in Wales.

> 'We had a fleet of steamers [wrote Sir Samuel Instone] both our own and time-chartered, which were costing a very large amount per day, and it was quite customary for these boats to arrive at North French ports a week or ten days before they could discharge, owing to the fact that the bills of lading had not arrived owing to delays in the post. We conceived the idea of purchasing an aeroplane and getting Government permission to carry our own letters . . . ships were consequently in a position to proceed to their berths and discharge their cargoes immediately on arrival—perhaps a week to ten days ahead of other vessels forced to lie off ports awaiting arrival of their documents. This was the means of saving for the Company thousands of pounds in ship-hire and demurrage. Out of that the Instone Air Line arose as a separate entity.'

This airline's first continental flight went from Hounslow to Le Bourget on October 13, 1919, piloted by Captain F. L. Barnard, who made his presence known on the other side by throwing out a number of greetings cards over Boulogne. They were decorated with the Union Jack and the French Tricolour and bore the proud message: '*À son premier passage à Boulogne-sur-Mer, l'Aéroplane de la Société Instone, 1 et 2 rue des Italiens, Paris, envoie à ses amis Boulonnais un salut fraternel* BARNARD *Lieutenant-Aviateur*.'

By the end of 1919, three main British rivals had emerged—Holt Thomas' Aircraft Transport and Travel, Handley Page Transport Company and Instone Air Line. There were other companies in Britain running unscheduled services to the Continent. There was also serious competition emerging from the Continent. Two French companies were already operating. K.L.M. had come into being. In fact, Britain's terminal airport at Hounslow was considered to be quite a busy place with at least four cross-Channel services a day.

In other respects, this old R.A.F. aerodrome, approached by a narrow tarmac road, was unattractive. It was irregular in shape, grass covered, with a crude, lightly tarmaced apron. It boasted one international touch. One gable of its twin sheds, bore the legend 'CUSTOMS': the other, triumphantly the word 'DOUANE'. In a converted wartime shed, a neat waitress in cap and apron served teas, cut sandwiches and was sometimes able to do a packaged lunch of sorts for adventurous travellers to enjoy during the two and a half hour trip to the other side.

At first Hounslow was the only aerodrome at which airliners could clear Customs. The services operated by Handley Page were obliged to run empty from their base at Cricklewood, to comply with formalities and pick up passengers. At a later stage, however, Customs opened at Cricklewood and the Handley Page services ran direct from there to the Continent. The aerodrome at Cricklewood was a grass field lying between the Broadway and Golders Green, bordered on one side by the Handley Page factory and on other sides by a railway line and built-up areas. There was little room for take-off. With luck the pilot found himself off the ground about one hundred yards before reaching the gap between the two hangars for which he aimed. A moment later he would be fifty feet above Cricklewood Broadway. Engine failure on take-off would certainly have been disastrous unless the pilot had gained enough height to make a circuit and land, for the Handley Page needed both its engines for climbing and indeed for maintaining level flight.

Edgware Road was their route to the Continent, and one of their great pilots was Captain R. H. McIntosh, who is still active in aviation and widely known as 'All-weather Mac'. As he came to fly this route regularly, he became a student of the red open-top Number 16 buses which thundered down the Edgware Road towards Marble Arch. He declares that he could sometimes overtake these—but only when they stopped to pick up passengers. All too often they seemed to be overtaking the heavily laden aircraft as she climbed. Only when he reached Marble Arch, and a height of some five hundred feet, could he start to breathe freely and feel that the long haul to Paris had begun. It should be mentioned that these early hazards left him undaunted. In 1958 he came second in the King's Cup air race.

Though such operations might seem somewhat over-adventurous, Frederick Handley Page, with his immense experience of long-range aircraft, was going about things with a shrewdness and thoroughness which certainly matched those of George Holt Thomas, particularly in his choice of staff and pilots. Having advertised for a manager, he was quick to secure the services of one of the first applicants for the job, George Woods Humphery, who at this stage first enters British civil aviation history, which from time to time he was to dominate. Another member of the newly-chosen team was H. G. Brackley, who was never to dominate but was destined to be an ubiquitous driving force in this story, a potent will-o'-the-wisp known and appreciated by all the aviation world as 'Brackles'.

A distinguished pilot who started with Handley Page was the late Captain Gordon P. Olley, who published his reminiscences in the mid-'thirties.

'One of my early trips on the London–Paris route will always linger in my mind, and it is hardly surprising that it should do so, seeing that I made as many as seventeen forced landings after leaving London and before I got to Paris; while by the time I neared the French capital it was so dark that I could not find the proper aerodrome and had to finish up eventually in a football field. Obstinate trouble with the petrol feed of my engines was the problem I was grappling with that day, and this meant that after perhaps a few miles' flying I had to alight and pump petrol by hand from one tank to another. But in each of these seventeen compulsory landings, I had no difficulty in finding a suitable field into which to glide and alight safely; while in every instance, also, I managed to fly out of that field again without the slightest mishap.'

From the autumn of 1919 till the spring of 1920, while Europe was still groping its way back towards civilian life and some sort of peace, the men who flew over from Hounslow and Cricklewood, hazardously lumbering into the unwelcoming skies, were supported by a great deal of faith, such money as could be raked together by private enterprise, and scant encouragement from a Government preoccupied with other things. There were, of course, rivalries: but the airline business was so small that everyone knew each other and a sense of shared adventure pervaded all. Moreover, the fledgling air services had sufficiently proved their reliability to be entrusted with His Majesty's mails.

The first Director of Civil Aviation, Major General Sir Frederick Sykes, a son-in-law, incidentally, of Bonar Law, was a voice crying in the wilderness, when he concluded his survey of 1919: 'It may be questioned whether civil aviation in England is to be regarded as one of those industries which is unable to stand on its own feet, and is yet so essential to the national welfare that it must be kept alive at all costs.' He suggested Government subsidies, pointing out that the French Government had already earmarked a large sum for their operators. He also suggested help in kind.

Passengers at this time were few and far between. Harry Harper, the world's first Aeronautical Correspondent, who had served with Northcliffe's 1917 Committee and joined Holt Thomas in the summer of 1919, recalls how anxiously they studied passenger bookings at this time. 'One would walk into the small office where the clerk concerned with this work was sitting and ask: "How many have you got today?" "Two," he would answer, with an air of satisfaction. "And how many for tomorrow?" "Three," he would reply, with an even greater pride.'

Yet those who worked Britain's first international airport at Hounslow did not go entirely without recognition. The Civil Air

Traffic Officer there was Major S. T. L. Greer, and there were occasions, naturally enough, when he had time on his hands. He was in fact, sitting in his office with his tunic jacket off and his feet on his desk when the Prince of Wales (afterwards Edward VIII) walked in. This, the first of all Royal visits, was pleasantly informal. The heir to the throne, ignoring the Major's somewhat dishevelled state, made a series of keen inquiries about the traffic and how it was run. 'You are a sort of Air Station Master?' he eventually concluded.

Major Greer humbly supposed he was.

'Station Masters usually at some time in their career receive a tie pin, but what we shall give to Air Station Masters I do not know!'

Royal recognition has followed over the years. There are many B.O.A.C. crew members today who sport cuff links and personal accessories which are personal rewards for serving Queen Elizabeth II on her overseas flights.

The airfield which the heir to the Throne inspected was about to reach the end of its days as London's international airport. It had been living ahead of its time. The land was required by the War Office, not as one might have thought for the development of tanks which had played such a decisive part in winning the First World War, but as a 'cavalry training ground'.

In March 1920, Croydon became the Customs Airport for London. The Hounslow period, however, was notable not only for what it inaugurated but for the spirit of those who were there. 'We had no idea that we were making history,' writes one of those pilots who was still flying for B.O.A.C. during the Second World War. 'Apart from the need to record our flying time for official purposes and perhaps noting the names of the passengers we carried, if they were in the public eye, we never troubled to keep any records, not even, I suppose, a diary. We all felt the uncertainty of flying and our chief concern was to get to wherever we had to without breaking anything or without killing ourselves. I don't believe that any of us had much idea of what sort of life flying was to offer us, or even whether it would turn out to be a career.'

CHAPTER IV

PIONEER CROYDON

DURING the three decades which saw first the birth of Imperial Airways, then of British Airways, and later the emergence of B.O.A.C. and B.E.A., London's international airport at Croydon was a famous place. It had been an operational base for the R.A.F. during the First World War. When it opened as a Customs airport in 1920, it was to serve a civil aviation consisting mainly of an assortment of converted warplanes shoestring-run.

Nature, not engine trouble, was the main enemy. A few of the young pioneer pilots gave up after only one winter. Many of the names recorded in the first year disappeared early in the nineteen-twenties. Some transferred to ground jobs. Some were casualties—and this early period of aviation is not without its roll of honour. There were those also who won fame in after years as pilots and in key positions in British and foreign air services.

Not only courage and fine airmanship were needed, but also money. Behind the statistics of men and machines aloft without radio or much more technical equipment than that of the motor-cars of the period, there was a very shaky financial background. 'Flying by itself' was a Churchillian phrase which was not achieving the authentic ring of history. Holt Thomas had gone into the business with acumen and resource. If he had been premature, it was owing to lack of technical equipment to support the flyers. 'The day of the luxurious "aerial liner" may dawn in due course,' he wrote, 'there are possible economies in operation which may change appreciably the financial aspects of aerial transport. But when we . . . calculate in terms of existing aeroplanes, or of those we know we shall have, say, next year, then Utopian dreams have certainly to be banished from our thoughts.'

No craft which could by present standards be described as a luxurious 'aerial-liner' was to alight at the new airport for some time—though that time was not so distant as some imagined. Nevertheless, when international traffic moved there, 1,155 passengers had already been carried overseas by British operators with only one fatal accident. When in 1958 the closure of Croydon was under discussion, B.O.A.C. alone was sometimes carrying overseas more than eleven hundred passengers in a single day from the London International Airport, back once more near Hounslow. Croydon enjoyed its heyday as the most up-to-date and efficient airport in the world, having exceedingly reliable radio and meteorological services. It met all London's civil aviation requirements till the beginning of the Second World War, in which it was bombed. Its former glories were never regained.

There was little glory about it when the Hounslow men moved there early in 1920.

> 'Actually the first little party of pioneer airwaymen to invade Croydon, driving in an old Ford car, lost themselves in a maze of roads between Sutton and Wallington [wrote Mr. Robert Brenard] and it was some time before they located the aerodrome—then known as Waddon aerodrome—which had housed a war-time fighter squadron. This military aerodrome they set to work to turn into a proper commercial airport. One of the most urgent needs was office accommodation. This was provided by purchasing old wooden army huts and erecting them on either side of what became a sort of "main street" leading from Plough Lane to the aeroplane alighting-ground. Other people followed the first arrivals, erecting their particular type of temporary wooden building. These were all of different shapes and sizes, until the final appearance of this "main street" reminded one forcibly of a Wild West township.'

It was a gold-rush atmosphere: but very little gold was struck. Even the honour of carrying H.M. mail was without much profit. A. T. and T. had been granted a six months' monopoly, receiving two shillings of the two and sixpenny surcharge for each 1-oz. letter. Their revenue from this did not exceed £25 a week.

Sefton Brancker, running the airline for Holt Thomas, pressed on. The daily service, carrying two passengers in each direction had been improved by the introduction of specially ordered de Havilland 16 four-passenger commercial aeroplanes. The Company had begun two services a day in each direction. Fares had been reduced to £15 for the single journey. Costs were still too high and the operation did not pay. Eight-passenger de Havilland 18 aircraft were then introduced. They cut down the cost per passenger mile but increased establishment charges. The airline still did not pay. An arrangement was made with the Royal Dutch Air Line (K.L.M.) to work a service to Amsterdam in May 1920. This failed because fares were too high and the Post Office withdrew its support.

Bill Lawford left a record of these days of struggle.

> 'One could enlarge *ad lib* on the enthusiasm of the staff of A. T. and T. from the highest to the lowest—and the highest, General Brancker, had that magnetic personality which he radiated to all, revealing himself at once as a great chief and friend. After any particularly nasty flight, there was always awaiting his great hearty grip of the hand with a twinkling: "Well done—Cheerio and stick it, old lad," or a polite little note to that effect. . . . His great secret was that he was *human* and showed appreciation for those who worked for him, and as a natural result received one hundred per cent unswerving loyalty and affection in return.'

Croydon began on a small scale. It was transitory and unconventional. Men of the three rival British airlines discussed their problems and their triumphs. The great year of hope had passed but 1920 still had about it a climate of experiment and enterprise. Handley Page, as well as A. T. and T., introduced £120 season tickets on their London–Paris service, valid for twelve single journeys in either direction—but there were few, if any, customers for these. For the 1920 Easter holidays, Handley Page offered special return fares of 25 guineas. They were running passenger and freight services to Brussels in collaboration with a Belgian company. They also started an air mail service to Amsterdam in 1920. The Instone Air Line was flying to Paris twice weekly in each direction. Another, short-lived, British competitor was Air Post of Banks Ltd., which represented the interests of a number of banking houses. This service started early in September 1920, mainly for the carriage of documents. It ceased after only two months' work.

The French, more enterprising than any other nation in pioneering flight, started a London–Paris service in September 1919. Their first concern, Cie. des Messageries Aériennes, known as C.M.A., operated under a pool arrangement with Handley Page. Another company, the Cie. Générale Transaérienne, which began late in 1919, made a similar pool arrangement with A. T. and T. In March 1920, a third French line, Cie. des Grands Express Aériens, joined the cross-Channel competition with a fleet of twin-engine Farman Goliaths, each capable of carrying twelve passengers. The British Air Ministry report of the period somewhat wistfully quoted 'handsome Government subsidies' which were going to French civil aviation. It also noted that passengers and mail were being flown from France to Morocco with stops in Spain and that among their activities the French had a bi-weekly service to Turkey. 'The policy of carrying out long-distance flights in order to connect France with her colonial possessions by air is still being actively pursued, and a successful flight has been made across the Sahara from Algiers via Timbuktu to Dakar.'

This must have been disturbing reading to those who visualized British aviation on an Empire-wide pattern, knew of long-range and intercontinental flights made during the war and afterwards, and found themselves forced meanwhile to be content with modest crossings of the English Channel.

In spite of such frustration there was a strong sense of comradeship among everyone close to the business on both sides of the Channel.

> 'Pilots, mechanics, ground staff, were all at the time belonging to the same great family [writes Robert Michel, a Frenchman who worked for the British at Le Bourget], both staffs English and French were strongly united and formed a strong team who had most of the time to work under sometimes most difficult circumstances. The task was particularly hard for the pilots who had to fly on converted war machines, with no wireless, practically no weather reports, in gales, rain and snow, with single engines. I was at that time the only staff dealing with the traffic. My duty was to weigh the passengers and their baggages, collect their excess, their passports, help to load the machines, make load sheets and Customs manifests—and to have all services leave on schedule.'

The year 1920 came to an end with an uneasiness about the future which could no longer be concealed, but with an amazing record of safety. Since the opening in August 1919, there had been only two fatal accidents on the British scheduled air services. There was no great cause for public anxiety with the safety of the new airlines. The trouble was that there was relatively little public concern for any aspect of the air lines in Britain. Unlike their neighbours across the Channel, neither the Government nor the nation had been imaginatively stirred. There was none of that enthusiasm with which the Elizabethans had supported the pioneers of sail. British merchant airmen were left to their own meagre resources even when it was apparent that these would fail and that that failure would not only discourage a vital new industry but bring discredit upon the country.

Just about the time that Croydon Airport opened, a Government Committee, under Lord Weir, recommended direct financial assistance to the British air transport companies on approved routes across the Channel and on routes where flying-boats could be operated. No Government grant came through in 1920. The French meanwhile with State assistance could cover their operating expenses, even without pay-loads. They were able, too, to cut fares.

'The French Government,' protested Brancker, 'has increased its subsidies to commercial aircraft, which has enabled them to reduce the London–Paris fare to £6 6s. od. She has already run a most efficient service from Toulouse to French Morocco for more than a year. She is organizing a service to Warsaw which starts shortly. Germany is operating various internal services. One of her air transport companies has flown more than all our services put together.'

British private enterprise could not face Government-subsidized foreign rivalry. Nor could civil aviation in this country be run like a series of rival bus services each backed with limited funds and the motto 'winner takes all'. It began to dawn upon people that British civil aviation was more important than that. There were the aspects of prestige and strategy which some had foreseen, upon which few had acted, but which too many had ignored. When this realization came to the point of action, it was almost too late for the fledgling industry. Certainly it was too late for George Holt Thomas, who simply had to give up and go out of business. His interest passed into the hands of the B.S.A.-Daimler combine.

With the new masters emerged a vigorous character, Colonel Frank Searl, who had run London's buses as private enterprise and was afterwards to become first Managing Director of Imperial Airways. 'Until the advent of this man, it was generally accepted that aeroplanes had to be treated gently and not flown too hard or something might go wrong,' writes Captain W. Armstrong. 'So we would bring a plane out of the hangar in the morning and fly it to Paris, where it would be pushed into another hangar to receive some obscure but very necessary grooming. It was quite certain that having flown from England, it would be entirely wrong to fly it back on the same day. Searl changed all that. I remember the consternation we felt when he brought his hard business mind to bear on the subject. Seeing an incoming plane from Paris, he followed it round to its hangar.

' "Is this plane going back to Paris today?"

' "Oh, no!"

' "Why not?"

' "Well, you see, it needs inspecting and tuning up."

' "What is there to do?"

' "Oh, the plugs have to be removed and cleaned."

' "Well, let's clean them."

'So they were cleaned; not a very long job.

' "Now, what else?"

' "We shall have to look at the magnetos."

' "Anything else?"

" 'The filters must be looked at; and we—er, we shall have to fill up with petrol, oil and water. And yes, then give the rigging a look over."

' And so on until all the tasks were done.

' "Now, is that all you would do? It is! Well, it can go to Paris after all."

'And with reluctance, it had to be agreed that it could.'

In December 1920, the new masters from the Midlands lost heart. All the A. T. and T. services were withdrawn. Handley Page also felt the pinch and closed down their Amsterdam service that autumn. By the end of the year, they were the only regular operators on the London–Paris route. The other survivor, Instone, operated on demand only.

Then the whole thing collapsed. There were no scheduled British cross-Channel services whatever from February 28 till March 19, 1921. Only the French flew into Croydon. British pilots had to stand by and suffer for a failure that was not theirs. Some of them offered their services for nothing in order to keep the propellers turning during this period of shame. 'All-Weather' MacIntosh, representing his fellow pilots, told Frederick Handley Page that the men were willing to fly without pay to help out. H.P. replied that it was the Government which should be helping, and the offer was regretfully declined.

Brancker, who had given up the security of a Service career in the interests of civil aviation, wrote: 'The last ten years of my life have had their chief interest in aviation. I had the pleasure of seeing all my dreams come true during the war, and have now had three rather heart-breaking years in endeavouring to modify the magnificent engine of war which we had created in 1918 to the requirements of the British Empire during peace.'

That statement, in fact, contained an element of truth which Brancker, for all his fine qualities, together with many other men of vision, had failed to recognize. It had been a mistake to regard civil aviation as a service which could simply be adapted from the machinery of war. This, incidentally, was to be brought home to the British again at the end of the Second World War, when another attempt was made to beat swords into ploughshares.

Though other European nations may also have suffered such illusions, they had seen to it that civil aviation received sufficient Government support. The British were forced on to the touch line to witness the triumphs even of their former enemies.

> 'Eighteen months ago [wrote Brancker in *The Times*] a British aerial transport firm carried on certain international negotiations at The Hague for the organization of a through service from London to Stockholm and Oslo, with halts at The Hague, Hamburg, and Copenhagen, and in connection with a line from Hamburg to Berlin. Holland, Denmark, Norway and Sweden naturally have few pilots and no aircraft of their own. It was therefore practically certain that all these stages would be manned and equipped either from England or from Germany, and it was fairly certain that the British, in

the first instance, would have the running of four, if not five, of the six stages involved. The British firm concerned has since gone into liquidation, largely because of the delay in any guarantee of Government assistance; the result is that Mr. Fokker, the designer of the most efficient fighting machine which Germany produced during the war, is to have the order for the equipment.'

The British collapse was really a first step to the doubtful system of trial and error by which civil aviation progressed in its earlier years. It was a sacrifice which saved money but cost much in men and prestige. There were many human casualties but the loss of Sefton Brancker himself as a commercial operator became ultimately a gain to the British Merchant Air Service when he 'went over to the Government', to become Director of Civil Aviation, for a very vital period of years.

The Government came to the rescue, too late and not very efficiently.

Towards the end of his term as Secretary of State for Air, Winston Churchill, in March 1921, had appointed a 'cross-Channel Subsidies Committee' to furnish first-aid treatment. This was done by means of a temporary scheme of subsidies granted to Handley Page and Instone for the London–Paris route. Handley Page flew its first subsidized service from Cricklewood in March 19, Instone from Croydon on March 21. Each Company thereafter operated on alternate days, giving six British services a week in each direction with fares brought down to the French level of £6 6s. od. single and £12 os. od. return. In the humiliating interlude in which no British service operated, the French had looked after mail. This was now handed back to the British Companies. This temporary subsidy, afterwards described in a Government white paper as 'tending to encourage extravagance and to limit flying', ran from March 1921 till March 1922.

When it was superseded by a so-called permanent scheme setting a total subsidy at £200,000 a year for three years on a system of payment by results the subsidies went to Handley Page, Instone and the newly-formed Daimler Hire Ltd. for the London–Paris route and to Instone for the London–Brussels route. Later that year there was a new division of the field.

It should be explained that Daimler Hire Ltd. had been a member of the B.S.A. group which had operated A. T. and T.

during the latter part of that airline's existence. When the end came, in 1920, the B.S.A. group disposed of all the assets. None of these was taken over by the new concern, Daimler Airway, which emerged in 1922 with Mr. George Woods Humphery, formerly of Handley Page, as General Manager and Colonel Frank Searl as Managing Director. The new Company started from scratch with the delivery of the prototype DH 34 at Croydon on March 31. It went into service on April 2, carrying newspapers to Le Bourget flown by the famous W. S. R. Hinchliffe, who had been appointed Chief Pilot.

This Hinchliffe, with a patch over one eye, was one of the aviation 'cards' with which Croydon abounded in those days. He had a habit of putting on his bowler hat immediately on alighting and, thus adorned, would taxi across to the landing apron. After Lindbergh's solo flight across the Atlantic, he became restless with the operation of short scheduled hops and joined the Hon. Elsie McKay in her attempt to fly the Atlantic from east to west, from which they never returned.

Daimlers suffered an unusual stroke of misfortune, when one of their brand new DH 34s landed on top of another, smashing both machines. Somehow or other, for five long weeks, Woods Humphery managed to operate his Paris service with his sole remaining aircraft.

The Government of the day, having at long last conceded that British civil aviation could not 'fly by itself', was soon forced to realize that it had been foolhardy to pay subsidies to several airlines competing with each other on the same route. In May 1922, for instance, there were seven British services a day between London and Paris all qualifying for subsidy. Three were flown by Daimler and two each by Instone and Handley Page. Though Handley Page created a record that summer by carrying 260 passengers in one week, foreign subsidized competition weighed heavily against British operators. In August, Instone withdrew one of its Paris and one of its Brussels services, gave up the carriage of goods and dismissed some of its pilots. By the autumn, it was clear that public money was being wasted in subsidizing British rivalries against foreign competition.

The 'permanent scheme' therefore was revised by another, effective from October 1, which for the operators led to a friendly free-for-all. Mr. Woods Humphery recalls that he and

Colonel Searl made a great show of self-denial. They pointed out to the authorities that Handley Page had been operating a London–Paris service long before Daimlers came on the scene, and that Instone had great experience of the Brussels service with its extension to Cologne. Daimlers therefore offered to break new ground with Manchester–London–Amsterdam service, with a connection to Berlin. Their reward for this was the largest slice of the subsidy, £55,000. Instone received £25,000, and Handley Page only £15,000, with £10,000 for a new concern, The British Marine Air Navigation Company Ltd. for a service from Southampton to the Channel Isles, which they did not in fact begin to operate until 1923.

From that October, British services out of Croydon really did begin to show both some variety and to range further afield. At the beginning of the month, Instone took an inaugural service through to Cologne and appointed their first manager in that city. Daimler started a Croydon–Rotterdam service which it extended to Amsterdam. It also opened the London–Manchester section of the route. It did not extend to Berlin, however, until 1923 owing to political obstruction—the ever familiar overtone of civil aviation.

In Britain there was evidence that at long last the public was catching on to the new air services. The total number of passengers carried on the Paris route in 1922 was 10,025, of which 7,566 flew British—Handley Page carrying more than half of these.

To foster this public interest, and indeed to get customers, all the airline operators indulged in every form of publicity. Press flights were frequent. American publicists and journalists were particularly welcome. When the famous American lecturer Lowell Thomas wanted a flight to Germany, Woods Humphery himself saw to it that the visitor would have red-carpet treatment. When he came to make the final arrangements, however, Woods Humphery realized that the American was to be the sole passenger aboard and was thus unlikely to be impressed by the popularity of the new service. Orders went out at once for members of the airline staff to be mustered and dressed as passengers to join the airliner at Croydon and accompany the great man on his journey. It was a good flight and Lowell Thomas was duly impressed. The bad moment came with their arrival when the members of the airline staff in Germany were suddenly confronted by a troop of their own English colleagues doing their best to act the parts of passengers and diligently cutting them dead. Some years afterwards, Woods Humphery revealed this cheerful little ruse to Lowell Thomas, who liked it well enough to put it into the text of his lectures.

The airlines saw the value of putting themselves on show. There were conducted tours of Croydon Aerodrome, with specially organized visits for school children. Joy-rides were a popular feature of the business. Handley Page carried them in the early days when their aircraft had to travel between Cricklewood and Hounslow to pick up the cross-Channel traffic. At Croydon Aerodrome, Instone started 5s. joy-rides in their airliner *City of London* and carried 386 people in 3½ hours one Sunday afternoon.

Freight, which is the subject of another chapter, had its publicity value. Alexandra Roses went through the streets of London in a specially decorated motor-car for conveyance to the Continent in a specially decorated aeroplane. Luxury items such as Devonshire cream, Scottish grouse and grapes from Lord Londonderry's garden, carried across the Channel by air, made what were thought to be useful paragraphs in the newspapers.

Imaginative writers had never been loth to take air transport as their theme. When Croydon airport in particular and continental air travel in general were beginning to achieve a certain glamour in the minds of that post-war generation, Gilbert Frankau created a delightfully period picture of the scene in *Gerald Cranston's Lady*:

> 'Putting on his travelling-cap, leaving the office, stepping into his car, telling Havers, "Croydon Aerodrome, and you'll have to look sharp," Cranston's primary sensation was relief. . . .
>
> 'The successful man's car spun on, beyond the river through the desert of suburban shops, across the railed green of Clapham Common. . . . But presently, as leaving the Common behind them, they came out of shopland into vale land, he forgot, in expectation of his actual journey, the purpose which had driven him to undertake it. Air-travel—he had flown more than once during the war—ought to be distinctly enjoyable. Profitable, too—once people like the Instones had done the pioneer work. . . .

'In five minutes they came to the railway bridge; and in three more, crossing it, to the big white signboard of the 'drome. The car veered down a narrow road; and so arrived, through unpretentious gates, along a concrete roadway, at the Instone Office. "Just on time, I think, sir," said Havers, glancing at the clock on his dashboard as Cranston stepped out.

'A young ground-officer in the white sea-cap and dark uniform of the Instone service, who had obviously been awaiting the passenger's arrival, saluted; asked Cranston's name; whispered to a subordinate, "Tell 'em he's here"; signalled a porter for the suit-case and—Cranston having given the interested chauffeur his final instructions—led him past the office into the wood-walled concrete-floored Customs hut.

'The suit-cases were already on the bench.

' "Chalk 'em up quick, Evans," said the Instone man to the Customs official; and to the porter, the chalking done, "Take 'em aboard, while I get Mr. Cranston through C.I.D." He led to the left; and Cranston followed into a narrow wooden corridor, where a second official, in a bowler hat, rose from a plain wooden table, to examine his passport.

' "We don't waste much time, you'll observe," commented the ground officer, guiding him back through the Custom-house and out into the open aerodrome.

' "Apparently not."

'Cranston, interested as a traveller newly arrived at some foreign railway station, had halted for a moment to survey the scene. Fifty yards ahead of him, he saw the big Vickers-Vimy bi-plane with the long narrow cabin underslung between its yellow wings and the "G.E.A.R." painted in prominent white letters all over its blue fuselage. Mechanics stood at its lower wing-tips. High and forward, where the two leather caps of pilot and observer just showed in silhouette above the triplex-glass wind-screen, another mechanic was twirling at the stiff propeller . . .'

Observe that it was a '*successful* man's car' which made this dashing journey. An atmosphere of success was being created but there was no stampede of eager passengers to share the convenience and glamour of international flight. The 12,400 carried in 1922 was a disappointingly slight increase on the 10,800 carried in 1921.

Foreign competition became keener in 1923 with the amalgamation of the two main French Companies to form Air Union, from which ultimately Air France emerged. Croydon also witnessed the arrival of the first German aeroplane to land in the United Kingdom since the war. It brought German airline officials to discuss the setting up of the London–Berlin air route, which opened in April that year with Daimlers working in collaboration with the Germans.

In March 1923, *The Aeroplane* stated: 'The ding-dong struggle for the target number of passengers carried was won this week by the Air Union who carried 76 passengers to H.P.T.'s 61.'

During the summer, the French again cut their rates. Air Union announced a single fare of £4 10s. 0d. between London and Paris, while Handley Page maintained their charge of £6 6s. 0d. In May, the newly-formed Belgian air line Sabena flew its first service from Brussels to Lympne, but did not operate a regular passenger service into London till 1926. Instone began a new non-stop service to Cologne and were only prevented by political difficulties from building up a regular service to Prague. Handley Page started a new service in August to Zürich. In September the British Marine Air Navigation Company started their regular service between Southampton and Guernsey.

For all these activities and the jockeying for position which went with them, the system of so-called permanent subsidies was a failure. By this time, however, the Government and the nation were beginning to be aware not only of the existing air services but of the need for their extension to cover the British Empire. There were statesmen at Westminster who could see this larger aspect of things, especially Sir Samuel Hoare (later Viscount Templewood) who took over the Air Ministry in October 1922. He was particularly inspired by the pioneer work in Australia of Qantas which had been born in 1920: and with this in mind, he set to work upon the problems of British civil aviation:

> 'It was clear that precarious doles were useless for the purpose. The essential condition was some kind of long-term agreement. Without security of tenure for a substantial number of years, the companies could not be expected to make far-seeing plans or undertake the great expense of buying new machines and improving their services. At this point I found

myself in trouble with the Treasury. The Treasury did not believe in civil aviation, and strongly objected to long-term commitments to companies that were obviously in financial difficulties. This opposition, which seemed very reasonable to many people at the time, made it necessary for me to produce a plan that avoided the objections to the doles that had hitherto proved useless and extravagant. It seemed to me that the best way to convert the critics was to invite two or three well-known business men to look at the problem from a practical angle, and to give me their conclusions with the least possible delay. This was the origin of what was known as the Hambling Committee.'

Sir Herbert Hambling was Deputy Chairman of Barclays Bank. His son, Sir Guy Hambling, tells the writer that it was the Prime Minister, Bonar Law, himself who urged his father to take on the job of investigating the situation of the competing Companies, saying: 'Can't you get them to amalgamate?'

The Committee worked fast.

'The unanimous recommendations were on the lines that I expected [Sir Samuel Hoare wrote]. First, that there must be greater security of tenure if there was to be any substantial development of civil air transport, secondly, that in the early days of civil flying, a single organization was more effective than the cut-throat competition of several small companies, thirdly, that a single company should be formed with a capital of a million pounds, and with Government nominees on the Board to take over the existing services and to expand civil air transport, fourthly, that the Government should guarantee a subsidy of not less than a million pounds, spread over ten years, and that the public should raise a corresponding million pounds as the capital needed for research, development and supply.'

This was well received by the public and soon accepted by the Cabinet. In spite of the fact that he had been one of the earliest passengers, Bonar Law might have proved to be a stumbling block. In the nick of time, however, he was succeeded by Baldwin as Prime Minister. 'I doubt whether Bonar Law would ever have approved a vote of a million pounds for civil air transport,' wrote Sir Samuel Hoare, 'even though it was to be spread over ten years. His successor knew nothing about aviation, but the romantic streak in his complex character had reacted to the wide horizon and undiscovered opportunities of the air.'

The Hambling Committee also envisaged the air services flying one million miles a year: and its apparent obsession with the magic of a million caused some wry comment at the time. Finding a name for the new concern had its lighter moments. The suggestion that it should be called British Aircraft Transport Service was killed when Woods Humphery pointed out that the initials spelt BATS. In its place he proposed 'Imperial Airways'. Such was the birth and naming of the immediate forerunner of B.O.A.C.

CHAPTER V

AIR MAIL

AIR MAIL in these times represents something like eighteen per cent of the revenue of the B.O.A.C.

The idea of sending letters by air was well in advance of aeronautical invention. Letters had been carried in balloons across the English Channel in the eighteenth and nineteenth centuries. The first official British acceptance of mail for transmission by air was advertised by the Postmaster General in 1870. Paris at that time was besieged by the Prussians and the mail was to fly by pigeon post from Tours into the beleaguered city. At Tours the messages were reproduced in quantity by microphotography before being handed over to the pigeons which risked their lives by flying over the German lines.

In Britain the first air mail operation to be recognized by the Government ran from September 9 to 26, 1911, flying mail in each direction between London and Windsor. The cards that were carried bore the wording: 'Coronation A.D. 1911. First U.K. aerial post by sanction of H.M. Postmaster General,' together with a drawing of a biplane over Windsor Castle. During that period more than 25,000 letters and 90,000 postcards were carried. The *Manchester Guardian* described the effort as 'an amusing enough game for the silly season'.

Northcliffe's 1917 Civil Aerial Transport Committee saw possibilities in an air mail service, 'one machine being run each way daily, weather permitting, between London and Glasgow, via Newcastle and Edinburgh.' It was thought to be a possibility worthy of being put to experiment as soon as hostilities ended.

Counting the Windsor flights as part of a pageant, and ignoring the special carriage of Forces mail after the First World War, we come to the first British regular air mail service. It was not an internal service within Britain. Aviation was not developing along those lines. It was on November 10, 1919, that the G.P.O. and the French Post Office granted A. T. and T. a six months' monopoly for the carriage of official air mail between London and Paris. There was a ceremony the next day when the first air mail pennant was attached to the rudder of the DH4A aeroplane which left Hounslow with eight bags of mail destined for Paris. Alas, it was a false start. Bad weather forced the pilot to turn round at Epsom: and that day's mail had to go by surface transport. The Company had better luck the next day and flew their load through to Paris.

The charge to the public was 2s. 6d. an ounce. 'I think it is cheap to charge a man 2s. 6d. for carrying a letter from London to Paris by air,' wrote Holt Thomas, 'though with a sufficiently large guaranteed load one might reduce these charges as to make them surprisingly low in view of the speed of transport obtained . . . an average of quite one hundred miles an hour. . . .'

Soon after these words were printed, the rates were cut to 2d. an ounce, but even so there was no great success for some years to come.

The British Post Office was not slow in taking to the air. A. T. and T. had been flying a scheduled service for less than three months when they were awarded their mail contract, receiving 2s. out of the surcharge on every letter. In its attitude generally towards the new element of the air, however, the Post Office was cautious. It was prepared to follow the development of civil aviation without making any specific contribution towards its cost, whereas it had directly contributed towards the early development of steamships. Eighty years before the opening of the London–Paris air service, the Post Office had attached so much importance to the speed promised by steamships that in 1839 it started a subsidy payment to Mr. Samuel Cunard to encourage the policy of bigger and faster steamships. No such contribution ever went to aviation. The Post Office was prepared to use air services just as soon as they were established with reasonable regularity. Each extension of the air network was faithfully exploited.

Little real benefit besides prestige came to operators from Post Office revenue in the earliest days; its impact only became beneficial after the first decade. Apart from the novelty, there was no rush by the public to use air mail during the early years. The gain in time had to be considerable to make it worth while to the sender. In 1925 the total weight of first-class mail despatched from the United Kingdom by air was only about six tons. The mail bags which appeared, not without pride, in the early records have been described by one of the pilots who carried them as 'Small bits of sacking just a few inches long, containing some half a dozen letters or so.'

In the development of air mail, the Post Office claimed that they were not seeking to make any profit. The revenue from the surcharge had to be sufficient only to pay the air conveyance charges. These were fixed in terms of weight and distance to each port of call—the basis which still persists at the present day.

The first chairman of Imperial Airways, Sir Eric Geddes, was at some pains to point out to his shareholders that the Post Office was in fact making a profit. 'The general policy of the Postal Administration seems to be that not only is the air mail a luxury to which the public is not entitled without a special payment, but that it is a luxury which is taxed in addition.'

The fees which the public paid at the outset were twofold. First the normal surface rate to cover the Post Office's ordinary costs on a foreign letter: secondly the air mail fee which was made to cover the conveyance charges. This duality was a continual headache to the Post Office counter clerks since the scales of payment and weight were different for surface and air. Where a special air mail fee was charged, the mail became known as 'surcharged'. In 1928, for instance, the charges to individual countries in Europe varied according to distances. It was not until 1930 that a general postage rate for Europe was introduced: 4d. for the first ounce and 3d. for each additional ounce. In the same year, surface and air mail postage rates were merged, the amount of the postage rates intended to cover the air conveyance being concealed.

In February 1933, George Woods Humphery, as Managing Director of Imperial Airways, summarized the relationship between the airline and the G.P.O.:

> 'In regard to air mail, we are in the somewhat peculiar position, to use a manufacturing analogy, of being producers of a commodity, selling through a sole wholesale agent, but

without any voice in fixing the retail price or any contact with the users.

'We carry at a pre-arranged bulk contract rate, but with no guarantee of minimum loads, such air mails as the Post Office gives us. Moreover, the Post Office fixes the rates to be paid by the public, and so the entire commercial risk rests with the air carrier.'

In 1934, the G.P.O. introduced a 'zonal' postal rate. To any Middle East country the charge was 3d. per half-ounce. For India, Malaya, East Africa, etc., the charge was 6d. per half-ounce. These far-flung services operating outside Europe in the 'thirties had a common origin in the early 'twenties—the 'Desert Furrow' of the R.A.F.

Both Palestine and Iraq had been mandated to Great Britain by the 1919 Peace Treaty. British troops had been garrisoned in Egypt since 1882. Egypt, proclaimed a British Protectorate during the war, did not attain even limited independence till 1922. Thus Britain was heavily committed in the Middle East and much responsibility fell upon the R.A.F., which was required to maintain security in the mandated territories, taking the place of ground forces. This was Trenchard's plan for 'control without occupation'. Squadrons were stationed in Egypt, Palestine and Iraq, but there was no direct communication along the three sides of the triangle. To reach Baghdad, there was a caravan route between the Euphrates and Damascus which offered the shortest desert crossing: and the camel was the accepted means of transport. But with the French occupying Syria, some other way had to be found within the British zones of influence. A proposal to build a trans-desert railway linking Palestine with Baghdad was turned down because of cost.

So a conference, held in Cairo in March 1921, decided on an air route, to be used primarily for mail and communications. The first move was a service run by the R.A.F. between Amman and Ramadi on the Euphrates about 65 miles west of Baghdad. It was valuable training but it was a tough proposition. The distance between the two places is about 470 miles with an average elevation of about 2,000 ft. above sea-level. The cruising speed of the aircraft was only about 100 miles an hour and their endurance not more than six hours. Their water-cooled engines were not sufficiently reliable to rule out the possibility of fairly frequent forced landings. High temperatures and altitudes, both causing loss of power and lift, also reduced performance. Airborne radio was in its infancy. All flying across the desert, therefore, had to be done by visual contact.

In June 1921, a survey of the route was made by two Royal Air Force motorized convoys equipped with Crossleys, some of them converted into armoured cars by the mounting of Lewis guns. One convoy went eastward from Amman, the other westward from Ramadi. Each struck out on a roughly predetermined course assisted by Arab guides and, wherever possible, following traditional Arab caravan tracks. Their task was to select suitable areas for emergency landing grounds, not more than twenty-five miles apart. At night the parties, which included surveyors, meteorologists, motor transport experts and radio operators, fixed their position by the stars. The correct time was obtained from a portable radio set. Maps were prepared for the pilots of the aircraft accompanying the two convoys.

Plenty of suitable landing places were found. The party from the west marked their grounds A. to R. and Cairo was responsible for the administration of these. The eastern party marked theirs in Roman numerals from I to XI and these were administered by Baghdad. It was a tough job: but there were compensations still recalled by one of the radio operators:

> 'The pleasure of swimming in the pools, some hot and some ice cold, in the Azrak marsh, the joy of sitting round a camp fire varying the normal bully and biscuit diet for a stew of gazelle meat, the pleasure of being able to draw unlimited water from the wells of El Jid and to remove the caked dust and grime from the long days spent in the desert. In my own case, the joy of knowing that on the arrival of the next DH 9A I should be changing over with the Radio man to return for a well-earned respite in the cool green hills around Amman.
>
> 'The credit overall goes not to the man behind the theodolite, not to the men flying out on the provisions and spares, nor to the men keeping the parties in radio communication with one another and the base camps, but to one and all who formed a disciplined understanding and willing team no matter how menial his share in the total result.'

Nobody now knows who first had the brainwave of ploughing a

furrow the whole length of the route. Ploughs, suitably weighted, were dragged at the rear of each column. The continuous furrow so readily visible from the air was enhanced at various points by the cutting in the sand of large arrows pointing in the direction of the next landing ground. At the end of 1922 and again in 1923, the track was straightened in places and generally improved. The pilots who flew the furrow had to report on the visibility of the track, and great care was taken to keep it in good order. In fact pilots flying along that route years after the furrow had been superseded by radio and navigational aids reported that some of it was still visible. From 1923, the Nairn Transport vehicles running between Damascus and Baghdad joined the track about half-way and added the pattern of their wheel tracks to the line of the furrow.

To make use of the desert route, Air Ministry planned to send Government mail from Britain by sea to Egypt, thence to Baghdad by air. Not too much trust was placed in the service. Only duplicates were sent, the originals being despatched by surface transport, which at that time took anything from 25 to 32 days from London to Baghdad. The air mail gave twelve days outward and fourteen days inward. In spite of the 'enormous saving of time', much quoted in Government circles, only one letter was in fact sent by the first service in June 1921.

It was a fortnightly service. The aircraft, in pairs in case of trouble, flew one way one week usually taking two days, and returned the following week. That went on for five and a half years. On October 8, 1921, the R.A.F. facility was opened to the public, a fee of 1s. per ounce being surcharged. It was poorly patronized. On December 7 that year the G.P.O. reported to Air Ministry that 'the largest consignment consisted of 354 private and two official letters, weighing 30 lbs.' The G.P.O. proposed to advertise the Christmas mail and to reduce the surcharge to 6d.

The Nairn Transport service, connecting with the Mediterranean at Haifa, hit the air service badly. The G.P.O. informed Air Ministry that the public was to be offered the use of the Nairn service for mail from the coast to Baghdad at a surcharge of 3d. per ounce. The Ministry had to agree to a similar reduction. There was indeed no alternative in view of the fact that the time in transit by Nairn was about the same, or even slightly less, than by air. Moreover, the surface mail was running weekly whereas the R.A.F. continued to provide only a fortnightly service.

When Brancker made a technical report to Air Ministry covering the whole operation of the route in 1922, he recommended that outward mail should ultimately be routed through Constantinople (Istanbul). This was rejected at the time. More than three decades later, however, during the Suez crisis when B.O.A.C. left Cairo, the services were routed through Istanbul. Brancker also criticized the desert track:

> 'The present means of navigation, by which the pilot is absolutely ordered to follow a motor track across the desert by eye, is to my mind most derogatory to the training of pilots in navigation. I realize the necessity of this system at present as a safeguard against the chance of a pilot and machine being lost in the desert and its occupants dying of thirst. I feel very strongly that a really efficient system of wireless telegraphy should be established on this route as soon as possible. The present system is likely to spoil a good pilot.'

After some years, the R.A.F. itself had misgivings about the continuation of the service. Their squadrons had become more dispersed. The training commitment in that area was less demanding. That the experience had been valuable could not be denied. Apart from the training of aircrew, the service had been put to many tests: and there had been casualties. The water-cooled engines had given their share of trouble and forced landings had been fairly common. Spare engines had been flown out to grounded aircraft and engine changes carried out in the desert at the height of the hot season. Refuelling was not without its rigours. To put five hours' fuel in the tanks sometimes meant handling 60 tins of petrol, 12 tins of benzol, and 2 five-gallon drums of oil—and two of the fuel tanks were under the top wing about thirteen feet from the ground.

Ballads about aviation have a way of being cynical. One which celebrated the line of the furrow in 1922, written under the initials J.O.P.E. was no exception.

The ashes of a fire—lit all in vain—
A Thing that breathed and lived but yesterday,
The charred and blackened wreckage of a 'plane,
Are all that mark the Man Who Lost His Way.

An error of a minute; a side-slip in a cloud;
He failed to see the Track he thought he knew,
The endless days of waiting—by fear and hunger cowed—
Ere the jackals took the meat that was their due!

In the bitter cold of Winter, when the sullen engines fret,
And the leaden sky above them bids them stay,
In the storm or in the sunshine; in the dry or in the wet;
The Air Mail passes swiftly on its way.
In the hottest days of Summer, when the water-holes are dry,
And the Desert's full of things that are not there,
The gaunt and weary jackal sees the shadows passing by
Of the Mail 'planes as they hurry through the air.

We have placed at your disposal all the arts we learnt in war,
And for ninepence you can purchase, if you're wise,
The same efficient service of the Man who Yesterday,
Chased the black-crossed Birds of War from out your skies.
The letters that they carry from Cairo to the East,
Bear little slips of paper, coloured blue,
And the loss of crew and pilot doesn't matter in the least,
If the Mail Bags see the Desert journey through.

The grimmer aspects of this ballad might well have raised eyebrows in high places: but not those of the Air Minister, Sir Samuel Hoare. He wrote a foreword to the volume in which the poem appeared in 1925, recalling his own journey over the route, 'Eastern cities in the dim light of early dawn, fleeting glimpses of Judaean hills through shifting banks of clouds. . . .'

One of the results of his visit was the decision which came in that year to commercialize the route. It was logical that the newly-formed Imperial Airways should make a beginning with this 'ready-made' mail run and in 1926 the transfer was made. It was the first step for Imperial Airways towards the mail line to India, which is reviewed in more detail in later chapters, and which was already extended to Delhi by 1931.

In that year there were two notable though premature experiments shared with the Australians in flying mail through to that continent. The rate of postage was fixed at 1s. 4d. per half-ounce and the first air mail for Australia left Croydon on April 4, 1931, by one of the regular mail planes, *City of Coventry*, which arrived at

Karachi on April 12. There the mail was handed over to the crew of a specially prepared Hercules airliner *City of Cairo* with extra fuel tanks. Captains Roger Mollard and H. W. C. Alger took turns about as captain and co-pilot, carrying as crew an engineer and a radio operator for the onward flight towards Darwin, through Calcutta, Rangoon, Singapore to Surabaya. On April 19, Alger was flying the aeroplane from Rambang in Indonesia with strong head-winds reducing the speed to 70 miles per hour when a petrol leak was discovered. They were nearly out of fuel when they spotted the racecourse at Koepang and put down at once on what seemed a useful stretch of tiger grass beside the track. Too late they saw that the grass was the innocent cover for scattered rocks. In seconds their wheels were ripped off and the *City of Cairo* crashed down on her belly, a total loss. The crew got out safely and rescued the precious mail intact. For the next six days it remained in the custody of the Dutch Post Office at Koepang.

The Australian postal authorities had chartered a plane from Qantas to be ready at Darwin to rush the mail south on a two-day flight to Brisbane. From there they had arranged for Australian National Airways—the famous Charles Kingsford-Smith with his partner Charles Ulm—to fly the mail on to Sydney and Melbourne.

The men on the spot were undaunted by the news of the crash. They were determined that the mail should get through *by air*. The Kingsford Smith concern was given a charter to fetch the stranded mail. 'Smithy' himself, flying his renowned record-breaking *Southern Cross*, left Sydney on April 21 and was across the Timor Sea by the 24th, taking on 290 lb. of mail, comprising 15,000 items. The next day he flew back to Darwin, giving a lift to Mollard, who had received instructions from London to buy another aeroplane and also to 'take the next train to Perth'. Mollard saw the mail fly off in a Qantas DH 61 for Brisbane where it arrived on the 28th. Then he ignored orders by taking a ship to Perth—for the good reason that London had overlooked that there was no railway. In due course he purchased a DH 66 Hercules from West Australian Airways, one of the conditions of sale being that one of that airline's pilots was to be in command on the return journey as far as Darwin—but that was to be the second of the experimental flights.

The return of the first Australia–England mail flight was made by Kingsford-Smith flying his *Southern Cross* under charter to Imperial Airways, replacing the *City of Cairo* on the run from Darwin to Akyab in Burma. Twenty-five bags of mail, weighing 663 lbs. had been flown through by separate services from Melbourne to Darwin for the take-off on April 27. 'Smithy' handed over his load to the Imperial Airways' *City of Karachi* at Akyab on May 3. It arrived at Croydon on May 14.

On the second outward flight, Imperial Airways carried the mail, described as '5,000 articles', as far as Akyab, whence Kingsford-Smith, still on charter to the company, took it across to Darwin for onward transmission by Qantas. Mollard in the newly-purchased Hercules flew the return service through to Karachi where the mail joined the established service to Croydon.

These were gallant but expensive experiments. Not stout hearts alone, but more powerful aircraft, were needed. Two years went by before there was another survey, mentioned later in these pages together with the Qantas-Imperial Airways partnership which established the regular mail service in 1934.

At Croydon airport in May of that year, the Postmaster General, Sir Kingsley Wood, formally presented to Imperial Airways the first royal air mail pennant. The consent of King George V had been given to the pennant being flown by all aircraft carrying Royal Mail. It has a deep blue ground with a device in yellow representing a crown over a posthorn. It was first flown by the airliner *Hengist* carrying the Indian mail over the London–Paris sector of the route on May 26.

Also in that year in London appeared the special blue pillar boxes for air mail, together with the famous blue 'stream-lined' postal van which made impressive dashes from the G.P.O. to Croydon. These were passing manifestations. The blue air mail label which was—and is—a sign to the sorter that a letter must immediately be diverted into the special air mail channels had come to stay. Air mail from London at long last covered every continent except America: and both in the Ministry and in the boardroom of Imperial Airways there was talk of a service between Europe and America via the Azores and Bermuda 'in conjunction with foreign air interests'.

More immediately significant, however, was the talk of an exchange of mail on an un-surcharged or 'all-up' basis between the United Kingdom and all the Commonwealth countries now joined in the Imperial Airways network. Hints of such a scheme were made in 1933 by Woods Humphery in his lecture at the Institute of Transport. 'Letters to India cost 6d. per half-ounce, as compared with 4s. 7d. per half-ounce to South America by the French line. I believe that the day is not far distant when all the letter mail for most destinations in the Empire will be carried by air at little or no more cost to the public than the ordinary mail rates.'

The late S. A. Dismore, for many years Secretary of Imperial Airways, conceived the Empire Mail Scheme. Its first practical details were worked out in mid-air aboard a Hannibal airliner which was being flown on a demonstration and flag-showing flight to South Africa in 1933. The pilot was Captain 'Taffy' Powell, later as an R.A.F. Air Commodore a leading figure in the war-time transatlantic air 'bridge'. Travelling as passengers were Sir Eric Geddes and George Woods Humphery. All the way to Cape Town, these two men chewed over ways and means. At their destination, they decided that Imperial Airways could in principle carry all the mail—but the idea was likely to meet with a cool reception at the G.P.O. and it would have to be 'sold' to Air Ministry. They were business men running a commercial undertaking, even though their company was subsidized and recognized as the 'chosen instrument' of the Government. They therefore returned from the Cape at a more leisurely pace, by ship, but making use of every waking hour—in Woods Humphery's words—'working it all up'.

In March 1933, Geddes signed a memorandum to the Cabinet containing this significant paragraph:

> 'Imperial Airways has conclusively demonstrated its reliability and dependability already, and the Board has every confidence in its ability to carry a vastly increased volume of Empire letter mail. The Board therefore invites H.M. Government to investigate, in conjunction with Imperial Airways, the carriage by air of letter mail in bulk on the London–Cape Town and London–Australasia routes in the next four or five years' time, on revised rates of conveyance to be negotiated.'

The scheme was approved by the Cabinet. It went through the House of Commons on December 20, 1934. In postal history many regarded it as paralleled only by the introduction of the

Penny Post in the nineteenth century. Politically it was important—though it may well have proved to be financially unsound. In British civil aviation history, it ranks as one of the boldest and most imaginative measures ever undertaken. It started in 1937, as promised. The outbreak of the Second World War in 1939 killed it. At the time of its demise, the territories within the Scheme included the Dominions, except Canada, the subcontinent of India, Burma, East Africa, the majority of the colonial dependencies as well as Egypt and Sudan. New Zealand was about to join as soon as the trunk route could be extended to Auckland. From the date of the full operation of the scheme, July 28, 1938, Imperial Airways was to receive a fixed subsidy of £750,000 per annum for the first three years with a system of gradual reduction afterwards. Actual payments, however, were to be based on operating costs. In addition the British Post Office was to pay for mails carried at the total annual rate of £900,000 with a special grant of £75,000 for Christmas mail. At the outset, it was calculated that over 2,000 tons of mail would be moved annually. This caused a dramatic reorientation in the workings of Imperial Airways. Until this time, the long-haul routes had been served by land planes, except for flying-boat services crossing the Mediterranean referred to in a later chapter. For the new responsibility, it was considered that the existing airfields, most of which were primitive by the standards of the nineteen-fifties, were inadequate. Viewed as a pattern, they did not seem to offer sufficient flexibility for the new mail services. The decision was therefore made to switch to flying-boats. Southampton was the chosen base in Britain.

A fleet of 28 flying-boats of the Empire class was ordered from Shorts 'off the drawing board'—without waiting for a prototype to be built. Empire routes were transformed as the boats were delivered. The first came through in 1936. In June 1937, the Empire Mail Scheme was inaugurated between Britain and South Africa 'without surcharge and without air mail label'. In October of that year, was the first flying-boat service between Southampton and Karachi. In June 1938 the Empire flying-boats *Cordelia* and *Camilla* left Southampton on the first through service to Australia. Within a few weeks, the Air Mail Scheme was extended to New Zealand and to Hong Kong.

When the Scheme came into full operation, there were five

services a week between England and India, three of which went on to Australia. Egypt at the junction of the African and Australian routes had sixteen through services east and west every week.

Imperial Airways was now, in the last full year of peace, the world's largest carrier of external air mails. But nobody can tell whether the scheme would ever have proved a lasting success. There were snags and time was too short to prove that they could be overcome. Even the more optimistic experts maintained that there was no mean pattern of guesswork in the planning of the venture. It was comparatively easy on paper to plan aircraft capacity over a period to move what from past records had been the known weight of mail. But there were new unknown elements, one of which was the postage rate. By surface mail this had been 1½d. for the first ounce and 1d. for each additional ounce. This had to be changed to 1½d. per half-ounce, the sender having no option whether he paid this rate or not. Though half-ounce letters suffered no change, heavier letters cost the sender a great deal more than they had done in the past and he could not save himself by sending them by sea. What would be the effect of the rates as planned? Would the increased cost ultimately reduce the amount of commercial mail?

Another problem lay with human habit. For years the public had been aware that surface mail for the East and for Africa went on Thursdays over land or by air to Marseilles, thence by P. & O. steamer, and that on Fridays there was the regular Union Castle boat to Cape Town. In spite of energetic publicity by the Post Office, the public could not be persuaded that the air services went at more frequent intervals. Up to the bitter end in 1939, weekly postings continued to be concentrated on the Thursday and Friday departure days of the sea mail. This end-of-the-week postal habit swamped certain aircraft with mail to the exclusion of any other traffic, and ultimately it had to be controlled artificially. The advertised posting times for specific destinations were then withdrawn. It was announced that all first-class mail would be carried by air at frequent intervals and that it would be carried on the next available outlet. 'What happened behind the scenes,' wrote one who worked there, 'was that Imperial Airways and the Post Office reached agreement as to the limiting amount of mail which each flying-boat would carry and, when that weight was reached at the Post Office, the bags were made up and sent down to Southampton for despatch. Even so, at least two of the eight Empire flying-boats leaving Southampton per week had room only for four passengers.'

These two factors, the increase of postage and the impossibility of forecasting a specific transit time, attracted so much criticism that they overshadowed many of the advantages that the Empire Mail Scheme had to offer. Real trouble—and a foretaste of what might have become disastrous but for the war—came with the carriage of the first Christmas mail in December 1938. A normal total weekly load of fifteen tons rose to a peak of nearly a hundred tons in a week, which is little enough judged by present standards, but which was at that time an unforeseen scale of increase which might well have led to total breakdown. The fleet of Empire flying-boats, each having a capacity of about three tons, was quite inadequate. Every aircraft in the fleet of Imperial Airways was mustered. Even the Mercury pick-a-back seaplane designed to be carried by and launched from the Empire flying-boat *Maia*, whose story is told later in these pages, flew non-stop from Southampton to Alexandria loaded to her modest gunwales, including stowage in the floats. When the full resources of Imperial Airways were still insufficient, more aircraft had to be chartered from private firms. For a fortnight the sky between London and Egypt saw a strangely mixed fleet of mail carriers, aircraft of different capacities, different speeds, different ranges: some overtaking, some lagging behind, particularly those chartered aircraft whose crews found an irresistible necessity for a refuelling night-stop in one of the gayer European cities.

The task of the London staff was to keep the mail moving in chronological order by means of this variegated fleet. With the two Empire routes splitting at Alexandria and with heavy loads for the Middle East itself, the exercise developed into an airlift from Southampton to Alexandria with separate operations east and south of that point. Two clearing dumps were established, one was at Airways Terminal by Victoria Station with direct access to Platform 17, from which Imperial Airways then ran special trains for passengers and mail to Southampton. The other was in Alexandria.

Mr. E. V. Dolby, Mail Adviser to B.O.A.C., who was in charge of the operation, writes:

'The Post Office delivered each evening to Airways Terminal all the mails available for both routes, the mails to each country and each destination within that country having its own serial number. The air companies' staff, working in conjunction with a representative of the G.P.O. selected, according to capacity of the aircraft waiting at Southampton or Croydon, the appropriate load of mail for each, taking care that the bags selected bore the earliest serial numbers in the dump. Thus Airways Terminal became a virtual sorting office in terms of mail bags rather than letters.

'The task of the Alexandria dump was even more difficult. Mails were continually arriving in Alexandria, having taken any time from three to ten days to reach there, and their arrival was, therefore, completely out of chronological order. Every detail of the load, including serial numbers, on board each aircraft leaving the U.K. had to be cabled to Alexandria, so that Bob Stapleton, the officer in charge there, could plan in advance. Again the process of absorbing into the dump and selection therefrom in terms of weight and of the earliest serial numbers had to be made for each aircraft leaving east-bound or south-bound. It is worth while recording, however, that, in spite of these difficulties, with only one exception, all the mail posted by the advertised posting date for Christmas reached their destination by Christmas Day.'

With the outbreak of war, the Empire routes could no longer cope with the loads they had been carrying and the scheme was abandoned even before the routes themselves had to be curtailed or modified because of enemy action. To reduce the loads, the surcharge system for air mail was reintroduced. The Atlantic air mail service which had been inaugurated only a few weeks before the outbreak of war was also discontinued in circumstances which will be described in a later chapter.

The use of microphotography introduced the British public to air mail during the Franco-Prussian war. The Second World War brought back microphotography in the form of airgraphs. The process was to reduce the mail to micro film so that a single roll of film would contain 1,700 letter pages weighing only a hundredth of the original 1,700 pages. This multiplied the mail capacity of any given aircraft by approximately one hundred times, though, of course, it broke the cherished principle of privacy in correspondence and was quite arbitrary in its restriction of length—considerations which might be irksome in times of peace but which were acceptable to a world at war as they had been to the beleaguered Parisians in the 'seventies.

The airgraph idea was not new. There was correspondence on the subject on the files of Imperial Airways in 1932 which dragged on for a number of years. It was the planning of the first mail-carrying flights across the Atlantic in the late 'thirties which brought the idea within the scope of practical possibility. Airgraphs Ltd. was a Company formed by Imperial Airways (afterwards B.O.A.C.), Pan-American Airways and the Eastman Kodak Co. It was first established in the United States and afterwards in England. Flying-boats were then the only aircraft considered capable of crossing the Atlantic. Their load, especially in winter, between Bermuda and Lisbon, would be limited either to a small number of passengers and no mail or a load of mail which compared with that moved by sea would be almost trivial. Both the British and the American airlines which were working very closely together on the Atlantic venture realized that the adoption of the airgraph would result in their getting a much higher net figure for the carriage of mail.

In spite of the fact that Imperial Airways and Pan-American carried out a series of successful scheduled transatlantic mail flights before the war, nothing came of the airgraph scheme until the war itself altered the situation, first for Britain, later for America. It was therefore Imperial Airways' successor, B.O.A.C., which first came to handle this process, when matters were precipitated by agitation by British troops in the Middle East about delays in mail from home. Processing equipment had already been shipped to Britain and more equipment was immediately sent to Cairo. In April 1941, the first airgraph mail was introduced from Cairo to Britain; the first outward-bound load went in August of that year. The airgraph service was extended to the public to cover the Middle East, North Africa, India and Ceylon in 1942. It worked smoothly and Airgraphs Ltd. began to make a profit.

When the United States came into the war, their military authorities at once became keenly interested in the scheme, They stated, however, that they would not pay the fees charged by the Company and threatened to take it over unless it was ceded to them. They had their way and in due course a very large system was set up with hundreds of microphotograph machines established at key points all over the world. The name was altered to V-Mail, which became a potent factor in postal communications in the Armed Forces everywhere.

The original Company lingered on till the post-war years. Woods Humphery, who had long since severed his connection with British civil aviation and had become one of the organizers of the transatlantic supply and ferry services, wrote to Lord Knollys, Chairman of B.O.A.C., in March 1946, regarding the suggestion to dissolve the joint company, or to give up the British interest in it: 'I suggest you do neither; airgraphs were not intended as a substitute for air mail but came between air mail and cable—not so quick as cable but cheaper—slower than air mail but again cheaper.'

Lord Knollys replied: 'Not dissolving, holding dormant.'

But in any case airgraphs had served their purpose. Other companies had copied their processing, apparently without infringement of patents, and in August 1949 Airgraphs Ltd. was dissolved.

The carriage of air mail continues to present its own peculiar problems. The first of these arises from the priority which has to be given to mail over passengers and freight. In any mail-carrying B.O.A.C. aircraft, for instance, the space necessary to accommodate H.M. mail has to be set aside before it can be known what capacity is available for passengers and freight. This involves knowing beforehand what mail the public is going to post. In earlier days, this was relatively simple because the loads were small, but at the time of writing when anything up to twelve tons a day are handled outward on B.O.A.C. services alone at London Airport, occupying space for the accommodation of at least 150 passengers, the system necessary for capacity reservation becomes a science of its own.

This science—or inspired guesswork—involves estimating the rate at which the public are going to post for every country of destination at every hour of the day. When the impending departure of an aircraft demands an accumulation of the mail in hand for the destination which it serves, a reasonably accurate forecast must be made of the total weight. To do this, an elaborate system of records has been built up over the years. It is claimed that the mail requirement for any proposed frequency or change of schedule can in fact now be assessed in advance.

In general it may be said that mail has ridden on the back of the development of air services primarily designed for passenger traffic, the progress of which has been due to technical developments, incentives for lowering fares and the persuasion of the public to fly. Naturally the economic value of speed in air mail has been proved to the point where the air mail service has become really competitive with the cable services, bearing in mind the full length of the letter compared with the abbreviated staccato of the telegram. As in every other aspect of air services, the speed of handling on the ground cannot keep pace with the greatly accelerated passage through the air. The Deputy Director General of the G.P.O., in a recent lecture, gave an example from the Korean war. For the troops' mail, B.O.A.C. ran Argonauts providing four deliveries a week. When the speedier Comets were introduced on the run, the transit time was greatly decreased, so much so that the effective deliveries of mail were telescoped into two per week which naturally caused complaints from the Forces and gave strength to the motto 'More haste, less speed'.

The period after the Second World War saw once again a build-up of intensive air services over the world's main trunk routes, in which B.O.A.C. actively participated, with the exception of South America. The immediate post-war years were difficult because the only aircraft available for the British derived from bombers. True civil types did not take shape till five or six years after the war ended.

No attempt was made to return to the conception of all-up mail except in Europe. It was obvious in post-war years that any scheme for carrying all-up mail between the continents would need much greater resources than those offered by the original Empire Mail Scheme. Despite the fact that all mail outside Europe is surcharged at the time of writing, in the late nineteen-fifties, the normal loads carried by B.O.A.C. are comparable with those carried under the old Empire Mail Scheme during the famous peak Christmas week of 1938. B.O.A.C. handle anything up to 110 tons a week during a Christmas period: British European Airways even more. It would be impossible, therefore, to conjecture the immensity of the task if an international all-up mail service were contemplated.

Finally, a feature of the post-war period is an extension of the cheaper rates for second class and parcel mails as well as the special rate for newspapers and periodicals—an important element in the dissemination of knowledge and culture, if we rule out the increased circulation of comics. Such rates are now available world-wide, with the air letter at 6d. to every country in the world. The lightweight air letter is in original thought a direct descendant from the airgraph of the Second World War. Its advantage, of course, is the privacy conferred by its adhesive edges. Its popularity is such that the Post Office estimate the number sold per year in the United Kingdom to be in the neighbourhood of 50 million.

CHAPTER VI

THE FIRST CHOSEN INSTRUMENT

IMPERIAL AIRWAYS began in a frigid climate of good intentions not unmingled with hostility. Its genesis was a Government Committee. Having borne the ensign of the British Merchant Air Service to the ends of the earth, it expired, after some sixteen years, at the instance of another Government Committee—but only in name. In its final amalgamation with British Airways to form the war-time B.O.A.C., Imperial Airways was able to offer a proud legacy of experience, man-power and organization. Those sixteen years created the whole basic long-range pattern which B.O.A.C. and others were to expand, accelerate, and consolidate when the great age of air transport came in the 'fifties. During those years, a commercially inept, half-heartedly subsidized, haphazardly planned system of competitive cross-Channel services was transformed into a massive network of world air routes which stood up to the stresses of war and in peace fulfilled the vision of those who had foreseen a new integration of the British Commonwealth through air power. In its first full year, Imperial Airways flew some 853,000 miles. In its last full year of peacetime operation, 1938, it flew just under 6½ million miles. Such was the expansion in mileage alone of what was surely one of the most significant British achievements between the wars. Though it began badly and ended unhappily, the prestige and experience of the service built up during those lean hard-working, often discouraging, years became an international force and a national asset. There are many who, even twenty years after, look back upon Imperial Airways with affection and a certain pride.

When the Prime Minister said at the outset: 'Can't you get them to amalgamate?' Sir Herbert Hambling went about the task of working out a formula not only for that but for a novel essay in Government-sponsored private enterprise. It was in fact a half-measure compromise between the free-for-all commerce of 1919 which had failed, and the State ownership which was to come in the 'forties with B.O.A.C. and B.E.A. A significant phrase was born when the new Company was referred to as the 'chosen instrument' of the Government. Nevertheless there was still a slightly old-fashioned ring about another phrase in the contract providing for the formation of a 'Heavier-than-Air' transport company.

A capital of one million pounds was to ensure 'that the Company itself would be concerned in the risking and expenditure of its own resources'. The Government subsidy was also one million pounds spread over ten years, 'beginning high' with £137,000 a year, decreasing to £32,000 in the closing years. The Government gave the Company full and unfettered control except that the State's interest was to be assured by the appointment of two Government Directors.

Though the Hambling recommendations had been popular and the idea of the chosen instrument had been well received, there was no rush for the shares. 'The City regarded air transport as a dangerous gamble,' the Air Minister, Sir Samuel Hoare, afterwards admitted, 'and it was only after considerable pressure from Whitehall that we found a financial house willing to underwrite even so small an issue as the £250,000 that was needed to start the Company. Civil air transport became even less popular in financial circles when the shares at once fell to a heavy discount.' The present Sir Guy Hambling, who was among those willing to back a venture of which his father was one of the Government Directors, recalls that he was paid some hundreds of pounds to take up a large block of shares and for a time became the largest private shareholder. If the shares started at a discount in the 'twenties, they were to move out of the speculative field during the 'thirties, reflecting ever-increasing public confidence in the build-up of the airline.

At the take-over, the price paid for the four Companies as going concerns was £148,750. Each Company had one Director on the new Board of Imperial Airways: Colonel Frank Searl from Daimler, Sir Samuel Instone from Instone, Lieutenant-Colonel J. Barrett-Lennard from Handley Page and Mr. Hubert Scott-Paine from the British Marine Air Navigation Company. Sir Samuel Hoare has given his own account of his selection of the Chairman:

'As my chief object was to make flying a normal method of travelling, it was essential to have as a chairman of the board someone who was a recognized expert on transport questions. Eric Geddes, formerly General Manager of the North Eastern Railway, and afterwards the very successful Inspector-General of Military Transport in France, seemed to me the man best fitted for the post. It was true that he knew nothing of aviation. The need, however, at the moment was for someone whose wide knowledge of existing transport could be particularly applied to the economic and commercial problems that were certain to arise in the new chapter of air travel. Somewhat reluctantly he accepted the post, but only on condition that he brought with him Sir George Beharrell, the chartered accountant upon whom he always depended for financial advice. I gladly accepted this condition, as expert financial advice was greatly needed.'

Geddes was a big man—in every sense. 'I once flew him in an Argosy to Paris,' writes one of the original sixteen pilots. 'When he came into the cockpit his corpulence was such that the Engineer's seat was really too small for him. This made itself very evident when I came to land and was unable to take the control back to its full travel. He reacted violently, trying to writhe back in his seat. In fact he was still struggling when we landed. . . .'

The Chairman need not, of course, have travelled in the cockpit: but Geddes, as the same pilot bears witness, numbered conscientiousness among the first of the qualities in his somewhat formidable character. He believed in first-hand experience. He took the earliest opportunity to fly over the new Empire routes as they were developed. In spite of his combining active chairmanship of Dunlops with that of the new airline, he had the affairs of Imperial Airways very much at heart, and to many became an 'inspired leader and guiding star' as one of his old staff describes him. Though he had enchanted Britain's wartime Prime Minister, Lloyd George, by his singing of Welsh songs, he could be irascible, forthright and fearsome on occasion: and he had his critics.

Lord Reith, who was one of Geddes's successors in the chair, suggested, in his book written many years later, that 'Imperial Airways was closely associated with Dunlops. The board met in the Dunlop office, employed the same solicitors, auditors, architects; Geddes was the autocrat of Dunlops; his closest associates there, Sir George Beharrell and Sir Hardman Lever, both sat on the Imperial Airways board.'

If Geddes was something of a tycoon, he was just the kind of powerful leader needed by an airline that must expand or expire. Moreover there is plenty of evidence that he was accessible to those who needed contact at the top, until his death in 1937. If indeed he had lived a little longer and had been able to take part in the controversy which raged round Imperial Airways just before the Second World War, this story might well have had a different ending. As it was, his reluctance to accept the Chairmanship from Sir Samuel Hoare was understandable, for he certainly went in to bat on a sticky wicket. Not only did the City show an indifference amounting almost to hostility towards air matters but there was still an almost Edwardian outlook in Government circles.

The Air Minister, for instance, did not even have a seat in the Cabinet until Bonar Law was superseded by Baldwin, who raised the status of Sir Samuel Hoare to full membership of the Cabinet, equal in rank to his colleagues at the War Office and the Admiralty. This happened during the period of the Hambling Inquiry and helped the Air Minister in furthering his plans for civil aviation. Even with this promotion, the Air Minister was up against an Air Staff that was still fighting for its existence. The 'service side' was ambitious and naturally jealous. It was headed, moreover, by the rugged Trenchard who had his own consolidation programme for the R.A.F.

> 'I had also to reassure the Air Staff that my civil programme would not be at the expense of the military requirements [wrote Sir Samuel Hoare]. Their fears were not without foundation. The Air Estimates for 1923, including civil aviation, were restricted to £12,100,000, and it looked at the time as if any new subsidies for civil air transport would have to be found from reductions in the very small sum to be allocated to the Air Force. With the Air Force cut in this way to the bone, it was only natural that Trenchard and his Staff should look suspiciously at expenditure on civil aviation. . . .'

The Air Minister was sometimes embarrassed by the high flying of his Director of Civil Aviation:

> 'Brancker had the faults of his great qualities. He was a superb propagandist, and when he spoke or wrote in public, his enthusiasm swept away the words of caution in his official briefs. It was a time of international aviation meetings, and the Director of British Civil Aviation was not only the outstanding figure in the world of civil flying, but also a very good speaker. Curzon and the Foreign Office were shocked by his unorthodox style and I had constantly to explain away his flights of oratory. Even if I agreed with what he had in mind, and this was often the case, it was very important in these days of civil aviation for the junior Secretary of State to avoid an open clash with any of his more powerful colleagues. No one, however, could bear any lasting resentment against Brancker's indiscretions. They were obviously the effects of his burning zeal. He would be the first to say "*mea culpa*" and the first to commit them again.'

Personalities counted in that small struggling community of civil aviation. At the time of Imperial Airways' formation in 1924, the staff numbered only 250. Many of these had won their posts only after some jockeying. There was fierce competition at all levels. The four amalgamated companies had all contributed staff; but inevitably some had fallen by the wayside. There was an uncomfortable shakedown.

The announcement, for instance, that George Woods Humphery, who had been General Manager of the Handley Page Company immediately before the amalgamation, would hold the same post in Imperial Airways, was the occasion for a serious dispute between the pilots and the management. There were protests that Woods Humphery lacked the experience and knowledge required for the job. But this was only one of several issues which led to a strike by pilots and mechanics. The new management committed the indiscretion of offering the pilots quite unacceptable terms consisting of a retaining fee of £100 a year and a mileage rate. These were rejected out of hand. The sixteen pilots who had been taken on demanded a guaranteed figure of £450 a year and flying pay based on time instead of mileage. The dispute grounded Imperial Airways. The new Company was unable to start operations on April 1, 1924, as contracted. Throughout the whole of that month, all services were suspended. During the following month only skeleton services were flown.

The conflict became acrimonious, complicated and personal. Woods Humphery remained at loggerheads with the pilots who had formed a Federation at Croydon. Lawyers were brought in: writs were issued. It was only the emergence of Major H. G. Brackley—the popular and trusted 'Brackles'—as an intermediary between the pilots and the management that staved off disaster. The pilots chose him as their representative to deal directly with the Board. The Company created for him the post of Air Superintendent.

Something of the atmosphere of this critical period was recalled by Mrs. Brackley in her biography of her husband.

> 'Keen and interested as Brackles was in the proposed new post—for which his past few years' work had given him the right experience—it was a difficult position and he felt it keenly because W.H. and he had been colleagues at Handley Page. To be called, at this juncture, to a position to represent his fellow pilots on the Board and have *direct* access to the new Chairman, Sir Eric Geddes, and the Managing Director, Col. Searl, when the pilots were virtually in a state of strike on account of their attitude to the General Manager, was a difficult and an unpleasant situation for someone of my husband's type and temperament. I look back over the past years, with my experience of both these men, and my knowledge of the inside story. Both were young, enthusiastic, ambitious, self-made and single-minded in their devotion to their ideal of work; temperamentally poles apart, with a new science and unexplored business to pursue. I can only wonder more and more—despite all the difficulties, disillusionments and misunderstandings of others, mostly, and at times between themselves—what an amazing record they both achieved. . . .'

Brackley's appointment created a much-needed bridge of understanding between the flying men and the management on the ground. Though Brackley himself began with a typical Air Force suspicion for mere men of business, he soon established himself in the confidence of the management. With his personal charm and nervous energy he mingled a very practical all-round ability. It was said of him that he would never issue an order to a pilot that he could not carry out himself. This side of his character was noted by Lloyd C. Ifould, for many years the Station Engineer in Paris:

> 'Early one morning, I was waiting on the aerodrome for a pilot to come along and do a test flight. We had installed a new port engine in a machine and a short test flight was necessary before it could go on the 9.00 a.m. service to London. Major Brackley happened to be in Paris, and had to come out early to Le Bourget. "I am afraid the service will be delayed, sir," I told him. "No pilot is here to test the machine." With these words scarcely out of my mouth, Major Brackley said: "Start the engines, I will test her for you!" Within fifteen minutes we were in the air.'

That incident, so characteristic of Brackley, belongs, of course, to a somewhat later period when the new services were already well established. His actual appointment and his first actions in taking over are mentioned in a letter he wrote at the time. Better than any official document of the period, this conveys something of the briskness of the atmosphere and of his own contagious enthusiasm.

> 'Yesterday I spent three hours with Sir Eric Geddes and met the Board of Directors. I was duly appointed and left Pall Mall immediately for Croydon to try and get the flying personnel together. . . . At Croydon I found more difficulties than expected. Questions of insurance, withdrawal of writ; making up and signing of agreement; inspection of machines; insurance of machines, and the hundred and one questions connected with the taking over of a new job and meeting new staff. . . . Instone and Handley Page had not handed over their machines officially and we could not touch them. This morning I had to get out temporary agreements for all the pilots, sixteen in number, to cover the period during which the proper agreements are being drawn up. Timetables for all routes, terminal aerodromes and accommodation—all these things have to be thought out and action taken. . . . Difficulties arose between pilots' solicitors and Humphery's solicitors over the writ question, the pilots naturally demanding that Humphery should withdraw the writs. After a great deal of discussion, I have got this settled. . . . Then I had to interview disgruntled men who had been thrown out of employment and demanded

work with the new Company. After a great deal of talk with the Managing Director I got him to send letters to them stating that they will be taken on as soon as there is work for them to do. . . . There are tons and tons of freight waiting to go.'

Those accumulations of freight were among the lesser problems. With the grievances of the pilots settled, there remained for the new management the headache of the eighteen machines inherited from the four companies. While many of them were old and well tried, they were mostly single-engined and incapable of development. This mixed stable consisted of seven DH 34s, one Vickers Vimy, one Vickers Vulcan, one Handley Page o/400 (a modified First War bomber), three Handley Page W8s, two Sea Eagle Flying-boats, two Westlands and one DH 4A (another First War aircraft). Five of them were more or less unserviceable when taken over. On one occasion during the first year of operation there remained only two single-engined aircraft serviceable.

Looking over that mixed stable, it was evident that the whole future of the Company depended on bigger and faster aircraft. With these the demand was for safety and reliability—excellent qualities which were later to threaten the Company with the epithet 'Slow coach'. British manufacturers were invited to submit plans and tenders for aircraft with at least two, and preferably three, engines.

In March 1926, Imperial Airways paraded a new fleet of five twin-engined Handley Page airliners at Croydon for a naming ceremony and inspection by Dominion Prime Ministers. These aircraft, finished in the then standard colours of the Company, dark blue fuselage with white lining and lettering and aluminium doped wings and tail unit, formed the first fleet of its own choosing: and it went into service in Europe.

In the summer of that year were delivered three Armstrong-Whitworth Argosy three-engined biplanes, seating eighteen to twenty passengers and carrying a steward, then known as a 'waiter'. This functionary who served coffee, sandwiches and biscuits was an immediate success, not least with the crew who, it must be remembered, were still occupying open cockpits. Even at 95 miles an hour, hot coffee was feasible and welcome.

The Argosy also provided a special hazard of its own for those who flew it. The nose engine was 'dirty', shedding oil which spattered back on to the pilot's windscreen, blotting out his view. His sole companion in the open cockpit, the flight engineer, had to keep working with rags to keep the windscreen clear. As the engines got older, the wiping had to be carried out every few minutes. When it rained the mixture of water and oil spread across the screen in an opaque film, defeating even the human windscreen-wiper. The Argosy offered a standard of comfort which encouraged the Company to introduce a midday London–Paris service—the famous 'Silver Wing'.

Apart from its buffet, which had a glamorous appeal to travellers in the mid-'twenties, this service became renowned for its punctuality. Within a few months of its introduction there were pleasing reports in the Press of people in the fields of Kent setting their watches by the three engines of the Argosy pounding through the skies.

> 'This may have been slightly exaggerated [wrote Lloyd C. Ifould], but not in the case of Captain Jimmy Youell. Providing his departure was anywhere near schedule, his E.T.A. would be 2.25 p.m. The Croydon Control Tower knew that even before they received the message from the machine, as they were aware immediately a machine left Le Bourget, of the captain's name, number of passengers, quantity of baggage, and freight on board. News would soon get around as to who was bringing in the "Silver Wing". At the Airport, there are caricatures of all airline pilots, and Captain Youell, possibly the most romantic and best known of all Europe's airline pilots, is caricatured peering over the side of the cockpit of an Argosy, which is coming in to land. He is looking at the clock in the Control Tower, which points exactly to 2.25 p.m., five minutes before the bar is due to close. People on the aerodrome are running like hell for the bar, to have "one" before that happens. They are not looking at the clock in the Control Tower—they know the time—it's Jimmy piloting the Argosy from Paris, and they have just five minutes to go.'

Here is an indication of fares and routes operated in the summer of 1927. London–Paris £5 5s. od. single and £9 9s. od. return and on the 'Silver Wing' services £6 6s. od. and £11 11s. od.; London–Brussels £5 single and £9 return; London–Cologne

£5 15s. od. and £10 5s. od. London–Le Touquet £3 and £5 15s. od.; and London–Ostend £4 and £7 5s. od. In October the Paris fares were reduced to £5 5s. od. single and £10 return on the 'Silver Wing'; the Brussels fares became £4 10s. od. and £8 5s. od. The Southampton–Guernsey fares were £3 and £5 10s. od.

During the following winter, there was an interesting new fare development when first and second class travel on the London–Paris route was introduced. Second class flights had no bar service or stewards, and they went at less popular times. The first class services, with all comforts laid on, were a few minutes faster in the air and took off from London and Paris at midday. By that time the 'chosen instrument' was beginning to justify itself. In 1927, the airline carried 70 per cent of all passenger traffic on the London–Paris route in both directions, and the total number of passengers on this route was 19,762. In that year Geddes told his shareholders: 'Your fleet in Europe consists of 15 aircraft, eight of which are so closely similar and have so many interchangeable components that, for practical purposes, they may be taken as being of the same type . . .'

Even with the steady build-up which followed from the late 'twenties through to the 'thirties, efforts to popularize flying were essential to everybody in the business. The Secretary of State for Air gave a lead. Of the many flights he made in the 'twenties, Sir Samuel Hoare wrote:

> 'What better in those days when every civil flight was regarded as a foolhardy adventure than for the Secretary of State for Air to start the use of aeroplanes for his official journeys? "Fly yourself, and whenever possible with your wife, and show that you can keep to a definite time-table in carrying out a flying programme"—that was the marching, or rather flying, order that I gave myself. . . . The idea that the Secretary of State for Air should normally use air transport for visits and inspections was entirely new and, in the minds of many people, mad. The *Morning Post* particularly objected to it. The place for Ministers was, it declared, Whitehall, and when Ministers travelled, they should keep to the established methods of transport. My flights they regarded as dangerous and objectionable stunts. In actual fact, they were the very opposite of stunts. Their whole object was to prove

DH4 of A.T.A. about to take off for Paris, the first scheduled air service in the world

Scene at Cricklewood with O/400s of the Handley Page air fleet

Refuelling Sir Alan Cobham's aircraft before departure with Sir Sefton Brancker on their great Eastern survey flight

First India–England air mail arriving at Croydon, 7 April 1929 (Sir Samuel Hoare second from the left)

that flying was not a stunt, and I did everything possible to make them appear as humdrum and unsensational as possible.'

Imperial Airways also took up propaganda during this period. There were, for instance, 'tea flights' over London. For a guinea or thirty shillings, passengers could book seats in a standard air-liner for a sight-seeing flight over London and down the Thames while tea was served. In the early 'thirties, there were also special Sunday day trips from Croydon to Le Touquet. There were light refreshments on the way out: luncheon and tea were taken on French soil: dinner was served on the plane during the return flight. Over Paris, too, propaganda flights were of immense value to British prestige and custom when the first four-engined Handley Page airliners were delivered in the early 'thirties. Thousands of people received their *baptême de l'air* on these short sight-seeing trips over Paris during which refreshments were served in seats equipped with individual electric lights and hot and cold air ventilators.

It was this great breed of Handley Page airliners, known as the Heracles class in Europe and the Hannibal class on the Empire routes, which first carried the British Civil Air Ensign, established by Order in Council, in August 1931, after approval by King George V. This ensign, which may be flown by all British aircraft registered in the United Kingdom, is of light blue, having a dark blue cross edged with white and with a Union flag in the first quarter. It corresponds with the red ensign of the Merchant Navy. It was hoisted immediately an aircraft touched down, and flown to the point of disembarkation. It was also flown on departure, from the time of embarkation to take-off, which, in the early days when crews were still unaccustomed to the retractable masts, caused a good deal of anxiety. Recalling the early appearance of the new ensign at Le Bourget, Lloyd C. Ifould writes:

'The lowering and hoisting . . . was carried out by the First Officer or Radio Officer, at the command of the Captain. This was part of the cockpit drill, but, occasionally, some captains omitted to give the order, and other members of the crew would forget it prior to the take-off, as each member had various duties to perform. The machine would go haring along the 'drome, take off, climb, reduce engines to cruising r.p.m. and on course, still flying the Ensign, with the mast bent straight back, looking as if it would snap off at any moment and possibly go into the airscrews. Someone would rush to the Control Tower, and a radio message would be sent to the aircraft, "Your flag". The reply would come back, "Thank you". Other airlines were not long in following our example. Air France, Lufthansa, Dutch, Belgian, Swiss, Italian, all commenced to fly their flags from their machines. All those different flags fluttering gaily in the breeze made of the airport a pretty and colourful sight.'

They were also a constant reminder of the lively competition that was springing up everywhere in Europe. With the introduction of the Handley Page 42, claimed by its makers to be the world's first real airliner, Britain was well in the lead. In 1931, Imperial Airways possessed a fleet of eight of this type of four-engined aircraft. They carried 38 passengers with an operating crew of Captain, and First Officer and two Stewards, and their motto was 'safety first'. No passenger came to harm throughout their nine years' term of service which carried them on to the beginning of the Second World War when they were transferred to active service transport duties with the R.A.F. For all their many great virtues, they were slow and this was to cause much criticism later. Flights made against strong headwinds between Croydon and Paris often took over 3½ hours. 'Frequently we would suffer the indignity of seeing trains moving faster than we were,' writes one of the pilots who flew them. But when the first four of the Heracles—the type specially designed for European traffic—came into operation, the pilots took well to them. 'We had been caught up in what was probably the most thrilling period in the history of civil aviation. All the while the need for the maximum commercial efficiency was a driving force. The result was that salaries were low, and increases hardly come by; but staff were commercially minded in the right sense, and, despite the discomforts, the poor working conditions, the poor pay and allowances, there was a keen measure of zeal. Keenness to have a job well done carried Imperial Airways through many a difficult patch. Well for the country, and British flying, that it was so.'

For many years the Heracles class airliners enjoyed international fame. Wherever they appeared in Europe, they attracted intense curiosity, and assuredly they were the most visited British airliners until the B.O.A.C. Comet came along in the 'fifties. An indication of the faith of Insurance Companies in the operation of these and other Imperial Airways craft came in March 1933, when the premium rate for accident insurance for passengers travelling on the Company's services was reduced to that charged for surface transport.

The European pattern in 1934 was similar to that of 'previous years but new routes were planned and for these new aircraft were ordered.

From Short Bros. came two four-engined landplanes called *Scylla* and *Syrinx*, each with a capacity for 39 passengers, not liked by the pilots owing to their heavy control. Nevertheless they were safe and steady and served their purpose well on the European routes. Another acquisition by Imperial Airways was a number of DH 86 Diana-class short-range airliners which were also put into service on the Empire routes which are the subject of the next chapter.

For the moment we must leave the European services as they were, well established in the mid-'thirties, with an unequalled reputation for comfort and safety. For them it was becoming a period of consolidation rather than progress. Much of the creative ability and energy of Imperial Airways was being directed to the building up of the world-wide network.

CHAPTER VII

A WORLD PATTERN

WHEN Imperial Airways acquired its resounding title, the dream of H. G. Wells of 'Air Services planned on a world scale' was far from fulfilment. At the time of their amalgamation, none of the subsidized operating companies was flying outside Europe. The established conventional trunk communications had changed little since the time of Queen Victoria.

A decade and a half later when the Second World War broke out, the airline was operating nearly seventy aircraft in all parts of the world—South Africa, India, Burma, Malaya, Australia,—in association with Qantas Empire Airways—linking Bangkok with Hong Kong, Kano with Khartoum, and was about to start commercial transatlantic flights. This achievement stemmed not only from visionaries and from competent management but also from men of action who sweated out the long-distance routes—the R.A.F. and civilian pioneers who made record flights in converted service aircraft immediately after the First World War.

An air route to India was agreed by all to be the necessary first feature on any pattern of Imperial air communication. The Egypt–Iraq service of the R.A.F. offered a ready forged link in the chain, to be extended onward to India and ultimately across Europe from London to Cairo. But even with the R.A.F. already at hand as a potent ally, much of the groundwork had to be done from scratch—and money was tight. 'When the India service was first contemplated,' wrote Woods Humphery, 'we were urged by the Secretary of State to make it as cheap as we possibly could, because he expected to encounter great difficulties in getting the larger subsidy required.'

Even with a subsidy in hand and machines and men to do the job, an airline is helpless without the outlay of many resources on the ground. These, as both the Government and the new company realized all too soon, must be not only concerned with aviation and geography but also with politics. That was the basis of an expedition made by Sefton Brancker, piloted by Alan Cobham, in a DH 50 in 1924. The task was to survey every aspect, political as well as physical, of the route across Europe to India. At that time there had been changes at Westminster. Brancker had been working for the first time for a Socialist Air Minister, Lord Thomson, the chief with whom he set off ten years later, with misgivings, on another trip to India, in the airship R 101, in which both of them lost their lives.

There was a General Election while Brancker was making his final preparations. He outlined to Thomson his programme for contacting all the authorities, political and aeronautical, along the route. 'Forgive me for bothering you in the midst of a lightning election,' he wrote in a personal note, 'but I want to get you to set this progressive policy into motion—before you desert us—if indeed you do! But you may, and I do want to get things going before the post-election period of stagnation sets in.'

Neither Thomson, nor Hoare who came into office again with a new Conservative Government, was likely to stagnate in this matter. Politics aside, the two men were friends and both enthusiasts for an air route to India. It was in the ways and means that their views differed. From Thomson's first brief span of office and from subsequent events, it was clear that he favoured the airship as a vehicle—a predilection which led to his death.

Brancker's trip with Cobham was a fantastic mixture of goodwill, adventure and mischance. He cut his head open on the roof of the cabin. The aircraft tipped on its nose in Asia Minor. He collapsed with pneumonia in Calcutta. None the less, he recovered and went on to Rangoon where he finished his job. On the way back, encountering a European winter, he and his crew force-landed in Germany in a snowstorm. A less stout-hearted Director of Civil Aviation might have been tempted to finish the last leg of his journey in a *wagon-lit*. Not so Brancker. He and his companions set about dismantling the machine with the aid of the German police. Three large lorries transported it fifty miles by road through the snow, to an airfield near Stuttgart where they arrived at midnight. The next day they re-erected the machine in a shed with the aid of German mechanics. That same evening they flew to Strasbourg. They reached Croydon on March 17, 1925, and it is left for another generation to marvel at that fantastic interlude in the snow.

This was not, however, just an adventurous test for men and machines. Foundations had been laid for the civil air services which were to follow. There had been successful contacts throughout Europe. The Iraq Government had said that they were prepared to help, particularly in the establishment of a station at Rutbah Wells, half-way across the desert between the Mediterranean and Baghdad.

In Persia things were not so easy. The German Junkers Company was already established in the confidence of the Government and things might not go well with the British—which indeed they did not. In India, Brancker managed to arouse interest and promises of support, but noted a lack of local initiative. His summary of it all was crisp and encouraging:

> 'I have returned impressed with the fact that the operation of air transport in the East will be very much easier than it is in Western Europe. Generally speaking, the route between London and Rangoon is an extremely easy one for operation. I believe, therefore, that an aeroplane service along this route will fly with extraordinary regularity. I had anticipated that the journey might be a difficult one in places. The nearer we came to our anticipated difficulties, the less serious they appeared. . . .'

One immediate result of Brancker's report was a Government decision to make a practical start on the route to India by commercializing the R.A.F. service from Cairo to Basra with a view to extending it to Karachi. For this there was a new subsidy. 'The agreement with the Air Ministry,' Geddes told the shareholders, 'under which your company will receive an annual subsidy of £93,600, is for five years and the Government is to provide aerodromes, hangars, and other accommodation.'

There had been a joint survey for Air Ministry and Imperial Airways carried out by the late Charles Wolley-Dod, one of the great pioneers of the airline, over the route, which was taken over in October 1926. At this time, the range of all civil aircraft was small. Though a direct flight across the desert from Cairo to

Baghdad was, of course, desirable, and possible with a light load, it was out of the question economically. Emergency landing places had to be devised: and a substantial refuelling station set up somewhere near the half-way mark. Brancker had persuaded the Iraq Government to co-operate over this and a commodious fort was built on the oasis at Rutbah Wells. It had to be well fortified as the behaviour of local tribes was then unpredictable. Within the fort was a rest house for a permanent staff presided over by a manager and his wife: and there were all facilities for controlling the adjacent airfield. Food, fuel and all the necessities of life came by motor transport from Baghdad some 240 miles across desert tracks. There was an excellent water supply from an artesian well. Pilots who flew that route often speak of the fresh quality of that water so miraculously abundant in the midst of the desert. By the time Brancker made his fifth journey along that route, the fort was in full operation:

> 'Where previously there had been bare desert, with a few water holes around which gathered the camels and goats of some wandering tribe, we now found Rutbah Post, a stone-built caravanserai provided with an hotel, a powerful wireless set, a good water supply and a courtyard full of cars and lorries plying between Damascus and Baghdad. The only detail that the architect had forgotten was the provision of fire-places. Rutbah must be nearly 3,000 feet above the sea, and is often bitterly cold in December; we dined in overcoats and had a very shivery night in the hotel.'

Elsewhere along the route the accommodation planned for passengers was crude. This was to be expected in view of the uncertainties of the future and the remoteness of the airfields. Imperial Airways used R.A.F. airfields as much as possible. Heliopolis in the suburbs of Cairo became the Egyptian terminus, and Karachi, where there was the huge airship shed, was planned as the terminus in India. The Rutbah Wells oasis was but one of several stations where night stop accommodation for passengers and crews had to be available.

Imperial Airways machines were equipped with radio and were not forced to follow the Desert Furrow of the R.A.F. They all carried desert rations, nevertheless, and an emergency water supply, for there was always a possibility of pilots becoming lost in that featureless waste and there was an ever-present risk of the aircraft running short of fuel, particularly westward bound against strong prevailing headwinds. Emergency fuel dumps were laid down to be kept supplied by motor tankers. For the nomadic tribesmen of the desert, these were an irresistible lure. Though the nomads of those days had no use for petrol, they had a great liking for the cans, which they put to every kind of domestic use. They also took a childish delight in using the dumps for target practice.

To thwart them, the emergency fuel had to go underground in locked tanks. The nomads, however, did not lose their interest. They amused themselves by using the locks for target practice and they continued to loot the dumps. As a final countermeasure, the airline had to resort to secret locks. There then remained only the hazard of human error—the possibility of the aircrews not carrying a key. Woods Humphery, who had been a marine engineer before going into aviation, overcame this by providing for the secret locks keys which also fitted the cabin doors of the aircraft, and as such were indispensable at take-off. This scheme worked well on the relatively rare occasions when pilots were forced to land beside the emergency tanks. The only hazards then were the scorpions which set up house in the sheltered spaces between the tanks and the desert surface.

A pilot of those days, Captain Roger Mollard, recollects unscheduled stops out in the blue along the old line of the furrow: 'Passengers took the whole thing in a spirit of adventure. They all got out and helped with the refuelling. On occasion when I landed beside one of these tanks, I can remember passengers standing out in the open, holding out their coats as windshields while we were refuelling.'

There was one emergency landing just before nightfall beside a disused fort. Desert rations, water, bully beef, biscuit and a medicinal tot of brandy were unloaded with all the warm clothing that the passengers and crew could muster. The fort was open to the skies but with some cover from the night winds of the desert. There was no sign of any human being in that desolate spot but there was evidence of a visitation by camels. Having no light or fuel, with immediate prospect of darkness, Mollard persuaded his stranded passengers to hurry forth to collect camel dung in their hats. Fortunately the passengers of those days were more addicted to hats than they are now. A sizeable pile of camel dung was collected, dipped in petrol and used as a camp fire. That the passengers felt none the worse for this adventure was shown later when they met for a reunion dinner at the Trocadero in London and sent Mollard a signed menu card 'From the Camel Dung-Burners Club.'

For this route Imperial Airways had made a good start by ordering from de Havilland three-engined Hercules aircraft robustly constructed and specially designed for tough desert conditions. A Near East division was set up for the administration of the new service, with headquarters at Heliopolis. The terminal at first was merely a marked-out area of sand with a one-time hangar and a large shed which served as workshops and administrative offices. The first batch of the new Hercules were ready at the end of 1926 and enjoyed a dramatic first appearance. The Air Minister *and his wife* went out to India with the first flight.

> 'Five new de Havilland aeroplanes [he wrote], each equipped with three 450 horse-power Bristol Jupiter engines, had been designed and ordered for the Indian service, and the opening flights fixed for the beginning of 1927. As soon as the plan took this concrete shape, I determined to make the first journey over a route that was obviously destined to become a great Imperial highway and, since the line was civil and not military, and a woman was, therefore, not contraband, my wife was equally determined to go with me.'

Samuel Hoare was flying in the face of convention. He was reminded of another Minister, William Huskisson, the unhappy President of the Board of Trade, who had been run over and killed by a locomotive at the inauguration of an earlier transport service—the Liverpool–Manchester Railway 1830. Hoare, however, argued that the trip was a contribution to much-needed propaganda. 'We were both intent upon proving to a doubting world that flying was a normal and dependable way of travelling for women as well as men, and no longer an adventure that only men could undertake.' Without question this 10,000-mile flight had all the best propaganda elements.

The Prime Minister, Stanley Baldwin, was not enthusiastic about Ministers hitting the headlines during Parliamentary recess. 'What with F.E. winning diving competitions in Madeira, and Leo Amery ski-ing in the most mountainous regions of the Alps and Sam Hoare flying to India, I feel like a circus manager whose performing fleas have escaped.'

Others in high places were deeply stirred. The Khan of Kalat, ruling Prince of Baluchistan, offered the Hoares 'a carpet as a symbol of your conquest of the air—a conquest such as King Solomon made when he flew over these regions on his magic carpet.'

This particular conquest of the air was an achievement shared by many varied talents. The R.A.F. had made a major contribution: but the new service would have been impossible without the survey pilots, the engineers, the radio and meteorological experts and the many others who go to make up the complex team which enables an airliner to fly with punctuality and safety. This aspect of team work was recognized by Samuel Hoare in his own vivid accounts of his journeys. He claimed no personal glory for what he did. He was at some pains to emphasize a sort of amateur status.

King George V sent a message to the Hoares on their arrival in India. 'My hearty congratulations on your safe arrival in India after your most successful and enterprising flight. I hope that you and Lady Maud enjoyed your journey . . .' This was a well-merited acknowledgement of long-range civil aviation—particularly in that the King wrote of 'enjoying' the journey, not of triumphing over dangers and difficulties. It was the first time that a British Minister had actually made a positive use of one of the Empire links, of which there had been so much talk for so long. By taking his wife, he had emphasized the civilian nature of the new air route.

Many people in the business were already speaking of an extension from India through to Australia. All seemed set fair for consolidation and expansion. The joker in the pack was international politics. As Brancker had feared German interests had begun to influence the Persian Government, which suddenly refused to implement the agreement with Imperial Airways which Brancker himself had been negotiating during a secret trip to Tehran. There was no alternative but to stop short the India service at Basra while bargaining with the Persians continued. The first service on this shortened sector started in January 1927. It began on a somewhat leisurely fortnightly basis but in the following April the frequency was increased to a service every week. The Persian troubles, however, went on for some years.

In 1929, the situation eased slightly and the service from Cairo was extended to Karachi—but not for long. The Persians wanted the airline to operate through the more populated parts of their country: and Imperial Airways found the aerodromes unsuitable. Central Persia was a difficult mountainous terrain. They could only offer to continue to fly the coastal route. Persia replied with a notice to quit.

Politics aside, there was a good measure of adventure. During the summer of 1931, for instance, Captain Roger Mollard was outward bound to India in a DH 66. With him, flying as supernumerary, was a Captain—we must call him Captain 'X'—who had recently joined the airline and was learning the route. Between Lingeh and Bushire, engine failure caused them to make an emergency landing on a salt pan some twelve miles short of Lingeh.

'The landing was successful but, probably due to iron ore in the hills, we were unable to contact Lingeh by radio. I considered that as Captain "X" was new to the route and did not even speak a few words of the local language, it would be best for me to go to Lingeh to despatch messages and get assistance. Leaving him in charge, I explained that I expected the walk would take me about four hours but that, using donkeys, the journey from the village to the aircraft should take about two and a half to three hours and consequently I expected to return before nightfall.

'Threading my way through the foothills took longer than I had counted on and five hours had passed before I reached Lingeh, where our agent was somewhat alarmed to see me arrive on foot. He was most helpful, however, and started at once to collect donkeys and arrange for a supply of bedding, food and drinks. Armed guards also had to be provided and as I was not in a fit condition for the return ride I suggested that an interpreter should also be included in the party. The agent himself volunteered for this duty and the party set off for the salt pan. It was some time after dark before they approached their destination.

'Meanwhile Captain "X" had arranged that in the event of my not returning before sundown he and the passengers would keep watch during the night as bandits were not unknown in that locality. Two passengers were in possession of revolvers and the aircraft was equipped with a Very signal pistol.

'Captain "X" was himself on watch after an evening meal when in the moonlight he saw advancing towards him over the salt pan a body of mounted figures several of whom had rifles or guns slung over their shoulders.

'In case they were hostile, he promptly challenged them with the time-honoured "*Halt! Who goes there?*" to which the interpreter in the party promptly replied, "*Mesopos-A.P.O.C.*" which were well known abbreviations for the Mesopotamia Trading Company and the Anglo-Persian Oil Company. Unfortunately Captain "X" was not aware of this and thought that the words were in a foreign language and as the party continued advancing he fired a signal cartridge into their midst. The immediate result of this was that the donkeys taking fright stood on their hind legs, shedding their burdens on to the salt pan, and started to stampede off towards Lingeh. Fortunately the required bedding and food was easily retrievable and the misunderstanding having been put right the passengers were able to spend a not too uncomfortable night beneath the wings of the aircraft. The next day the engine was put right, the aircraft was flown off the salt pan without difficulty and we went on to Basra.'

In 1932 the service was transferred to the Arabian side of the Persian Gulf, which was not without advantage as the new route could be shared with the R.A.F. who were already on terms of friendship with the Sheikhs on the Trucial Coast. The Air Force had found a particularly good friend in Sheikh Issa and it was through him that the long and delicate negotiations were conducted in time for the transfer.

The Sheikhs agreed to Imperial Airways making use of that coastline for flying-boats or for the construction of land bases. It was not easy to find sites for airfields, but finally it was decided to use the Isle of Bahrein, south of Basra, a sheikhdom in Treaty relationship with Britain, in which oil had just been found, and Sharjah lying on the flat desert almost at the foot of the bare and rugged Oman Peninsula. This peninsula faced the Persian coast overlooking the bleak and sunscorched end of the Persian Gulf close to the borders of Baluchistan. It was here that the new route joined up with the old line of flight to Karachi.

Political troubles with Persia were not the only ones. The balance between geographical possibility and political expediency was always precarious. The European leg of the new trunk line was threatened when Italy refused to allow flying-boats to use Brindisi as a point of embarkation for the flight across the Mediterranean to Egypt. For a time indeed, Imperial Airways was turned out of Italy altogether: and was forced to use a Central European route through Vienna, Budapest, Belgrade and Salonika. For a time, also, the Greeks refused the use of Navarino.

When the Mediterranean troubles were settled, the air link between Europe and Asia was provided by Scipio-class flying-boats, the first four-engined passenger aircraft to be used by any airline in the world. Egypt, of course, became an important junction not only for flights east but also for traffic south into Africa.

Cobham had carried out a flight known as 'The Empire League Imperial Airways Survey' to South Africa in 1925. In 1929 he made another survey flight in the *Youth of Britain* as far as Salisbury. These opened up the territory and created public interest. By the mid-'twenties there were already a number of airfields in existence along the line. In 1926 a company called The North Sea Aerial and General Transport Ltd., in which the Blackburn Aeroplane Company had an interest, obtained a contract from the Colonial Office to operate an experimental service between Khartoum and Kisumu. Their first aircraft, a seaplane, came to grief on the Nile and sank. When the news of this reached Sir Samuel Hoare in Cairo on his way through to India, he made arrangements for the R.A.F. to loan another seaplane in order that the experimental flights might be continued. While the Air Minister was in India, Brancker went down to Khartoum to join Captain Gladstone who was in charge of the experimental work and who had already completed two flights in each direction. At this point Auriol Lee, a talented actress of middle age, whose name was publicly associated with Brancker, makes an almost official appearance in the pages of aviation history. She joined Brancker, Gladstone and the engineer, as 'supercargo and publicity to prove that the flight was easy and comfortable'. The party was duly greeted at Malakal by the Deputy Governor and 'a party of completely naked natives—Shelluks—fine, hearty men, with carefully dressed and red-tinted hair, and a few bead necklaces'.

It was when they stopped at Jinja that the supercargo became an embarrassment.

'Jinja is nearly 4,000 feet above the sea, and at that time of year very hot; so the air about midday is peculiarly dead and lacking in lift. We refuelled and taxied into the lake with a view to getting off. Gladstone opened up the engine and away we went over the surface of the water, but do what he could the machine would not leave the water. . . . Then the water in the radiator began to boil furiously. Now, inadvertently, the overflow pipe was situated on the top of the centre section; it pointed into the passengers' cockpit, and before we realized what was happening, the lady passenger, engineer and I were enveloped in showers of scalding water. Yelling blue murder, we covered ourselves with every rug and overcoat we could find, while Gladstone was thoroughly alarmed as to what he might find when he came to get us out. That stream of hot water seemed endless, but at last it stopped, and we emerged sadder, wiser and very wet. Finding that we were not parboiled like lobsters, Gladstone made another try to get off, with exactly the same result! And then he stopped the engine. The engine, being thoroughly overheated, then refused to restart, and we drifted slowly across the lake, with Gladstone and the engineer struggling fiercely with the starting handles while I took over the controls. Eventually we arrived on the jungly shore, which we knew was shared between a particularly fierce herd of buffalo in the forest and numerous hippos and crocodiles in the water. Here we wrestled with the engine, and, in the midst of our struggle, a large thermos flask, containing iced drink, burst with a loud report. For a moment we thought we were being shot at. We had assembled on the deck of the floats and our lady passenger, who had been unwittingly tempting the crocodiles with a very attractive pair of legs, nearly fell in! Jinja did not boast a launch, but eventually an antique steam ferry, supported by a native canoe, came to our rescue, and we were towed ignominiously back to Jinja. There seemed nothing for it but to lighten our load, so we handed the lady and most of the baggage over to a kindly Uganda official, the Director of Survey, with a motor-car.'

When Captain Gladstone eventually joined forces with Cobham to form the Cobham-Blackburn Airline, Imperial Airways at first considered having this company operate a section of the African route for them. They decided instead to acquire the interests of this concern and operate the whole route themselves.

At the time of Cobham's second African flight in 1929, Imperial Airways and Air Ministry were carrying out a joint survey beginning in South Africa and working north. Air Ministry was represented by Captain (later Sir Frederick) Tymms: Imperial Airways by Charles Wolley-Dod, a pilot with a phenomenal sense of direction who rarely carried a map when he flew over the European routes. He had given up his studies to join the Air Force in the First World War. Instead of returning to the blackboard, he had afterwards become an instructor in the Spanish Royal Air Service. He had made his start in civil aviation when the Spaniards formed a Seville-Morocco air service in the early 'twenties. At the time of his survey of Africa, he was recognized as an authority in airline development and was put in charge of the newly-created North African Division. Later he went back to work in Europe and was killed on flying duty between Brussels and Cologne just before the Second World War.

The African survey resulted in an agreement between the Government and Imperial Airways for a weekly service in both directions between Egypt and Cape Town. It was a more ambitious project than the Indian line but with the advantage that it passed through and linked up territory which was under the Crown or within British political control. There were, for instance, 27 main aerodromes and 30 intermediate alighting points along the 5,600 miles of the route. It was the task of local administrations to provide these, either from existing accommodation or by construction, in some cases hacking them out of virgin bush. Even if these places had been surveyed and carefully planned, they were still known to be unserviceable during the rainy seasons. The section between Khartoum and Kenya was particularly bad. Many of the landing strips had to be built on swamp and it was some years before the problem of reliable landing surfaces in Africa was overcome.

The whole of the route was to be protected by a chain of radio stations. It was planned that no aircraft would ever be outside the range of these. Some of these stations were already in existence but many new ones had to be built: and a meteorological service had to be organized to work with them. Except in a few places where local resources could be used, Imperial Airways had to build and maintain rest houses for passengers and staff and indeed soon found themselves running a chain hotel business—some of it under canvas—right down Africa.

As much of the new territory, particularly from Kenya to the south, is high and also subject to high temperatures, it was essential to have aircraft with exceptional performance for take-off. Atalanta monoplanes, carrying ten passengers, were ordered. While they were being built, however, the traffic on the route increased so rapidly that they were in fact outmoded before they arrived.

The northern half of the route opened in February 1931, with a service from Croydon to Mwanza on Lake Victoria in Tanganyika, taking ten days to do the trip of just over 5,000 miles—a good comparison with the twenty days then taken by surface transport. It operated in several parts. Passengers and mail traversed the European sector partly by air and partly by rail. The Cairo–Khartoum sector was flown in Argosy aircraft transferred from the European service. The next sector from Khartoum to Mwanza was done in the old Calcutta three-engined flying-boats which had started the Mediterranean service (a far cry from the old Channel Islands service which they had originally operated).

In December 1931, the second half of the African route, the extension to Cape Town, started experimentally with Hercules released from the India service. The through weekly service from London to Cape Town opened in January 1932, taking ten and a half days for the 8,000-mile flight.

The Indian service had been extended by a charter arrangement with the Government of India to Delhi in 1929. In the spring of 1931, there was the interesting if over-ambitious experimental flight by a specially prepared Hercules from Cairo, intending to reach Australia, which stopped short in Timor Island owing to lack of fuel. Two months later, there was the second experimental flight to Australia which went as far as

Handley Page *Hannibal* at Sharjah, 1934

Captain Horsey receives the first Royal Air Mail pennant from Sir Eric Geddes, Croydon, May 1934. Sir Kingsley and Lady Wood (*left*)

Caledonia over New York at the end of her famous Atlantic crossing

Return Ferry Service—Liberator emplanes passengers during a Canadian snow storm

Horseshoe Route—Ops. Room, Cairo

Akyab. It was not till 1935 that there was any substantial development of the Indian and Far Eastern traffic, when the weekly Delhi service was extended to Calcutta. It was operated by a new company, Indian Trans-Continental Airways, which in itself was a break from Imperial Airways' policy of dependence only upon themselves. India, however, had insisted on participation and the new company, using the Atalanta airliners originally built for the African route, extended the service through to Rangoon and later to Singapore.

Australia now comes into the story with characteristic vigour and self-assurance. Existing long-haul services on other routes had been created by London initiative. There had been co-operation and active support in some areas, passive and even active resistance in others. Australia had long since been working on her own account. For more than a decade she had been gaining in popular airmindedness and in experience of civil aviation. 'Queensland and Northern Territory Aerial Services Ltd.'—familiar to all the world as Qantas—had been registered in November 1920 to promote air-taxi and joy-riding work, to gain public confidence in aviation and ultimately to run regular air services. The first of these was between Charleville and Cloncurry in November 1922. The distance, 557 miles, was too great to be flown in one day: so a night stop was made.

Aviation is never without its characters, and Australia produced a vivid bunch of personalities. Qantas stemmed from the efforts of two First World War pilots and a Queensland farmer. The pilots were the late Paul J. McGinniss and W. Hudson (now Sir Hudson) Fysh, for thirty-two years Managing Director of Qantas. The farmer was Fergus McMaster (later Sir Fergus) who became the first Chairman of the Company. He was a wealthy and influential man in Queensland pastoral circles, who remained convinced through thick and thin that aviation had a special future in Australia. There were thin times in 1921 and 1922, when Qantas shareholders, backing the faith of the founders with additional cash, marked their cheque butts 'donations' when making their contributions.

McMaster was a determined leader and relentless in his search for capital. For instance, he tackled Alexander Kennedy, one of the Queensland pioneers who had first crossed that country by bullock dray. At the age of 83, Kennedy might have seemed an unlikely shareholder for a new airline, but he offered to take £200 worth of shares. On McMaster urging him to make it £250, Kennedy surprisingly agreed on condition that he should become the first passenger when the regular air service started. So with Hudson Fysh, who was the pilot for the second leg of the first journey from Longreach to Cloncurry, went as the airline's first passenger Kennedy, by that time aged 85, and already a director of Qantas. In the first year of regular services, Qantas carried 208 passengers.

This greatly influenced Sir Samuel Hoare, when he came into office in 1922 to face the problems of British civil aviation.

> 'Unlike the European lines that started from the great cities and concentrated upon transport between them, Qantas came into being at the country end and to serve the scattered districts of Queensland, where a distance of a hundred miles between two country towns might take as long as four days to cover. The new airline had immediately created so wide a demand for its service that branches were already being started in many directions. In spite of primitive machines, no radio, no night flying and no weather forecasts except an occasional telephone message from a garage proprietor in Charleville the flights had been sufficiently dependable for the company to obtain a contract for carrying the mail.
>
> 'These evidences of success were arriving in London at a most opportune moment. I urgently needed some striking example of practical air transport with which to persuade the Government and the Treasury that there was much to be gained from civil air services.'

By 1930 Qantas had flown one million miles. Their friendly association with Imperial Airways in the experimental mail flights of 1931 has already been described. These flights had not been entirely successful from the British point of view in spite of the fact that the mail had got through. In Australia they had appealed much more to the public imagination and had evoked practical interest in the rapidly widening aviation circles. Approaches were made to Qantas to initiate an Australian service to fly all the way to Britain. But already a more realistic scheme was forming in the thoughts of people at both ends of this longest of air routes—the idea of a partnership. Imperial Airways were already flying their Atalantas as far as Singapore: Australia would go to meet them.

Brackley was chosen by the management of Imperial Airways as a flying ambassador to promote the idea. His craft was the *Astraea*, then Britain's most modern airliner. He left on May 29, 1933. Between Koepang and Darwin he met the old trouble of headwinds and shortage of fuel crossing the Timor Sea. It was a miracle of foresight on the part of an Alsatian Roman Catholic missionary which saved Brackley and his men from disaster. They already knew they would not make Darwin when they sighted the Australian coastline and were reconciled to a forced landing at Bathurst. Approaching that settlement, looking desperately for somewhere to put down, they were amazed to see a cleared landing ground in the jungle. There was just enough space for the *Astraea* to land crosswind on her last reserves of petrol. It was Father Gsell, the Franciscan who was later Roman Catholic Bishop at Darwin, who had thought of working with the Aborigines to make an emergency landing ground for airmen who might find themselves in distress over the Timor Sea. He welcomed the crew to his mission where radio contacts were made with the outside world. The mission lugger, the *St. Francis*, was despatched on a thirty-hour trip to Darwin to fetch petrol. Even when that little vessel returned after a tempestuous trip, the *Astraea* remained weather-bound for several hours. When at length she set out for Darwin, Father Gsell went along too.

In Australia, Brackley's goodwill mission was a resounding success. He said in a broadcast that the journey of some 14,000 miles from London had taken one month.

> 'During this time we have spent some fifteen days on the ground, paying many official calls and making many inquiries into Met. and local conditions *en route*, as well as doing many short flights, carrying hundreds of guests, so that those who have not already sampled air travel could try for themselves the comfort that modern British air transport has to offer on our Empire Airways. For those who have been used to the older and much noisier form of air transport, I think that *Astraea* has proved a revelation and many have expressed their delight and surprise at the ease with which they could carry on conversation in the cabin without even raising the voice. This is so on all airliners now employed on our Empire

Airways from the time one starts from London on the four-engined Heracles class, which carry thirty-eight passengers in two comfortable cabins with tables, to the four-engined Scipio flying-boats from Brindisi to Cairo which is now completed in one day. Now all passengers on Empire routes should have the same facilities and standard of comfort throughout the routes—whether the Australian routes are to be operated by my Company or other Australian operators.'

The questions raised in that last sentence were settled by the remarkable partnership which followed, and which, tempered by the fortunes of war, flourishes on a more ambitious scale at the present day. Hudson Fysh flew back with Brackley in the *Astraea* as far as Karachi, where the aircraft remained. He travelled on to London by the normal Imperial Airways services. His mission was to obtain aircraft from de Havilland and to work out the basis of the partnership with Woods Humphery. The result of this was the creation of Qantas Empire Airways, a new company incorporated in January 1934 in which half the stock was held by Qantas and half by Imperial Airways. The financial structure was modified later when both Qantas and B.O.A.C. became State-controlled. The principle of the partnership has remained through the years. It has been said that the full terms of reference have never been put down on paper. Though an umpire was appointed, he never, according to Hudson Fysh, 'had to blow his whistle'.

At first Qantas operated the Brisbane–Darwin sector. In 1935 it took over the Darwin–Singapore sector. In April of that year the first passenger service went from Croydon to Brisbane, taking twelve days, a gain of twenty days over surface timings. The partnership was working the longest airline in the world.

CHAPTER VIII

REORIENTATION

THE first ten years' trading by the chosen instrument, celebrated in 1934, had been successful. The world-wide mandate was well on its way to being accomplished. Financial prospects were sufficiently good for the declaration for the year 1934/35 of a dividend of 6% plus 1% bonus. The following year the bonus was raised by 1%.

With the opening of the 12,750-mile London–Brisbane service, the airline had become a force in international and Commonwealth affairs. The 7,885-mile flight from London to Cape Town took nine days. Experimental flights were made to connect Empire routes with Hong Kong and also to cross the centre of Africa from Khartoum to Nigeria. North Atlantic air services were under discussion. One of the most dramatic moves in the whole of British civil aviation history was the order of the fleet for the Empire Mail Scheme, hailed even by the American Press, when it came into operation in 1937:

News Week Magazine wrote: 'Since its organization twelve years ago, Great Britain's Imperial Airways has been one of the world's greatest air transport systems. It was one of the first airlines in the world to show a profit . . .'

The American journal *Aviation* made this comment: 'Call it long-nurtured strategy, or a triumph of "muddling through", as you prefer, Imperial Airways' programme for the immediate future if carried out as announced can scarcely fail to give Great Britain a position in air transport equalling her leadership in ocean commerce.'

The chosen instrument was not without honour also in its own country. Of the Empire Mail Scheme, *The Times* wrote: 'The effect of this scheme upon the commerce of the country and the outlook of its people will be incalculable. As seafaring has brought a wider outlook to the maritime states, so will air-faring create a more international outlook.'

Within the United Kingdom the four principal railway companies combined with Imperial Airways to start a series of internal services known as Railway Air Services Ltd. In Europe in 1934, Imperial Airways flew more than seven and a half million miles, which was in fact over three times the effort required for the subsidy. In 1935 the European end of the trunk lines was speeded up by express services to Budapest and Brindisi, bringing these cities within a day's flight of Britain.

The number of passengers carried from Croydon across the Channel on the regularly operated air routes to the Continent showed a steady increase through the 'thirties. They also revealed a slight flaw in the operational pattern. In 1932 the Company carried 59% of all the pasengers who travelled. In 1935 the figure had dropped to 50%. In 1937 it was only just over 36%. With the prodigious increase of intercontinental responsibilities went a weakening of Imperial Airways' position in Europe. The chosen instrument was not a monopoly. Indeed there was soon more than one chosen instrument.

The Hambling Committee of 1923 had recommended 'a commercial organization run entirely on business lines'. Yet in the mid-'thirties there were already murmurs about increased dividends being paid out of increased subsidy. The achievements of Imperial Airways may have been magnificent but the organization itself was vulnerable because it was a compromise between capitalism and State ownership, between a form of national service and a dividend-paying public company quoted on the Stock Exchange. Controversy between private enterprise and public ownership in the operation of air services still continues, and it is no part of the purpose of this narrative to join issue, except to show the changing status of the airline as it evolved. With the Empire Airmail Scheme well on its way, Imperial Airways might have seemed all set for another ten years of successful trading, when in August 1935, the Air Minister, Lord Swinton, went to lunch with Geddes, who then heard of a proposal that

> 'we should surrender our exclusivity north of the London–Cologne–Budapest line in Europe, and that the Government

should be free to support financially another civil aviation Company between this country and that area, without compensation to us. . . .

'The Secretary of State assured me most emphatically that there was no feeling on his part against Imperial Airways, nor any feeling on his part that we had not faithfully and efficiently performed our duties, indeed he admitted that we had generously performed those duties.

'He assured me that we were, in his opinion, fully deserving of support and of the continued confidence of the Government and of the Air Ministry, but he impressed upon me that although he did not know the reason, there was dissatisfaction both within the Government and in the House of Commons, with Imperial Airways' so-called monopoly, and that this dissatisfaction really amounted to hostility which he was persistently combating, both among the members of the House of Commons and outside, and he felt that it was in the best interests of Imperial Airways that this hostility should be met by allowing some other operator to come into the area reserved to us under our existing Agreement. . . .

'I impressed upon him the departure which the present proposals made from the principles of the Hambling Report. His reply was that the Hambling Report, while accepted at the time, could never be put forward as an irrevocable policy for all time, and that if the Hambling Committee were reporting today, it might take quite different views.'

This significant conversation was carefully put on record by Geddes. It ended almost with a sense of foreboding:

'I made some play on what I had in fact been feeling of recent months, namely, that, owing to changes at the Air Ministry and otherwise in their channels of communication with us, we were drifting from the position of being their principal chosen civil aviation agent and were becoming one of a lot of competing operating Companies. . . .

'He most indignantly denied any such intention, and said that our position was not only maintained, but maintained with his whole-hearted goodwill and support, and he hoped to strengthen it. He said that he wished to keep in personal touch with me, and we have arranged that we will, from time to time, meet informally.'

It was a time when personality counted for much. Personal contact and informal meeting, even so, did not stop the drift. While the bold scheme for re-equipping the Imperial Airways' fleet went forward to the admiration of other air-faring nations, criticism of every aspect of the airline increased in the home country. Was the personality of Geddes himself partly to blame for the crisis he never lived to see?

The late C. G. Grey, editor of *The Aeroplane*, at once the most candid and controversial aeronautical journalist of his day, believed that Imperial Airways' first Chairman was, in fact, responsible for much of the difficulty which came later:

> 'The cause of the present troubles of Imperial Airways Ltd. can be told in six words. It is the shadow of Sir Eric Geddes. His principle, which may have brought him to his outstanding success in the material things of life, was to build up a system of almost inhuman mechanical efficiency. And the one thing that is needed when you are dealing with such temperamental people as the pilots and crews of aeroplanes is the intimate personal touch. They need a dictator, but he must be a *Führer*, a personal leader, which Sir Eric Geddes was not.
>
> 'To the employees of Imperial Airways he was a machine to be feared rather than a human being to be loved and followed. Even many of those who admired him because of the kind of outward efficiency which he forced on to other people, could never quite bring themselves to regard him as a human being.'

Other strong personalities were emerging in British civil aviation. These have an immediate bearing on our story because they affect the destiny of Imperial Airways and contribute a good deal to the pattern that ultimately became B.O.A.C.

One of the more robust characters was Edward Henry Hillman, a motor coach operator who went into airline business in a fit of pique because the authorities had restricted his road services. His airline was formed in 1931, and started operations the following spring. For a time his fleet consisted of two-seater, three-seater and four-seater Moths. Then he became, in his own view, the designer of the de Havilland Dragon, which later developed into the famous Rapide. In the light of history, he should perhaps be described as the sponsor rather than the designer, according to the recollections of the late Captain John H. Lock, who was one of his pilots for a time:

'Though these aircraft were designed by the de Havilland Aircraft Company, Hillman always claimed that he was the designer! He said that had he not gone to de Havilland's with a specific order for six machines and with firm ideas in his head as to what he wanted, the Dragon would never have been built. It was very amusing to hear Hillman telling people how he designed the Dragon, it went something like this: "It was like this, mate. I went over to old de Havilland and I ses to him, 'look here, mate, I want an aeroplane that carries ten people, must have two of those Gipsy engines of yours,' and I draw him out a sketch of what I want, and there you are, mate, the *Dragon!*" '

Hillman was a rough diamond, a rugged hefty individualist with wild hair and a preference for working in shirt-sleeves. He greeted his pilots with the words 'Hello mate!' At first he dealt with 'tripper flights' from Romford to coastal resorts such as Clacton and Margate. Very soon, however, he developed more ambitious routes across the Channel, and to Liverpool, Glasgow and Belfast. He was most in his element on a Bank Holiday:

'I remember my being startled after my first return trip from Clacton at finding him at my elbow with a cup of steaming tea, shirt-sleeves rolled up, blue waistcoat unbuttoned [Lock wrote]. I did not once see him in anything but a blue serge suit.

' "Here you are, mate, I reckon you deserve this."

' "Thanks a lot," I said. I certainly wanted it.

'Hillman was looking very fat and red in the face: he was a victim of blood pressure, and I believe it killed him eventually, for he died from heart failure.

' "We look like being busy, don't we?" I said.

'He clapped his hands.

' "Busy's the word, mate, busy's the word. We can't keep the passengers waiting, can we? . . ." '

Hillman created a new popular approach to aviation. Just before he died, in 1934, he had a public issue. Many people of modest means who had been users of his buses subscribed for shares in the aviation enterprise. 'Most of those who subscribed were people who put their small savings in,' writes one who was subsequently a Director. 'At the Annual General Meeting it was most distressing when it had to be explained to these shareholders that the fact that they had put their money into a company did not mean that automatically they would receive dividends.' Hillman himself had taken a large block of shares which his executors subsequently had to offer for sale on behalf of the family. At the instance of Gerard d'Erlanger, these were purchased by the Banking House of Erlangers, who from that time till its amalgamation with Imperial Airways never failed to put up their proportion of whatever capital was required. The rest was supplied by Whitehall Securities through the personal interest of Clive Pearson, who later became Chairman of British Airways. During the year after Hillman's death, his Company, under the chairmanship of Ronald McCrindle, increased their Paris frequency to four daily and also operated services to Le Zoute, Brussels and Antwerp. It was one of the several independent companies operating without subsidy which by October 1935 were covering 22,000 miles of route, serving more than twenty-five centres in the British Isles and Western Europe.

Some of these services catered specially for holidaymakers, particularly on the Belgian coast. Others specialized in freight and the delivery of London newspapers. There were cuts in fares between Britain and the Continent. There was indeed a certain amount of cut-throat competition among the 'independents', most of whom were in some measure competing with Imperial Airways. In the autumn of 1935, Hillmans amalgamated with Spartan Air Lines Ltd. and United Airways Ltd. to form British Airways to which in the following year another Company which had specialized in traffic to Northern France, Holland, Belgium and Southern Sweden, British Continental Airways Ltd., added their forces.

The Managing Director of the new Company was Ronald McCrindle and one of the directors was Gerard d'Erlanger, both of whom were to appear later on the Board of the B.O.A.C. Another director was Harold Balfour, who became Under-Secretary of State for Air and afterwards Lord Balfour of Inchrye. The Company had an issued Share Capital of £363,204. The British Government had no financial interest. The shares were all held by private interests. Additional finance as required by the Company came from Whitehall Securities and Erlangers in equal proportions. Its objects, defined in the Memorandum of Association, were:

(a) To establish maintain and work lines of aerial conveyance between such places as may be from time to time selected by the Company in any parts of the world, and generally to carry on the trades of businesses of Aerodrome and Air Transport Service Proprietors:

(b) To carry on the business of carriers of passengers, troops, mails, goods, merchandise, bullion and treasure of all descriptions, whether by air, land, or water, in any part of the world.

From the time when Geddes noted the drift of his management out of official 'confidence', it seems that the Government, for a variety of reasons, including pressure from private enterprise and fear of monopoly, had already accepted the notion of a second chosen instrument. Imperial Airways, having their hands full with the immense developments of the Empire routes, were quite ready to surrender the rights mentioned in Geddes's note of 'exclusivity north of the London-Cologne-Budapest line in Europe'.

The Government was then free to subsidize the newcomer and the arrangements were duly reported in the Air Ministry Progress Report for 1936. 'In preparation for the establishment, with Government assistance, of a regular passenger and mail service between England, Holland, North Germany and Scandinavia, a preliminary experimental service was inaugurated by British Airways Ltd. on 18th February, 1936, over the route London–Amsterdam–Hamburg–Copenhagen–Malmo.'

British Airways was a strong and vigorous growth. Many felt that its independent spirit was welcome in British civil aviation. In one respect, at least, it was less inhibited than the first chosen instrument. It could buy aircraft of foreign manufacture, if it could be proved that there were no British-built aircraft available to do the job, whereas Imperial Airways was under a definite obligation to fly only British aircraft. British Airways, therefore, brought Fokker aeroplanes into their services to France and Germany during 1936. In the spring of 1937, the company began to operate German Junker aircraft on their Hanover line and American Lockheed Electras on the lines to Paris and Malmo.

The shadow of the Second World War had already fallen on Imperial Airways. Though Shorts delivered their magnificent fleet of Empire flying-boats, the Ensign landplanes ordered from Armstrong Whitworth were very late in delivery. Hitler was marching in Europe. The rearmament programme in Britain had started. There was urgent demand for warplanes. Civil aircraft came a bad second: and in Europe Imperial Airways were forced to continue to fly their well-liked comfortable, safe, but slow and obsolete Hannibals:

> 'The European services have been operating under severe handicap [Geddes told his shareholders in the last speech he made as Chairman in 1938]. New aircraft were ordered in 1934. . . . Not one was delivered in the year under review and in fact the first has only now been delivered—four years after the order. Instead, therefore, of having new aircraft, larger, faster and more comfortable than those of its competitors, the Company with its old aircraft has to compete against the new aircraft of foreign companies and of British companies using foreign aircraft.'

British Airways consolidated their European services in the latter part of the 'thirties. They operated a night service via Cologne to Hanover jointly with Deutsche Lufthansa. Their night mail to Germany flew in all conditions. No passengers were carried and this was the only regular British air service on which aircrew were provided with parachutes. Just before the outbreak of war in 1939, a daily passenger service was inaugurated between London and Warsaw via Berlin. Apart from their London–Paris service, which they ran in direct rivalry with Imperial Airways, the airline also operated a number of unsubsidized services within Britain.

Their Government subsidy in 1937 amounted to £25,000. It was increased to £73,500 for the ensuing year when the Company was entrusted with the development of a new route to Lisbon and South America. During the next two years, survey flights were made to Lisbon and West Africa: and ground surveys were made to Brazil and the Argentine. The second chosen instrument was to open up an inter-Continental air route. A London–Lisbon service was planned as a first step in 1939. It was stopped by difficulties with the Spanish Government. The Second World War altered the face of things in that sector, a story which must be left to another chapter.

For British civil aviation 1937 looked good. British Airways was well on its feet, and Imperial Airways was making a higher profit and increasing dividends. Yet the situation, with these two chosen instruments, was somewhat bizarre. In his essay on nationalization the late John Longhurst, a protagonist of private enterprise, described it in this way:

'Modification of the Government's "chosen instrument" policy by the subsidization of the new British Airways Ltd. to run a number of services to European capitals, was made on the recommendation of the Government inter-departmental Warren-Fisher Committee, which decided in 1936 that Imperial Airways had enough on its hands and that at least in Europe a second British company should operate, if necessary with subsidy. The growth of British Airways was a welcome sign that private enterprise was taking more interest in the possibilities of developing the industry, and the Government appreciated the need for adopting a less restrictive approach to the subject. Though no one has ever explained why subsidized Imperial Airways was restricted and subsidized British Airways was virtually unrestricted in its purchase of foreign aircraft, the event certainly served to underline the advantages of truly free enterprise. Incidentally, the Government, in subsidizing British Airways and allowing it to take away Imperial Airways' traffic, was losing money with both hands. A peculiarly un-Treasury-like procedure.'

In the House of Commons a Conservative Member, W. R. D. Perkins, referred to the London–Paris services as a 'Gilbertian situation of two British airlines, both subsidized by the Government, competing with each other, cutting each other's throat, on the same route.' That remark, with which so many men in the business agreed, was but a particle in the dust storms of controversy and criticism which enveloped civil aviation in general, and Imperial Airways in particular, during 1937. Comment came from all sides of the House. It was not confined to policy or to technical matters. Personalities and individual actions were criticized. No airline, and indeed few if any public services, have ever been subjected to such many-sided attacks.

For instance, in June 1938, after a Government Committee had passed highly critical comments on the organization of Imperial Airways, F. Montague, Labour Member for Islington, formerly Under-Secretary of State for Air and afterwards Lord Amwell, brought remarkable charges in the House. He alleged that an overseas operating manager of Imperial Airways had been excluded from seventeen clubs for drunkenness and for insulting the wives of pilots. He went on to suggest that this man had attempted to force his way into the bedroom of the wife of one of the pilots. 'That person continually wrote adverse reports on pilots. These reports were accepted without any question and the demand of the pilots to see them was refused.'

Such unsavoury charges were never in fact proved. In April 1939 the Air Minister said in the House that they were investigated 'in great detail, and have not been substantiated'. They are mentioned here simply as an example of the degree of public criticism to which the foremost British airline has been subjected in the course of its history. No other major airline in the world has had to contend with the same degree of Parliamentary and public interference in the day to day running of its affairs—with such damage to international prestige.

Another charge made by Montague at the time concerned an alleged statement by a high official of Imperial Airways that if trade union practice came in, he would get out. On being pressed by Mr. Aneurin Bevan to name the individual, Montague stated that it was Brackley.

The row in the House really started over the discharge by Imperial Airways of a number of pilots and aircrew, including the Chairman and Vice-Chairman of the newly-formed British Air Line Pilots' Association. Woods Humphery, as Managing Director, denied the alleged victimization, but, amid a great deal of publicity, the charges developed into a general indictment of the whole of the affairs of Imperial Airways. It was alleged that there was grave dissatisfaction among pilots, that the Company was doing everything in its power to break their union, that wages had been cut at a time when directors' fees were being increased, that the equipment was not good enough. Perkins, who was at that time a Vice-President of the Association, said: 'Imperial Airways service in Europe is the laughing stock of the world and the Paris services are operated by obsolete aircraft.'

Geddes's chairmanship of Dunlops was implicated in a charge that Imperial Airways had not used a de-icer made by the rival Goodrich Rubber Company. Brabazon, then a Conservative M.P., referred to the ordering of the flying-boats from Shorts as 'a great gamble'. From the Labour benches, Montague inferred that pilots were forced against their better judgement to fly under conditions that they considered unsuitable. Mander, from the Liberal benches, stated that the Company had refused for eight years to recognize an organization representing Wireless Operators. Other critics denounced the whole system by which a company receiving a State subsidy was paying out increased dividends to the shareholders. Imperial Airways met the attacks with reasoned answers and explanations on these and many other issues that were raised. Yet, as Longhurst has it, 'a comparatively innocent squib developed into a conflagration'. The Government accepted the need for an inquiry and set up a small Committee under the Chairmanship of Lord Cadman of the Anglo-Iranian Oil Company.

At that time the name of Imperial Airways stood high in the world not only in the minds of the airfaring public but in the opinions of other airline operators. The Company already had an unparalleled record of achievement in every field of civil aviation. It had entered a phase of rapid expansion at a time when its every move was hampered by the rearmament programme. A scattered but devoted staff in the air and on the ground, who had grown up with the organization, viewed with dismay the mounting scale of hostile criticism. Geddes had died, and was succeeded as part-time Chairman by Sir George Beharrell. Without Geddes, the major responsibility not only for running the airline but for meeting public criticism lay with the Managing Director, George Woods Humphery, who was described even by such a candid critic as C. G. Grey as having 'more influence on the continent of Europe today than any man in Air Transport, and probably more than any but a few of our political people'. Such was the position when the Cadman Committee went to work. Its recommendations, published in March 1938, affected the whole field of civil aviation.

The Committee said that the Department of Civil Aviation should play a much more important part in 'the initiation of policy and in forward planning', and foreshadowed the creation of a Ministry of Civil Aviation seven years later. Another recommendation was for State assistance to the aircraft industry for the promotion of civil machines, with liberal financial aid for research. On the financial side, the Committee wanted the subsidies to British air transport operators doubled.

Imperial Airways were to concentrate on the Empire routes and

British Airways should in general develop European services. To avoid indiscriminate competition the same external routes were not to be operated by more than one United Kingdom company. The London–Paris services of the two companies were to be run by a joint organization.

Comment upon the management was outspoken.

'We particularly stress the appointment of a whole-time chairman, because apart from any directorial duties which will fall to him, close personal intervention on his part is immediately necessary to restore the mutual confidence and goodwill which have been seriously prejudiced but are essentials in the relations of the management to Government Departments, the Company's staff and outside organizations.' More detailed criticism followed.

'Although the carriage of air passengers in safety and comfort and the conveyance of mails and freight have been achieved by Imperial Airways with considerable efficiency, we cannot avoid the conclusion that the management of Imperial Airways has been defective in other respects, in particular not only has it failed to co-operate fully with the Air Ministry but it has been intolerant of suggestion and unyielding in negotiation. Internally its attitude in staff matters has left much to be desired.

'It appears to us that the Managing Director of the Company, presumably with the acquiescence of the Board, has taken a commercial view of his responsibility that was too narrow and has failed to give the Government Departments with which he has been concerned the co-operation we should have expected from a company heavily subsidized and having such important international and imperial contacts.

'There should, in our opinion, be an immediate improvement in these respects and this may well involve some change in direction of personnel.'

The Company defended their General Manager and their own record in a circular letter to shareholders.

'. . . Mr. Woods Humphery has been condemned by the Committee as above without having an opportunity of saying a word in his defence on the matters in question. . . .

'The Report states that the considerable increase during the last two or three years in the number of pilots and other operating personnel is rendering personal contact between employer and employee ineffective for the adjustment of grievances and recommends that personal contact be now supplemented by collective representations of employees. The Report after drawing attention to the fact that your Company had stated that it had no objection to "collective bargaining" points out that it is essential that any organization formed with those objects should be in a position to negotiate authoritatively on behalf of a substantial proportion of the class it claims to represent. This is the principle upon which your Company has acted in the past and in fact your Company had adopted collective bargaining in regard to one of its groups of employees a considerable time before the Cadman Committee was appointed. Unfortunately there have been rival associations claiming to represent certain groups of the staff.

'. . . There is the bald statement that your Company is operating in Europe with obsolete aircraft. This is entirely beyond the control of your Company and it is to be regretted that no explanation as to why obsolete aircraft are running on certain European services is given, although evidence as to the causes was tendered fully before the Committee, and no reference whatever is made to the fact that for over 90 per cent of the routes operated by your Company, the services are maintained almost entirely by the most up-to-date flying boats in the world. . . . There was no lack of foresight on the part of the Board in this matter, for in 1934 an order was placed with an important British Company for twelve large landplanes, comparable in every way with the Flying Boats which are now so successfully operating the Empire Routes. The first of these landplanes was due for delivery in September 1936, but in spite of the efforts made by the Air Ministry and your Company not one of these has yet been delivered. . . .'

The Government of the day, which was Conservative, was itself not unaffected by the wider criticisms implied in the Report. The Air Minister, Lord Swinton, was succeeded by Sir Kingsley Wood, a change which had some bearing on the choice of the last Chairman of Imperial Airways. The recommended increase of subsidy to three million pounds a year went through. The Government also began by accepting the principle that Imperial Airways and British Airways should work in separate orbits. Then in November 1938 it decided that the two airlines should be merged into a single public corporation, obtaining their funds by the issue of fixed interest stock guaranteed by the Treasury. This merger, which created B.O.A.C., was subject to an Act of Parliament which received Royal Assent only a month before the outbreak of the Second World War in 1939.

There are former members of the staff of Imperial Airways, who are still serving B.O.A.C., who regard the Cadman recommendations as censorious and punitive. After their publication, there were more debates in Parliament during which charges were made against the organization as a whole which were regarded by people in the business as being not only discouraging but irresponsible and damaging to British prestige overseas. Throughout the rumpus, Imperial Airways—as if there were nothing wrong behind the scenes—continued to run the world's greatest inter-continental airline, a matter of vital importance to the British Empire then on the brink of war. If feeling in Parliament ran high, it ran much higher among the staff of Imperial Airways. People were bewildered and angry by the stigma which they felt had been placed upon a public service of which they had every reason to be proud. The Chairman of the Captains' Committee for instance wrote to the Chairman of the Board after a meeting held to discuss the Report:

> 'As a result of our Meeting, the views of all serving Captains were sought and it is on behalf of my Committee and the Captains that I am writing to express their unanimous satisfaction in the Management of Imperial Airways, with particular reference to the Managing Director, who has been subject, in their opinion, to unwarranted criticism by the Committee of Inquiry.
>
> 'Indeed they are glad if there have been times when the Management have been intolerant of suggestion and unyielding in negotiation with the Air Ministry, which is considered by the Committee of Inquiry to be lacking in virility and in the initiation of policy and forward planning with regard to both the development of new routes and suitable aircraft.
>
> 'The Captains, in particular those who have served since the inception of the Company, greatly regret the decision to disassociate the Company from the European services which have been, to some extent, built up by the pilots' efforts;

> nevertheless, in whatever sphere they may be called upon to serve, they wish to assure the Board of their continued unswerving loyalty and goodwill, and they feel that in so doing they are expressing the views of the whole of the Company's staff.'

The Chairman of Imperial Airways was, of course, affected by the Cadman recommendations. Beharrell had succeeded Geddes as Chairman of Dunlops. As a part-timer he therefore qualified for replacement. The irrepressible C. G. Grey had ideas with which many were in sympathy:

> 'Precisely what is the difference in function between a full-time Chairman and a Managing Director I cannot imagine. My idea of a Chairman is a Director who comes to a Board meeting, swings a bit more influence than the other Directors do, and goes away. But a full-time Chairman must be much the same thing as a Managing Director. That is to say he is the Director who does the managing. So the best thing to do would be to make George Woods Humphery full-time Chairman and let the Board then find a couple of other full-time Directors. The great thing is to find some way of taking some of the work off his shoulders. But, quite definitely, his resignation would be the very worst thing that could happen for Imperial Airways Ltd. and for British civil aviation.'

No such promotion seems to have received serious consideration outside the lively mind of C. G. Grey. A new figure, unconnected with aviation, but by a curious chance personally associated with the early life of Woods Humphery, entered the scene at this point. J. C. W. Reith had built up British broadcasting from scratch. As Sir John Reith he found himself Director General of the new form of public corporation—the B.B.C. which became the model and envy of the whole world. His organizing spirit was restless. Years later, as Lord Reith, he told, with a good deal of candour, his own story of his entry at top level into civil aviation. A writer of fiction would hardly dare to invent the coincidence of his personal association with Woods Humphery. It would seem far-fetched were it not true that these two men who now came into conflict had sat next to each other as apprentice engineers in a drawing office in Glasgow. Woods Humphery, moreover, became a member of Reith's father's church. When he was married there by Reith Senior, John Reith was 'urgently summoned to function as best man'. They lunched together occasionally in after years when, in the words of Reith 'our respective roads had led to peculiar but comparable heights'. In those days of more or less casual contact, Reith observed that Woods Humphery had a slightly envious regard for the B.B.C. but an even stronger sense of his own duty towards the Imperial Airways shareholders.

The conflicts between the two of them were fundamental. Reith himself expressed this as a contrast between the 'dividends motive and public services motive'. When it came to their outlook on Imperial Airways, there was the basic difference between one who cared greatly for something which was his life-work and one who saw just another job to which he would devote his duty, which he regarded as one of almost ruthless reconstruction.

Some months before the Cadman findings, Reith recorded an uneasy interview with Woods Humphery.

> 'In the autumn he came twice to see me. Though he said nothing about it, I was sure on the second occasion in mid-November that he had heard of the possibility of my being asked to go to Imperial Airways. He went so far as to tell me that he could not possibly have a full-time chairman; there would not be nearly enough for him to do. He was, in fact, booming me off. But it was unnecessary, I had no desire to go there. Even if the idea had been attractive otherwise, we were not likely to get on together; his ideas and mine were radically different and I could not have contemplated putting an old friend out of a concern which was largely of his own creation. I reminded him of what I had often urged on him before; for I knew what he did not—that a government committee would soon be appointed to investigate his company and his management.'

When the Report was published, Reith's view was that Woods Humphery 'might either resign of his own volition or be asked to do so'. Three months after its publication, Woods Humphery went to see him again 'and this time it was obvious that he had heard I might be offered the chairmanship. He told me what the chairman should do and should not do; the chairman's first responsibility was to the shareholders; he had to serve them, no one and nothing else. He was surely trying to boom me off.'

Neville Chamberlain's Government, reeling from crisis to crisis during the last year of uneasy peace, was, in fact, having some difficulty in finding a full-time Chairman for Imperial Airways. That in itself was surely symptomatic of the gross neglect of civil aviation by the State for nearly two decades. The full-time chairmanship of Britain's main trunk airline was regarded by many as a lesser office. Reith, for instance, made no bones about this. In the light of his ambitions, he saw such a job as something of a step-down from the B.B.C. Broadcasting had a shorter history than civil aviation. Yet because it had been integrated as a monopoly by the Government of the country while retaining creative independence it carried greater prestige than the British Merchant Air Service. Reith made it clear from the start that he wanted and deserved a more stimulating job than the running of Imperial Airways.

That he wanted some job was never in question. From King George VI downwards it was known to everybody that Reith, having built the B.B.C., was restless at having too little to do. He was also being criticized by supporters of Neville Chamberlain, who felt that he carried impartiality in broadcasting too far. Sir Kingsley Wood, who as Postmaster General had been associated with him at the B.B.C. and had good reason to revere his managerial qualities, became Air Minister. Sir Horace Wilson, who had been described by some, including Reith, as the *alter ego* of the Prime Minister, became the spokesman of the Government in its insistence that Reith should go to the airline. On June 3, 1938 Reith, who had a number of other irons in the fire, was forced to the point with a request to visit Wilson.

'It was as feared. The Prime Minister and the Secretary of State for Air had authorized him to "instruct me to go to Imperial Airways—tomorrow if possible". A full-time job; no other interests at all. Chamberlain and Kingsley Wood had seen Beharrell at noon that day and told him I must be made chairman; the rest was for me to settle with Beharrell; and Beharrell was expecting me in his office now. Woods Humphery, Wilson said, must go; I should insist on that.

'That was how it was put to me. They had taken a lot for granted; I said so to Wilson. He replied that I had made it very clear that I had not enough to do in the B.B.C. and wanted to be busy; this would make me busy. Quite true. But I had never been asked if I would go to Imperial Airways. Nor, however, had I ever said I would not. I had listened to Fisher and Wilson talking about it and, in default of any flat refusal, acquiescence had been assumed; now the whole matter had been arranged. I definitely did not want to go to Imperial Airways. I realized its importance, immediate and potential; was not disturbed by my ignorance of air transport. It was just not the sort of thing I wanted, particularly with the Woods Humphery complication; and now, worst of all, it would mean leaving the B.B.C. altogether.'

On the same day, Reith met Beharrell at the Athenaeum Club—not the most likely spot at which to form the destinies of British civil aviation.

'I asked why he and his Board had accepted the Cadman recommendation about a full-time chairman, but there was no answer. I inquired about Woods Humphery and was told that he was certainly staying on; the Board could not contemplate him leaving. I asked Beharrell to face up to the situation: the post I was going to was that of full-time, executive chairman, that is chairman and managing director; but there was a managing director already who, according to him, must stay. He replied that there would need to be some allocation of work between Woods Humphery and me. I told him there could be no restriction of my authority if I went there; I would not be content with what any official decided to refer to me; how would he feel himself in such a position? He said he certainly would not like it; most invidious. When he inquired what my answer was I said he could provide the answer himself; the whole situation was distasteful and embarrassing to me, especially as I had known Woods Humphery for so long. When he asked what salary would be required, I said I was getting £10,000 from the B.B.C. and would not require any increase on that. He "thought they might be able to go to that figure but no more". He did not mention that Woods Humphery was already getting £7,000 plus £1,500 expense allowance, and that if he had still been there in September he would have had £10,000 plus £1,500. There was a B.B.C. Toscanini concert in Queen's Hall that Friday night which I had meant to attend; did not; went home feeling utterly miserable.'

Toscanini was denied the company of Reith in the doomed Queen's Hall and Imperial Airways had the great man thrust upon them. His personal impact upon British civil aviation might have had prodigious long-term results but for the war which was just round the corner. As it was, his first impact was melancholy.

'I was brought to the door of an old furniture depository behind Victoria Station. It was Imperial Airways; a plate on the wall said so. Inside were some counters, luggage on the floor, a few people standing about—a booking office evidently. I inquired of a young man behind one of the counters where the head office was. He pointed to a dark and narrow staircase; up there, he said. The Managing Director's office: Second floor he thought. Having ascended thither I went along a passage, also dark and narrow, between wooden partitions, peering at the doors and wondering which to try first. Here it was—a bit of paper with "Managing Director" written thereon. From Broadcasting House to this.

'And the first decision demanded of me was an indication of what had happened to me otherwise. Would I approve the expenditure of £238 on passengers' lavatories at Croydon? I inquired politely if such a matter and such a sum had in the past required the approval of the Managing Director personally. Yes, indeed. It seemed I was to work in very low gear; I doubted my capacity. A few minutes earlier I had made a courteous signal to Woods Humphery on coming aboard. If he had not gone I should have been tempted to tell him of this unexpected strain on my mechanism.'

It was inevitable that Woods Humphery should go. Air Minister Kingsley Wood made the announcement: 'In view of the fact that the appointment of a whole time chairman must obviously carry with it the position of chief executive of the Company, the present Managing Director, Mr. Woods Humphery, has placed his resignation in the hands of the Board.'

With Reith as Chairman and Managing Director, there could be no position for Woods Humphery on the Board. Reith was willing for him to continue as General Manager without a seat on the Board, which, for a man of Woods Humphery's record and ability, would clearly have been intolerable. What happened was the disappearance of Woods Humphery from Imperial Airways and indeed from Britain. He went right out of the whole business to reappear, as we shall see later, only for the duration, in the war story of B.O.A.C.

Reith observed: 'When I left the B.B.C. no one need have noticed it. Without Woods Humphery no one in Imperial Airways knew where they were.' He added a sting to the tail of this comment: 'In later years these conversations seemed to pass from his mind; he accused me of smashing up his organization—the organization which, in fact, I had not been able to find.'

The organization was not perhaps keeping up with the physical expansion of the airline. It may have needed overhaul. It could hardly have been so elusive, however, when considered in the terms of day-to-day operation. At that time Imperial Airways was concerned with one hundred and eleven stations all over the world—in East, South, West Africa, Sudan and Egypt, Palestine, Iraq and Iran, India, Burma, Malaya, Indo-China, Hong Kong, Europe and the West Atlantic. There were eight associated companies, twelve subsidiaries. There were 77 aircraft. There was a staff of more than 3,600—about the same as the B.B.C. Many of these resented Woods Humphery's departure. Cables from staff in all parts of the world poured in. A telegram was drafted at a meeting in the Café Monico in London to every engineer on the routes calling for a twenty-four hour strike as a protest. It was not sent as it would have brought every aircraft on the Empire routes to a standstill and caused world-wide inconvenience to passengers who could not be expected to be aware of the issues involved.

Uneasiness was not, however, limited to the Company's staff. Hudson Fysh of Qantas cabled: 'Resignation Woods Humphery at this stage inauguration Empire Air Services fantastic and feel unacceptable to all interested in Australia. Do hope British stability will prevail.'

Imperial Airways was continuing to make history overseas and was indeed creating the last inter-continental link, between Europe and America, which is discussed in the next chapter. Its destiny as an organization was being decided in the in- and out-trays of a Whitehall obsessed by rearmament and in the strong managerial hands of Reith, the organization expert who admitted that he knew nothing of aviation, but knew everything about public corporations. His predecessors who had run the chosen instrument had had to think of shareholders. In November 1938, Reith thought differently.

'Here I was face to face with . . . the need to please the hundred or so shareholders assembled on that occasion by announcing a large dividend. They had 7 per cent, and I felt they should be well content though they had had 9 per cent before. The year under review had ended before my advent, but that did not matter. I gave them the usual sort of statistics; explained that the Company was already severely hampered, and would be still more hampered in future, by shortage of aircraft and by shockingly late deliveries; it was operating aircraft that in normal circumstances would long since have been replaced. I questioned, in the circumstances, the Company's policy of using only aircraft and engines designed and built by British manufacturers.'

Significantly, he went on:

'Actuated therefore by no political prejudice or predilection but by straightforward considerations of efficiency, I had felt a non-commercial constitution was necessary for civil aviation, particularly as it required State support. The present position was neither commercially nor constitutionally satisfactory; the Company neither wholly free nor wholly secure.'

The outcome of this was the merger between Imperial Airways and British Airways to form a single Corporation.

Step by step Reith and the Conservative Government welded and moulded the two chosen instruments. The transition from private enterprise to State control was accelerated by the outbreak of war, when both Companies under their subsidy agreements placed their aircraft and equipment at the disposal of the State. The 'Appointed Day' for the new Corporation to take over the two concerns was April 1, 1940, which thus became the date of birth of B.O.A.C.

This was not effected without some reshuffling. Brackley, for instance, who had been Air Superintendent since he was called in to solve the pilots' strike in 1924, was moved. A new post of Operations Manager had been created: and Brackley soon went off to make a survey across the Sahara, through Central Africa and along the West African Coast—an important mission, as it turned out soon afterwards when the Second World War closed the Mediterranean.

New people were brought in. One of Reith's early appointments was that of the Hon. W. L. Runciman, who eventually took up the newly created post of Director General, the title which Reith himself had held at the B.B.C. Runciman became one of the first members of the new Board, with the Hon. Clive Pearson, the former Chairman of British Airways, serving as Deputy Chairman and I. C. Geddes, who was in shipping, Harold C. Brown and a future Chairman of B.O.A.C., Sir Gerard d'Erlanger. Reith also created two Assistant Directors General, one for the eastern hemisphere, to which Colonel H. Burchall of Imperial Airways was appointed, and one for the western hemisphere to which Major J. R. McCrindle of British Airways was appointed. 'The basic principle of organization was, as in the B.B.C.,' wrote Reith, 'functionalism tempered by a considerable measure of regionalism.'

The British Government paid £262,500 for British Airways. For Imperial Airways the figure agreed was £2,659,086. Since the shares which British Airways owned in internal companies were not included, the price worked out that their shareholders had 15s. 9d. for each £1 share. The stockholders of Imperial Airways received 32s. 9d. for each £1 share, which was considered by Reith as being 'fair-to-generous'.

Thus these two Companies, the younger and the older, which had carried the flag of the British Merchant Air Service throughout the world, came to an end. A new phase of public enterprise began, only to be stunted at birth by the Second World War. The change was born of expediency. It grew from neglect, since the end of the First World War, by successive Governments of the great potential of the British Merchant Air Service. Many loyalties were taxed by the manner rather than the fact of this change. Parliamentary debate, newspaper publicity and the strong language of the Cadman Report had not only done much damage overseas but had struck at the confidence of the men on the job. Long afterwards there lingered the feeling that much of the criticism had been ill-directed and unfair—and that some of the mud, unjustly, had stuck. Time might have cured these feelings: for the new set-up was starting with far greater resources in money and with a new status in its Government support and with the undoubted capacities of Reith.

But money, status, and a less critical atmosphere came too

late. B.O.A.C. was already at war at the time of its birth. Before exploring the war record, we must return to deal with one of the last but most significant of the efforts of Imperial Airways—the laying of the foundations of the air bridge across the Atlantic.

CHAPTER IX

ATLANTIC BRIDGE

THE air crossing of the Atlantic was a project which came early into men's minds. Slightly less than ten years after the first aeroplane flew over the sand dunes at Kitty Hawk, Lord Northcliffe was offering a £10,000 prize to 'the first person who crosses the Atlantic from any point in the United States, Canada or Newfoundland to any point in Great Britain or Ireland in 72 continuous hours'. This offer, published in the *Daily Mail* in April 1913, startled the world and was, of course, ridiculed by many as a stunt.

Before the First World War, nevertheless, two serious attempts were actually planned. In Britain the famous pioneer pilot Gustav Hamel, with private backing, commissioned a special monoplane from Martinsyde. It was to be fitted with an undercarriage which would be jettisoned after take-off (an idea adopted by Hawker and Grieve when they made their Atlantic attempt in 1919), special buoyancy tanks for keeping afloat in the sea and a telescopic mast for signalling to ships in case of a forced landing. Only the sudden death of Hamel himself stopped the plan. In America, a British pilot, J. C. Porte, was engaged by the millionaire store owner, Rodman Wanamaker, to make an attempt in a Curtiss flying-boat. Porte made a series of successful test flights and was about to start for Newfoundland when it was found that his flying-boat would not take off with the full load of fuel needed for the crossing. Then, with the outbreak of the First World War, came the suspension of all thoughts of an Atlantic crossing and, of course, the withdrawal of the Northcliffe offer.

That war led to an appreciable increase in the power and range of aircraft. Even before it was over, indeed in its darkest days

in 1918, Lord Northcliffe renewed his offer, in order to stimulate the production of more powerful engines and more suitable aircraft'. Alcock and Brown in a converted Vickers Vimy bomber won his £10,000 prize with the first non-stop flight in June 1919. The British dirigible R 34 made a two-way crossing three weeks later. The Americans had made the first crossing in stages a little earlier. Lieutenant Commander Read flew the flying boat *Liberty* across in May 1919. They also made the first east to west crossing by single aircraft in 1924, using Iceland, Greenland and Labrador as staging posts. For almost two decades it was regarded—justly—as a heroic feat to cross the Atlantic by air. Charles Lindbergh, more than any other, appealed to the public imagination because he flew alone in a single-engined machine. Today we take Atlantic flight by jet airliner for granted. As in any suburban train, the occupant of the next seat in a Comet may be somebody's grandmother aged eighty or somebody's grandchild aged six. Forty years after the first flight of British civil aviation, there were some B.O.A.C. Captains who had flown the North Atlantic over six hundred times and B.O.A.C. aircraft were making regular flights across fifty times a week in each direction.

What we take for granted now may well seem nursery stuff to a future generation: but it has been won the hard way. Desperate expediencies in the Second World War accelerated the general use of the North Atlantic air—and this was an achievement in which British and Commonwealth airmen excelled. Something of their story will be told in the next chapter. Its foundations go back to the 'thirties. They were international: they were built on goodwill between nations in spite of the fact that the North Atlantic crossing by sea as well as by air had already aroused the keenest competition between nations. Individual record-breakers brought honour to their countries, to themselves and to their aircraft constructors. Their achievements were important. Nevertheless there was a great gap between a specially prepared and always risky individual flight with little or no ground organization and a scheduled air service. This could be closed by international co-operation, by a completely integrated ground organization, and above all by a deep study of weather conditions carried out by every nation involved.

In 1930 Woods Humphery and a Pan-American Airways representative, went to the Azores for talks with Aeropostale, one of the four French operating companies. They contemplated a southerly crossing of the Atlantic through the Azores and Bermuda, where the British Colonial administration was already awakened to the possibilities of an air link with New York. Nothing came of these talks at the time. Horta was used as a flying-boat base later, but it was never considered satisfactory even in summer. The southerly route was used in after years, particularly during the war, by landplanes.

The Atlantic bridge first took shape at a conference in Ottawa in 1935 attended by delegates from Britain, Canada, the Irish Free State and Newfoundland. As soon as they reached basic agreement they went on to Washington where an understanding was reached based on the principle of full reciprocity, which it was hoped would lead to the early establishment of a transatlantic air service connecting all participants.

Foynes, on the River Shannon in Ireland, close to Shannon Airport, once familiar to so many transatlantic passengers, was chosen as the eastern terminus, to be staffed by weather men provided by the British Air Ministry. The western station at Botwood in Newfoundland was run by the government of that country. The Canadian Department of Transport provided a flying-boat base for Montreal at Boucherville, with control, radio and navigational aids at St. Hubert airfield some two miles away.

At these three points the staff and equipment were installed late in 1935 and calibration of direction-finding apparatus was continued throughout that winter. Study of the North Atlantic weather was conscientiously and indeed adventurously carried out. Some of the men wintered at out-stations in Newfoundland. A British Air Ministry observer spent months travelling to and fro across the Atlantic on the s.s. *Manchester Port*, measuring winds and gathering data on clouds. Two weather zones were mapped out: the westerly allotted to the meteorologists of Newfoundland and Canada; the easterly to the British staff at Foynes. After all this work had been collated on both sides of the Atlantic, and it was believed that a good idea of the weather could be depicted, more than a year elapsed before agreements were finalized and official permits granted which secured for

Imperial Airways and Pan-American Airways the right to use certain airports.

The first survey flights provided an imaginative essay in Anglo-American goodwill and co-operation. The Pan-American Airways' flying-boat *Clipper III* took off from Botwood punctually at 2100 hours G.M.T. on July 5, 1937. Imperial Airways' flying-boat *Caledonia* took off from Foynes at 1800 hours on the same day. The flights were to be simultaneous and the differences in take-off times had been arranged to make allowances for the prevailing wind which favoured the Americans on the first crossing. It all went according to plan. *Clipper III* duly alighted at Foynes and then flew on to Southampton. *Caledonia* alighted at Botwood and flew on to Montreal and New York. Both aircraft then completed the round trip, returning to their respective countries, the whole operation having been carried out, according to the official report, 'without mishap and indeed almost without incident'.

It was a success which owed much to ground organization and training, as Captain Wilcockson, who commanded *Caledonia*, emphasized afterwards. Not only had these flights required the building and operation of airfields, flying-boat bases, radio and meteorological stations throughout a vast area, but also the co-operation, arranged by the British G.P.O., of shipping on the North Atlantic run. The training of the crews themselves was of great importance. International law, for instance, required a first-class navigator to be carried on any aircraft on a flight exceeding 600 miles over water. This called for a knowledge of celestial navigation and a special class had to be started at Imperial Airways School at Croydon. 'Several of us attended the school for eight or nine months. . . . Some months were then spent on the routes, getting experience on the "C" Class flying-boats and practising practical navigation.' The crew for this first commercial survey flight consisted of a Captain, First Officer and two Radio Officers, the latter being on duty during the whole of the flight, 'one being able to check on the other'.

Scattered among the facts and technicalities of Wilcockson's account of his crossing are some nice human touches. It was raining hard, for instance, when they gathered on the jetty ready to board *Caledonia*, 'not at all the sort of night that one would choose for a jaunt of this description'. Nevertheless

President de Valera himself and a large crowd of people waited in the rain to witness the departure. When they passed Loop Head just after seven on that inclement July evening,

'It was to be our last sight of land for two thousand miles, but I can honestly say that we all experienced a certain sense of relief to see it disappear in the rain, and know that we had finished with the waiting and preparations. . . . There is a distinct easing of the tension when one actually gets into the air and can settle down to the routine work on the aircraft. Other worries naturally occur on a flight of this description, but they seldom assume the proportions of the imaginary ones previous to starting.'

They spoke by radio to shipping, but only twice was their Atlantic loneliness broken by the sight of vessels.

'At midnight we sighted a ship's lights on our starboard bow. I told my Radio Officers to try and contact with him if it were possible, as his position would have been extremely useful to us as a definite check on our navigation. We had at this time been flying for five hours without a sight of the sky, and although we were satisfied that our D.R. navigation was correct, a definite fix from a surface vessel would have cheered us up immensely. Some time passed without a reply and finally we had to return to our radio schedule without contact having been made. It seems strange that with all the help given us by shipping on this trip, the only two vessels sighted gave us no help at all.'

For many long hours even the celestial sky was denied them.

'At 3.26 we obtained our first sight of the sky since leaving Ireland; it was only a brief glimpse, but it gave my First Officer and me time to get our sextants and obtain a run of sights on two stars which happened to be in ideal positions; one was the planet Jupiter and the other the bright star Arcturus; they gave us an accurate latitude and longitude.'

Their arrival was a historic occasion in transatlantic aviation, but there were no heroics.

'At 9.15 a.m. we obtained our first sight of land about 25 miles distant. Twelve minutes later at 9.27 a.m. we crossed the coast at a point which we identified as Cobbler's Island about six miles south of our plotted track. We were now flying very low and received quite a welcome from the fishermen of the village over which we passed. . . . At 10.03 a.m. we arrived over Botwood. After circling the town we landed on the Bay of Exploits at 10.08 a.m., having accomplished the first scheduled Atlantic crossing in 15 hours 10 minutes; this was 50 minutes less than the estimated time. . . . Our flights from Botwood to Montreal, New York and back to Botwood were more or less routine. . . .'

That year *Clipper III* carried out two more round trips, one of which was made on the southern route by way of Bermuda and the Azores. *Caledonia* and her sister aircraft *Cambria*, under the command of Captain Powell, made four more round trips between July and September, the latter making the record run of 10 hours 36 minutes homeward bound. There was considerable public enthusiasm for these first survey crossings, and *Caledonia* made a three-day flight round the coasts of Britain visiting seaside resorts, where she was seen by thousands who had followed the reports of the Atlantic flights.

Shipping in the Atlantic continued to offer human contact during these long experimental flights. Of a flight of his in August Captain Wilcockson wrote:

'On our way out we had met the Captain of the s.s. *Geraldine Mary* at Botwood; he was leaving for London on the Tuesday, 17th; we were leaving at 9 a.m. for New York. I asked him for his probable position at midnight on the Friday when we hoped to be making our return crossing over from Botwood to Foynes. After a few minutes with a chart he estimated that his position would be about 30° W. or approximately in mid-Atlantic. I told him I would see him there some time after midnight; he was rather sceptical but promised to be on watch and we had a drink on the strength of it. We actually passed directly over him at 04.00, his position being 29° 38′ W., or 22 miles from his estimated position he had given us before leaving. We switched on our wing searchlight which was answered by a white flare from the *Geraldine Mary*, "whose passengers had stayed up in the hope of seeing us pass over".'

But these shipping contacts were sometimes more sociable than useful. On his next flight:

'We were about 500 miles out from Newfoundland and made contact with a Norwegian ship. We asked him for his position and told him we wanted a bearing. His reply rather shook us: it was "Will you first send a private message to Oslo free of charge?" We felt stumped for a minute but as I rather wanted the bearing, I asked my Radio Officer to try again. After a lot of explanation we finally got our bearing. The only thing necessary now was his position to enable us to plot the bearing on our chart. There was another long wait but at last our patience was rewarded; my Radio Officer passed the message with a large grin; the position given was "500 miles from Cape Race". As far as we were concerned, it might just as well have been "somewhere in the Atlantic".'

Two years later, when the Second World War imposed radio silence on shipping and aircraft alike, no doubt everyone concerned looked back on even that conversation with a certain amount of nostalgia.

At the present time B.O.A.C. employ a staff of more than 1,100 in their North American offices and stations. Headquarters in New York and Montreal are administratively responsible, within their respective areas, for the scheduled services in and out of New York and Montreal, on the North Atlantic, the trunk line across the United States and the services to Bermuda and the Caribbean. They also administer the wide and energetic network of Sales Offices throughout the Continent. This is by far the largest overseas commitment of B.O.A.C. and it is largely the creation of the post-war years. Before continuing the story of the pre-war experimental flights across the Atlantic, something must be told of the beginnings of this organization on the other side.

Daimler Hire opened an office in New York in 1922. It was primarily concerned with the hire of automobiles to Americans visiting Europe. Such travelling Americans were also among the most eager early supporters of the cross-Channel air services. In 1929, by which time Imperial Airways had taken over the air interests of Daimler Hire, Paul Bewshea, now Sales Adviser, North America, was sent to New York to represent jointly the air interests of Imperial Airways and the automobile hire business of Daimler Hire. It is not without interest that Bewshea's background was not in aviation. Geddes, in making the appointment, stressed his need not for a flying man but rather one whose approach was that of an experienced traveller who could sell the virtues of air travel as an enthusiastic layman. Working alone from a small office in the Plaza Hotel, Bewshea sold seats on

Imperial Airways flights between London, Paris and Cologne in the early days, and later on the Empire services. He worked very closely with the pursers of ships leaving New York with tourists for Europe. At a later stage, just before the war, the Cunard Company took over the whole of the sales representation.

Apart from actual sales, however, the prestige of the British Merchant Air Service in North America has always counted for much, and this also came within Bewshea's orbit during the pre-war years. The first flight of the *Caledonia*, so tersely described by Wilcockson, was an occasion where prestige was a deservedly important element. It was Bewshea's task, of course, to make arrangements for the arrival of the *Caledonia* in New York.

> 'Wilkie got me on the telephone from Montreal in the morning and . . . asked me what I wanted him to do. I told him when he got to the George Washington Bridge to hold back as much as possible to give the flying photographers a chance to get some good pictures. I remember Wilkie saying "How do I know where the George Washington Bridge is?" and I told him to get a map. Also I mentioned to him it was very hot and humid in New York and he had better come in tropical uniforms, whereupon he informed me they only had the heavy winter blues.'

Caledonia duly alighted at Port Washington and the Americans were so enthusiastic that the coastguards put a cutter at the disposal of the triumphant aviators for the last lap of their journey into the heart of New York, where a Pan-American reception awaited them. Here they encountered the first ill-luck of their journey. One of the cutter's propellers became fouled on a steel cable. Members of the crew had to dive over the side to cut the cable clear. When they got under way and attempted to explain the delay by radio telephone, the instrument broke down. For the first time since they set off on their historic journey, they were 'lost'.

Apart from showing the flag and selling space on Imperial Airways services, the small office in New York became the terminal point of an enterprise which was a testing ground for much of the experimental work across the Atlantic—the Bermuda–New York service which opened in June, 1937. In 1934 an arrangement had been made between Imperial Airways, Bermuda and the British Government for a passenger and mail service between Bermuda and New York. From the first it was regarded as a co-operative venture with Pan-American. One of the new flying-boats being built by Short's for the Empire mail scheme was earmarked for the Bermuda operation. It was given extra fuel tankage. It was named *Cavalier*.

The base offered by the Bermuda Government was a small rocky island in the Great Sound, called Darrells Island. This romantic spot is conveniently close to Hamilton, the capital, but accessible only by water, which ultimately proved to be costly in time and money. It was used during the Boer War as a prison camp, and after the Second World War as a film set. For its use as a flying-boat base in the 'thirties a hangar was built, just large enough to accommodate the *Cavalier* and the Pan-American flying-boat.

When this had been made ready, Imperial Airways were faced with the problem of getting the *Cavalier* there. Even with its long-range tanks it could not be flown out, whatever route were chosen. It therefore went by sea. The hull went in a packing case 100 feet long—said to have been the biggest of its kind ever to be put on board ship. The wings were packed in individual crates. This bulky cargo had to be unloaded at the Royal Naval Dockyard at Somerset, Bermuda, five miles away from its ultimate destination, since the Navy possessed the only crane capable of lifting such weights. The unpacking and the towing of the components five miles across the water to Darrells Island, where they were reassembled, was a lengthy task, calling for much ingenuity.

Eventually *Cavalier* took to the air, was tested and made a proving flight to New York. When the commercial services started, it flew turn and turn about with the Pan-American *Clipper*. Members of the American Press flew to Bermuda by *Clipper* and returned by *Cavalier*, and many were greatly impressed by the first British aircraft to fly scheduled services in North American skies.

> 'Impressions? Plenty of them [wrote Wayne Parrish in *American Aviation*]. But in all frankness, and in all deference to the host on the outgoing trip, the revelation came on the return. We've been on the receiving end of a lot of subtle insinuations that the British were far behind in commercial aviation, but we can say in all candour that one of the great

experiences in flying scheduled air transport lines was the New York-bound flight on the *Cavalier*. It is not a matter of being unpatriotic and certainly we are well appreciative of what Pan-American have done, but the British really have something!'

Cavalier impressed everybody. This Empire flying-boat could hold its own for performance and comfort against any contemporary landplane. The passengers enjoyed an interior roominess which has rarely been matched since. The promenade deck with its footrail and high windows where passengers could stretch their legs and pass the time of day was a feature which is nostalgically remembered by all who flew in *Cavalier* and indeed by many who travelled in the Empire boats of Imperial Airways. For eighteen months, *Cavalier* successfully operated the Bermuda route, a solitary British aircraft alternating with the Clippers of Pan-American Airways. There was, however, a whisper of trouble. It was a matter of the icing in the air intakes. It was noticed in the winter of 1937–38. It could be overcome by the pilot varying the height and flying into warmer strata or by manipulating his throttles. On a flight on January 22, 1939, Captain Alderson, encountering wintry weather *en route* from New York to Bermuda, found *Cavalier* in this particular difficulty. He had experienced icing trouble before—the falling off in the performance of one engine and then another. He had countered this by turning back into warmer air, losing height and manipulating his throttles.

There were thirteen people on board, eight of them passengers, when Captain Alderson with two dead engines nosed *Cavalier* down towards the Atlantic swell. The Radio Officer sent out a distress signal giving the estimated position of the aircraft during the last few minutes of the descent.

'The First Officer went back and shouted instructions to the Steward to have lifebelts all ready, and then came back and took his seat for landing [stated Captain Alderson]. It was certainly a calmer sea than I had seen over the Atlantic for several weeks . . . but there was a pretty big swell, and no advantage to be gained by landing in any particular direction. It was a very lumpy sea. As I say, I hoped to get down all right, but I could see there was a chance of being damaged. There was no alternative but to make the best use of what wind there was. That was very little, I should say about seven or eight miles an hour. I got the First Officer to agree my estimate of the wind direction, which was not very easy to pick out at that particular time, and we agreed that it was south. I made a normal landing, using some flap, as slow as I could, but having the two inner engines dead, of course, made a good deal of difference, and I had to put the boat on the water fairly fast. I had the two outer engines, and picked up my spot as well as I could, but we did, as it proved, damage the hull on the first impact. Actually this was not very severe, and neither the First Officer nor the Wireless Operator imagined any damage had been done at all.'

There was no panic. Indeed there was no fear of any impending disaster. Passengers who were waiting for lunch at the time were told by one of the stewards that the meal would be served after alighting.

It did not occur to the Radio Operator, who had not even been wearing his safety belt, that the landing was abnormal. Alderson himself, however, realized that the hull was damaged by the impact:

'I immediately left my seat, went back and personally ordered all passengers out of the ship, as I knew that she would fill with water very quickly. I went on top of the hull and took off the emergency hatches. I had already given a message to the Wireless Operator—the ''Sinking'' message—and he went on repeating this and the distress call until his radio was affected.'

Some of the passengers went out through the two cabin entrances. Others went through the navigating deck and emerged on the top of the hull. An elderly passenger had received a severe head wound owing to the fact that he had insisted on standing up at the moment of impact after the stewards had requested all passengers to remain seated. Lifebelts were distributed. Some passengers and crew remained on the hull but *Cavalier* soon sank and with it one of the passengers disappeared. The remaining survivors managed to form themselves into a circle with linked hands.

For ten long hours, fading from daylight into night, they clung together working their limbs against the numbing cold and talking and singing to one another. Not all of them survived the night.

The elderly passenger with the head injury, 'slipped off very quickly, about an hour after darkness set in'. One of the stewards, Robert Spence, having given his own lifebelt to one of the passengers and exhausted himself by swimming to the help of others, became delirious and later died from exhaustion. Twice during the night, the ten who remained alive saw lights and shouted themselves hoarse. On the third occasion, two members of the party broke away and swam shouting towards a ship's lights. Their cries were heard by the captain of the *Esso Baytown*, who eventually rescued them all.

This vessel was one of many which had been alerted by the base staff in Bermuda who had worked out the estimated position of the stricken aircraft at the moment of its descent. It was, nevertheless, an act of magnificent seamanship which brought Captain Spurr of the *Esso Baytown* to the right spot in darkness and amid the heavy seas which had risen after the crash. Many years afterwards, Miss Nellie Smith of Bermuda, described as a dauntless lady who still enjoyed flying, recollected the disaster in these words: 'It is still vivid in my mind. I have suffered no ill-effects from it. I would like to say how brave all the crew and passengers were at the time. We all mourned the loss of the *Cavalier* as well as those who were drowned. She was the most beautiful plane I have ever seen.'

The loss of the *Cavalier* on its 290th scheduled flight was not only a disaster for those involved but a severe blow for British aviation in the North Atlantic. The New York–Bermuda run, built up in friendly rivalry with the Clippers of Pan-American, had been an achievement of importance in laying part of the foundations of the Atlantic Bridge. Now, in January 1939, this enterprise had to be abandoned, for *Cavalier* could not be replaced. There were no Empire flying-boats available fitted with the necessary long-range tanks. The shadow of war had fallen upon the British aircraft industry: no replacement could be built.

Problems of range dominated the Atlantic air throughout these years before the Second World War. The feasibility of Atlantic flight for scheduled mail and passenger services had been proved: but neither the British nor the Americans had been able to develop machines with enough range for regular non-stop crossings. History would repeat itself and another World War would accelerate aircraft development and establish Atlantic flight as an everyday routine. Meanwhile, in the last remaining peaceful years of the 'thirties, Imperial Airways and Pan-American continued to strive to find ways and means.

There were three possible expedients for overcoming the difficulty. One was the use of catapults—particularly favoured by the Germans who successfully employed catapults for launching aircraft from ships. This was rejected by the British as being too inflexible for regular service use. The other two expedients were flight refuelling and the use of 'pick-a-back' composite aircraft. Both these were tried by the British.

A distinguished consulting aeronautical engineer, the late Robert Hobart Mayo, was for many years associated with Imperial Airways and for a time served as their General Manager (Technical). His most famous achievement was the invention and construction of a 'pick-a-back' aircraft, known to the world as the Short-Mayo Composite, the lower compartment being called the *Maia* and the upper the *Mercury*.

Mayo's first memorandum describing this project was put forward as early as 1932:

> 'It is well known that an aircraft can fly quite safely and efficiently when carrying a load considerably in excess of the load at which it can safely take off. An attempt to take advantage of this fact is to be seen in the proposal to use refuelling in the air as a means of enabling longer stages to be tackled, but this scheme has obvious and serious limitations and cannot be regarded as a real solution to the fundamental problem. In the Composite Aircraft, which I now propose, full advantage is taken of the general improvement which can be effected in speed and load-carrying capacity by the use of high wing loading and correspondingly high stalling speed, but the aircraft embodying this feature is not called upon to take off. . . . The aircraft with high wing loading is mounted on another aircraft of very low wing loading to form a composite aircraft which has a relatively low resultant wing loading and is capable of taking off at a relatively low speed. Both aircraft forming the composite aircraft are provided with power plants, the total power being such as to ensure a quick and easy take-off for the composite aircraft. . . . My invention includes special means by which the upper component can be detached from

the lower with complete safety and without involving any risk of unintentional release or collision or fouling after release.'

At first it was thought that this invention would serve Australia as well as the Atlantic mail service. Its practical application, however, was made on the Atlantic. The price of the composite was quoted as £60,000. A crane lifted the upper component into position. If for any reason a launching of the upper component did not take place, the composite could alight again as one unit. The one and only composite to be built was put to the test on an Atlantic flight in July 1938, with Captain D. C. T. Bennett in command of the upper component, *Mercury*, who reported, 'the aircraft was loaded to approximately 20,650 lb. and at this load the separation was perfectly satisfactory and felt in every way to be safe.'

Bennett flew from Foynes to Montreal and then went on to New York. He made the return journey without, of course, the aid of the lower component, via the Azores and Portugal. His report mentioned the fact that the composite idea had been 'particularly well received both in Canada and the United States'.

Mayo's invention offered one solution to the problem of range. Proposals were put forward by Imperial Airways for the construction of a modest fleet of such machines. It was suggested at the same time that these might easily handle a large proportion of Atlantic mail carried in the form of airgraphs. In the autumn of 1938, however, Air Ministry decided that no case had been made for such a scheme. The objections which caused 'great surprise and regret' to Imperial Airways, were that the composite 'will be outclassed on the Atlantic by competitors; that it will not be a sufficient advance over possible Atlantic competitors; that its value will be seriously impaired by not carrying passengers; that it prejudices the use of boats; and that Messrs. Short Bros. are already too heavily engaged to deal with the upper components.'

In his letter of protest to the Director of Civil Aviation, the Secretary of Imperial Airways wrote:

'Capital expenditure of about £200,000 would cover four upper components, the alteration of two Ensigns to form lowers, and the modification of two others for conversion at short notice. The cost would not be wasted if the composite principle were used anywhere, e.g. a 24-hour service to South

Africa or South America, a 48-hour service in three or four stops to Australia, or as a precaution against interruption of normal Empire services by war or other emergency, when their high speed and great range would be very valuable.'

The Minister's objections were finally upheld in a letter of March 31, 1939:

'It is clear . . . that unless the principle of segregating passengers from mails was established and admitted as long-term policy, there would be no point in developing further the ideas contained in the composite aircraft. The principle of segregation remains unacceptable to the Secretary of State. . . .'

This letter killed the idea but not the composite itself. . . .

'In view of the present shortage of equipment, pilots and trained mechanics, the Secretary of State would be willing . . . to allow the composite to be incorporated in Imperial Airways fleet if the Company could make good use of it for commercial purposes.'

Mercury, as we have already noted, played a gallant part in the Empire air mail rush in Christmas 1938. It was handed over to the R.A.F. in May 1940. *Maia* was used for the training of land-plane pilots converting to flying-boats and was eventually destroyed by bombing in Poole Harbour in May 1941.

Apart from the construction of bigger aircraft with a longer range the only remaining pre-war alternative to composite aircraft was flight refuelling, and Imperial Airways turned to this on the eve of war. Converted Harrow bombers were used as flying tankers over the two terminal points at Foynes and Botwood. The flying-boats they served were the *Cabot* and the *Caribou*. After taking off, the flying-boat and the Harrow would get into formation. A grapnel on a long cable was wound out from the flying-boat's tail. The Harrow, flying to starboard, then fired another cable by rocket to catch on to the grapnel. Then a hose pipe was wound out from the cables from the Harrow to the flying-boat and drawn tight into an airproof fitting. Climbing above the flying-boat, the Harrow released 800 gallons of petrol through the hose. The First Officer and the Radio Officer of the flying-boat controlled this operation by flag signals from a window. The process took about twenty minutes while the flying-boat steadily proceeded on her course.

During the few summer months of 1939, *Cabot* and *Caribou*

made eight experimental round trips across the Atlantic, flying a total of 50,000 miles without mishap, and ended with a high standard of regularity. No passengers could be carried before this experimental service had to be brought to an end owing to the outbreak of war. For the honour of British civil aviation, it was particularly unfortunate that war prevented the carriage of passengers in these British aircraft. Not for eighteen years, till the first long range Britannia came into the service of B.O.A.C. in 1957, did any British-built aircraft on a scheduled service carry fare-paying passengers into New York.

When Britain went to war against Hitler, the Americans continued to enjoy the advantages of neutrality, and to Pan-American Airways went the honour of carrying the first paying passengers across the Atlantic by way of Newfoundland and Ireland in the summer and by way of Bermuda and Lisbon in the winter. After the declaration of war, their services had to terminate at Foynes, and the British maintained a shuttle service between that point, Hythe and Whitchurch. Thus it can be said that all the foundations of the Atlantic Bridge were laid by international collaboration in the years of peace, and the first traffic was started by the nation that was soon to become Britain's powerful ally. The development of the traffic across that new bridge is part of the war story shared between the two nations.

CHAPTER X

THE SHORT-HAUL WAR

WHEN the lights went out in September 1939, the British Merchant Air Service had already disappeared from the skies of Europe. All aircraft had been recalled from the Continent. Atlantic flights soon lapsed. There remained the main trunk traffic through the Middle East to Africa, India, the Far East and Australia. Croydon itself was stilled. Imperial Airways and British Airways were in the throes of amalgamation. The two companies, not yet officially joined, placed at the disposal of the State a mixed fleet of 82 aircraft.

Two days before war was declared, these streamed into Whitchurch near Bristol, a modest airfield where there was a small clubhouse used by a country flying club, where young men and women were enjoying a quiet drink when the British Merchant Air Fleet began to arrive. The place was just big enough for a single aircraft to land and take off. There was very little hangar space. As the Imperial Airways aircraft came in, they were dispersed round the edges of the airfield. When the British Airways craft arrived, parking arrangements on the perimeter were double banked.

By the time Chamberlain's broadcast was heard, the staff was settling down in tents, their meals served from field kitchens. Though Whitchurch as B.O.A.C. headquarters was greatly improved during the war, the first hard winter there was tough going.

> 'Life at Whitchurch [writes Charles Hartnoll of B.O.A.C.] with anything up to twenty-three degrees of frost became largely a fight to keep from freezing rather than to keep aeroplanes flying. Yet engines had to be started and run regularly:

the work of maintenance had to go on. This question of starting engines was a snag of the toughest order.

'One day in March 1940 we had a gale. It gave little warning, but there was no need to consult "Met" to realize that this was no ordinary wind. All hands made a rush across the flying field to the dispersed aircraft and hung on grimly. There were DH 86s, Hudsons, Ensigns, DH 91s and HP 42s. The latter, with their huge wing area, were the biggest problem. By the time Foreman Griffiths and F/E Caseley had reached them, the mooring pegs had already been wrenched out and *Heracles* was lifting, first one side, then the other, with the opposite wing tip hitting the ground finally to heave backwards through a barbed wire fence into the next field. She never flew again.

'To save *Hanno*, Griffiths climbed into the cockpit and Caseley managed to get the two-stroke going and started the top engines. The idea was to hold her against the wind. Before the lower engines could be started, however, the two-stroke wheezed and cut out with the huge machine rolling over on to its wing tips like a ship in distress, and the wind shrieking through the rigging as if she was in actual flight. It was while Caseley was striving to turn the two-stroke handle in an effort to restart it that *Hanno* came back on to an even keel; a heavy gust caught her and she rose in the air flying backwards with the Flight Engineer still hanging on to the handle. This aircraft, too, after nearly ten years of excellent service, finished up in the next field wrecked beyond repair.'

While Whitchurch served as the landplane base for the duration, the flying-boat terminus was moved from Southampton to Poole, Dorset, only the maintenance base remaining at Hythe.

B.O.A.C., and indeed the whole of the British Merchant Air Service, became entirely and directly engaged in the war effort as hostilities spread throughout the world. Their identities became all but submerged. It was the policy of the Government, agreed with the Americans, that all transport aircraft would be built in the United States—none in Britain—an expediency of war which was to have profound effects upon B.O.A.C. in after years.

The tasks assigned to the British Merchant Air Service during the war years were so diverse and so widespread that it is difficult to do justice to them in full. Fortunately the Government promoted a paper-bound volume entitled *Merchant Airmen*, published in 1946, while many facets of this great story were still fresh in the minds of those who took part. Dudley Barker was the anonymous author of this rewarding work which is recommended to those seeking a more detailed account than these pages can offer. In this and the next chapter incidents have been selected, told if possible in the words of eye-witnesses, to illustrate the temper of the times and something of the hazards of a great airline at war.

Operationally, aircraft and crews were involved in military duty even before hostilities started. It was a period of sealed orders. One of the first of these was carried by Captain H. H. Perry aboard an Ensign the day before war was declared. His aircraft was crowded with R.A.F. men and equipment. When, after take-off, he opened his orders, he found that his task was to dump his somewhat bewildered passengers in an open field near Rheims, there to await the war and the arrival of their machines from England. This was the first of many ferrying flights.

All such operations were organized by a special war-time body, National Air Communications, whose task was the co-ordination of all civil aviation activities. While the trunk routes overseas remained unchanged during the static period at the beginning of the war, National Air Communications reorientated the internal and European services. They were responsible, for instance, for the birth of Air Transport Auxiliary, headed by the present Chairman of B.O.A.C., Sir Gerard d'Erlanger, and charged with the ferrying of aircraft from the factories to the R.A.F. bases in Britain and abroad where they were needed for operations. B.O.A.C. seconded flying, engineering and other specialized staff to this formation: and in June 1941 assumed responsibility for its administration. A.T.A. started with 30 amateur pilots. At the end of the war there were 700 pilots, women as well as men, operating from 15 bases in the United Kingdom. They delivered 310,000 aircraft to the R.A.F. and the Fleet Air Arm during the course of the war: 154 A.T.A. pilots were killed on duty.

Within a month of the outbreak of war, twice-daily Ensign services between London and Paris were re-established. For these aircraft and their crews there were exciting times to come with the fall of France, to which we shall refer later.

It will be remembered that Hitler's 1940 offensive began with Norway, and it was there that two of Imperial Airways' most famous flying-boats, *Cabot* and *Caribou*, were involved. These craft had completed their summer programme of Atlantic flying, with the aid of flight refuelling, after the outbreak of war in 1939. That winter they had been transferred, with their crews, to R.A.F. Coastal Command for long-range reconnaissance work. Their Captains, changing from their dark blue uniforms into the lighter blue of the R.A.F., remained in command—Captain S. G. Long in *Caribou* and, in command of *Cabot*, Captain Gordon Store, to whose reports we are indebted for many of the details of events in Norway.

It had been hoped that the two flying-boats would have been put back on the Atlantic run in the summer of 1940 and that they might indeed have inaugurated the first British passenger service to America. Hitler's invasion of Norway put paid to that. Armed with seven guns, 'rounded off by a battery of two blackened broomsticks which protruded in a threatening manner from the tip of the tail,' *Cabot*, with her sister ship, broke off routine reconnaissance work and went on special missions to Norway. Their task was to take in R.A.F. parties with Norwegian officers and equipment to set up radar stations. Their first objective was Harstad, the main Allied base for operations against Narvik.

When *Cabot* arrived there on May 4, 1940, her crew saw a little port crammed with naval vessels and transports. In the streets were British, French and Norwegian troops. Though the town had already been bombed and there were air raids while *Cabot* lay moored to a buoy in the harbour, the townspeople were out and about and children were ski-ing on the slopes round the town. The R.A.F. told them that the construction of fighter bases was already well ahead. After refuelling and a night spent by the Captain and crew aboard *Cabot*, they were detailed to fly on to Bodo, a small port south of Narvik. They were to remain there for ten days assisting the R.A.F. with the radar equipment and the search for airfield sites. *Caribou* was also to drop its load and then return to base in Scotland.

Store duly alighted at Bodo the next day, a clear and sunny Sunday morning. Switching off the engines, the crew listened to the pealing of church bells and the radio operator ran up a Norwegian flag, civil fashion, as a mark of respect. Then they watched a policeman being rowed towards them in a small boat. He held up his hand with four fingers extended. They took this to be a local victory sign and grinned at him cheerfully and made the same gesture back. These amiable exchanges were interrupted by the Norwegian interpreter on board, who spoilt the sunny morning for them by announcing that the church bells were sounding an air raid alarm and the policeman's four fingers meant four Nazi aircraft.

These enemy planes passed over and the church bells had pealed an All Clear when the *Caribou* arrived. The two Captains went ashore for a conference. They learned that apart from a Scots Guards Company some miles away they were the only Englishmen in the place. There were some Norwegian troops in Bodo but no anti-aircraft defences. The equipment was off-loaded and the Captains were just giving their attention to the vulnerability of their flying-boats when the church bells pealed out another alert. This time they had been seen by the Germans. Glinting in the sun, a Heinkel was descending in a wide spiral. The two Captains made a dash for the dinghies. Captain Store reached *Cabot*, slipped moorings and started taxiing before the Heinkel came in, low, for its first attack. His crew were already manning their guns, one of them abandoning the cooking of steaks in the galley in the absence of the Airgunner-Cook who had rowed over to *Caribou* to borrow some gravy salt.

'Jerry now came in for his first attack, very low, just as *Cabot* was passing the lighthouse at the harbour mouth [wrote Store]. Frost acted as Fire Control Officer in the astro dome, and as the Heinkel approached we opened up to full throttle at right angles to his line of flight, at the same time giving him all we had with what guns could be brought to bear. His bursts spattered the water clear of us so these tactics seemed to have rattled him and we repeated them again and again. Our Jerry seemed a plucky and determined fighter, and well protected evidently, as we drilled him full of holes every time he passed over—oil streamed below his wings and fuselage. I think about eight attacks were made. To take off and continue the battle in flight seemed senseless as this formidable opponent could have attacked from below and astern, out of the field of fire of our guns.

'Long had meanwhile been having some trouble getting

Caribou's engines started, but now was taxi-ing across the harbour. Taking stock of *Cabot*'s position, I had stopped a bullet in the left foot which was feeling wet, warm and crunchy inside the flying boot, but everyone else was O.K. although several had had narrow escapes with one crew member having his belt shot away and Frost's steel helmet deflecting a bullet. Smoke was coming out of the wing-roots and the starboard outer engine refused to answer to the throttle. The bow mooring hatch was shattered. I expected the bottom to have suffered several bullet holes, so considered the sensible thing to do was to run *Cabot* gently on to the mud at the north end of the harbour. As we did this Jerry put in a parting burst at *Caribou*, replied to by a long and accurate one from Williams, Long's waist gunner. Jerry's last burst had been an unfortunate one, as four members of *Caribou's* crew were wounded. George Bowes had a bullet in his thigh-bone; young Buck got one which made a nasty hole in the calf of his leg, Dupe had been drilled across his back clear of the shoulder blades and Williams had a clean hole through the fleshy part of one arm. Fuel was gushing from the centre section tanks, down to the bilges.

'We got ashore by the simple though chilly process of wading and a girl with a Morris Eight on the shore road, who at first had been frightened and had hidden as she thought us Germans, until we hailed her, offered in perfect English to run those who were hurt up to the hospital, which was only about three miles distant.'

Cabot and *Caribou* were winged. They needed considerable attention before they would be able to fly off. After the wounded had been despatched, therefore, the two flying-boats were stripped of equipment and armament. When *Cabot* had been dealt with, her crew joined forces with the men of *Caribou*. They were wading, ankle deep out to the aircraft when the Germans struck again, first with bombs, then with machine-gun fire which threw up the sand on the heels of the scattering crews.

The tide receded and left the two flying-boats high and dry on mud. As she lay there helpless *Caribou* was bombed and completely burnt out.

By the light of the northern summer night, the three uninjured officers, with the aid of motor boats from Bodo, set to work to salvage *Cabot*. They towed her out of the harbour into the open sea. 'Expecting aerial attack at any moment, this ghostly convoy proceeded several miles up the coast to a sheltered spot between a high cliff and a tall island rock where with much difficulty owing to the steeply shelving sea bed, she was eventually secured by her own and some borrowed anchors from the bow and by a tail line to the cliff foot. The roundels were covered over, using service blankets, and bushes, and altogether *Cabot* was well camouflaged, being visible from only directly above. Thus she was left while the crew returned to Bodo to have stands made for the 'K' guns so that protective armament could be placed upon the cliff above, whilst engineers worked below patching up the aircraft and engines.

> 'Early next morning along came a German plane with obvious intent to destroy *Cabot*, but instead only found a small Norwegian float-plane, which she destroyed, and the Nazi pilot gave vent to his feelings at being thus thwarted by machine-gunning the streets of Bodo. Nazi reconnaissance and intelligence had, however, been at work, and that same Monday morning a Dornier flying-boat passed close by the hospital and proceeded straight to *Cabot*'s hiding place. An immense column of black smoke announced that our beloved *Cabot* had now received a Viking's funeral.'

The crews of the two flying-boats with their wounded were brought back from Norway by the Royal Navy. The loss of their craft may have seemed a relatively slight calamity against the whole tragedy of the Norwegian campaign. Its immediate effect upon British civil aviation was to postpone still further the prospect of a British transatlantic air service.

With the German invasion of Western Europe, and the entry of Italy into the war, the story of the airline in Europe takes a melancholy, if heroic turn. The very existence of an airline is a symbol of peaceful living and international goodwill. Wherever violence encroaches, it is robbed of this character. Harnessed to the war machine, its own identity lost, the airline continues to participate in such vital matters as ferrying and maintaining communications even at extreme risk. Conversely, it is involved in the rescue of people and equipment threatened by encroaching violence. The word *evacuation*, which now comes prominently into the story, is one which has continued to figure in airline history long after the ending of that war and is still, alas, topical today.

The years 1940 and 1941 presented a sad series of evacuations from Scandinavia, France, the Low Countries, Italy, Greece and Crete, in which men and machines of the airline participated. It is not possible within these covers to do justice to them all. One or two examples, therefore, must serve to illustrate the theme of rescue and retreat.

As all the world knows, the German break-through in 1940 was sudden and staggering in its impact. The services of K.L.M. and Sabena to London, resumed soon after the war started, had been running normally on the day before the invasion came. The British services to Paris continued even after the invasion started. Some airliners belonging to K.L.M. and Sabena just escaped the Nazi onrush by flying across the Channel and landing in Britain, there to work closely in war-time association with the British Merchant Air Service.

As soon as the victorious German armoured divisions poured into France, every aircraft in the British Merchant Service fleet other than those on the long-range routes, became engaged in running supplies to the retreating forces of the Allies. Their main task was the flying of food and ammunition to forward troops. They plied back and forth unarmed and without armour. Towards the end of May 1940, for example, Captain G. R. Buxton carried a cargo of food by night in an Ensign to an isolated pocket of British troops at Merville. Returning to England he was shot at by a trawler in the Channel. Immediately after landing he took on another cargo for the same destination and joined a formation of civil aircraft flying by daylight with an escort of Hurricane fighters. At Merville in an open field, the crews stripped to their shirts and had begun unloading the supplies when German Messerschmitts appeared overhead. The Hurricane escort engaged them and in the course of a running fight of about twenty minutes drove them off, after which they had to retire themselves as their fuel was exhausted.

The merchant airmen went on discharging their cargoes: but not for long. Two Messerschmitts came in low out of the sun firing their guns. The men scattered as best they could. They lay and watched the Ensign *Elysean* machine-gunned from wing tip to wing tip while the Radio Officer crouched for shelter beneath its tail. The airliner burnt out: most of the other aircraft were holed but they were still able to fly. Unarmed as they were, without any protection for their field, the crews raced for their aircraft. The Radio Officer, who had miraculously survived the strafing, jumped aboard an Ensign which was taking off with its door open.

On the way back across France, they flew into intense anti-aircraft fire. Two of the airliners were hit near Calais, some of their crew killed and some taken prisoner. Captain S. T. V. Cripps limped across the Channel on three engines, one of which cut over Folkestone. He landed at Lympne on two engines and one wheel.

In spite of this adventure, one of the Ensign pilots, Captain Allen Andrew, took off again that same day for Rouen carrying fully charged aircraft batteries to R.A.F. fighter squadrons who were so heavily engaged with the enemy that they were unable to recharge their own batteries.

This was the beginning of the end. The dearly loved Le Bourget, to which the first British merchant airmen had flown in 1919, was soon threatened, and with it the whole long-standing pattern of the airline's operations in France.

It happened that the same Captain G. R. Buxton was there with *Ettrick* which needed attention because of engine trouble.

> 'We had decided to investigate the trouble when the air raid warning sounded [writes Lloyd C. Ifould]. We stood spell-bound looking towards the terrific explosion which hurled bits and pieces up into the air. For a moment we did not realize that it was the result of bombs, as the warning had just sounded that very instant. . . . Usually, one had plenty of time to go and lie down under one's favourite tree, or to find oneself a ditch or cellar. . . . When more thuds, followed by explosions, occurred, all in the same vicinity, and within a few seconds of each other, "Boys, this is it!" someone shouted, and we decided to make for cover, or at least protection of some kind from the flying fragments.
>
> 'We had just made a dive for the main airport building, only forty yards away, when great lumps of the aerodrome began to go up in the air. There was only one thing to do—make for the cellars under the Customs, which was in the main airport building. There were many cellars, all on the same level, but

they did not afford much protection, as they were only a few feet below the ground. However, that was better than nothing. Our only defence was a few machine-guns, there being no anti-aircraft guns on the aerodrome. Hell was let loose. The very earth trembled. The din was terrific. Bombs were literally raining down on the aerodrome.

'The first bomb to strike the building landed on the north end, putting what little light we had in the cellars out, and leaving us in darkness. Another direct hit, and then a lull until the next wave of bombers came over. They scored three direct hits on our building. The nearest bomb fell within a few yards of us. Walls cracked and started to cave in. Doors were blown off. I found myself lying flat on my stomach between the legs of a man who seemed to be very powerful, but whose legs were trembling in accompaniment with the walls of the building, and in that position I stayed, and so did he. As he was wearing leggings, it passed through my mind that he must be a Garde Mobile. During the next lull, when we had started to breathe freely again, he struck a match to see what was between his legs. In the flickering, eerie light, we just looked at one another. I could not see him very distinctly, as by now, the floor above us, which was the Customs, and stacked with articles of all kinds held in bond, was on fire and crackling. The blasts from the bombs had blown the smoke and dust down into our cellars, but I could see him well enough to realize that I had been right. He was a Garde Mobile, and it gave me a perverse feeling of satisfaction to see one of those swaggering, domineering men with the insolence scared right out of him. We continued to stare at each other until the match flickered out, but neither of us spoke or moved from the position in which we had found ourselves. We just waited for the next wave, and possibly death, but we did not have to wait long.

'Things were beginning to get pretty bad in our cellar. The air was foul, and we were half choked with smoke, but we hung on. There was nothing else to do, with the shower of bombs that were dropping around us. The worst thing about this raid was the knowledge that the very building we were in was the objective the Luftwaffe was trying to destroy. . . . During a lull I decided to make a dash for the shelter, which had been built for the use of the official administrative staff of the airport. The Luftwaffe had a full knowledge of this particular shelter, as in peacetime, the Lufthansa crews, who landed at Le Bourget, had watched it being built. However, they failed to score a direct hit, although they left bomb craters all around it. . . .

'It took me some time to recognize the place, as it was in semi-darkness, due to the clouds of dust and mortar caused by the destruction. I eventually found the great iron door, on which I struck several times with an iron bar that happened to be handy. The door gradually opened, much to my relief, and I went in. Officials crowded around me and eagerly asked me what I had seen. . . . I then found that running through the smoke and dust had so clogged my nose and throat that I could not speak. My mouth opened and closed all right, but not a sound would emanate. The first aid attendant soon put that right, and I then made a tour of the shelter to see who was there. The lighting arrangements were functioning here, as the shelter had its own small electric power plant, in case of such an emergency. At the end of the passage, there stood my Garde Mobile, against the wall. He seemed a little reassured now. When we saw each other, we had to smile. "Nous sommes mieux ici," he said.'

Captain Buxton was wounded in the thigh. There were many hundreds of casualties in the area and many aircraft damaged. The Ensign had a burst tyre and no serious damage that could not be repaired but the authorities would not agree to her being moved, though Buxton climbed aboard, tried the controls and thought he could take off. Eventually the machine had to be abandoned—but not before a final ceremony:

'As we all felt considerably the worse for the day's experiences, we decided to drown our feelings in the bar of the Ensign, which the Luftwaffe had very kindly opened up for us. We helped ourselves generously, and handed out drinks to any of the boys who happened to come around. Needless to say we did a roaring trade. We were determined that if the Germans should capture the Ensign, they were not going to get any free drinks. We were going to take care of that ourselves.'

It was a tale of confusion, defeat and breakdown of communications: but much of the spirit of loyalty to the airline which coloured so many similar misfortunes in so many different countries, comes through in the eye-witness accounts:

'On June 10 [wrote Ifould] the Germans were very near Paris. Early that morning we piled sandbags around the main wheels of the Ensign to protect us from the sudden explosion of delayed action bombs that might go off, as we had to change the wheels, and wanted to pull the machine to a less exposed position at the other end of the aerodrome, where we could proceed to make the necessary repairs, but a message arrived from Flitcroft (of Air France) asking me to go to see him, at once.

'He said: "The French Government is moving to Tours. Some of the members have already left, and Air France is leaving as soon as we can load. I have told Monsieur Monteux that we are getting out of here, and you had better do the same. I think you would be wise to start packing all the equipment you think you ought to take with you. I will see if I can spare a few men to help your staff load your trucks, but, you know, we have a hell of a lot to do ourselves and very little time in which to do it, so don't expect too much help." '

Maurice Monteux, who had been Paris Manager for Handley Page Transport Co. in 1919 and was still serving B.O.A.C., had not yet lost direct touch with headquarters: 'I rang up Bristol and suggested that if it was decided to continue the London–Paris services these should be operated to an aerodrome on the South of the Loire. Later in the day it was decided that the aerodrome of Tours should be used. I rang up Bristol again at 7 p.m. that night and informed them of what was happening.'

The seat of the French Government had been moved to Tours and it was to that airfield that Winston Churchill flew on June 13, 1940, on his last visit to France before the end. No one came to meet him or seemed to expect him, 'but we borrowed a service car from the Station Commander and motored into the city. . . .'

When these melancholy discussions broke up, Churchill took his leave of the French Government for the last time. One of the airline captains watched him pacing back and forth on the cratered airfield with Paul Reynaud, the French Prime Minister, noticing his old grey coat and grey felt hat and that he looked 'terribly haggard and worried'. Nevertheless Churchill's own description of that day mentions the fact that he 'slept sound' on the flight back to the task of building a fortress Britain.

The French Government retreated to Bordeaux and the ground staff of the airline went with them. Everything was then concentrated on rescue and evacuation. Fortunately everybody connected with the airline had been fitted out with the blue uniforms of B.O.A.C. This helped them in situations where roads were blocked and communications broken down, but in which men in uniform could still claim some slight priority.

Every serviceable aircraft controlled by National Air Communications was to bring home to Britain as many key men as possible for the continuation of the war. Those who flew on these missions went unarmed over burning cities, battle areas and roads pathetically choked with refugees. They landed on panic-stricken and sometimes already abandoned airfields. Captain Cripps, for instance, went to pick up a party from Nantes. He landed his Ensign on an airfield which was deserted, with numbers of aircraft lying about abandoned and burning. His First Officer left the airliner for a few moments to salvage a bicycle, and, with this solitary souvenir, they left. They did not, however, return empty. They landed at Jersey where air evacuation was already in full swing, organized by Jersey Airways Ltd., filled their Ensign with Channel Island families, and carried them across to Exeter.

Paris fell to the Germans on June 14. Three days later a small fleet of civil aircraft was sent out to help with the evacuation of an R.A.F. Squadron from an airfield near Lyons. They were to refuel at Bordeaux and Marseilles. Bordeaux itself was in jeopardy as Captain Perry saw it when he landed his Ensign:

> 'I spent some time taxiing back and forth across the airfield, trying to get some petrol out of somebody, getting none, and damaging my tail wheel in the process. Suddenly a French officer whom I knew came out of one of the hangars and told me, with a white face, that France had given in. By this time the airfield was an extraordinary sight. Some other Ensigns and some DH 86s of my party were coming in from the north, all seeking petrol. An R.A.F. Bombay came in from the south. I gave it up for a few minutes and slipped into a shack to get

a cup of coffee. Inside I met my son who, unbeknown to me, was flying one of the other aircraft in our fleet [Captain Perry's son was later reported missing from an R.A.F. operational flight]. I asked him what he was doing, and he said, "Same as you, Dad."

'Then I started to look for petrol in earnest. I taxied over to a dump, seized a bowser, and managed to get the Ensign filled before the angry French bowser-crew found out. It seemed hopeless to try to push on to Lyons, so I went across to ask the R.A.F. crew of the Bombay how things stood. They turned out to be part of the squadron we had been sent to help; they said they were the last aircraft out, and the Huns were already in the place. Some of the other captains decided to try to push on nevertheless, but they had to put back to Marseilles, and most of the aircraft were later destroyed by the Germans at Bordeaux.

'By this time a lot of French aircraft were coming in. They came from all sorts of directions, putting down where they could, and the crashes were mounting rapidly. I decided to make for home, managed to get off in spite of my broken tail-wheel, and got home without incident.'

That day marked the beginning of real confusion. The rest of the story is most fittingly told in the words of the report made by Maurice Monteux to B.O.A.C. Headquarters only a few days after his arrival as an exile in Britain. Biscarosse, to which he refers, was a flying-boat base south-west of Bordeaux to which we shall refer again later.

'On Monday, June 17, I had an interview with the manager of Air France. He had been able to contact Colonel Genain who was then between Algiers and Fort Lamy, travelling on this route. Colonel Genain had informed Air France that the stock of petrol on the Sahara route had been exhausted and that in some places like El Golea there were only 7,000 litres of petrol left. Air Afrique were of the opinion that we could not possibly use the Sahara route and that the only thing to do was for our flying-boats to fly on the West African coast to a terminus to be fixed by you. I tried to have this information checked by Shell in Bordeaux, but they knew absolutely nothing about the position of the petrol stocks in Africa.

'I waited until Wednesday, June 19, before sending you a

message asking you to stop any landing either at Biscarosse or Bordeaux for home-bound services and saying that only one or two machines would be able to come from England so as to take up position somewhere in Africa. I understand that this message never reached you.

'On Wednesday afternoon I was in Bordeaux aerodrome where I got news that the Germans were in Périgueux and nearing Poitiers on the other side, that meant the taking of Bordeaux within 48 hours and Biscarosse about the same time. It was imperative that all services should be stopped across France. Air France had sent all their flying-boats except *Ville de St. Pierre* to Marseilles and Algiers on the night between Tuesday and Wednesday, June 18/19. Their landplanes left Bordeaux on Wednesday morning for Marseilles and Algiers too, with the exception of two Dewoitine which were placed at the disposal of the Director of Civil Transport.

'I got in touch with the staff at S. Nazaire and instructed the British Station Superintendent to evacuate to England as soon as possible. The British staff at Lezignan was also recalled and left Bordeaux by boat on the morning of June 20.

'It was then obvious that the activities of the Corporation in that part of the world had come to an end: Bordeaux was bombed in the early morning of June 20. It was more than dangerous to continue to remain in Bordeaux. On the morning of June 19, a German reconnaissance machine flew above the base at Biscarosse, circled at very low altitude and flew back without any shot being fired at her.

'In those circumstances I decided to discharge all French staff. I paid them the current month and for released staff I gave everyone two months' salary. I burned out all my confidential files and the deciphering codes. On Wednesday evening, when I came back from Bordeaux, Captain Loraine who had arrived earlier in the day on a Special Charter had not yet left Biscarosse. I asked him whether it was possible for him to take me over to England with my family as I felt I would be of more help to my own country and the Corporation in England than in remaining in France under German domination. Captain Loraine said he would ask the charterer, Mr. Monnet. On the morning of June 20, when it was heard that Mr. Monnet wanted to go back to England by 9.0 a.m.

we were driven to Biscarosse base. Mr. Monnet agreed to Captain Loraine taking me over and we left Biscarosse. . . .'

The flying-boat base at Biscarosse was also the scene of one of many political wartime operations carried out by the men of B.O.A.C. Captain D. C. T. Bennett, famous later for his work on the Atlantic ferry and for his leadership of the Pathfinder Forces of R.A.F. Bomber Command, took the Empire flying-boat *Cathay* there during the last fateful days when France was being overrun. His passenger was the Polish leader General Sikorski whose mission was to contact the remaining formations of the Polish Army who were still fighting their way back across France. When the General went ashore in a dinghy about midday, Bennett pointed out the risks entailed in keeping a flying-boat in that exposed position for more than a few hours. Sikorski said that he could not possibly complete his mission before five o'clock the following morning, which meant keeping the *Cathay* in dangerous idleness for some seventeen hours. The flying-boat was unarmed. Air bombardment of the whole area was going on intermittently. After the departure of the General, Bennett taxied his craft along the coast for about six miles, ran her on to a sandy beach under cover of some trees turning her in order that she might rest facing open water in case there had to be a quick getaway.

During the afternoon, members of the crew went ashore. Villagers warned them to keep clear of the roads. German tanks and motor cyclists were already coming through the village streets. The crew returned to the flying-boat, taking it in turn to keep watch throughout the night on the wings, listening to the rumble of victorious German armour fanning out through the countryside.

They remained undiscovered and Sikorski kept his rendezvous at five o'clock the following morning, bringing with him his daughter and members of the Polish general staff. Taking off, *Cathay* passed directly over German tanks, the Polish officers being stationed at the windows ready to open fire with their personal weapons. *Cathay* was intercepted once or twice by enemy fighters but none of these pressed an attack, probably mistaking *Cathay* for one of the formidably armed R.A.F. Sunderlands. When enemy fighters seemed as if they might in fact attack, Bennett managed to lose them in a thick pall of smoke drifting from burning oil tanks on the French coast. In the midst of this manœuvre, he calculated his estimated time of arrival in Britain. Being Bennett, he brought his passengers down to the safety of British waters punctually to the minute.

The Battle of France was over and the Battle of Britain began. Captains and crews seconded to Air Transport Auxiliary ferried aircraft from the factories to the fighter squadrons. Others, flying the now well-proven Ensigns, actually participated in the Battle of Britain, moving ground staff and equipment of Fighter Command in and out of the battle positions as needed. There were other instances of evacuation and rescue work in Europe, particularly in the Mediterranean, before the Germans and Italians were contained and the war became world-wide. With the Battle of Britain won, and the British war effort gradually developing from the defensive to the aggressive, new patterns of short-haul work from British bases developed. It is perhaps proper to break strict chronological sequence to mention some of these before passing on to the story of the trunk routes and events in the Middle East.

When the Germans completed their occupation of Scandinavia, Sweden remained neutral but cut off from the United Kingdom by land and by sea. There were many reasons, political and strategic, for maintaining contacts with that country and this could only be done by air. The original route, opened before the war by British Airways, had continued to operate from Perth to Stockholm till the Germans moved. When this was abandoned with the loss of some of the aircraft, there was for a time no communication with neutral Sweden except by cable. This situation was bad politically, for it meant the withdrawal of all British influence from Sweden. There was also a very pressing material necessity—that of ball bearings. War-time Britain urgently needed the finest ball bearings in the world, which Sweden produced. It was equally important to deny them to the Germans. B.O.A.C. was therefore asked to restart the service between Scotland and Stockholm early in 1941.

The aircraft were to fly by night, though in summer there was little enough darkness in those northern skies. They were to fly unarmed and their route lay through the Skagerrak, both sides of which were flanked by some of Germany's most powerful anti-aircraft concentrations.

At first the route was operated by only one aircraft, a Lockheed which had been rescued by the Poles when their country was overrun. Its identification letters were BG and it was soon known as *Bashful Gertie—the terror of the Skagerrak.*

When this aircraft broke down after several months' service, the R.A.F. released some Hudsons to take its place and the ball bearings continued to roll in despite early misgivings at the neutral end. By 1943, Norwegian exiles based in Britain were doing much of the flying. They were followed by British crews in Whitley bombers converted into freighters, which proved to be unsuitable for the job. They were followed in turn by Dakotas flying at about 20,000 feet over the dangerous flak of the Skagerrak, and a single Curtiss Wright 20, a prototype aircraft. Though these carried many useful loads, they presented dangerously slow-moving targets for flak, searchlights and night fighters. An alternative route was therefore worked out for them across the Norwegian–Swedish border to the north. With this change came also the introduction of Mosquitoes into the B.O.A.C. fleet. These fighter-bombers, made famous by the R.A.F., carried a crew of two with two bomb-bays into each of which a single passenger equipped with oxygen, flying kit and a flask of coffee, could be fitted, or an equivalent amount of cargo. The Mosquitos flew high, fast and unarmed, with civil markings, and they continued to use the Skagerrak route. They were so successful that for a time they even flew in daylight and many passengers on urgent missions were carried safely between the Scottish base at Leuchars and Stockholm.

They did not fly without danger. Captain Gilbert Rae, on one occasion, had to force-land in Sweden after being attacked by an enemy fighter at a height of 17,000 feet. He was intercepted on another occasion at 23,000 feet on a night of bright moonlight over the Skagerrak and this time he was carrying a passenger in a bomb-bay. Being unarmed, he dived in a series of tight turns to sea-level where with full throttle he managed to pull away from the enemy fighters. This evasive action was so violent that his Radio Officer needed a fortnight to recover from his injuries. Communication with the passenger was possible by inter-com, and Rae began to make tender inquiries as soon as he was out of enemy range. From the passenger there was no reply. He had passed out, mercifully, and remained unconscious for some twenty minutes. He had recovered, however, when they released him from the bomb-bay at Leuchars.

Seven B.O.A.C. men were lost on these hazardous Mosquito operations, among them Captain Rae, who was killed on the subsequent flight.

The Dakotas were severely handicapped by the much longer distances of the northern route and it was decided later in 1943 to lay on converted bombers such as Lancasters, Yorks and Liberators. Throughout these operations, the Swedish authorities were much concerned with the risk of shooting down British aircraft which were not always able to keep to the rigidly marked air corridors that had been agreed. There were a number of incidents and complaints, the most serious of which was caused when a British Liberator put down by mistake at a military airfield in Sweden. The Commandant of the airfield instructed the machine to take off again immediately, but this action was regarded as un-neutral in allowing a belligerent aircraft to use a military base in Sweden. There was a row in the Press followed by fierce debate in the Swedish Parliament.

Nevertheless, the base at Leuchars continued to operate to Sweden until the end of the war. The traffic, which was a B.O.A.C. commitment throughout the period, was of immense importance, fully justifying in the terms of war effort the risks that were run. Apart from the essential cargoes of ball bearings and other vital equipment, there were movements of people whose presence in Britain could be said to have altered the course of the war. One of the Mosquito passengers, for instance, was Professor Niels Bohr, who had made his way from occupied Denmark into Sweden, and whose work for the Allies on the atomic bomb undoubtedly contributed to the shortening of the war.

CHAPTER XI

THE LONG-HAUL WAR

THE only Dominions not completely served by the fleet of Imperial Airways engaged in long-haul traffic when war broke out in 1939 were Canada and New Zealand. Twice a week Empire flying-boats plied between Southampton and Durban, taking four and a half days. A third service ran weekly between Southampton and Kisumu on Lake Victoria in Kenya. There was a weekly connection for these with flights across Central Africa to the West Coast. At that time West Africa could only be reached by way of Khartoum and this Central African route.

Three times a week flying-boats left Southampton for Singapore, whence Qantas Airways extended the line to Sydney, the full journey from the Solent to Sydney taking nine and a half days. At Bangkok there was a twice-weekly branch service to Hong Kong with landplanes. Flying-boats also ran a twice-weekly service between Southampton and Karachi, with landplane connections to Calcutta. This pattern was being extended, as war broke out, by the experimental flights across the Atlantic of *Cabot* and *Caribou*, both doomed, as we know, to become early war casualties. *Cabot* took off from Southampton for the United States just after Chamberlain made his broadcast, and on the way over picked up an S.O.S. message sent out from s.s. *Athenia*, Britain's first major war casualty at sea. *Cabot*'s cargo included a present of grouse for President Roosevelt.

Long-haul operations were not greatly disturbed by the hostilities, which were of course confined to Northern Europe. They were disrupted later by the closing of the Mediterranean, and then greatly affected by the entry of Japan into the war. These two events, together with the opening of the Atlantic Bridge, mould the whole course of their war-time story.

There were a number of preliminary moves. Three days after war was declared, the R.A.F. in Egypt asked for a civil landplane service to carry documents and Government officials between Britain and Egypt. A trunk line was immediately opened with Frobishers, later replaced by Lockheeds, running from Shoreham, Sussex, through Bordeaux and Marseilles to Tunis and Malta, thence by way of Sollum to Alexandria. This service was extended eastward to India and continued to operate twice weekly until Italy entered the war.

The possibility of the Mediterranean being closed by war had been foreseen. One of the objects of Brackley's 1939 survey across the Sahara through the Belgian Congo, returning by way of West Africa, had been to decide on alternative routes. Brackley's flight, however, had carried him across France to Algiers on the way out, returning through French West Africa to Marseilles. The collapse of France had not been envisaged. Now a much wider detour was required to avoid the West Coast of France and Franco's Spain as well as Italy. A route between Britain and West Africa was urgently needed to join up with the existing line across Africa to Khartoum. Without it, there could be no all-air communication between Britain and her forces in the Middle East. It was a job for flying-boats.

On the evening of August 5, 1940, the flying-boat *Clyde* lay at her moorings in Poole Harbour ready to start one of her experimental Atlantic crossings. Captain A. C. Loraine was making his final preparations for the flight when he was called to the telephone to be told that his destination was to be Lagos, West Africa, instead of New York. He was to carry eight important passengers. He was faced with a journey of some 5,000 miles which had never been flown by flying-boats. After the first stop there would be no facilities whatever. Owing to the war he would have to maintain radio silence and there would be no weather reports. He was not to alight in French colonial territory—and the distance from Lisbon to Bathurst in the Gambia in itself was equal to an Atlantic crossing.

The passengers turned out to be members of General de Gaulle's newly-formed Free French Army headed by Colonel (afterwards General) de Larminat. The second pilot on this flight was Captain W. S. May, the only other member of the crew being Radio Officer Cheeseman.

They reached Lisbon on August 6. That evening a flare path was laid in the harbour and *Clyde* started her run, using her forward lights for take-off. With her extra fuel and equipment she was carrying 53,000 lb., a greater load than she had ever lifted before. Sitting in the second pilot's seat, Captain May concentrated on the water ahead while Loraine was engrossed in lifting *Clyde* clear. Then May saw 'what I took to be a thin searchlight of the kind that we have for testing cloud-height, on the hills across the harbour ahead of us. Suddenly I realized that this "searchlight" was on the water immediately on our path; that a small ship, probably a fishing vessel, lay directly in front of us, and what I saw was our own lights shining on a sail furled round her mast.

'I shouted to Loraine, but he was concentrating on take-off, and I was not sure whether he had heard me, for the ship was slightly to my side, placed so that he could not easily see it. Just then we became airborne, flying only a few feet above the water straight for the vessel. It seemed impossible to miss it. I shouted again.'

May acted 'as I have never done before and hope I shall never have to do again'. He seized the controls and flung *Clyde* hard to port, so hard that the port wing could have missed the water by only a few inches.

After flying all night, and for many daylight hours, monotonously down the West Coast of Africa, May went below to speak to the French passengers, who, of course, had no steward to look after them. It was only then that he became aware for the first time of a large v-shaped tear beneath the starboard wing just beyond the outer motor. A whole section of the aileron had been torn out—by the mast of the ship in Lisbon harbour.

At Bathurst, nevertheless, they alighted safely, tying up at the small quay at Half Die, the once notorious settlement whose name commemorates the sufferings of its first European inhabitants. A few miles up the Gambia River, the Germans had abandoned an airfield and it was from there that they obtained raw material to mend the aileron.

At the next stop, Freetown, there was a refuelling crisis. The fuel was there all right; but Loraine saw it being propelled towards him aboard a steel barge of several hundred tons. The slightest brush with such a barge might well have sunk *Clyde*. By frantic signalling, he managed to keep the barge clear of his moorings. Then he found a quiet bay upstream where *Clyde* could be moored. The petrol which was in drums was brought alongside in native canoes, hoisted on to the wings and poured into the tanks through a funnel. Loraine's raincoat was held over the funnel all day to keep out the tropical rain which persisted while they took on a thousand gallons of fuel. The flying-boat was, of course, a novelty in those parts. The refuelling natives called her 'A canoe that goes for up'. With this fuel on board, *Clyde* just managed to reach Lagos to accomplish, as the Captain and crew thought, the task that had been set. In fact their adventurous mission was by no means over.

They were involved in political and strategic issues of high importance. French Equatorial Africa was in favour of the newly-formed Vichy Government. The existence of this solid pro-Vichy bloc threatened the whole structure of Allied communication. Colonel de Larminat and his men were on their way to avert war in Central Africa. Brazzaville, the Vichy French capital, faced the Belgian capital Leopoldville directly across the Congo. De Larminat was to use Leopoldville as a base for his negotiations.

But there was no ship at Lagos to carry him on this urgent mission. The Governor of Nigeria, in consultation with the B.O.A.C. Regional Manager at Lagos, signalled London to seek permission for *Clyde* to make the hazardous trip into the interior. As soon as this was cleared, another signal went to the British Consul-General in Leopoldville requesting him to provide a mooring. The Consul-General at once got in touch with Mr. Ian Scott-Hill, now a member of the staff of B.E.A., who at that time was already deeply involved in Central African adventure as assistant to Mr. Vernon Crudge, B.O.A.C. Regional Director in Nairobi. Crudge had made his way by car and river steamer from Kenya to the mouth of the Congo, surveying the possibilities of a flying-boat route. Having reported, he had returned to Nairobi, leaving Scott-Hill to await developments. Nobody in Lagos, in fact, knew that he was still in Leopoldville. The request coming from the Consul-General late in the evening to prepare to receive a flying-boat the next morning astounded Scott-Hill.

Strong currents run in Stanley Pool between the two Congo cities. There are many shallows and rocks. At first it seemed quite impossible to find a safe mooring during the hours of darkness for a large flying-boat arriving early the next morning, and Scott-Hill told him to advise Lagos that it could not be done. The Consul-General, conscious only of the acute political need for action, deliberately withheld this advice, insisting that the reception arrangements should go ahead with all speed, to which Scott-Hill naturally agreed. The mooring was assembled and Scott-Hill was only just about to rush it out on to the river the next morning when *Clyde* arrived overhead. Loraine had to be told, in fact, to fly round while the mooring was thrown overboard and secured.

The first Lagos to Leopoldville flight, which had to be done without stopping to refuel in any French territory, made history in more senses than one. *Clyde* became the secret rendezvous for the de Larminat party and anti-Vichy French officials from across the water. Scott-Hill himself contributed a shrewd political manœuvre. He was already acquainted with Colonel Carretier who commanded the French Air Force units across in Brazzaville. The Colonel was an enthusiast in matters of long-range aviation and had himself flown the South Atlantic. Bearing this in mind, Scott-Hill sent him an invitation to cross the river to look over *Clyde* and see for himself the flying-boat that had made the astonishing journey from Britain to the Congo.

Carretier was met on board by de Larminat. In *Clyde*'s saloon these two men worked out the plans of the *coup d'état* which startled Brazzaville and won over French Equatorial Africa to the Allies a few days later.

Clyde's mission of adventure and high politics was followed almost a month later—during the period of the Battle of Britain—by a trio of flying-boats with the double mission of surveying the Congo route through to Durban and reinforcing what was known as the Horseshoe Route from Durban to Sydney which we shall mention later. The trio consisted of Captain J. C. Harrington, in command of *Corinthian*, Captain J. Davys following a few days later in *Cassiopeia*, followed in turn by Captain F. J. Bailey in *Cooee*. To the second of these, Captain Davys, we are indebted for an eye-witness account of this trip. With their passenger cabins loaded with extra petrol and pumps, they went first to Lisbon, then to Las Palmas in the Canaries.

'The next day we set off for Bathurst. It was easy, we had the whole of Africa on our left and couldn't miss. We crept gingerly round Dakar and arrived at Bathurst in a shower of recognition signals—the signallers were a bit touchy as Vichy Dakar was very close and they hadn't much else to shoot with.

'The next day I picked up an Army Officer who thumbed a ride and said he knew the way. It was just as well we had him on board, because my instructions said to land in a salt creek about ten miles from Freetown—in which case we would probably still be there as there was only a foot of water in it. He, however, knew better as he had seen our mooring laid in the harbour only a week before.

'Lagos was a pleasant relief—we had our own staff and were able to relax at our mess and tell all the landplane blokes about the war they had never seen (they saw plenty afterwards).

'The next morning the Governor of Nigeria tried to impound our flying-boat as a local transport so we had to get away quickly and headed for the dreaded Congo with our guns and dinghies at the ready.

'We found the mouth of the Congo at a place called Banana and headed up the river through mountain gorges looking for a native village called Leopoldville when suddenly a vast city burst on our astonished gaze—the last thing we expected. Not only was there a modern city but a buoy waiting for us.

'We set off for Stanleyville, cutting across the great loop the Congo makes to the north. For hour after hour we flew over dense jungle with occasional glimpses of water underneath and, feeling rather sorry for the pygmies, finally struck the Congo again well to the west of Stanleyville, to make sure of not missing it, and so presently we came to a small township and there was a buoy and there was a launch—so we alighted and inspected them both.

'The buoy was a massive iron structure bravely breasting the current and we reckoned if the moorings could hold it it could hold us as well without noticing it—the launch required further study.

'The order had gone forth that we must have a buoy, petrol and a *motor* launch. The buoy was easy—the petrol not too difficult, but the launch was a different matter as there was no motor boat at Stanleyville. However, the Belgians were not to be beaten. They had got a boat and they had got an old "T" model Ford so they just put the two together. Having removed the wheels and the back axle, they put it in the boat in the back of which they drilled a hole in which they inserted a bit of piping through which ran another bit of pipe connected at one end to the transmission and presumably at the other end to a propeller—and I never saw it but am prepared to believe anything. In the front part of the boat was a 20-gallon drum connected to the top of the radiator, the bottom being piped over the side while beside the drum was a small boy with a dipper to keep the drum full of Congo. The last piece of equipment was a large boy who stood beside the small boy to beat him on the head, whenever he noticed that he was not dipping Congo but looking at "fly bateau".

'The driver sat in the driver's seat driving the normal gears and throttle and blowing the normal horn—the only thing that didn't work were the brakes—a pity!

'The next morning when we arrived with our baggage at the river side we were tearfully informed that the carboat "it worked not"—perhaps the big boy had either killed the little boy or had just forgotten to notice, anyhow, there were we and there was the "fly bateau" and in between a hundred yards of raging muddy torrent full in our imagination of crocodiles and other nameless horrors—we were stuck.'

Native canoes took them aboard the flying-boat and they left Stanleyville for Lake Victoria. There were other incidents and minor adventures before the three flying-boats arrived in Durban to join the main fleet operating the Horseshoe Route.

Only a glance at the map at this point can convey the extent and significance of this famous route which carried the flag of the Commonwealth throughout most of the war in spite of the encroachments of the Japanese in the Far East. At one end of the horseshoe was Australasia. Thence the curve came up through India to the Middle East, roughly at the top of the shoe. The other curve went down through the Sudan and East Africa to Durban. This pattern with a somewhat different context was already in existence before the war—with the one all-important addition of a thick black main trunk line between the Middle East junction and the United Kingdom. The loss of this could only be remedied by a prodigious detour. First by flight from Britain to West Africa, then by two services across Africa, by landplane to Khartoum and by flying-boat through the Congo to Lake Victoria.

On the Horseshoe Route itself, Durban had already been selected as the engineering base for the flying-boats. The staff was on the way there before the Mediterranean closed. The whole maintenance programme was shared with Qantas who had their base at Sydney at the other terminal of the route. The planning went well. Only nine days after the Italians entered the war, a weekly service was running from each end of the Horseshoe Route. Some weeks later, when the engineering parties had established themselves at Durban, these services were duplicated.

When on June 10, 1940, Italy came into the war, sixteen flying-boats were on service east or south of Alexandria. They switched at once to the new arrangement. Others were caught in the new area of hostility, though they had been warned already to avoid all Italian territory. *Cathay* flew safely from Ajaccio to Britain. *Caledonia* flew from Corfu to join the Horseshoe fleet. Captain Lock, passing through the Mediterranean, was told politely by an Italian ground radio station that as they were at war they could not give him any more bearings. *Clyde* lay at her moorings in Malta homeward bound with a party of R.A.F. officers: and the Captain, Kelly Rogers, agreed that he would get them back to Britain in spite of a hostile Italy across their path.

Just before take-off on the morning of June 11, it was discovered that one of *Clyde*'s engines was only giving half power but it was decided nevertheless to fly the machine. More serious was the heavy swell outside the smooth waters of Kalafrana Bay. It was enough to overturn the flying-boat, bearing in mind her heavy load and the faulty engine. Kelly Rogers therefore made a daring decision to defy the conventional rules of take-off. He taxied the flying-boat out through the entrance of the bay. When the swell began to affect her, he swung right round and took off directly into the bay, clearing with only 200 feet of water to spare. He flew non-stop to Biscarosse where, in his own words, 'we had difficulty in getting fuel . . . and were the last civil registered aircraft to traverse Europe for a long time.'

In spite of such adventures as these, *Clyde* met her end through natural causes. She operated the new regular route between Britain and West Africa from October 1940 till February 1941, when at her moorings in Lisbon she was struck by a hurricane which devastated the whole area. There was a single Portuguese workman on board when it struck. For a long time she rode it out with waves breaking right over her. Her crew tried to reach her by boat but were forced back. For hours her seaworthiness upheld her and it seemed likely that she would survive. Then a piece of floating wreckage was hurled against her port wing, puncturing the float. She turned turtle. The unfortunate Portuguese was drowned, and she was a total loss.

The closing of the Mediterranean to through-services in 1940 did not mean that the men of the Merchant Air Service were entirely moved from the area. B.O.A.C. aircraft and crews continued to pass through Malta during the worst bombardments. They had to land and take off under cover of darkness sometimes while bombs were falling round them on Luqa airfield in Malta. Another perilous individual task which fell to the long-range airmen was the Crete evacuation.

> 'When Germany invaded Greece [writes Captain Davys] we on the Horseshoe Route had no idea that anything was going seriously wrong until one day when I was on stand off at Cairo, I was called into the office and told in great secrecy that I was to take a "C" class boat to Crete and bring back various personnel. Still not realizing that anything much was wrong but impressed by the secrecy, I went down to our Nile base, where I found that everyone else knew all about it as the aircraft was being loaded with packing cases marked Crete!
>
> 'Our first stage was to Alexandria where the R.A.F. were to brief us and also disguise our boat with camouflage paint to look like a Sunderland.
>
> 'The briefing was rather alarming—everything in Greece had collapsed. German fighters were everywhere and our job was to get as many R.A.F. personnel out of Crete (where the Sunderlands were dropping them from Greece) as possible. The only cheerful part of the briefing was their assurance that as we looked like a Sunderland in our war paint, no one would come near us.
>
> 'The plan was to arrive at Crete at last light escorted if possible by a Sunderland, stay the night and leave again as soon as it was possible to see. So, in the late afternoon, only half painted, we set off tucked in alongside our escort which had a comforting lot of guns.
>
> 'The chief disadvantage of all civil aircraft in war-time is that it is impossible to see anything behind. So as we neared Crete

I watched the Sunderland's tail gunner who kept pointing at things behind us to one of his pals and swinging his guns about, which gave us a creepy feeling up the spine of something nasty just behind us. Nothing, however, happened and in due course we crossed the island and alighted in Suda Bay—one of our peacetime refuelling stops.'

The crew bedded down for the night on board *Coorong* moored among the wrecks of Allied shipping. Before dawn their passengers were brought alongside, thirty-five R.A.F. men evacuated from Greece.

'We had only twenty seats but nobody seemed to mind though we were a bit horrified—no seats—no weights—no load sheet, no paper work—not at all the things we were used to. However, we soon got used to that! And so at first light we set off back to Alexandria.

'The next four days were a pattern of the first—sometimes we had an escort. Sometimes we didn't. There were the constant air raid sirens which never materialized into anything—they went once while we were refuelling and the tanker crew hopped into their dinghy and rowed ashore leaving us feeling very naked in the middle of the harbour. Then there were the night guards who walked round with Tommy guns shooting out any lights which showed, also the same sort of load of passengers early every morning—we were carrying fifty a time at the end.

'The last morning the starter on our No. 3 engine seized up—so we tried to wind it to start but could hardly move it. We all had a go, still with no success, what time daylight grew apace and the morning air raid was about due. Suddenly the sirens went and the First Officer, Ernie Bicknell—one of the strongest little men I know—said "Let me get at it" and seizing the handle wound it at a terrific rate—bang!—the engine was away and so were we like a flash hugging the valleys across the island and down on to the wave tops the other side all on our own and, of course, it would be the morning we met our only Jerry. We met almost head-on at nought feet, took one look at each other and bolted in opposite directions. . . .'

Two flying-boats *Coorong* and *Cambria* brought out 469 passengers between them, making 13 return trips in all. The

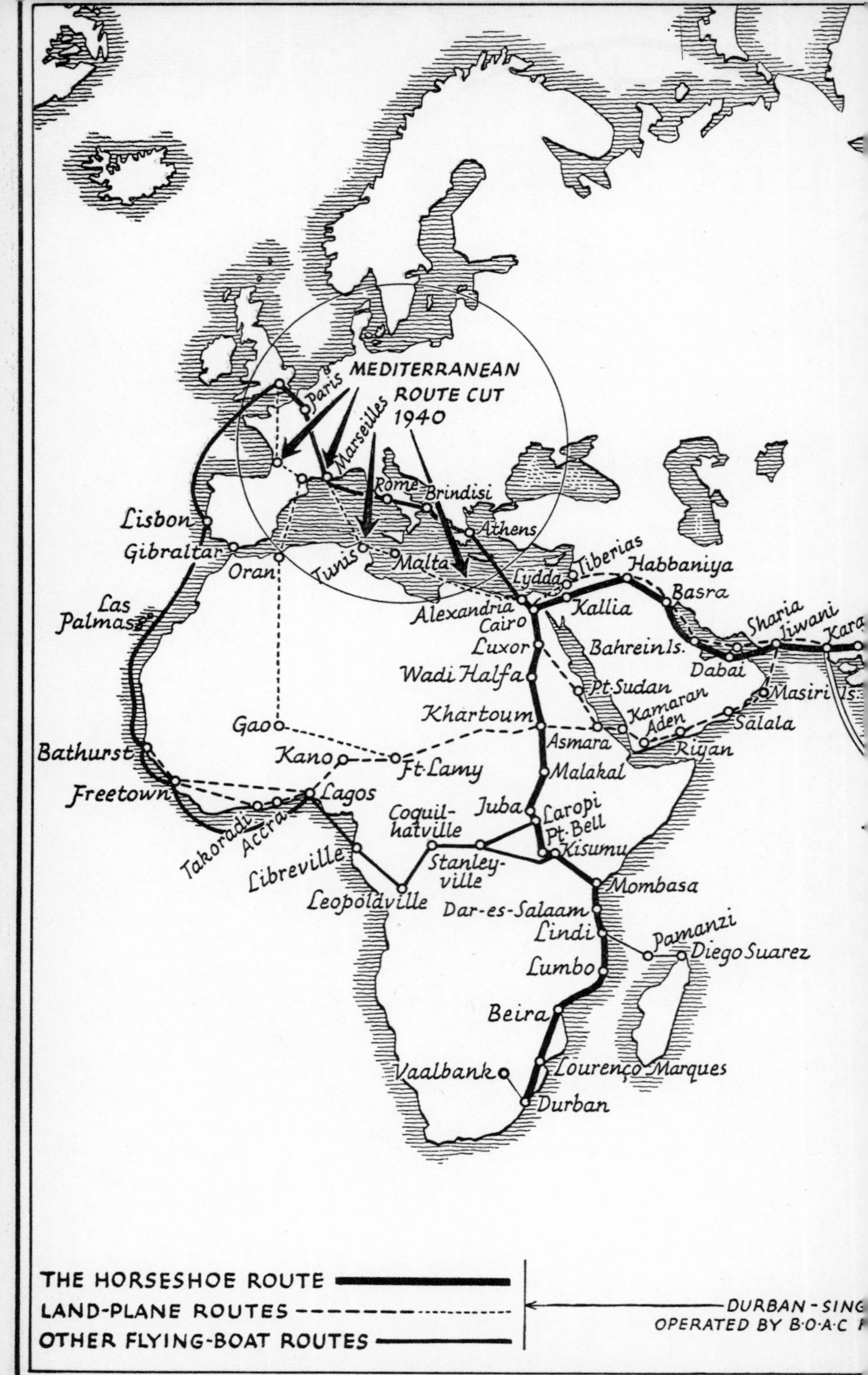

MEDITERRANEAN ROUTE CUT 1940
Paris
Marseilles
Rome
Brindisi
Athens
Lisbon
Gibraltar
Oran
Tunis
Malta
Tiberias
Habbaniya
Lydda
Basra
Alexandria
Kallia
Cairo
Sharia
Jiwani
Kara
Luxor
Bahrein Is.
Dabai
Wadi Halfa
Pt. Sudan
Masiri Is.
Kamaran
Khartoum
Aden
Salala
Gao
Asmara
Riyan
Las Palmas
Bathurst
Kano
Ft. Lamy
Malakal
Freetown
Lagos
Juba
Laropi
Coquilhatville
Pt. Bell
Takoradi
Accra
Libreville
Kisumu
Stanleyville
Mombasa
Leopoldville
Dar-es-Salaam
Lindi
Pamanzi
Diego Suarez
Lumbo
Beira
Vaalbank
Lourenço Marques
Durban
THE HORSESHOE ROUTE
LAND-PLANE ROUTES
OTHER FLYING-BOAT ROUTES
DURBAN-SING
OPERATED BY B·O·A·C

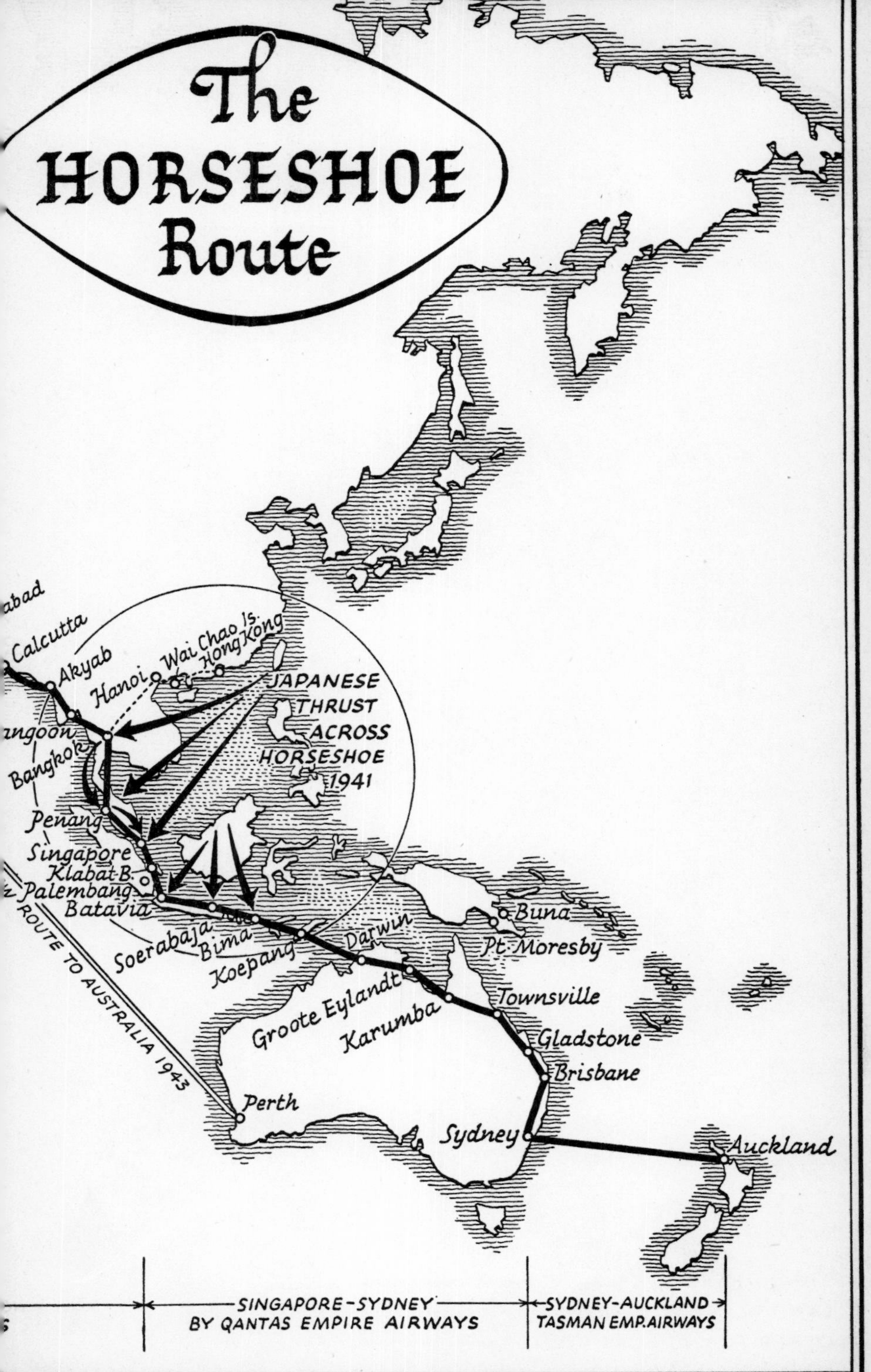
The HORSESHOE Route
abad
Calcutta
Akyab
Hanoi
Wai Chao Is.
Hong Kong
JAPANESE THRUST ACROSS HORSESHOE 1941
angoon
Bangkok
Penang
Singapore
Klabat B.
Palembang
Batavia
Soerabaja
Bima
Koepang
Darwin
Buna
Pt. Moresby
Groote Eylandt
Karumba
Townsville
Gladstone
Brisbane
Perth
Sydney
Auckland
ROUTE TO AUSTRALIA 1943
SINGAPORE-SYDNEY BY QANTAS EMPIRE AIRWAYS
SYDNEY-AUCKLAND TASMAN EMP. AIRWAYS

crews worked these on a roster system. When one of the flying-boats operating the Horseshoe Route alighted on the Nile in Cairo its crew was rushed by car straight to Alexandria to take a turn on one of the camouflaged flying-boats running the Cretan ferry. The car returned with a crew who had operated to Crete and who then took over the routine Horseshoe flight either to Durban or Singapore. For these men, the Cretan interlude was in violent contrast to their normal operations. The flying-boats, built to carry 21 passengers, averaged 36 on all the flights out of Suda Bay, which meant that on some trips up to 47 passengers were taken—so many that on some occasions when the rescued Service men filed on board, the forward door sank so low that seawater slopped in.

Though these pages are devoted to aviation, they would not be complete without a reference at this point to a ship, M.V. *Imperia*, originally a Dutch fishing research vessel in the North Sea. This diesel-engined craft was bought by Imperial Airways to serve as a floating base, meteorological and radio station for the flying-boats crossing the Mediterranean. For many years her station was in Crete where she was a familiar and hospitable stop for crews and passengers in transit between Italy and Egypt. In command of her was Captain Francis Grant Pool, who had lived long in those waters and spoke the local dialect fluently. In fact his identification with Crete was such that when *Imperia* received a pre-arranged code signal to up-anchor and sail for Port Said on Italy's entry into the war, Captain Pool elected to stay behind. After the flying-boats made their last run, Pool, disguised and riding a donkey, started his own operations, rounding up and organizing the evacuation of large numbers of Commonwealth troops. He continued this work so long as there was need and at the end of it all was rewarded by a well-deserved D.S.O. and D.S.C., and the post of Consul in Volos—an appointment dear to his heart in which he ended his days.

Imperia, obeying her code signal, sailed right through the naval patrol off Port Said, to the delight of some and the embarrassment of others. After being refitted, her next duty was at Akaba, which was to be used by the flying-boats on the Horseshoe Route as an alternative if Rommel's forces came near enough to Cairo to prevent them from alighting there. Except for experimental flights, the services of *Imperia* were not actually used at

Akaba and for a time she was moved to Hurgada on the Red Sea coast again as an assurance against German advance in the Western Desert.

Her last service with B.O.A.C. was a happier one. With victorious British forces advancing along the North African coast in 1943, it became possible once again to contemplate some kind of merchant air route through the Mediterranean from Lisbon and Gibraltar, if a suitable Allied area in between could be found. The idea was put to the R.A.F.—Lord Douglas was at that time Commander-in-Chief Middle East—and the waters between the Island of Djerba and the mainland were chosen. A tented camp was built for passengers and staff and *Imperia* sailed in, once more to play her part as a floating meteorological and wireless station.

Soon after that, Italy fell and the flying-boats from Britain which once had to go by way of the Congo came through Syracuse in Sicily, and the *Imperia* had had her day. She was sold to the Secretary of State for War for £12,500. One of the many who knew her and liked her states that she was subsequently purchased by two British Army officers. Then the story goes that she was picked up in the Mediterranean drifting with nobody on board. Certainly she played a notable part in British civil aviation in peace and in war.

Reverting to the period of the Crete evacuation of 1941, it will be remembered that the Germans fostered an armed uprising in Iraq in order to further their drive towards the East. This started the first serious disruption of the newly established Horseshoe Route. The map indicates the importance of Lake Habbaniya, some 60 miles west of Baghdad, as a refuelling-point for flying-boats over the route. The revolution, which started towards the end of April 1941 under the usurped premiership of Rashid Ali, at once placed this important link in jeopardy. The Royal Air Force possessed a large permanent base on the shore of Lake Habbaniya. At the time of the rising it was manned largely by trainees who were equipped with obsolete aircraft with which they had to fight for their lives.

A mile or so away from the base, along the shore of the lake, was the B.O.A.C. rest-house, well equipped as a regular port of call for the flying-boats on the route to the Far East, but, of course, quite unfortified.

As soon as the trouble started, the B.O.A.C. Traffic Superintendent for Iraq and Persian Gulf, Mr. Alistair Thomson, sent away all women and children aboard two flying-boats. There remained six Europeans belonging to the ground staff, together with half a dozen Assyrian and Armenian employees.

Themselves unarmed, they watched Iraqi troops dig themselves in on the plateau which dominated the R.A.F. cantonment and which stood roughly 150 feet above the level of the rest-house. There were some two thousand airmen within the cantonment. They were holding forces at least 15,000 strong. The men in the rest-house remained in communication with the R.A.F. by telephone. By May 2, they had made all preparations for departure: 'bags packed, codes burnt, cash distributed, rations prepared'. No flying-boat came from Cairo to take them off. The next day they were still in touch with the R.A.F. when a lorry approached containing armed Arabs. The approach was cautious. The Arabs disembarked and hid whenever an aircraft appeared.

Eventually the lorry drew up in the B.O.A.C. compound and the armed men disposed themselves at various points of vantage. There then emerged from the lorry Sheikh Afti Khan, with his son Mishrif, who was courteously entertained according to the custom of the country, but who left no doubt in Thomson's mind 'that he was out to enrich himself as best he could'. Observing B.O.A.C. possessed no guard, his first move was to suggest that his men, in charge of his son, would remain as guard for the rest-house. He named his price, which was to be paid four days in arrears, but then inquired tenderly about transport saying that his own truck had broken down. There was nothing for it but to let him have a B.O.A.C. vehicle as he promised to return with food the following day. That night the Sheikh's guard remained and there was constant bombardment of the R.A.F. camp from up on the hill.

The next day, May 4, a flying-boat alighted at the far end of the lake. The B.O.A.C. men were able to put out in their launch but failed to attract the attention of the flying-boat which made off before they could approach. That day the telephone was cut.

'During the afternoon [Thomson afterwards wrote in his report] it was noticed that two Arabs were hanging about the place talking to the Sheikh's men, but on being told to send these men away, the guard said that they were friendly.

'Just before sundown, however, these Arabs were seen to go up on to the Plateau, and communicate with some soldiers there, two of which came down into a ravine. After dark the Sheikh's son asked to see us. He was asked what he thought of the situation and seemed to favour our going to Ramadi for internment, but to gain yet more time, we said we would not decide until the morrow. While this talk was going on, one of the guards came in and told Mishrif that he was wanted outside. Mishrif returned in a few minutes to say that six soldiers were outside and about to fire a volley into the rest-house, but that he had told them that we were unarmed. He said we were to go outside. The soldiers would not allow us to take anything at all with us, and as soon as we set foot outside the door, we were seized, hustled into a double line and searched by the Arab guard, who took anything they wanted.

'All staff lost their wrist watches, and three their money. Two staff were then blindfolded, and there was every indication that we were going to be shot, but instead we were marched on to the plateau, where a most excited officer waved a revolver at us and told us they (the Iraqis) were fighting for their freedom—from what bondage they did not say. He then threatened us with the revolver and made us put up our hands for a further search.

'More personal belongings were removed from our clothing both by Arabs and soldiers, and then an order was given to tie our hands behind our backs which was done, though actually very inefficiently. A motor truck then arrived and after the Traffic Superintendent had been lifted into it, an R.A.F. aircraft came over and bombed and machine-gunned a position about 200 yards off. The party scattered, leaving prisoners to take cover as best they could. Fortunately the aircraft did not spot us and after all had been pushed into the truck, we proceeded to Falluja via the desert.'

On the following day, May 5, the men were pulled out of the truck and marched into a house at Falluja where they were interrogated and then bound. They were then pushed into a filthy truck which was covered with bitumen and sent off to

Baghdad. After interrogation at an Iraqi army headquarters, to which they were led blindfold, they managed to speak to the British Embassy, which was still operating. After that they were blindfolded again and taken to the Ministry of Defence.

> 'On arrival at or near the Ministry of Defence, the lorry was parked at the side of the street and remained in the sun for three-quarters of an hour while the populace again were allowed to view the prisoners. We were then hauled out of the lorry and hustled down between two rows of soldiers two deep, amid shouts and jeers from the onlookers. The party was then placed in a wet stone cell devoid of any furniture and left to meditate.'

Conditions for these men improved but they were kept in custody until the end of May when an armistice was declared.* Ultimately that part of the Horseshoe Route was restored.

During the whole of this period before the Battle of El Alamein and for some time afterwards, while a German and Italian break-through to the Middle East was still a possibility, West Africa and the trunk lines across the centre of Africa were of strategic importance. Not only were they the chief means of communication with the United Kingdom, but they also served the ever-increasing stream of supplies coming from the United States by sea and later by air across the South Atlantic. Britain found herself desperately short of long-range flying-boats after the loss of *Cabot* and *Caribou* in Norway in 1940 and *Clyde* at Lisbon in February 1941. Two more flying-boats, *Cathay* and *Champion*, sister ships of *Clyde*, were brought in during the following month. Meanwhile the British had to lay their hands on anything they could get, and this brought a curious, indeed a unique, craft into the fleet. She was called *Guba*, and she was the early version of the familiar Catalina flying-boat. This machine had been used for an expedition to New Guinea in 1939 to study flora and fauna for the American Museum of Natural History. She was afterwards commissioned by the Australian Government to make a survey across the Indian Ocean. She had just made an appearance at the New York World Fair, having completed 24,000 miles'

* B.O.A.C. staff once again met trouble in Baghdad in 1958, when the British Embassy there was sacked. On this later occasion, however, they were not molested, though some of them witnessed the killing of the Prime Minister and the dragging of his body behind a lorry through the streets.

flying, when the British Air Commission in Washington purchased her. She was at first intended for training in Canada, but the need for long-range aircraft on the West African route was so great that it was decided to fly her across the Atlantic with a cargo of aluminium tubing needed in the war factories of Britain.

Under the command of Captain I. G. Ross, she set out from Botwood in October 1940, and made the crossing in sixteen hours and twenty-one minutes to Stranraer. She carried no heating: in fact, she was still equipped with electric fans from her tropical journeys. Some seven hours out of Newfoundland at 13,000 feet, the propellers iced up and the ice thrown off broke the windows of the navigator's compartment. Freezing draughts cut through the aircraft and the crew had to hold down everything with weights, their numbed hands almost unable to grasp pencils and charts. Then all the cockpit windows iced over and Ross was only able to see through the navigator's broken windows. At that height, for long without oxygen and half frozen, Captain and crew became light-headed, but *Guba* plunged on. When at last they came down below 5,000 feet after fourteen hours to look for a landfall and broke cloud, they found themselves above the liner *Empress of Britain*, slowly sinking after attacks by enemy aircraft.

At Stranraer, nobody knew they were coming in, owing to security silence, and their reception was so chilly that the Captain was heard to say with some asperity: 'Fill the goddam thing with gas and we'll fly it back.' But *Guba* went on to fly for many years more, carrying passengers and freight on the West African route.

A further reinforcement of the West African route was made by the purchase of three Boeing Clipper flying-boats from Pan-American Airways. These were not secured under lease-lend arrangements, but were bought for cash. It is said that the American Company, already certain in their minds that their future lay in landplanes, and therefore only too ready to dispose of flying-boats, nevertheless made a profit of a quarter of a million dollars on each of these craft. To the British at that time they were invaluable at any price, being capable of flying not only across the Atlantic non-stop, but from Britain to West Africa without calling at Lisbon. During the earlier years of war there was always the threat that Spain would join the Axis powers and

Portugal be over-run. Detailed preparations had been made for B.O.A.C. to vacate Lisbon at short notice.

The Boeings, named *Bristol*, *Berwick* and *Bangor*, could not be serviced in Britain. The Corporation therefore set up a maintenance base for them at Baltimore, U.S.A., to which they returned for servicing after each round flight between Britain and West Africa. In that way, an unscheduled transatlantic service was initiated in 1941, and the Baltimore base remained in use, as we shall see, until the post-war years.

The landward aspect of the West African route was strengthened by a fleet of landplanes, including Flamingoes and Ensigns, built up for the trunk line across Africa to Khartoum. There was heavy traffic in supplies and passengers for Egypt, the Western Desert and the Mediterranean. On the return run they carried back ferry pilots who had taken aircraft reinforcements from the wharves of West Africa to R.A.F. bases in the Nile Delta. The Empire flying-boats were brought in to assist in this traffic by flying the Congo route, which made a wide sweep to the south before coming up to Khartoum and the Nile.

Geography and weather were not the only problems that had to be overcome. At Lagos, for instance, the flying-boats made use of a lagoon which natives were accustomed to fish by night.

> 'Nothing could persuade them [relates *Merchant Airmen*] that there was any danger in unlit fishing canoes wandering about a lagoon on which flying-boats were alighting; one delighted fisherman, indeed, was discovered with his canoe tied to one of the alighting flares, finding the lights served admirably to attract the fish. When the fishermen realized that they were really to be forbidden their night waters, they grew angry, and employed a witch-doctor to put a ju-ju on the lagoon. This would not have mattered, except that the native employees of British Overseas Airways then refused to go near the place, until the Corporation employed another witch-doctor to "de-ju-ju" it. (The Airways witch-doctor did not seem to be particularly powerful, since the Airways depot ship caught fire on the lagoon a few nights later, though that may be laid to the blame, perhaps, not of witchcraft but of a watchman who decided to refuel a petrol engine by the light of a hurricane lamp.)'

In the autumn of 1941, the Americans, though not yet themselves at war, took over the burden of much of the trans-Africa route. Pan-American Airways made regular landplane flights from New York by way of Brazil and across the South Atlantic and from the West Coast of Africa to Khartoum, thus releasing some of the pressure on our own services.

That same autumn, a daring, though temporary, return to the Mediterranean was made. Five flying-boats were taken off the West African run in order to fly through Lisbon, Gibraltar, Malta and Cairo. With the Axis powers still on both sides of the Mediterranean, this was a hazardous business for unarmed, comparatively slow craft flying directly across the enemy's lines of communication. They had to be called off when the Germans made their final great advance across the Western Desert in the summer of 1942.

Emerging from these long-haul operations of supply to the Middle East and communication within the British Commonwealth and the Allies, there was a short-haul pattern of operations within the Middle East area which became widely known as the 'Tedder Plan'. At that time, Lord Tedder was in command of the R.A.F. in the Middle East and the idea for a marriage of resources of civil aviation with the needs of battle was his. In the summer of 1941, when he took over, Tedder found himself almost without R.A.F. air transport. It has been noted already that civil aircraft helped out R.A.F. movements during the Battle of Britain. In the battles which developed in the Western Desert, the R.A.F. and the Army were woefully lacking in freight and passenger craft. With no new transport machines being manufactured in Britain, all had to come from America.

Tedder's need was not only for air transport in and across Africa but also throughout the Levant and to Iraq. The plan was for the use of airline machines organized on regular services by experienced airline people. The existing capacity was not adequate in itself. Tedder needed far more transport than could be supplied by B.O.A.C. alone, so service aircraft with their crews were diverted to B.O.A.C. These machines were mainly Lockheed Lodestars, which had been ordered originally by the French but delivered to the Royal Air Force. B.O.A.C. took them over, trained the crews and set up a large maintenance base at Asmara in Eritrea for the servicing of the combined fleet.

Flexibility was an essential element in the Tedder Plan. The aircraft had to assemble from time to time at moments of emergency for mass operations carrying men, supplies and casualties within battle areas. Crews would be called off routine operations in the peaceful parts of the network to do ferry jobs right into the front line, carrying live ammunition, fuel, blood plasma, senior officers, evacuating wounded, important prisoners or such precious cargo as a captured enemy cipher machine. On such duties the merchant airmen served in the Battle of Alamein. They continued until there was no further need of them.

When Japan entered the war on December 8, 1941, quite detailed plans were already in existence for three separate variations of the Horseshoe Route between Burma and Australia. The phases of withdrawal are best seen on the map between pages 201–202.

At the same time as the various phases of withdrawal were being worked out, B.O.A.C., with ever-increasing world-commitments, came up against a grave shortage of air crews. Two months before Japan entered the war, therefore, arrangements were made that the Australian crews of Qantas, who had been going as far as Singapore, should fly on to Karachi. The burden of carrying on in the face of Japanese aggression in constantly worsening conditions fell almost entirely upon the Australian merchant airmen. It is to their credit, therefore, that the life-line between Britain and Australia over this critical area remained open for as long as it did.

The carefully planned phases of withdrawal were telescoped into a few days of frantic rearrangement owing to the speed with which the Japanese struck out. The B.O.A.C. Director General, Mr. W. L. (now Lord) Runciman, together with the Regional Director for India, Mr. J. W. S. Brancker, son of Sir Sefton, were almost trapped in Bangkok where they had been studying the new arrangements at first hand. They were intending to leave on the regular east-bound flying-boat on that Monday morning when Japan went to war. In the early hours, however, the local office learned that the Japanese were already in Siam and were expected in Bangkok within a couple of hours—and the flying-boat had, of course, been diverted to one of the alternative routes which these officials had come to study. Japanese troops arrived that evening. There was no resistance, indeed there was pleasantness all round. Making the best of the atmosphere, the men of the airline then spent the night in Bangkok, went to the railway station the following morning and breakfasted in the restaurant in time to catch the 9.50 train to Pitsanulok in the north of the country. From there, by specially chartered aircraft, bullock and primitive canoe, and with a certain amount of walking, they made their way into the then safe territory of Burma.

The story now is a gallant one of retreat, withdrawal and rescue, punctuated by loss and disaster. The Japanese entered Burma on December 13. Penang in Malaya was evacuated a few days later. By the end of the month Singapore was threatened. During these days the flying-boats were busy ferrying ammunition and fuel to shore up our retreating forces, bringing out women and children. All reserve aircraft with crews and engineers were moved from Singapore to Batavia during the middle of the month. On December 22, Captain C. E. Madge took *Cassiopeia* by way of the Andaman Islands into Singapore with a load of urgently needed ammunition. Taking off from Singapore roads, the hull of the flying-boat struck a submerged object. *Cassiopeia* flooded and floated just long enough for the crew of the upper flight deck to scramble out. First Officer Blunt went back along the sinking hull and forced open the rear escape hatch. Diving into the flooded passenger cabin, he managed to bring out one of the four passengers, but she did not survive.

Within a week, the bombardment of Singapore started. The standby staff of the airline moved back to Batavia and organized shuttle services between that city and Singapore, all regular flying-boat services south of Rangoon having been suspended. The Australian crews now flying to Singapore in their unarmed craft carried out some of the most perilous civil air operations of the whole war and suffered many casualties, for the skies were crowded with enemy aircraft and there was frequent air bombardment in other ports of call. There was nothing which they could do to avoid air interception. Against the dangers of being caught on the surface, they developed a technique of tuning in to the radio station at the next port of call. If they received news of an alert, they would put down on some lonely stretch of coastal water until the all clear sounded. At a convenient distance from Singapore there was a little bay along the coast discovered by Captain O. F. Y. Thomas which became known as 'Thomas's Funk-hole'.

The British Minister of State, Mr. Duff Cooper (later Viscount Norwich) was brought out of Singapore in mid-January. In spite of ever-increasing air raids and later shelling from the mainland, the flying-boats continued to operate until February 3, when Captain W. H. Crowther took the last craft into Singapore, bringing out forty passengers in bright moonlight. After this the B.O.A.C. launch continued rescue work ferrying evacuees out to shipping in the roads, before itself escaping to Java.

Singapore before its surrender on February 15 was not by any means the only dangerous spot. For example, Captain A. Koch took the flying-boat *Corio* out of Darwin with reinforcements for Surabaya, intending to return with women and children. Just short of Koepang, which has already figured in this narrative in earlier adventures in more peaceful days, and which was then being bombed, Koch ran into a patrol of seven Japanese fighters.

He dived to sea-level, running for the nearest beach. The first few bursts from the fighters' guns killed most of his passengers and wounded him in the arm and leg. In spite of his wounds, Koch took what evasive action he could with cool deliberation, waiting till the stream of tracer bullets was beating against the windows of his cockpit then swerving violently towards them, a manœuvre which brought the flying-boat out of the line of fire. His wing tip floats were dipping into the surface of the sea every time he swerved. He was still some miles from land when the end came. With two engines on fire, *Corio* lost speed. When he tried to put her down, her nose plunged into the water.

Koch himself was thrown clear with two of his officers and three passengers. With one of the passengers, who like himself was a strong swimmer, Koch decided to attempt the five-mile swim to the beach to bring help to the others, though he was only able to use his arms. After several hours they reached the breakers and were joined afterwards by three other survivors. Eventually they managed to reach the Dutch authorities in Koepang and were taken off in a flying-boat.

After this the route from Surabaya to Darwin was abandoned. In its place a new shuttle service was opened from Broome to Tjilatjap. This service was intended for the transport of urgent supplies for the defence of Java and three flying-boats, *Circe*,

Coriolanus and *Corinthian* were used. But even as they began to operate, Java was being over-run by the Japanese and the flying-boats were engaged in rescue work. When *Circe* and *Corinthian* left Java on February 28, 1942, for Broome, only *Corinthian* arrived, *Circe* having been shot down by enemy fighters. By this time Darwin had already been bombed by the Japanese and Broome, crowded with refugees, shipping and aircraft, was threatened. There on the morning of March 3, the flying-boat *Corinna* was being refuelled. Passengers and crew were waiting on the jetty. Fourteen other types of flying-boats, most of them from Java, were waiting their turn to refuel—and Japanese fighters struck, burning and sinking every flying-boat in the harbour. Thus, with the greater part of the flying-boat fleet lost in that sector, the Horseshoe Route was broken—but only for a matter of months.

Catalina aircraft were being ferried over nearly 8,000 ocean miles from the Pacific Coast of America to Australia. These two-engined flying-boats, noisy but wonderfully efficient, were not in any sense airliners. They were to be used for supplying Australian troops fighting against the Japanese in the islands. They were also to be the means of mending the Horseshoe, for the experience in their long-range ocean use gained by Qantas resulted in their being suggested for direct flights across the Indian Ocean. The British and Australian Governments agreed on a direct flight to replace the Malayan sector of the Horseshoe. B.O.A.C. crews flew such Catalinas as Britain could spare to Ceylon, where they were handed over to the R.A.F. At first the spanning of the Indian Ocean from Ceylon to Perth, Australia, was a secret military operation. Then, in June 1943, the new route was handed over to B.O.A.C. and Qantas. Captain W. H. Crowther, the distinguished Australian pilot who had planned the new route, was placed in charge.

The first south-bound Catalina service was flown by Captain R. B. Tapp. He took 27 hours and 50 minutes, carrying diplomatic and troop mail as well as extra fuel. The next trip, in July 1942, took 28 hours 32 minutes, carrying a passenger, diplomatic mail and airgraphs. Soon they were able to carry three passengers on these trips. It should be added that these passengers had to have some degree of toughness as well as priority importance. They had to stand in the forward compartment for take-off, acting as ballast to trim the overburdened flying-boat. They remained in that position for some hours until enough fuel had been consumed to allow them to go aft and sit down. The only space aboard for a stretch was in the gun deck aft between the two semi-spherical blisters. There was no smoking and only scratch meals. There was, however, an unofficial honour which went with the trip. It was the 'Order of the Double Sunrise', for these flights took so long that passengers and crew enjoyed the distinction of seeing the sun rise twice in the course of the non-stop trip. When the last Catalina service came into Perth in July 1945, the record was 271 crossings made in an average time of 27 hours with over one million accident-free miles flown.

The service was started *ad hoc* by the R.A.F., then once weekly from July 1943 by Q.E.A. and three times a fortnight from October when the route was extended from Ceylon to Karachi. The route was reinforced in July 1943 with two converted Liberator bombers flown out to Australia by B.O.A.C. These landplanes provided a faster service with better facilities all round and the name Kangaroo, now inherited jointly by Qantas and B.O.A.C. was given to their service between Perth and Colombo. Captain O. P. Jones of B.O.A.C. flew as Commander on the initial service and adviser to Qantas.

The flying-boat remained the vital link in this chain of Commonwealth communications until 1945, when a new landplane service was started with Lancastrians which were civilian versions of the famous Lancaster bombers. This trunk line from London to Karachi was operated by B.O.A.C., thence via Ceylon to Sydney by Q.E.A. Its achievements belong to the post-war story. From this brief survey of the Horseshoe Route, we must now turn once more to the other side of the world pattern, the realization in war of the Atlantic Bridge.

CHAPTER XII

ATLANTIC AND BOARDROOM WAR

War having prevented Britain at the outset from carrying fare-paying passengers across the Atlantic, the honour of being the first had gone to the Americans (in the summer of 1939) who had shared with us all the earlier stages of the great experiment. The apparent loss of the first Atlantic fare-paying traffic was more than balanced by the B.O.A.C. effort in pioneering the Atlantic Bridge, in which Canada played a prominent part. Moreover, the management of B.O.A.C. itself was almost a war casualty. The war very nearly throttled the new organization at birth. While the honours of the Atlantic were being shared by merchant airmen and men of the R.A.F., the conflicts between the expediency of war and the claims of post-war progress were being fought out in filing trays, at conference tables, in Parliament and in the boardroom in London.

That British merchant airmen could, and did, fly the Atlantic even when Britain stood alone in 1940 was of immense prestige value. While the Battle of Britain was at its height, and German propaganda, powerful in the United States at that time, was proclaiming that London was in ruins, the flying-boat *Clare*, in her camouflage paint, calmly flew in to circle New York and alight at her moorings at La Guardia. She carried a relatively small item of especial significance—a few bundles of British newspapers dated September 15, 1940, the day of the turning point in the Battle of Britain.

The Germans had declared that British newspapers had been wiped out with the rest of our civilization. What better evidence to the contrary could be offered? The *New York Post* wrote:

> 'Bombs are dropping in or near Fleet Street every night, and the plants of two great London newspapers have already been

damaged, but all are continuing to publish more or less as usual. This copy reached New York yesterday aboard the flying-boat *Clare*, only three days after it had rolled off the presses around the corner from Fleet Street. It was edited and printed under the heaviest bombardment of the war to date, but its columns do not emphasize that. In fact, the traditional British under-statement is applied to the account of the raid then in progress. . . . It will be seen from the front-page headlines that there is no attempt to conceal bad news such as the bombing of Buckingham Palace.'

This was surely one of the most telling individual propaganda gestures of the war.

George Woods Humphery now reappears in a new capacity. Before the Battle of Britain began he had been telling the British Purchasing Commission in the United States that the twin-engined aircraft on order from American factories could be flown across the ocean. They had been going by ship in packing cases—a slow, dangerous and wasteful means of transport, particularly when Britain was in such dire need. In July 1940, the Commission sent a letter to Woods Humphery, which stated:

'I understand that as a result of your and Pirie's [Air Commodore Pirie, Air Attaché to the British Embassy, Washington] conversation with Sir Henry Self recently, it was agreed, subject to confirmation from Canada and England, that you will be responsible for flying across the Lockheed Hudsons, working with an organization in conjunction with the Canadian Pacific Railway.'

Just as Britain had active and enthusiastic support from Australian airmen at the far end of the Horseshoe Route, so the Canadians threw their energies into the Atlantic Bridge, which suddenly became such a vital factor in the strategy of the war. Woods Humphery was appointed assistant to the Chairman of a new Air Service Department set up by the C.P.R. to organize the departure end in Canada. At his suggestion, the organization of the flying and operational side of the new venture was put in the hands of some of his most experienced former colleagues of Imperial Airways, now B.O.A.C. Accordingly, Lieutenant-Colonel H. Burchall, who had been with Woods Humphery for so many years, was brought over to Montreal as General Manager with Captain A. S. Wilcockson, who had carried out the experimental Atlantic flights in 1937, as Operations Manager. Captains D. C. T. Bennett, R. H. Page, I. G. Ross and C. J. Powell joined the organization shortly afterwards.

Bennett and Page went to the Lockheed factory in California to take over the first two Hudsons, which were to be used to train the Atlantic crews. America still being neutral, these two experienced Captains belonging to a State at war had to travel as passengers in the Hudsons as far as the Canadian border. The bombers were not allowed to fly across the frontier into a belligerent country. They were therefore grounded and solemnly towed across by a horse.

This absurdity was the least of the problems to be faced. The aircraft themselves, which were coming through but slowly, had to be modified for the ocean crossing. There was an acute shortage of crews; particularly of navigators, though B.O.A.C. sent twelve complete crews across by sea. Canadians and Americans who volunteered had to be selected and trained. As always, the ocean weather was the greatest problem of all. The North Atlantic had never been flown in either direction in winter and there were many prophets of woe who said that this was impossible under war conditions of radio silence. The authorities themselves, on both sides of the Atlantic, were reconciled to a substantial percentage of loss, to be off-set against the heavy losses which were already incurred at sea and the great gain in time to be achieved by the air ferry.

Fortunately, Gander Airport, since familiar to so many Atlantic passengers, was sufficiently developed for use. Like Shannon, it was the outcome of the pre-war conference at Ottawa which laid the foundations of the Atlantic Bridge. It had cost the British Government a million pounds, of which Newfoundland had paid a sixth. At the time when the first Hudson arrived there, in the autumn of 1940, it was just serviceable as an airfield and only just habitable for airmen. It possessed one hangar and one administrative hut. For living accommodation, there were two railway sleeping coaches with a dining car.

D. C. T. Bennett, as Flying Superintendent, was in charge of all operational arrangements and was also to be the leader of the seven Hudsons which were to make the first crossing. C. J. Powell was responsible for all arrangements on the ground. It was thus very much a B.O.A.C. undertaking. As Bennett flew up from Montreal on November 10, 1940 he sent radio instructions that the whole formation was to be ready to leave that night. At Gander snow and ice had to be cleared away from the six aircraft that were waiting. They had to be thawed out.

The band of the military garrison, the Queen's Own Rifles, serenaded the crews in their dining car and afterwards played them off to '*There'll always be an England*'. Among their number were men from the United States, Canada, Australia and Britain; not only airline men but bush pilots, barnstormers, sky-writers and business men, all trained by B.O.A.C. As a gesture of confidence, each wore a red Remembrance Day poppy. One long dark night and the whole expanse of the Atlantic separated them from November 11 in the United Kingdom.

The twenty-two Canadian poppies were proudly worn the next day when the formation arrived intact at Aldergrove in Northern Ireland. In spite of the North-American accents, the ten-gallon hats and Texan boots, the weary unshaven men had to go through the pretence of having flown across from England. For security reasons, there could be no limelighted reception, in spite of the fact that they had pioneered a new route in the depth of winter under war conditions. After flying on to England, they were simply and quietly sent back by ship to Canada for further flights.

> 'They wanted to look around and go places [writes the officer who was in charge of the return journey]. But Headquarters wanted the men to go back quickly. There was then no return air service, but there was a ship for Canada due that day. The last of the seven aircraft landed at about noon, and the embarkation officials wanted all passengers to be on board at 3 p.m. Thoughts of "going places" were dashed to the ground; those pioneers of Atlantic ferrying stood only for about two and a half hours on the soil of England, and most of that soil was a hangar floor. They were on board just after three o'clock and the situation was saved by the Embarkation Officer producing a tray of whiskies and soda, this being the first liquid or solid refreshment these men had taken in England.
>
> 'It was evening before I had finished clearing up. We had just finished dinner when several of the men, who we thought were safely on board, came into the hotel at the port.

They were in much better spirits. Someone had tried to stop them leaving the ship, but when they found out that it was not leaving until the early hours of the morning they replied, "O.K. we'll be back", and protests from police and sentries went unheeded.

'While they were walking into the centre of the town, an air raid had started; they told me how they had been in a shelter and Hank had led the kiddies in singing. They had seen and heard a few bombs exploding, and they began to think that things were turning out according to plan after all. Their only desire then was to take back some souvenirs. "What sort of town is this," one said, "where you can't buy anything after 6 p.m." But he got his souvenir by buying one packet of every kind of cigarette in stock at the hotel, many of them brands that I had never heard of, and at last he was satisfied and went back to the ship.'

There were several more waves of Hudsons in flights led by Captains Page, Store and Bennett. The formation flying was abandoned owing to the difficulty of keeping contact between groups of aircraft, and also because navigational instruments and trained navigators were becoming available. Aircraft flew individually and in ever-increasing numbers. There was reoganization on the ground. Lord Beaverbrook's Ministry of Aircraft Production took over from the C.P.R. and formed Atlantic Ferry Organization. In the summer of 1941, this in turn was taken over by the newly-formed Ferry Command of the R.A.F. This organization was merged two years later into R.A.F. Transport Command.

Aircrews were never more precious than in those days, and it was unacceptable that they should cross the Atlantic in one direction at 200 miles an hour and travel back in the other at 10 knots. A service of Liberator bombers was therefore laid on to fill this need. Bennett carried out the first flight of this service in 1941 with a Liberator carrying Lord Dowding, of Battle of Britain fame, three other passengers and diplomatic mail. The first west-bound Liberator, operated by Captain Youell, was delayed at Blackpool by a bomb landing 25 yards away but made a successful crossing with seven ferry pilots as passengers a few days later.

During the next two months more than 20 flights were made in each direction, and in September 1941 B.O.A.C. were called upon to take over. They operated what became known as the Return Ferry Service with a fleet of 10 Liberators, Captain A. S. Wilcockson being in charge as Operations Controller.

At the beginning, these were not equipped for ocean flying at great heights in winter. Ice was the chief enemy and the Liberators had to go to 20,000 feet to avoid it. There was no system of heating for the interior of the aircraft. Only after various experiments had been tried was it found possible to harness the engines' exhaust system to this purpose. Until this was done, passengers, many of them middle-aged men on important war missions, travelled in discomfort and even danger. There were no seats in the Liberators in those days, the passengers simply bedding down on mattresses on the floor. A careless or a sleepy passenger might well go in danger of frostbite. On a west-bound journey, one traveller, who had removed his gloves, lost all the fingers of both hands.

Prominent among those who flew the Return Ferry was Captain O. P. Jones and one of the better stories about him relates to a Return Ferry trip.

> 'Midway across [states *Merchant Airmen*] the light at the instrument panel failed. The second pilot, making his first Atlantic flight, was at the controls at the time, and Captain Jones retired to the engineer's position, to write up his log-book by the glow from the dials on that panel. Flight Engineer Stack made way for him, and sat down on the floor to eat an apple.
>
> 'At that moment, over the middle of the Atlantic, all four engines cut out simultaneously. It transpired later that the pilot, adjusting the automatic controls in darkness, had accidentally pulled the master switch for all engines. They were then at about 14,000 feet, and they glided rapidly to 6,000 feet before the captain, striding forward, had remedied the mishap and brought the engines to life again. But before he did so, he closed his log book with some deliberation, laid his pen down beside it, turned to the engineer, and remarked, "Strangely quiet, isn't it, Mr. Stack?" '

By the end of the war (V.J. Day) B.O.A.C. aircraft on missions and services throughout the war had flown sixty-five million miles. The Corporation as a Government service had carried 325,000 passengers. Out of the total of 83 members of the Corporation's staff who died on flying duties during the whole war period, 29 Captains had been lost.

Throughout these years the higher management in London underwent many changes. There were times indeed when it almost passed out of existence. When Imperial Airways and British Airways were amalgamated by legislation and flung together by the impact of war, there seemed at least the dominating character of Reith to mould the new concern. But this was not to be. Reith himself, as he confesses in his memoirs, was awaiting day by day a telephone message which he hoped would call him to higher things.

'On January 3, 1940, I went to Bristol to take the chair at a board of inquiry into the loss of an aircraft near Malta. That evening and most of the night Runciman and I talked about the parlous state of civil aviation; we decided that one or other of us should immediately set off on a tour of all the routes; it would take some months to accomplish. Which of us to go? Next morning I attended the weekly meeting of the management committee and after lunch set out for home. Runciman came to guide me through the tortuous streets; between the centre and outskirts of Bristol it was decided I should go. It was a duty; it would be interesting; the staff along the routes, and the associated companies, would be glad to have a visit from the chairman. It was not at all what I would have imagined myself doing in war-time but the journey round the world would at least get me away from the exasperations of idleness, of continual waiting; the sooner it started the better. I told my wife what was to happen; naturally she did not like it; but her disquiet was unnecessary. For the telephone rang at last.

'Two days later I received a telegram: "*Congratulations on your appointment as a Minister of the Crown although it entails great loss to us. The very best wishes for the future from all of us.* Imperial and British Airways." I was sorry to leave them; they seemed sorry too.'

He left in charge Runciman, his Director General, a newcomer to the business. Apart from the diversity of the war pattern, some of which we have already noted in these chapters, the new man had to face an astonishing managerial situation. There were to be no new British civil airliners while the war was on. One of the most promising new promotions, the Fairey F.C.1, had to be dropped out of hand. With the whole existing fleet placed entirely at the disposal of the Air Minister, the Government was to pay the costs of the operations of the Corporation every year, offsetting them against the revenue from mails, passengers and freight. The London Headquarters had moved to Bristol, most of the flying-boat maintenance was moved from Hythe to Durban, and bases were established in Egypt at Cairo and Kasfareit, at Asmara, at Baltimore and Montreal and in several other places. These overseas units were connected with Headquarters only by cable. The Air Ministry's Department of Civil Aviation became the sole arbiter and initiator in all matters of air transport policy, taking its policy line from the Air Council and the Supreme Command. Of the 'initiative and responsibility' granted to the new Corporation under the British Overseas Airways Act of 1939, there was soon precious little to be seen.

With Churchill in power, Sir Archibald Sinclair had been appointed Air Minister. The Hon. Clive Pearson had succeeded Reith as Chairman of B.O.A.C. Something of the confusion that had grown up round the status and function of B.O.A.C. is indicated in extracts from a letter sent by Pearson to Sinclair in February 1943:

> 'Looking to the future, we envisage a rapid expansion of air transport both during and after the war, and we have considered whether we are well placed to meet it. The Corporation, as it appears to us, if they can be given full information regarding the intentions and requirements of the Government, can . . . make their plans and be responsible for putting them into execution. Alternatively, the Corporation can be given the limited responsibility of carrying out specific orders.
>
> 'We feel that we are not in either of the above positions and that, as your appointed members, we are in an anomalous situation. Moreover, not being an independent concern, we have not the discretion in directing policy such as would rest with a commercial undertaking; while, on the other hand, not being a branch of the public service, we have not the defined and regulated authority of a Service of the Crown. . . .'

He went on to suggest that the

'Board of Members should be strengthened and in particular the Chairman should be one who at least informally would have access to the Ministers of the many Government Departments with which the activities of the Corporation are concerned. . . .'

He pointed out that there was overlapping between the work of B.O.A.C. and Air Ministry, that specialist staff was being taken by the Ministry of Labour and that the future was obscure.

'. . . we believe that most post-war planning can be done without detriment to the prosecution of the war and without awaiting the settlement of international questions. We assume that whatever system of international air transport is established after the war, some part of it will be in the hands of British operators.

'Can we be informed whether it is intended that the Corporation should remain the sole British instrument for overseas air transport, or if not, then what limitations are intended?

'In sum, should we regard ourselves as a branch of the Air Ministry, which means, as we see it, that we are debarred from making as a corporation any contribution to the discussion of air transport policy? Or should we regard ourselves as a body under the Act free to formulate policy and express it?'

Air Ministry acknowledged this letter and invited Pearson to a meeting on March 1, 1943—where he first learnt officially about the formation of R.A.F. Transport Command. This, as we now know, was a world organization, in certain sectors running parallel with routes already operated by B.O.A.C. with whom clearly there had to be the closest collaboration.

As Director General, Runciman fought against the notion of Corporation subservience to the new Command.

'The Corporation's specialized skill was the operation of regular trunk services, and it was not equipped to do ferrying, airborne troop movements, taxi services and so forth with which the Command would be concerned. The Command had not the Corporation's knowledge of airline work. . . .

'The Corporation and the Air Ministry had . . . arrangements with neutral and Allied countries covering air transport services. These were outside the scope of the R.A.F. The Corporation would depend on the R.A.F. for the means of operating the services. . . . That these should be provided from one common source was right and economical.

'Similarly, the regular scheduled services on any route should be provided by one operator, the Corporation; there should not be two sets of such services.

'The Command would thus, as it were, manage the railway line, using it themselves for certain classes of traffic and providing the means for all classes of traffic. The Corporation, acting to the requirements of the Air Ministry, would run over the line such regular long-distance services as were needed. . . .

'In this way, associated in a common enterprise the Corporation and Command would each play an assigned part. The Command would not be free to tell the Corporation how to conduct its services any more than the Corporation could instruct the Command on other matters.'

The Brabazon Committee at this time had already been at work studying the question of building up a fleet of British civil aircraft after the war. This, with its hopes for the future, particularly weighed with the minds of those at the head of B.O.A.C. By 1943 the war had already begun to take a favourable turn. B.O.A.C. was acutely aware that American airline companies, their strongest potential rivals, were collaborating with the U.S. Transport Command in building up experience and services for use immediately war was over. Loss of identity and subjugation to R.A.F. Transport Command, though it might serve to rule out all possible duplication of effort in winning the war, seemed to be a direct threat to the present management and future development of the airline. The Board felt so strongly about this that when discussions with Air Ministry reached an *impasse* in the middle of March 1943, the Chairman, Pearson, the Director General, Runciman, and two other Members of the Board resigned, leaving only d'Erlanger, who at that time was running Air Transport Auxiliary.

Left virtually without Directors, the heads of Departments in the Corporation held an emergency meeting on their own and proposed that Reith, then a peer and out of office, should be brought back. The Air Minister requested the staff to withdraw this plea. Another meeting was held at which the staff decided not to withdraw. It was only a few days later when it became clear that the Air Minister had already invited people to serve on the Board that the request was withdrawn.

Sir Harold Howitt, a financial expert, as Chairman, Sir Simon Marks of Marks and Spencer and John Marchbank, formerly General Secretary to the National Union of Railwaymen, were then appointed to the Board and these appointments were debated in both Houses of Parliament in 1943. In May new appointments were made. Viscount Knollys became Chairman with Howitt as Deputy Chairman. Air Commodore A. C. Critchley became the new Director General and Commandant Pauline Gower, who had been in charge of the Women's Ferry Section of A.T.A., was appointed to the Board. The *Aeroplane* of May 28 made this comment.

> 'One conclusion to be drawn from most of the recent appointments to the Board of the Corporation is that the Air Ministry discounts experience of air route operation and believes air transport will thrive on business management. Banker, accountant, multiple shop proprietor, trade union organizer, an "A" licence pilot and a woman "B" licence pilot, now comprise the Board whose policy will be carried into doubtless vigorous effect by an officer who in civil life was a leader in popular sport. . . . To choose such a Board and to arm it with a chief officer who is said "never to have lost a friend or enemy" is either an extremely subtle method of obtaining startling results without appearing to plan them, or a naïve attempt to mix oil with water. Whether the Ministry would like to have its hand forced by the Director General who has a reputation for getting things done, we cannot tell. Nor, if that were so, could the Ministry have any guarantee with the Board so constituted, that the best things would be done or that things would be done in the best way. The difficulties which led to the resignation of the former Directors still remain to be resolved.'

The difficulties went fundamentally unresolved, though Critchley made sweeping reorganizations within the framework of management. Then, on April 1, 1945, civil aviation at long last was recognized as a force of sufficient significance to merit a Minister of its own. Viscount Swinton, who had been Air Minister from 1935 to 1938, was appointed as the First Minister of Civil Aviation, with Cabinet rank. Mr. W. D. R. Perkins,

'Operation India'

Transitional B.O.A.C. Lancastrian *Nelson* taking off from an uncompleted London Airport

Armstrong Whitworth Argosy *City of Glasgow* over London

De Havilland Albatross *Frobisher* over Croydon

whose questions in the House of Commons attacking the management of Imperial Airways had led to the Cadman inquiry, became First Parliamentary Secretary to the new Ministry.

There followed the Swinton Plan, which was a blue print for a post-war B.O.A.C. The Corporation was to be responsible for all Commonwealth routes, the trunk lines to China and the Far East and the North Atlantic. In all these activities it was to collaborate with British shipping interests. The European and United Kingdom air services were to be entrusted to another chosen instrument, which was to be founded upon the four main Railway Companies then in existence. Another organization was to be set up for services to South America. These proposals met with a mixed reception.

Before the plan could be implemented, the Labour victory of 1945 changed the face of things, and altered at least the framework of this story, with its plans for State control of civil aviation.

Whatever changes took place at the top, however, the achievements of the rank and file of the British Merchant Air Service in general and of B.O.A.C. in particular stood firm—so did problems of the future. Britain ended the war with a magnificent record in civil aviation but without her own aircraft with which to carry on. B.O.A.C. possessed a proud war record but its identity had been almost vitiated in the process. A letter published in the *Aeroplane* ventilated the feelings of what may be termed the senior rank and file for an organization which seemed at that time to be woefully run down.

> 'Today we are bitter and bewildered. We watch with amazement and envy, the steady flow into B.O.A.C. of Marquesses, Group Captains and Wing Commanders and first-class golfers, commencing in the highest of grades and at salaries that we, after 15 years of hard work, mainly overseas, still dream about.
>
> 'We, on return from many years' continuous overseas service, often without leave, find ourselves unwanted, often unknown to our new masters, and our wide and varied experience apparently rated as of little or no value.
>
> 'Many of us would gladly have joined up at the commencement of the war but were not allowed to do so, and, overseas, could do nothing about it. Today we feel that the new régime

controlling B.O.A.C. would be only too glad to see the last of us go and may even have decided to do so.

'Perhaps our last hope is that Viscount Knollys reads your columns and may want to know something of this matter. We seem to have no channels for presenting our case and, frankly, fear to do so!'

Such criticism, with its suggestion that the airline was recruiting the wrong kind of men, was one of the less happy hangovers of war which mingled with the proud war record. How the Corporation was, so to speak, unscrambled from that situation to hold its own against world-wide competition in the post-war years and indeed to make a profit by 1952 is our concern in the next chapter.

CHAPTER XIII

THE POST-WAR YEARS

B.O.A.C. came out of the war with renewed competition, a reinforced world-wide obligation, controversial legislation, chaotic finance and a very mixed fleet of aircraft. There were seventeen British and American types equipped with sixteen different types of engine in their two hundred and seven aircraft. There were seven types of flying-boat and ten types of landplane. Of the latter only the Dakota and Lodestar which were American, the York and the Lancastrian, which were developments of British bombers, could be considered as passenger aircraft. These machines were scattered at maintenance and operational bases at Hurn, Poole, Whitchurch, Durban, Montreal, Baltimore, and Cairo. As fare-paying passenger machines, except, perhaps, for the Dakotas, they were completely uneconomic—and even the Dakota was outdated for long-range work. There was no future in them, in competition with the new airliners already built in the United States whose aircraft manufacturers had become the universal providers for the world. One of Britain's greater sacrifices to the war effort had been the cessation of all development and manufacture of transport aircraft—and the handing of this side of the industry to the manufacturers of the United States. When peace came, B.O.A.C. felt the cold wind of this bitter war-winning decision which had had to be made in order that the Royal Air Force should fight its way to victory.

As in the First World War, however, when Northcliffe with H. G. Wells and other Members of his 1917 Committee had sat down to study problems of civil aviation in the peace that was to follow, so during 1942 and 1943 a committee of experts, under the chairmanship of Lord Brabazon of Tara, had met to make recommendations for future aircraft. In this lay the main hope for B.O.A.C. to rebuild almost from scratch during the post-war years. New aircraft in keeping with a new age of aviation were, after all, the first necessity for survival, whatever might be the managerial and political difficulties of a weakened, cumbersome and widely dispersed organization on the ground.

The Brabazon Committee, starting work in the darkest days of the war before the tide had turned in our favour, did its job well. The ideas it originated were not only in keeping with the new age which was to follow but, in respect of the Comet, enabled Britain to make a dramatic bid for world leadership in aviation. The Comet stemmed directly from Brabazon recommendations. This brilliantly conceived aircraft met misfortune which had profound effects upon B.O.A.C. in the post-war years.

The post-war period began with Lord Winster as Labour successor to Lord Swinton at the new Ministry of Civil Aviation. With the new Government came the Winster plan, from which developed the Civil Aviation Act of 1946 nationalizing the air transport industry and creating two new Corporations, British European Airways and British South American Airways to divide the field with B.O.A.C. As the air services within Europe reopened after the fall of Hitler, and civil aviation took over from R.A.F. Transport Command those intended to be maintained on a civil footing, B.E.A. was already virtually operating independently as the European Division of B.O.A.C. before the Act was passed. B.S.A.A. operated its first service to South America on March 15, 1946.

Before the changes had been officially made, however, Critchley sent in his resignation to Winster. . . .

> 'The announcement by the Government that we are no longer to have a national organization for the development of civil aviation, but three or more State-owned independent undertakings, renders changes in the organization of B.O.A.C. imperative, if it is to be run economically. We have now a Minister, a whole-time Chairman and a Chief Executive. For the reduced task to be undertaken this, I feel, is top-heavy and extravagant, especially at a time when we must preach and show an example of economy in all ways to junior grades

in this Corporation. May I, therefore, ask you to release me from my appointment as Director General. . . .'

Lord Knollys remained Chairman until 1947, when he was succeeded by Sir Harold Hartley who in turn was succeeded by Sir Miles Thomas in 1949. Echoing the thoughts of many people in the business, one newspaper murmured: 'Boards may come and Boards may go, but British air services go on for ever,' when in February 1946, a new Board—the third since the Corporation's birth in 1940—was announced, only to be changed again a few weeks later when British European Airways was formed.

It was recognized as a post-war necessity that the work of B.O.A.C. would have to be carried on by obsolete, stop-gap and makeshift aircraft, reinforced by purchases from America until such time as British-built machines would be forthcoming. Though the fleet had increased during the war, there were still not enough aircraft to go round.

'In the summer of 1946 [stated a Ministry report] the demand for air transport overseas, after six years of war, was so great that the available resources were entirely insufficient to satisfy it. The immediate task, therefore, was to select for operation those services for which there was the greatest need. Sometimes this entailed the withdrawal of a service in one part of the world in order to provide a more essential service elsewhere. Thus, a B.O.A.C. Dakota service to Karachi was withdrawn early in 1946 in order that the aircraft might be used on new services to Europe: similarly a Sunderland service to Calcutta was withdrawn and the aircraft put into service on a new route to Australia.'

The North Atlantic route offered both the greatest challenge and the greatest rewards. Based at Baltimore were the three Boeing flying-boats which had won fame during the war years in their flights across the Atlantic and thence to West Africa. They had carried very high priority passengers, including Winston Churchill, on occasions to which we shall refer later. They had had their day. They were put on to the Baltimore–Bermuda run where they were highly successful. Afterwards they were sold. Their departure from the Atlantic run left a gap during which Britain was without any aircraft capable of carrying commercial pay-loads. The Liberators on the Return-Ferry service did not qualify as commercial aircraft though they continued to run, training crews, carrying freight, mail and official non-paying passengers, which served the valuable purpose of building up still further Atlantic experience.

In spite of Britain's slender dollar resources, the Government authorized the purchase of five Lockheed Constellations. These American machines had not been built as airliners. They were converted for civil use and they began coming through in May 1946. The fact that a New York–London service was started on the 1st July was remarkable, bearing in mind the intensive training of crews and the reorganization of everything on a civilian basis. From outside, competition was fierce, with the Americans, of course, in a favoured position in being able to build their own aircraft. There were also French, Belgian, Dutch, Swiss and Scandinavian rivals in what was recognized to be a most lucrative field of operations.

The Corporation's Atlantic fleet remained in Montreal: and for the next few years, there was trouble about this. Complaints had been made as early as October 1945 in the House of Commons about the flying-boat base at Baltimore being an unnecessary drain on dollar resources when there was no longer a war risk in servicing aircraft in the United Kingdom. When the Boeing fleet was sold, the team of American and Canadian engineers who had looked after them had been transferred to Montreal. Protests in Parliament about the base remaining there continued until the beginning of 1949, when it was moved to Bristol—at a cost of about half a million pounds. The burden was aggravated by the severe loss of revenue from disruption of services during transfer.

While the North Atlantic route was being re-equipped with Constellations, the Commonwealth trunk lines were operated with four-engined Yorks, which were war-time transport aircraft; with Hythe and, later, Plymouth flying-boats, which were derived from wartime Sunderlands; and with Haltons and Lancastrians which were both converted bombers.

There was a clear and immediate obligation to renew the routes flown before the war by Imperial Airways. There was also a need for new services: and some of these had to be operated not because they were commercially attractive, but because they were required by Government policy. Early in 1946, the Corporation was instructed to extend its services to fall in line with the demobilization of R.A.F. Transport Command. Along the routes, R.A.F. staging posts and facilities had to be taken over and manned. The type of aircraft then in use and the lack of night flying facilities at many points meant the keeping, at least for the time being, of an uneconomic number of stations and the laying out of money on improving passenger accommodation where there were night stops. All this was costly in men and finance. At the end of March 1947, B.O.A.C. people were spread out over 47 overseas bases and stations.

If the flesh might be weak the spirit was willing. In spite of every frustration, the airline was rebuilding world communications. The old Empire flying-boat route, which had terminated at Calcutta because of the Japanese, was extended to Rangoon and at the beginning of 1946 to Singapore. The Lancastrian service to Australia inaugurated in November 1945, in partnership with Qantas, gave a 63-hour transit time from London to Sydney. In the same month came the first York Springbok service between Britain and South Africa in conjunction with South African Airways.

Late in 1946, the famous Horseshoe Route was wound up and the Empire flying-boats which had continued between Durban and Cairo had been gradually replaced by Yorks and had become redundant. They were followed by improved flying-boats operating from Britain to the Middle East, to Africa, Australia and the Far East—during the post-war years till 1950. The last of them were the Solents which were withdrawn from service in that year, bringing to an end a long tradition initiated in the great days of expansion of Imperial Airways. B.O.A.C. was forced to fall in with the mood of the times, which was against flying-boats. Basically they had been less economical to operate than their comparable landplanes. Their use had always been, and still is, a controversial issue among experts. For those who had been able to interpret it, there was a clear pointer to American thought on this subject when the Boeing flying-boats were sold to B.O.A.C. in 1940. At that time the United States had already acquired an interest in Bermuda, where Kindley Field, a base for landplanes, was being built. Even then the Americans, who would undoubtedly control the shape of things to come in civil aircraft design and construction, had already abandoned the notion of water-borne craft for their airlines.

It was not surprising that by 1950 Britain found herself alone as a flying-boat operator on the main international routes. This meant that there were no foreign Governments or other airline operators who could be induced to share the enormous expenses of world-wide flying-boat bases, with specialist staff and marine equipment in each place. It was obvious that the rest of the world would use wheels and that the cost of airfields would not fall heavily upon any one operator. Thus, flying-boats, to the great sorrow of many who had flown in them as crews or passengers, had to go. Whether this type of aircraft is likely to make a large-scale return to popularity as a tourist feature on the main trunk routes is still a point of debate.

Apart from such policy issues as the post-war controversy between landplanes and flying-boats which took five years before it was settled, there were many managerial headaches before B.O.A.C. was able to shake itself clear of war conditions and their consequences. One of those deeply involved in this period of reorientation during which the Corporation struggled towards a new life, says: 'For year after year till 1947 we were simply drawing deficiency payment from the Government. There could be no real accounting. It must be admitted that there was uncontrolled expenditure. We drew spares and fuel from the R.A.F. whenever and wherever they were needed. It was a situation which was bound to have its effect on the outlook of everyone concerned. A real effort had to be made to get back to commercial thinking. . . .' Relaxation of Government control was, in fact, less rapid than expected. While priorities still existed, the hoped-for commercial outlook could not develop. The operating costs of the flying-boat service were too high. Some of the other services by converted warplanes, though they were important in reopening and extending the essential lines of communication, were fantastically costly and could not be remotely economic. The Lancastrians on the United Kingdom–Australia run, for instance, were giving the fastest long-distance air service at that time in the world. But the bomber fuselage could only take nine passengers seated, or six in the bunks that were essential for a flight of 12,000 miles with only refuelling stops on the way. A comparable aircraft designed for civilian use would have carried say at least 36 passengers—with no additional staff to handle it on the ground.

With such operations in hand, and a staff swollen to nearly

24,500 scattered over the world, it is not surprising that the Corporation accounts for 1946/47 showed a huge deficit, amounting to over eight million pounds.

That year's report listed several main reasons for the loss. The multiplicity of types of uneconomical aircraft; the all too familiar delays in aircraft delivery; scattered and improvised maintenance bases: deficiencies in route organization: the cost of development work: and finally the programme of services in which commercial considerations were often subordinated to the national interest.

That first year of published accounts was not without promise of new ideas. Though the Tudors which were to form an interim fleet caused a crisis by coming through so slowly, the first Comet was built during 1947. Just as in the days of Imperial Airways, the Technical Development Department of B.O.A.C. was working closely with de Havilland, the manufacturers. But the order of progress was reversed. The manufacturers had prepared the project as a jet mail-carrying aircraft, as laid down by the Brabazon Committee. It was then 'developed upward' through direct discussions with B.O.A.C. as a transatlantic plane. It was finalized, however, as a medium long-range aircraft.

Meanwhile a fleet of Constellations was purchased for use on the trunk line to Australia. Twenty-two Argonauts were ordered from Canada. From Handley Page a new fleet of Hermes aircraft was expected shortly. This programme encouraged the Management to declare that these new machines would 'change entirely the Corporation's financial prospects and that with the economies made possible by the reorganization in hand, the Corporation should be self-supporting on its commercial routes within three to four years'. This period must not be allowed to pass without noting a revival, at least in part, of the notion of a Commonwealth airline. The field of operations was the Pacific Ocean. The Company, which existed from 1946–1954, was named British Commonwealth Pacific Airlines. It has been described by Sir Hudson Fysh as 'just an ideal'. Certainly it began with a strong mixture of idealism as well as expediency with talks at Wellington between New Zealand, Australia and Britain. B.C.P.A. as it was called during its brief lifetime, was to run a trans-Pacific trunk service between North America and New Zealand and Australia. Airline members of the concern were B.O.A.C., the Australian

National Airline Commission and the New Zealand National Airways Corporation.

None of the then existing British aircraft was regarded as suitable for this ocean crossing. Solent flying-boats were too slow for what was known to be a highly competitive route which the Americans would operate with much energy. It was realized already that the Tudor I would be too costly, and that the Tudor II might not be able to fly the critical stage between Honolulu and San Francisco with any regularity. B.C.P.A. therefore went for American aircraft. The first Annual Report made at the end of 1946 revealed difficulties over landing rights.

> 'On completion of the Bilateral Agreement with the United States, it is proposed to run three fortnightly return trips from Sydney, and one fortnightly return trip from Auckland to San Francisco. In view of the delay in completion of the Bilateral Agreement, approval was given by the Government to commence one fortnightly return service from Sydney to Vancouver via Fiji, Canton Island, Honolulu and San Francisco. As no right yet exists to pick up or set down passengers or freight in United States' territory, passengers and freight for the U.S. must be carried on to Vancouver, and returned to San Francisco by an American airline.'

The first service left Australia in September 1946, and an interim fortnightly service was run by Australian National Airways on behalf of the Company. There followed a regular scheduled weekly service—and Pan-American Airways, the main competitor, meanwhile increased their service to twice-weekly. In 1949, B.C.P.A. was running two services a week from Australia, and one from New Zealand, to San Francisco. The specifically Commonwealth aspect of things was a casualty, for by July that year Canadian Pacific Airlines were already operating their own service in rivalry between Vancouver and Sydney. In its last year of operation, B.C.P.A. terminated every fourth Australian and every second New Zealand service at San Francisco, but competition was fierce. A grant had to be made to meet an operating deficiency of over a quarter of a million sterling. Both B.O.A.C. and Q.E.A. then realized that their own plans for a round-the-world network would need to include the Pacific run. The continuance of B.C.P.A. stood in the way. That was one of the reasons for dissolving the airline. Several of those closely associated with the venture have since made no secret of the fact that the running of a single airline by three separate Governments is not the happiest of propositions, even when all concerned are friends.

Another casualty during the 'forties was the third Corporation set up under the Civil Aviation Act of 1946—British South American Airways, having the mid-Atlantic and South America as its field of operations. This concern had been incorporated during the war, in January 1944, as British Latin American Airlines Ltd., a private company representing five shipping interests, initiated by Mr. J. W. Booth of shipping fame. When the war ended, D. C. T. Bennett, who had left the R.A.F. with the rank of Air-Vice Marshal, was appointed Chief Executive of this airline, which had been created to exploit air services between Europe and South and Central America.

In September 1945, the name was changed to British South American Airways and at the end of that year the British Government sanctioned its beginning operations. When the new B.S.A.A. Corporation took over the assets on August 1, 1946, services were in operation between London and Buenos Aires and across the Andes to Santiago, by way of Portugal, West Africa and the Argentine. Another route covering the Caribbean connected with Portugal, the Azores and Bermuda. This was extended to Lima and Santiago where it joined up with the service across the Andes. At the outset, thirteen-passenger Lancastrians and twenty-one passenger Yorks were used; but in October 1947, the thirty-two passenger Tudor IV was introduced to the Caribbean section. Tudors had completed one-week testing in tropical conditions under the personal command of Bennett himself and these tests were 'fully satisfactory'. During that year B.S.A.A. bought a shareholding in British West Indian Airways Ltd. operating in the Caribbean and shortly afterwards formed a subsidiary which bought up the whole B.W.I.A. undertaking.

In January 1948 the Tudor *Star Tiger*, with 25 passengers on board mysteriously disappeared between the Azores and Bermuda and the Tudors were withdrawn temporarily from service for technical investigation.

When the first B.S.A.A. accounts were published in 1947, they showed a profit of over £30,000—at a time when both the sister Corporations showed heavy losses. An early public indication of trouble in the Corporation came with the termination of Bennett's appointment as Chief Executive. Questions in the House about this dismissal led to the disclosure that the accident rate of B.S.A.A. was inordinately high. The Parliamentary Secretary to the Ministry of Civil Aviation, G. S. Lindgren, Labour, admitted that one of the reasons for this was that the Corporation was working 'near to the bone'.

In January 1949, the Tudor *Star Ariel* disappeared without trace in mid-Atlantic. Again Tudors were withdrawn from service. The second year's trading had shown a deficit of over £400,000, attributed in part to delays in deliveries of new aircraft. The decision was then taken to merge B.S.A.A. with B.O.A.C. It had been a bold venture which might have developed into a powerful Corporation but for the catastrophic losses and mishaps to aircraft. It was not until 1958 that B.O.A.C. was able to restart a service direct between Britain and South America.

There was also an individual loss not directly connected with flying. When Bennett left, H. G. Brackley took his place: and it was a cruel fate that his appointment, where his talents were so much needed and welcomed should have been the occasion for his last appearance in this story. While paying a duty visit to South America, only eight months after taking up his new job, 'Brackles' was drowned in a bathing accident.

The absorption of a large number of B.S.A.A. staff into the framework of B.O.A.C. following this merger was one of several difficulties facing B.O.A.C. at this time. Another was that B.S.A.A. possessed no competitive aircraft for the Western hemisphere. Nor did B.O.A.C.; but to keep the services going, Yorks were used and later, Argonauts, then Constellations were transferred from other routes. The Argonaut fleet, however, was delivered in 1949 ahead of time; they had been introduced on the eastern routes to take the place of flying-boats, enabling flying-boat bases east of Cairo to be closed.

The Corporation was by no means out of the wood when Sir Miles Thomas became Chairman in 1949. His appearance, however, coincided with major reorganization and a degree of progress which was reflected in the results for the next few years. Surplus staff was steadily reduced. Revenue was increased and operating costs went down. As foreseen, the turning point came with the arrival of a really up-to-date fleet. These were admittedly interim aircraft but they were well able to stand up to foreign competition. They were all four-engined, pressurized aircraft, Stratocruisers, Constellations, Argonauts and British-built Hermes. In 1950/51 these were carrying more traffic than ever before at a lower cost per unit.

The new air age, which began with the post-war years, has produced as many of its own esoteric phrases as those thrown up by centuries of seafaring. It is not intended to burden the reader with many of these terms, which have their proper place in more technical publications. We must, however, introduce the 'load-factor to break even', which we believe to be self-explanatory. B.O.A.C.'s break even load-factor, for 1948, stood as high as 115 per cent, meaning, of course, that the Corporation could not break even at all. By 1950 it had been reduced to 75% and that showed the beginning of real progress. For the financial year 1951/52, the figure was down to 65% and for the first time B.O.A.C. made a profit.

There were other factors in turning loss into profit. It had been part of the post-war reconstruction to adjust the size and pattern of the Corporation to the volume of traffic.

> 'In the year 1947/48 [states the Annual Report] the combined staffs of B.O.A.C. and the former British South American Airways Corporation averaged 24,101 persons, each of whom on an average produced only 3,790 capacity-ton-miles in a year. Moreover, the total revenue of the Corporation worked out at an average of only £607 a head—an impossibly low figure, having regard to the fact that a considerable proportion of revenue must be applied to the purchase of aircraft and their supplies, and that all the other services an organization needs to buy from outside have to be paid for in addition to wages and salaries.
>
> 'By March 1951, the Corporation's staff had been reduced by as much as one-third; and by March 1952 the average output per employee had been increased from 3,790 capacity-ton-miles a year to 11,865, while the annual revenue earned by the Corporation had been raised from £607 a head to £2,047. This was achieved with the assistance of a greatly increased capital investment in aircraft, which rose from £396 a head at March 31, 1948, to £1,920 at March 31, 1952.'

Yet new fleets of aircraft, and a streamlined staff organization under the vigorous chairmanship of Sir Miles Thomas (who was also Chief Executive) were not enough. After the long war years it had to be emphasized at every level that the Corporation, though State-controlled, was essentially a commercial undertaking and that salesmanship was necessary in a highly competitive world market. The Report that followed the first year of commercial success, spoke optimistically of two forthcoming events, the start of tourist services across the North Atlantic and the introduction of the world's first civil jet airliner, the Comet—halving the times of most existing flights.

With its introduction, the Management declared in the Report for 1952/53:

> 'To halve the travel time across the world . . . is the most signal advance in international transport that we and our predecessors in title have been privileged to make in our history. B.O.A.C. has fathered the jet age in civil aviation, as in the past we pioneered the Empire routes and as in the future we intend to girdle the earth with all-British air services.
>
> '. . . the first phase of the jet age is now over, with the Comet 1 established in service and extending its operations along the main arteries of the Commonwealth. The second phase is soon to come with the Comet 2s and the Britannia in partnership providing express jet and tourist services. We plan a third phase in the battle for supremacy of equipment to bridge the Atlantic with long-range jets flying in step with time.'

This justifiable pride was humbled within twelve months as all the high hopes in the Comet were dashed by a sequence of three disasters—the most unexpected, bewildering and devastating misfortunes in the whole story of civil aviation.

It may be as well to recall the facts. Apart from a Ministry of Supply Comet loaned to the Corporation, the first service machine to be delivered came in February 1952, the ninth and last came in September of that year, by which time services were already running to South Africa and Ceylon. The services to Singapore followed in October 1952 and to Tokyo in April 1953. Then in May 1953, a Comet met disaster near Calcutta. None of the crew of six or the thirty-seven passengers survived. In January 1954 another was lost off Elba, this time with thirty-five passengers and six crew killed. After this the Comets were temporarily removed from service for modification. Then in March 1954 they were taken out altogether after a South African Airways machine was lost off Naples with seven crew and fourteen passengers. From the first service to Johannesburg in May 1952 to their withdrawal, the Comets had carried nearly 55,000 passengers.

What went wrong with these aircraft which gave B.O.A.C. the lead over the whole world?

The Comet had proved its ability to operate regularly and reliably. Its speed—twice that of most of its contemporaries—and its elegance captured the imagination. Moreover, it was comfortable to a degree hitherto quite unattained in any other aircraft. Its lack of vibration was amazing. A pencil could be stood on end on a passenger table and would remain unshaken while the aircraft cruised at over 450 m.p.h. at an altitude of anything up to 40,000 feet.

The disasters came without warning and were instantaneous. No distress signals were sent. Disintegration was such that at first it seemed that there would be few clues. It was small wonder that there was talk of sabotage, for the cause of failure remained a mystery for many long months.

These were not idle months, however. The Royal Navy and the Royal Aeronautical Establishment were working unceasingly and with great resources to solve the mystery. Sir Arnold Hall, then Director of R.A.E., Farnborough, was appointed by the Government to undertake a complete investigation of the whole problem and 'to use all the resources at the disposal of the Establishment'. When Hall and his team started work, very little of the wreckage of the Comet lost near Elba had been recovered and it was not known how much would ever be found. Technical investigations of the properties of the aircraft, nevertheless, were started at Farnborough and they went on as wreckage was received.

The Royal Navy's briefing was terse. Instructions went out through the Commander-in-Chief, Mediterranean, Admiral Earl Mountbatten, to 'recover the Comet. . . .' The special vessels H.M.S. *Barhill* and H.M.S. *Salvor* were fitted out to carry 200 tons of heavy moving gear. An observation chamber, television equipment, an eight-toothed grab and many other devices were sent from the United Kingdom to Malta where the ships were prepared. All this was done in a fortnight and the two vessels, together with H.M.S. *Wakeful*, in which the television equipment was installed, arrived at Elba on January 25, 1954.

Searches were made at depths between seventy and one hundred fathoms and it was the first time television had been used in that way. The first success came when a piece of wreckage was seen on the T.V. camera. This was a great triumph for the salvage crew—and their further efforts were afterwards recorded in *Blackwood's Magazine*:

'The chain caught round a chair from the Comet, the chair caught round some electric cables, the electric cables were attached to the after pressure-dome. We carefully dragged the whole issue to within twenty feet of the surface. Then, fearing to push our luck another inch, an ordinary soft-suited diver was sent down to get a stout sling round it. Within an hour it was safely on deck. . . .'

Again, acting on a hunch:

'Perhaps our trawl had indeed snagged something, but not quite enough to bring it to the surface. In that event, there could be a little heap on the bottom just to one side of us This proved to be exactly the case. It was Captain Polland's delight. That day he and his divers brought up six grab-loads of wreckage. Thursday, five grab-loads, Friday, one grab-load. Then the vein ran out. . . .

'. . . "After the Lord Mayor's Show comes the muck wagon." That is a well-known and true saying. Presumably the reverse is also true, because after the miserable week-end came sheer delirious delight. We found the long-sought vital centre section of the Comet; the part where wing spars pass through fuselage. . . .

'The diver in the chamber said he had seen the biggest piece of Comet ever. Down went the grab, expedited by many enthusiastic hands. When, at last, it re-emerged from the sea, normally taciturn men shouted with delight. The rear spar (or girder to laymen) was all there with numbers of jagged projections. The spar itself was about sixty-five feet long, by two foot six inches, and the projection made it an awkward customer to deal with.'

Perhaps the most rewarding grab resulted in bringing up 'the

DC 7C

Bristol Britannia 102

The second prototype de Havilland Comet 1

Some Chairmen of B.O.A.C.

Sir John Reith (*right*) and Mr. I. Geddes

Sir Miles Thomas

Sir Gerard d'Erlanger

entire forward end of the Comet, cockpit, flying controls, fire indicators—from the nose right back to the wings'.

The Royal Navy finally recovered some 68% in weight of the Comet, which was greatly in excess of expectations, as was the small amount of damage which had been caused to the structure of the aircraft either by salt water or the salvage process. As more of the wreckage arrived at Farnborough and as it was thought necessary to be satisfied with the structural integrity of the aircraft, Sir Arnold Hall decided that a complete loading test of the whole cabin ought to be made. In the words of the Official Report:

> 'The normal method of testing pressure cabins up to the point when they fail under pressure is similar to that used for vessels such as boilers. They are filled with water, and more water is pumped in until the desired difference between the internal and external pressure is reached. This method has two advantages over the use of air. Water is relatively incompressible, so that failure when it occurs produces only a mild form of explosion. The origin of the failure can be determined and the structure can generally be repaired and tested again. If air were used instead of water, the failure would be catastrophic (equivalent in the case of the Comet's cabin to the explosion of a 500 lb. bomb). Such a test would be dangerous, the cabin would be destroyed, and the evidence of the origin of the failure would almost certainly be lost.
>
> 'It is, however, necessary to prevent unrepresentative loading of the cabin structure by the weight of the water. This is ensured in practice by immersing the whole cabin in a tank, and filling the tank and the cabin simultaneously with water. Pressure in the cabin is then raised by pumping in water from the space outside it.
>
> 'Cycles of loading, to the same or different levels of pressure as desired, are applied by a suitable routine of pumping.'

A Comet aircraft was made available for Farnborough

> '. . . by the use of all the resources of R.A.E., repeated loading tests began early in June on aircraft G-ALYU (*Yoke Uncle*). The object of the tests was to simulate the conditions of a series of pressurized flights. To this end the cabin and wings were repeatedly subjected to a cycle of loading as far as

possible equivalent to that to which they would be subjected in the period between take-off and landing. In addition to one application of cabin pressure, fluctuating loads were applied to the wings in bending to reproduce the effect of such gusts as might be expected in normal conditions, although the contribution of gust loads to the stresses in the cabin structure, compared with that made by the internal pressure, was in general small.'

The cabin structure failed after making the equivalent of a total of 3,060 flights, the starting point of the failure being the corner of one of the cabin windows. The inference suggested by the tank test, that the primary failure was the bursting of the pressure cabin, was also confirmed by examination of the wreckage and other experiments.

There followed 'a line of experiment which produced remarkable results. Models of the Comet were made in light wood, suitably ballasted, and projected in the air at the appropriate speed. They were released from a kite balloon at a height corresponding to that at which it was believed the Comet structure failed. The model was so constructed that it would break at the point where the failure of the cabin was suspected. . . .' The descent of the fragments was photographed and it was found that they fell in a manner which agreed with the deductions made from the evidence.

After further deliberation, a further successful search for more wreckage was made, which provided important evidence about the bursting of the cabin, and enabled the investigation to conclude that 'the cabin had burst catastrophically in the neighbourhood of the front spar of the wing'.

Hall reported:

'I do not consider it possible to establish with certainty the point at which the disruption of the skin first began. But I consider that it is probable that it started near the starboard aft corner of the rear A.D.F. window, at a point where examination by experts showed that fatigue had existed. . . .

'It is my opinion that the fundamental cause of the failure of the cabin structure was that there existed around the corners of the windows and other cut-outs a level of stress higher than is consistent with a long life of the cabin. . . .'

From this exhaustive investigation the whole world benefited and the lessons learnt have been put into practice. Though the Comet disasters had been such a severe blow, the Corporation was not discouraged. Government approval was obtained for a programme which included an order for a fleet of new Comets.

Until these came through and the Britannias could be introduced, there was a period—and it was to be longer than estimated—of retrenchment and expensive make-do. The South American service taken over from B.S.A.A. had to go. South African Airways and Q.E.A., both partners in their respective spheres, were asked to extend their services to help out B.O.A.C. Even so, the Corporation was still very short of aircraft. Once again it had to turn to America for aircraft to fill the gap. These aircraft were second-hand. Yet because they were bought at a time when they could command 'top-of-the-market' prices, which in many instances was greater than the cost of the same aircraft when new, this was a very expensive deal. It left a legacy of high operating costs to be borne during the continuing life of these aircraft in the B.O.A.C. fleet. Moreover, they had to be modified and the Comet crews had to be trained all over again to use them. Revenue, which had been increasing owing to the enthusiastic passenger response to the Comet, now fell away.

These setbacks during the financial year 1953/54, were not felt till later. That year was the best to date in the Corporation's history, showing a profit of two million sterling. The Report ended with the words:

> '. . . We now wait with eager optimism and expectancy the delivery of the Britannia—which has shown good promise on its recent tropical trials—and later of the new Comet Mark 4. We appreciate that it may be some three years before a Comet is again cleaving the skies on the air routes of the world.'

This was too sanguine. In 1955/56, the Corporation again made a profit, but the loss of the Comets continued to cast its shadow. There were not enough suitable aircraft and that year's Report stated:

> 'Moreover, the only aircraft available for immediate delivery to fill the void . . . were unable to match, in passenger appeal and revenue-earning potential, the competition from airlines equipped with more modern aircraft. It was accordingly more

creditable that the number of passengers carried by the Corporation increased by 32% on the previous year.'

The recent innovation of tourist traffic was reflected in that increase of passengers. Fifty-three per cent of the Corporation's passenger traffic was derived from tourist class compared with forty-five per cent in the previous year. The tourist traffic, one of the newer developments of the air age, had a perceptible effect upon B.O.A.C. operations. The Corporation again made a profit in 1956/57. To this, tourist class travel paid an important contribution.

Sir Miles Thomas wrote a letter of resignation to the Minister of Transport and Civil Aviation on March 7, 1956, in which he made these points:

'I should be grateful if you would allow me to be released from my responsibilities as Chairman of the British Overseas Airways Corporation as soon as can conveniently be arranged.

'During the past eight years of my service with the Corporation I have, I hope, made some useful contribution to the progress of British civil aviation. From a substantial annual loss, the Corporation is now making regular profits. The operating plans for the future are settled; the administrative pattern is established. The Corporation has recovered from the tragic loss of the Comet 1 and is entering a new phase. The fulfilment of the operation programme with the Britannia depends only on the deliveries of the aircraft, which have now started.

'My own feeling is that I have completed the task for which I was commissioned in 1948. I can make a more useful contribution to trade and industry in other directions. Although the challenge of bettering the affairs of B.O.A.C. when it was costing the taxpayer £8,000,000 annually was good exercise, working in a Nationalized Industry is not my natural bent.

'Hence this request for release. . . .'

His successor was Gerard d'Erlanger, who stated in his first Annual Report:

'The air transport industry is one not only of rapid technical advance but has also been, and is likely to continue to be, one of very rapid expansion. In addition, the industry is one in which operating revenues exceed operating expenses only by a very narrow margin. The Corporation's average results for the year before remuneration of capital are, at 3.62 per cent of revenue, somewhat better than those of the industry as a whole, but as yet there is no margin to allow for adverse conditions, the setting aside of reserves to meet the high replacement costs of aircraft, or to provide for future development without requiring additional capital. The building up of reserves is therefore considered to be of prime importance for the Corporation.'

The operating revenue for this particular year exceeded the operating expenditure by a very narrow margin indeed. The medium-range Bristol Britannias belatedly came into service. Together with the new Douglas DC.7Cs which had to be brought in pending the arrival of the long-range Britannias on the North Atlantic, they were the first new types to fly for B.O.A.C. for over four and a half years. By June 1957, the DC.7Cs were operating eleven tourist and nine mixed class services a week, including twice-weekly services through New York to San Francisco. The Britannias started on the London to Johannesburg route in February 1957 and in March took over the thrice-weekly service between London and Sydney replacing the Constellation fleet, which was then offered for sale.

They were late coming into service because of icing at high altitudes in monsoon conditions. History was repeating itself—and this repetition is one of the most persistent and doleful overtones of British Civil Aviation history. The men who had been already trained to serve the Britannias in the air and on the ground, had to be re-allocated to Constellation and Argonaut fleets. As with the Comet setback, this Britannia delay had consequences which were reflected later. The 1957 accounts showed an overall deficit of more than £2,800,000. On the work of the Corporation there was a small profit, but there was a considerable loss on the Associated Companies which were still being built to become self-supporting. The fall in B.O.A.C. profits was attributed mainly to the late delivery of the Britannias but also to the effects of the fall in prices of primary commodities and to recession in North America.

The key to the profitability of any airline is the break even load-factor. B.O.A.C. during the 'fifties needed to fill their aircraft about 64% on an average throughout the year with its varying seasonal traffic in order to cover their costs, so that they might break even. Experience showed that it has been almost impossible for any airline to achieve all the year round load factors of about 65%. Thus B.O.A.C. and many others balance precariously on the edge of breaking even. And it was for that reason that the Corporation toppled over into the 1957/58 deficit, when they succeeded only in filling their aircraft 61%.

In such a situation, there is only one thing to do—to reduce costs and bring down the break even load-factor to below 60%. Because of the Comet 1 troubles and the long drawn out introduction of the Britannias, the Corporation was still unable in 1957/58 to bring down the break even load-factor which remained at about 64% as it was in 1951/52.

One of the most significant single events in the whole of this story of forty years was the return of the Comet in 1958. Though dramatic in its impact, this was an occasion which had deep roots in faith and confidence between maker and user. After the Comet 1 disasters, the Corporation declared its 'faith in the value and significance of the pure jet airliner is unshaken'. When the Comet 1s were withdrawn, Captain Peter Cane, who had been Flight Superintendent of the fleet, was specially appointed to act as a link between B.O.A.C. and de Havilland in technical and operational matters arising from the development of the Comets of the future.

His became more than a watching brief when, in 1955, the Corporation ordered their new fleet of nineteen Comet 4s. These machines were, of course, to incorporate all the structural design improvements which followed the Farnborough research investigations and the subsequent Court of Inquiry. Nearly every component and part of them were undergoing tests-to-destruction. To pave the way for their delivery in 1958, the Corporation acquired a pair of Comet 2Es in 1957. These were used to amass flying hours on the new Rolls-Royce Avon engines and to rebuild the Corporation's Comet organization. This latter human aspect was a massive undertaking in itself. For the fully operational Comet flight, 117 crews were required, including 261 Captains and Co-Pilots. The training of these men had to be accomplished in eighteen months.

A Comet Unit was re-formed in March 1957, with Cane as Manager. A few months later, this Unit was raised to Flight status, with Captain T. Stoney as Flight Manager. Twenty-one Captains who between them had shared 27,500 hours of pure jet airliner experience, started the Comet 2 programme, which began in September 1957, with flights between London and Beirut. The Comets made the 4,560 miles round trip every day of the week, and eventually the frequency increased to eleven return flights a week. Before this programme was extended to the Atlantic, some flights were made to Nairobi. A target of 3,500 engine hours on development flying was reached on schedule in June 1958. Only one day had been lost and that because of fog.

Then began an equally intensive Atlantic programme—at first between London and Gander, in order to give experience to Captains chosen for the Atlantic service. With the start of this in May 1958, B.O.A.C. made it abundantly clear to all concerned that they were going all out to fly the Atlantic with jets. Familiarization tests began on the continent of North America. There were instrument approaches and touch-downs at many Canadian and United States airports, including Idlewild. In spite of a growing sense of rivalry between British and American jets on the North Atlantic run, the Comet experimental flights into New York and other American airports were well received. The Americans regarded their comings and goings as valuable exercises for themselves in jet procedure.

During the summer of 1958, Comet 4s, still in the hands of de Havilland, made some spectacular proving flights to Africa, to South America, to New York for noise tests, between Hong Kong and Britain in a single day. Their delivery to B.O.A.C. was due in September. Meanwhile it was common knowledge that the Corporation's chief North Atlantic rivals, Pan-American Airlines, was planning their own introduction of pure jet services in Boeing 707s. Both the British and the Americans denied that there was any race to be the first across with a scheduled jet airliner service. In spite of this, the American Company published advertisements in the British Press stating that they would be the first and specified October 26 as the date of the commencement of their service.

This announcement galvanized the manufacturers and the airline. Certification for civil use was granted on September 29. On the following day, there was a hastily arranged handing-over ceremony at London Airport, at which Sir Aubrey Burke, Managing Director of de Havilland, said: 'I am sure I speak for everyone in the de Havilland enterprise when I say that this is one of our proudest and happiest occasions, because we have done what we were determined to do, we have brought the Comet back.

'Three and a half years ago we entered into a contract to build you bigger and better Comets and deliver the first one thoroughly tested, with a full certificate of airworthiness, on September 30, 1958. Well, here she is, and for good measure we have brought you two.'

A third Comet was delivered two days later. The same day came the welcome announcement from the Ministry of Transport and Civil Aviation that the Comet had been cleared for noise in Britain. On October 3 came the news that it was also cleared in New York. The following morning, on October 4, 1958, the first passenger-carrying Comet left London Airport for New York. Just after midday, Captain T. Stoney set off from New York on a counterpart flight, arriving at London Airport 6 hours and 12 minutes later.

The 52-passenger Comet 4, with an average speed of 500 miles an hour, and an air range of 3,000 miles, came into daily service over the North Atlantic in November 1958. If there ever had been a race, which both contestants continued to deny until the subject was forgotten, there was little doubt which side won—and the Comet 4 went on to prove its worth.

CHAPTER XIV

THOSE WHO SERVE

MORE than 330 Captains and 550 First and Second Officers are on the strength of B.O.A.C. at the time of writing. A Senior Captain may earn slightly over £4,000 a year; a Captain on the minimum rates slightly more than £2,300 a year. These men of responsibility may come into the limelight when they carry some important passenger or participate in some historic event: but mainly they carry their well-deserved prestige without ostentation. Though they mingle with their passengers on almost every flight and thus maintain the most intimate contact with the travelling public which is of immense value to all concerned, there is no 'star system' applied to them. Their names are not widely known to the public: yet their professional status is held in high honour wherever they carry the flag.

The first pilots to come to civil aviation in 1919 were those engaged by A. T. and T. and Handley Page, and they came from the Royal Air Force, many of them having flown in France in bombers and in the fighters that were then known as 'scouts'. Their civil machines by modern standards were simple to fly and operate. Navigation was limited to map-reading and to crude calculations involving compass, airspeed and wind. At first there were no technical examinations in proficiency for the very experienced men who were hopefully turning their swords into ploughshares. When these were first introduced by Air Ministry in the early 'twenties, they were of a cursory nature.

A pilot might be required to draw schematically the control and fuel systems of an aircraft and to recite a few elementary figures such as oil and petrol consumption. This part of the examination could be completed in about thirty minutes. It was followed by six short flights known as 'doing your landings'. The aircraft had to be taken off and landed three times without load and then three times with full load. These earlier craft, being designed for one pilot, did not provide for dual instruction, so that the pilot making his first flights for licence endorsement did so in a machine of which the characteristics were unknown to him. Nevertheless, it was not uncommon for a pilot to study the technical details, undergo his examination, complete his landings, obtain his licence endorsement and make his first service flight all in the same morning.

Contrast that simple procedure with just one of the exacting requirements in these times. Airliners are not only bigger but infinitely more complex. Today the pilot converting from one type to another spends four weeks in a classroom learning about the new machine—even though he may be a man with a good number of years' flying experience. At the end of the course, he must undergo a searching examination by the Air Registration Board. Then he enters a Simulator, which is an ingenious structure reproducing on a full scale and in the minutest detail the flight deck of the machine which is being studied. It also simulates all the conditions, contingencies, motions and sounds of flight. It is a fine teacher, much more economical to run than any aeroplane and more convenient to house.

The pilot converting to the new type 'flies' the Simulator for an aggregate of thirty hours, achieving handling and operating efficiency nearly, but not quite, good enough to take the new airliner into the air. His work with the Simulator, in fact, cuts down the airborne time he needs before passing his check from about seventeen to seven hours of actual flying. The last stage of his training will be to fly the aircraft on the operational routes under the supervision of a qualified Captain. All in all, it will have taken him about two and a half months to 'learn' his new aircraft.

This is not all. He will be checked by an instructor twice a year on matters such as technical knowledge, crew drills and flying skill. Every crew member undergoes such periodical checking, the purpose of which is to keep the men up-to-date and to eliminate any faults that may have developed. In no sense is there a spirit of picking holes.

'There is no easy road to qualifying as a crew member [writes

Captain W. Houston, Training Manager of B.O.A.C. and himself a veteran pilot]. The standard of instruction is very high. The man's competence is checked step by step by examination and test and when he is eventually checked out, his ability to do his job is as certain as human endeavour can make it. Length of service, past experience, reputation, are of no account in this process. Only the man's ability can gain the final signature which authorizes him to take his place as a fully qualified crew member. All this means that the crew member of today must be a man of higher calibre than was looked for then. This does not mean that pre-war pilots and crews could not operate today—many in fact do—but there is a much higher call on a man's brain today than there was formerly. He must know a great deal more and, equally important, his brain must be able to co-ordinate and translate into action, a vastly greater amount of information in a shorter time.'

The cost of training a B.O.A.C. pilot to the point when he takes charge of a regular flight may be as much as £8,000.

Because aviation has become such a normal part of everyday life and air travel has ceased to be an adventure in an age where anybody and everybody may fly, the full responsibilities of an airline pilot are not always appreciated. The increasingly sophisticated air-travelling public is inclined to think of him as one who is only concerned with taking an aircraft off the ground at the departure point and putting the wheels back on the ground at the destination, his reputation depending almost entirely on how smoothly this latter operation is performed. It may be appropriate here, therefore, to follow the routine movements of a B.O.A.C. Captain flying from London to a point in the Middle East, which is the first stage of his journey to Tokyo or Sydney.

To do this one should join him in his own home, some three hours before he is due to depart. Here he will already be in touch by telephone with three nerve centres—Movement Control, which keeps a check on all B.O.A.C. aircraft throughout the world, Operations Control, which arranges and regulates movements in and out of London Airport for aircraft on the first and last stages of their flights, and Service Control, which arranges the loading of mail, passengers and freight for each outgoing machine. His telephone conferences with these form his initial decisions and give the officers on duty an idea of what factors to consider in advance for the flight plans which they will formulate before the Captain himself arrives at the airport.

About an hour and a half before departure time, the Captain goes to the B.O.A.C. Operations Room, where he meets the crew, who will remain with him for the round trip to Tokyo or Sydney. He then receives up-to-the-minute information affecting his route, with a map showing the weather throughout, with forecasts not only for London and his immediate destination, but also for airports along the route. On the basis of these forecasts, he makes his final choice of the exact route to be followed, the amount of fuel to be carried, and the height at which to fly in order to use the most favourable wind. From these basic details, the Flight Plan is completed.

On this are shown courses to steer, distances, heights, speeds and times between points along the route—for example, London–Seaford–Dieppe–Paris–Dijon–Geneva–Milan and so on. The fuel required for the flight, already calculated, covers taxiing out, taking off, climbing, cruising, descending and landing at the destination. Percentages which must be added, cover the unexpected, such as variations in fuel consumption or in the selected route, changes in the winds or delays, such as those caused by circuiting a port of arrival owing to bad weather or heavy traffic awaiting permission to land. Extra fuel allowance is also made in case of diversion to alternative airports which may be anything from 150 to 500 miles away from destination.

When this Flight Plan has been finally checked by the Navigation Officer and the Captain, the whole crew pays a visit to the Meteorological Forecaster in his office to study the weather distribution in detail.

The Captain visits Service Control, where he will be told the number and identity of his passengers, the amount of baggage, freight and mail on board, and how it is stowed. At this point he checks the Load Sheet, which gives the exact weight of the aircraft empty, then shows in detail the weights of the crew and the passengers and their baggage, extra items, freight, mail, fuel, oil and water. It also indicates the trim of the aircraft—how these items have been loaded in relation to the centre of gravity. These figures are most accurately worked out. The only exception in these days is the individual weights of passengers, which is now given as an average of 65 kilogrammes for a woman and 75 kilogrammes for a man. If the Captain feels any uneasiness about accepting this, he can ask for his passengers to be weighed individually—which fortunately for the writer of this book is an uncommon occurrence.

Then the crew, just like their passengers, pass through Customs before going aboard the aircraft, where each in his own sphere checks equipment, radio, compasses, fuel tanks and provisions. The Load Sheets, the Flight Plan, the Passenger and Freight Manifests and some other documents comprise the Ship's Papers, and it is the Captain's responsibility to see that these are complete and on board before he leaves.

When the moment of departure approaches, with passengers in their seats and the Flight Engineer and Co-Pilot having completed their checks, the engines are started and permission to leave from the apron is requested, over the radio, from the Airport Controller. Further checks of engines and equipment are carried out as the airliner moves towards the runway. When the Captain is satisfied that everything is in order, he calls by radio for permission to take off. The Controller then gives him details of how his flight is to be conducted, so that he clears all other incoming and outgoing aircraft in the area. Occasionally the aircraft may be required to remain at some specified height. By the time it is over the English Channel, it will be granted permission to climb to that selected by the Captain in his Flight Plan.

There are Area Control authorities spaced at intervals throughout much of the world. On the flight from London to the Middle East, for example, they will be at London, Paris, Geneva, Milan, Brindisi, Athens and Beirut. During the flight, the Captain or the Co-Pilot is in continuous contact with each successive Area Control, being handed over from one to the next. The Area Controllers keep a fatherly eye on each aircraft passing through their domains and may instruct the Captain to make changes in his flight or may agree to such changes as the Captain himself may suggest—if, for instance, he should meet an area of bad weather.

Apart from this contact with the authorities on the ground, the Captain shares watch-keeping at the controls with the Co-Pilot, collects up-to-date information of the weather along the route and himself initiates weather information. He also checks navigation and, of course, when all is working smoothly at the 'front end' he visits his passengers. This social duty can take a large slice of his time. If there are only sixty passengers aboard—and there are soon likely to be a hundred—just one minute spent with each occupies him for an hour.

When the aircraft approaches its destination, the Control Authority again allots heights to which it may descend or gives special directions about the approach to clear other aircraft. The Captain awaits permission to land on a particular runway and this may be followed by further radio instructions about taxiing. Yet it is still the touch-down that counts!

The pilots of 1919 had to use a great deal of physical strength in managing heavy controls in unheated open cockpits weighed down by heavy flying clothing. In mist and rain they were obliged to raise their flying goggles and to peer round the windscreen into the teeth of the wind. It is not surprising that journalists and novelists of the period were wont to describe pilots as 'ruddy-faced'. The occupational strain of a pilot's calling was recognized at least by Holt Thomas, who in arguing that short hops were desirable in order that the pilot as well as the passengers should not suffer from fatigue, wrote in 1920:

> 'The alternative, for long stages, would be duplicated engine-power, which will come in time; also duplicate pilots. But the pilot resting in an aeroplane will certainly not rest as he would on *terra firma*; and taking an instance from other forms of transport, I think the reader will agree that to give an engine driver his "time off" actually on an engine would be a very poor form of comfort.'

Fatigue in pilots and aircrew was recognized as a problem first by the airlines and afterwards officially. Legislation was introduced in 1927 to set the maximum of 125 hours' flying in thirty consecutive days for pilots. The official maximum flying duty periods, which became legal in 1957, limit the flying duty of any two pilots or more operating an aircraft to sixteen hours; but if three or more pilots are operating an aircraft the period is limited to twenty-four hours subject to sleeping facilities being available on board. Crew members are covered by similar limitations somewhat less stringent than those applying to pilots. To provide adequate rest for crews on the long-haul services, a system of 'slips' is operated by B.O.A.C. The actual aircraft flying from the United Kingdom for instance, to South Africa, calling at Rome, Khartoum, Entebbe and Salisbury itself completes the full trip. The crew that takes it out of London, however, may be slipped at Rome and the next crew slipped at Nairobi. Those who get off at Rome remain there until the following day and take another machine on to Nairobi, where they stand off for several days before going on to Johannesburg. Thus to complete a round trip which takes an aircraft perhaps two complete days, the crew may spend nine to thirteen days away from London, according to the schedule operated. This system applies to all the long-range routes of B.O.A.C.

The single-engined aircraft of 1919 were, of course, flown simply by a pilot. There was a Flight Engineer on board the twin-engined aircraft which followed. Handley Page carried a third crew member, a rigger aboard the 0/400. The first four-engined Imperial Airways machine, the Hannibal, had a Captain, a First Officer, a Radio Officer with two stewards. During the Second World War, some four-engined aircraft carried a crew of five. During the post-war years, many B.O.A.C. aircraft carried a Captain, a First Officer (sometimes a Second Officer) with Radio, Navigating and Engineering Officers. In recent years, three or four cabin crew are usual—Stewards and Stewardesses, each of them costing £200 to £300 to train. The complement is likely to rise to six.

The relationship between those who fly and the management on the ground is of immense importance, as the history of this airline has shown. The start of Imperial Airways was delayed by a pilots' strike. The beginning of the end of Imperial Airways and the genesis of the Cadman inquiry was a controversy about pilots and aircrew forming their own representative bodies. Pilots and aircrews today are rightly protected by rules and regulations which are outside the scope of this story, but which afford them the status and security to which their responsibilities entitle them. With the increase in the size of aircraft and the volume of traffic, the pilot is still the man who has the final word as to whether any particular service shall fly and as to how it shall be flown.

He may not share the powers, or indeed the inclinations, of

some of his predecessors, such as Captain W. L. Hope who was a pilot employed by Handley Page in 1919 when the 0/400 was being converted for civilian use. One of the newfangled ideas was an enclosed cockpit, and it was Captain Hope's good fortune to be the first pilot to fly the machine with this luxurious addition. His flight did not go well. In fact, he became convinced that the contraption was dangerous, depriving him of the sense of feeling, seeing and hearing what was going on. On his arrival in Paris from London, he asked for it to be removed in order that he might fly back unencumbered. His wishes were acknowledged but not swiftly enough for his liking. He therefore armed himself with an axe—which took care of everything including the front windscreen. To take the place of that, Hope himself fitted a small piece of sheet aluminium to keep the wind off his face and the leopard skin flying helmet which he habitually wore. His resolute action earned him no rebuke: on the contrary, it held up the installation of enclosed cockpits in that type of aircraft for several years to come.

The management seemed to have regarded Hope's action as an indication that the pilot's personal comfort might be regarded as a matter of indifference. One of the old pilots recalls a plea for more comfortable working conditions, the elimination of draughts in the open cockpit and some protection from the rain being met tersely by the General Manager: 'What do you want? A bathchair?'

Yet the pilots' well-being was to become acknowledged as an important factor in the safety of flight. The closed cockpit which came at last with the Hannibal was an immense improvement. It is hard to say whether the pilots became more vocal with its introduction. Over the years since then, however, their views have been given proper consideration. It is recognized that the men who do the flying are best fitted to debate the ever-changing conditions of flight operation. It is unlikely that any B.O.A.C. Captain will be seen today wielding an axe to modify his aircraft. Nevertheless, the first-hand experience of operational pilots and air crew infiltrate all the major departments of B.O.A.C. Men with experience in the trunk lines of the world are to be found in the executive management and in the catering department, in operational control and in training, in passenger handling and in the actual selling of passages.

In spite of the wholly practical approach of the pilot to his job, there always lingers an atmosphere of *mystique*, a shared experience and authority which holds together those who fly. In the old days at Croydon, there was a Pilots' Room where, in the years between the wars, men of many European nationalities met regularly, and an international outlook became second nature to the pilot. It is not surprising that some of such men should find themselves occasionally sustaining friendships during the war years in spite of the fact that the British Merchant Air Services had thrown everything into the war effort. There were chance encounters between 'official' enemies who were old friends in such places as Stockholm and Lisbon—occasions when the ties of airmanship were stronger even than those of total war.

In the achievement of the present pattern of world air services, many pilots and aircrew have died—in peace as well as war. Some were pioneers who were consciously beating out new lines on the map. Others were ordinary men following up a line of country and doing their routine job. Pilot and aircrew are people who certainly accept an extra element of risk in their daily lives, like others engaged in public transport as a living. It is their service, backed by training and tradition, which makes air travel secure and amenable for a Prime Minister, a commercial traveller, a ballerina or an unaccompanied child.

CHAPTER XV

OF MACHINES

THE converted bomber, the DH 4A, which inaugurated the first service in 1919, carried a single passenger, travelling at 100 m.p.h. or less, powered by a single 12-cylinder Rolls-Royce 'Eagle VIII' engine driving a 4-bladed laminated mahogany propeller. This A. T. and T. machine was a simple aircraft, built of wood (ash and spruce) braced with steel wire and covered with linen fabric impregnated with a chemical 'dope' to make it taut and weather-resistant. 'We used to test the condition of this fabric on the wings by tapping it smartly with our knuckles. If it "drummed", it was considered satisfactory.'

Handley Page Transport Company began its operations with an HP 0/400 twin-engined machine. This was, of course, a converted bomber also, but Handley Page were the first to produce a twin-engined aircraft built from first principles as a civil air transport. This was the HP W 8 with twin Rolls-Royce Eagle VIII engines. It was shown in 1919 at the Paris Exhibition and went into service in 1923 as the W 8 B. It had 14 seats in a cabin provided with a toilet.

Single-engined planes which made their appearance in 1920/22 were the Napier-engined DH 18 and DH 34, both designed from the start by de Havilland as civil aircraft, each with eight passenger seats—and the DH 34 carried a cabin boy. Their speed was 103 m.p.h. and their working range some three and a half hours. The cockpit in the DH 18 was well down towards the tail and the unfortunate pilot had no direct view forward, the passenger cabin rising above his line of vision. The DH 34, which was very similar, had the cockpit in front of the cabin immediately behind the engine with a flight engineer as well as a pilot. From this new position, the pilot had an excellent view.

Progress in aviation has been in direct ratio to technical advance. Before the First World War it had been slow and erratic. During the war years, it received tremendous stimulus, leading to the amazing conquest of the Atlantic in 1919. With the coming of peace, the impetus fell off. Neither the public nor the State, as we have seen, was greatly concerned with aviation as a weapon of peace. The fleet inherited by Imperial Airways on its formation in 1924 was old, outmoded and mostly single-engined.

At the time of writing, a single airliner could cost the operator something like two million pounds. Some indication of the increased cost which has emerged with technical progress over the years is indicated by the following price list of the Imperial Airways inheritance:

	£
For the DH 34 an average of some	2,500
W 8 B	7,330
Sea Eagle	7,200
Vickers Vimy	2,500
Vickers Vulcan	1,000
DH 50	1,400

These were second-hand values and the rate of obsolescence was high: but if they were cheap in first cost, they were very costly to operate. They were limited in range, or 'endurance', a difficulty which Imperial Airways research was constantly trying to overcome. Clearly higher speeds were required, as well as ability to operate through the twenty-four hours of the day in all conditions of weather and to fly further without refuelling.

In 1923/24 Air Ministry had ordered the building of two types of three-engined commercial aircraft. One of these was the HP W 8 F, a modification of the W 8 B, which had made such a sensation in Paris. Its conception was unusual in that its engines were of two types, two Armstrong Siddeley Pumas of 230/240 h.p. mounted in nacelles in the wings and one Rolls-Royce Eagle of 360 h.p. in the nose. The Pumas were run at higher speeds than was normal for this engine. Because of this, and the fact that the engine in between them was of a totally different type, the noise was deafening. This aircraft, which was purchased by Imperial Airways, marked the first real attempt to provide immunity against forced landing. Hitherto engine failure in a single-engined plane had meant immediate landing. This was frequent enough in the early days and could be disastrous. The performance of these aircraft, however, was so good from the safety point of view that disaster from this cause was rare. Their manœuvrability combined with their slowness usually managed to keep them out of trouble, except where engine failure occurred in bad weather or during take-off.

The safety value of the twin-engined aircraft at first was held in doubt. Some said that if it had no single-engined performance, it offered no advantage over a single-engined plane. It was argued also that the potential source of failure being doubled, there was a greater probability of forced landing. The coming of three-engined aircraft therefore was universally welcomed.

During 1924, a study was made of a sleeve-valve engine which was to provide greater reliability, and a radial engine which was lighter than its predecessors and air-cooled. Three Armstrong Siddeley Jaguar radial engines were installed in the Handley Page Hampstead, another modification of the W 8 B, and also in the 18-seater Armstrong Whitworth Argosy, the first of the three-engined aircraft especially designed for Imperial Airways, three of them being ordered for the European services in 1926.

Because of the low weight per horse-power of the new radial engines, it was possible to increase the reserve of engine power to the aircraft, ensuring greater speed with no economic penalty. It was Bristol Jupiter engines, and not the early Jaguars, which went into the first de Havilland Hercules aircraft for service in the East. By this time, the radial air-cooled engine came to be adopted world-wide.

In both Argosy and Hercules aircraft operated by Imperial Airways in 1926, there was improved fuselage construction, in which steel tubes were used. Still built with wooden spars, the wings were also braced with steel tubes. At this time, the European fleet consisted of fifteen aircraft. Eight of these, though of different types, were so similar and had so many interchangeable components that for practical purposes they might have been the same type. This led to much reduction in maintenance costs.

The Calcutta, ordered as the Mediterranean link for service to the East, was Imperial Airways' first flying-boat. It had set a precedent also in being constructed almost entirely of metal. Powered by three Jupiter engines, each of 500 h.p., its hull and wings were of duralumin. Its total weight was just under 21,000 lb: and its draught was only 2 ft. 10 ins. With its maximum speed of 120 miles an hour, it gave good service until superseded by the four-engined Scipio class flying-boat, a much superior all-round development.

Metal construction had come to stay—so had the monoplane. In 1929, Imperial Airways ordered a Westland IV for charter work. It was a small four-seater with three 105 h.p. Cirrus Hermes engines. Though this machine anticipated the bigger monoplane liner which was to come belatedly, its acquisition at that period was not an indication of a change in the Company's biplane policy. In fact, the big four-engined biplanes, the famous HP 42s, were just about to come into their own. The first of this famous class, which was known as Hannibal on the long-haul routes and as Heracles in European service, was commissioned in 1931. It was the biggest aircraft of its day, with a wing span of 130 feet and a total all-up weight of 29,000 lb. giving accommodation in the European type for thirty-eight passengers and twenty-four passengers in the overseas type. It carried a crew of five including two stewards. Its normal range was about 580 miles. It was credited with a cruising speed of 105 miles per hour, though in service it was considerably slower. In fact, its slowness led to adverse criticism within two or three years of its introduction.

Nevertheless it was an exceptional aircraft for which many passengers expressed a marked affection. For the airline, it established a world-wide reputation for safety, comfort and excellent service. In its day it introduced many novel features. Its construction was light, mostly of aluminium alloy and steel, being fabric covered. It was the first airliner in Britain to have a tail wheel in place of a skid and air-operated brakes on its main wheels. Its galley amidships provided pre-cooked meals in flight. Noise was reduced by lining the cabin walls with a special material. Indeed it was one of the first airliners in which conversation was possible without effort.

Economically the Hannibal/Heracles was an outstanding success, in spite of early complaints about slowness and derisive quips from other operators. When an American airline operator commented on the 'built-in head winds', which were certainly a feature of this far from streamlined machine, an Imperial Airways man retorted with pride: 'Yes, but look at its built-in pay-loads'. Though this pride was undoubtedly justified, Imperial Airways went through a period in which 'safety first' was too much in mind. They had to accept large wing areas in return for ease of manœuvrability and slow take-off and landing speeds. Though this was admirable when these machines were airborne, it produced fantastic situations on the ground where the great wing surfaces were extremely vulnerable to wind. In Europe this was not a major hazard because there were hangars. In the Middle East, however, except at termini, there were no hangars at all and the machines were picketed in the open. On one occasion, at least, when the wind changed suddenly and blew from the rear of the machine, the wings folded forward and collapsed.

The monoplane first came into regular service when eight Armstrong Whitworth Atalantas were ordered and delivered over 1932/33 for the African service. It was a high-winged aircraft which gave passengers a good view. It was not large, taking only ten passengers and two crew, but its cruising speed was 118 m.p.h. Its range, considering the pressing need for longer-range aircraft, was somewhat disappointing at 590 miles.

The fast record flight of Scott and Black in the London–Melbourne air race in 1934 made people uneasy about the performance of British airliners. The official Air Ministry Report for that year stated:

> 'Hitherto a cruising speed of 100 m.p.h. has been considered satisfactory for commercial aircraft, but cruising speeds of up to 150 m.p.h. are now demanded. The economic limit which must be set to this increase of speed has been a much discussed question, but it is hoped that for flight at high altitudes, without excursion into the stratosphere, still higher speeds may be attainable without undue increase in operational cost. . . .'

Imperial Airways, with their highly successful, but slow, fleet of Hannibals and faster, but still too slow, Atalantas, was certainly a target for criticism. It was at this time, however, that the momentous decision was made to place an order for a fleet of twenty-eight Empire flying-boats, then regarded as of almost revolutionary design. This Short Bros. 'C' class flying-boat was of all-metal construction. It was a high wing monoplane, 88 feet long with a wing span of 114 feet. Its deep hull had two decks, the upper for the Captain, First Officer and Radio Officer, the lower for twenty-four passengers, the two stewards, mail and baggage. There were three cabins, more lofty and spacious than any before. The forward one was a smoking cabin. There was a small one amidships behind the galley and aft there was a promenade cabin, including a promenade deck running the full length on the port side where passengers could stand and look out. This flying-boat was very clean aerodynamically. Because of its lightweight construction, mostly of aluminium alloy, the all-up weight, despite its size, was only 40,500 lb. It was powered with four Bristol Pegasus engines of 920 h.p. for take-off. Cruising speed was 164 m.p.h. with a maximum of 200 m.p.h. To begin with, the range was 810 miles, but later the miles extended themselves first to 1,500 then to 2,500.

From this and later types, the S.30 and S.33, developed the Sunderland, as famous in its war service as the Empire flying-boats in peace. Some of their adventures and achievements have already been mentioned. There is another claim to fame which must not pass unrecorded. Many aircraft have taken their names from places. It was the unique distinction of one of the Empire flying-boats to give her name to a place.

The Imperial Airways flying-boat *Corsair*, homeward bound from Durban in March 1939, was forced off course over the Belgian Congo, and ran short of fuel. Searching for somewhere to alight, the Captain sighted a small patch of fairly straight water on the River Dangu. Here he came down: but before he could stay the flying-boat's run, she had collided with a muddy bank, staving in her hull. She sank in a few feet of water. Nobody aboard was injured, and all the mail was salvaged. She lay there in desolation amid swamp and bush. Even the nearest native village was several miles away.

Signals were exchanged with London. A flying-boat worth £50,000 (when new) could not be left to rot. To repair her on the spot, a party of engineers was flown out to the nearest possible point, some 200 miles away. They could only make part of the rest of the journey by road. The last lap was on foot over the swamp.

In hot humid conditions, they built a rudimentary dry dock

around the hull. Then they slipped a cradle under her and, with the help of scores of natives, they managed to haul her to firm ground, where her hull was made good and she was put in order. But the repair job was much less than half the battle. Getting her into the air was a far more formidable problem.

That stretch of the River Dangu on which she had alighted, though swollen by the rainy season, was still too narrow and too short for safe take-off—and half-way along its length there was a dangerous bend. Nevertheless it was decided to make an attempt. A stake was driven into the bank, to which the tail of the flying-boat was secured, while her engines were run up to full throttle. Then the tie-rope was slipped and she tore along down the narrow channel, both sides of which had been cleared of trees and undergrowth by native labour. At the bend she swerved and held her course, but she could not be got off in time and her engines were cut back. Before she pulled up, however, her hull came up against a rock and was holed.

Hauled once more on to firm ground, the hull was repaired again. Many long months had gone by since she alighted there, and Britain was now at war. *Corsair* was not only a valuable asset of the airline but an important war potential of the nation. The long months had already brought them to the dry season with the shrinking of the river and the prospect of not enough water to attempt another take-off for many months more.

Jock Halliday who was organizing the salvage then decided to dam the river and create an artificial lake. So much more native labour was needed that the first necessity was to build a village beside the river to house the workers, also to cut a road for haulage of timber for the dam.

It was not until January 1940 that the water rose sufficiently for another attempt. *Corsair*, with her tail tied again to a large stake ashore, bellowed with the full throttle of her engines and within a few seconds of being released from her tie-rope, was airborne in the early morning mist. She left behind her nine months of toil, a new lake, a new road and a new village—with a new name on the map, Corsairville.

This was not an achievement which can be said to have a direct bearing on technical development. It goes on record as an illustration of the adaptability and resource which are sometimes required in the men of an airline. No type of machine more justly earned the honour of giving its name to a place. No class ever attracted such affection from those who flew aboard as crew or passengers. When the time came to withdraw the Empire flying-boats from service in 1946, they had broken all records for long and useful service. After it was announced that these would be broken up for scrap in the foreign stations where their services had terminated, many former passengers wrote urging their retention.

Feeling ran so high among their admirers along the African section of the Horseshoe Route that a proposal for breaking them up in that area had to be abandoned. Leaving behind them affection and high regard, they were in fact flown back to the United Kingdom to meet an undignified end as scrap.

When these aircraft were first ordered for the Empire mail scheme in 1934, it will be remembered that Imperial Airways also ordered a new landplane fleet of twelve Armstrong Whitworth Ensigns. These were all-metal, high wing monoplanes powered with four Armstrong Siddeley Tiger ix engines, each developing 925 h.p. for take-off, which gave them a cruising speed of 165 m.p.h. The European version had accommodation for forty passengers and the Empire version for twenty-seven, the latter being intended for a landplane service between London and Calcutta only. We have already referred to the lateness of delivery of these aircraft which had a critical effect on the affairs of Imperial Airways. The first delivery was expected in 1936, but it was not till 1938 that the first aeroplane was ready to undergo official flying trials. By the end of that year, five Ensigns were completed and put into service temporarily, only to be withdrawn for modifications. The Ensigns eventually served long and well. A few of them at least were still on the books at the end of the war. As a class they were an interesting illustration of technical development. From their first operation till 1942, the payload (plus crew) increased from 9,580 to 12,000 lb., the fuel capacity from 650 to 1,064 gallons, the cruising speed from 165 to 180 m.p.h., the service ceiling from 18,000 to 24,000 feet and the operating range from 650 to 1,000 miles.

While the Ensign fleet was still being built up, Imperial Airways had to make do with minor additions to its European fleet. Two fast Boulton and Paul twin Jaguar-engined P 71A aircraft were bought. These, named *Britomart* and *Boadicea*, could accommodate seven to thirteen passengers. A fleet of twelve equally fast DH 86 fourteen-seaters were also acquired for the Far East and West Africa as well as Europe, and two Avro 652 twin Cheetah-engined six-seaters. During this pre-war period, the Atlantic had set its own special problems of range which have been discussed, together with such ingenious devices as the Mayo Composite, in another chapter.

The last type of aircraft Imperial Airways introduced was the fast and graceful DH 91 with a cruising speed of around 200 m.p.h. Five of these built for the Company were known as the Frobisher class. A number built specially to the order of the Air Ministry were called Albatross. The Frobishers, which had a range of 1,000 miles and carried twenty-two passengers, were a return to wood construction. The main plane embodied box spars and a cover of spruce planking and plywood. The fuselage was a monocoque built of a sandwich of plywood separated by a layer of light stabilizing material.

In 1938, both Imperial Airways and British Airways had in mind further advanced designs for aircraft. Air Ministry placed orders for two new types and entered into commitments to subsidize the early production of a third. The first was to be a four-engined all-metal landplane intended for carrying passengers and mails on the North and possibly South Atlantic routes. Imperial Airways collaborated in the drafting of the specification and in supervising this new machine which was ordered from Short Bros. The second of the new types was a four-engined metal landplane intended for European services. The detailed specification for this was drawn up in close collaboration with British Airways and the order was placed with the Fairey Aviation Co. Ltd.

British Airways had been operating services within Europe with the excellent fast Lockheed 10A and 14 aircraft, typical of the newer machines then built in the United States. They were also using British DH 86 aircraft. This latter type, which Imperial Airways had flown since 1934, was a biplane powered by four Gipsy VI engines giving a speed of 141 m.p.h.

The war brought civil aircraft construction to a standstill, but for two projects, the 'G' class flying-boat and the DH 95, the Flamingo, of which the newly formed Corporation acquired eight. The 'G' class flying-boats had originally been intended for Atlantic operations but were requisitioned for military use. They were much bigger than the original flying-boat with a cruising speed of 180 m.p.h. and a range in still air of 3,000 miles. The Flamingo was a twin-engined landplane with accommodation for twenty passengers and a speed of 200 m.p.h.

The fact that transport aircraft for the Services, from 1941, had to be obtained from America added greatly to B.O.A.C.'s responsibilities in that new acquisitions constantly added to the number of types in the fleet. In 1943, for instance, the Corporation was coping with 117 aircraft of 23 types with 25 different types of engines.

After the war, making do with what it had been able to acquire, the Corporation had to settle for conversion of service aircraft, chiefly Yorks and Lancastrians. Though the latter was soon replaced, the York was kept in service for several years, at first as a passenger aircraft, then as a trainer and later as a freighter. At the time of writing, it is only a couple of years since B.O.A.C. disposed of the last of its Yorks, but a number of them are still being worked in various parts of the world as freighters and for high-density passenger traffic.

The Lancastrian deserves mention because of its adaptation for the fast post-war Britain–Australia service. It had, in fact, been used as a V.I.P. aircraft as early as 1943. Trans-Canada Airlines improved its furnishings and operated it across the Atlantic in 1944. B.O.A.C. in the following year equipped it with sleeping berths and a galley. As a passenger aircraft it had no hope of commercial success, but its performance as a stop-gap was impressive.

The very useful Argonaut, a development of the Douglas DC 4, was powered with Rolls-Royce Merlin engines, as was also the Lancastrian. It was used as an 'interim' airliner seating forty passengers, cruising at 250 m.p.h. at 20,000 feet, with fuel reserves and a range of 2,400 miles. Its reliability and usefulness were such that it served admirably as a stop-gap later when the Comet 1 had to be taken out of service.

Before flying-boats were abandoned in favour of an all landplane fleet, three more types went into service during the postwar years. The first and second of these were the Hythes and Plymouths, which were adaptations of the Sunderland. The other was a further development, the Solent. This, the last of the flying-boats, continued in service on the trunk line to South Africa until 1949 when the change-over to landplanes was completed.

There being no British-built landplanes immediately available, the Corporation purchased American Constellation 049s for the North Atlantic and later Stratocruisers, as well as Constellation 749s, for the Commonwealth services. The former is a very large span aircraft with two decks, carrying up to seventy-two passengers with a cruising speed of 340 m.p.h. and a range of 4,200 miles.

With the introduction of the spectacular but unfortunate Comet 1, the first pure jet civil aircraft to be built, B.O.A.C. set new standards for the commercial aviation world. The Comet was built throughout of light alloy and four de Havilland Ghost jet turbines were installed in the wing roots. The development of this engine was highly satisfactory. It began its life with an overhaul interval of 250 hours and the elimination of difficulties in service resulted in an extension of hours to 750 within two years. The disaster which overtook the Comet 1s and the research into its cause have already been noted in another chapter.

The Bristol Britannia, a turbo-propeller aircraft, exists at the time of writing in three forms, with varying capacities and ranges. The 312, which is the largest, has a wing span of more than 142 feet, and its length is just over 124 feet. Cruising at 385 miles an hour at 30,000 feet, it can carry a payload of 28,000 lb. for 3,400 miles. Its arrival was the answer at least to the problems of range over the Atlantic so far as Britain was concerned. It was to be the first British aircraft to operate a regular scheduled service from London to New York non-stop both ways and all the year round.

Mechanically its Proteus engines were highly satisfactory, but, owing to its unique 'reverse air-flow' which after entry to the engine is directed forward, its development preparatory to going on service was greatly prolonged because of the tendency of ice to form in the air intake system in certain conditions of tropical weather. By the aid of television, it was possible to observe this phenomenon in all stages of its development when the reasons for it became evident, and means for overcoming it were evolved.

In 1957, B.O.A.C. bought ten Douglas 7c aircraft of very long range, eminently suitable for North Atlantic operation. They were intended to serve as an insurance against the possibility of late deliveries of the Britannias. While it was generally anticipated that the jet engine would oust the piston engine, determined efforts were made, especially in the United States, to develop some of the older types and these were particularly successful in the DC 7cs.

At the time of writing, in the summer of 1958, there was much promise on the threshold, including a fleet of Comet 4 aircraft, to the inauguration of which we refer on page 232, a fleet of Boeing 707 aircraft powered by four Rolls-Royce jet engines, and an order in hand for Vickers VC 10s. Prophecy being no part of our terms of reference, these newcomers must be left without further comment. They belong to another phase of development.

This steady growth of the machine in its power, capacity and size over the years has had to be matched by ever-increasing responsibility and organization in ground engineering. At the beginning, technical responsibility for an aircraft was normally vested in one man holding a Ground Engineer's Licence. His task would cover checks, inspections, rectifications, repairs and final certification that the aircraft was fit for flight. Overhauls were similarly covered by one person holding the necessary licence.

Specialization began during the 'thirties. Now in the 'fifties, the ground crew for a minor check has grown to include on occasion thirty mechanics, three supervisors and three inspectors. For a major check there may be eighty mechanics, seven supervisors and eight inspectors. For operations on this scale, the flow of work must be controlled. Moreover, the demand for faster maintenance and overhaul is greater than ever in order that the fullest possible use can be made of the very costly aircraft in service. To achieve this, the most accurate forecasting of work processes against a time schedule has to be devised.

Until recently, a Certificate of Safety had to be prepared and signed daily for every airliner. Now a Certificate of Maintenance covers the aircraft for thirty-one days or for an agreed period of flying hours. Repairs *en route* may be covered by a Certificate of

Compliance signed by an engineer, not necessarily licensed but recognized as competent by B.O.A.C.'s Chief Inspector.

An engineering project arose out of the war years but was not mentioned in the preceding pages dealing with the Second World War. This is the overhaul and repair base at Treforest near Cardiff, which began in 1940 as a war evacuation measure but which has continued as the Corporation's main repair base. During the war years it operated not only on behalf of B.O.A.C. but for the Ministry of Aircraft Production which, of course, looked after R.A.F. aircraft. At one time twenty-six variations of different types of engines were passing through the shops. In addition, more than 3,700 wrecked or burnt engines were dismantled and tens of thousands of engine parts salvaged. During the peak output of the war, in November 1944, more than 2,300 people were employed at Treforest, including 800 women. When post-war reorganization was complete, the base became known as Repair Factory, Treforest, and throughout the 'fifties this organization undertook the overhaul of engines and accessories not only for B.O.A.C., but for other airline operators as well as the Ministry of Supply and the United States Air Force. At the time of writing, Treforest is fully employed on turbo-prop jet engine overhauls and the factory in the Welsh valley is well equipped for the needs of the jet airliner age.

In making this brief reference in this non-technical book to the vast and intricate technical organization of B.O.A.C. one can only use the old analogy of the iceberg—a great structure unseen beneath the surface which supports what is visible in the sky. Engineering, significant and vital though it may be, is but one of the many facets of airline operation, which are no less efficient for being submerged, as it were, from public view.

The new science of meteorology, for instance, has grown up side by side with aviation, from the times when Hounslow and Le Bourget used to exchange notes on the weather by telephone twice a day.

The craft of navigation began with a few primitive instruments on a dashboard in the cockpit, a map which implied that the ground ought always to be visible and such visual aids as place names painted on the roofs of railway stations. From such early beginnings have evolved the systems of great complexity required by fast-moving jet aircraft often called upon to operate in areas of great traffic density and also flying thousands of miles at a single stretch. Navigation is now closely identified with radio and increasingly with radar.

Radio itself is another complete science which has grown up with aviation. At the end of the First World War specialists in the Services had produced the basic ingredients of the fixed and mobile radio-communication and radio-navigational systems still in use on the airways of the world. Some of the de Havilland and Handley Page machines in the R.A.F. Communication Squadrons flying after the Armistice in 1918, were equipped with wireless telephony. The first airline to order Marconi sets was A. T. and T. By 1920, all Handley Page Transport's 0/400s and the DH 16s of Instone airlines had been fitted. When the pioneer companies were merged to form Imperial Airways almost the only item which was common to all was their Marconi wireless equipment, which at that time was a great asset in such a mixed fleet.

It was, of course, an Air Ministry task to look after civil aviation in the early days: and few at first realized that the official responsibility for commercial radio services had been vested in the G.P.O. by an Act of Parliament in 1912. It therefore came as something of a shock to the struggling airline community when officialdom announced that the Law demanded the licensing of airborne wireless stations *and the people who operated them*. To the pioneer pilots, already proficient in the daily use of wireless, the prospect of an examination by grave middle-aged post office officials, who had never 'been up', was received with some indignation. To add to the humiliation, stamps to the value of ten shillings were demanded from examinees. One pilot, at least, while adhering to the letter of the Law, registered his protest. He handed his examiner 240 halfpenny stamps—all of which had to be cancelled and then affixed to the examination form.

Though the vagaries of red tape beset aviation radio at the beginning, the need for international control and standardization was soon obvious. The British were ahead of their foreign competitors when, in 1922, radio was made compulsory in all commercial aircraft carrying passengers and goods. The French and Dutch operators had to fall in with this later.

Wherever the British trunk lines spread throughout the world, there went with them radio stations and systems of communication, for speed of flight and speed of communication must go hand in hand. At the end of the Second World War, B.O.A.C. collaborated with Air Ministry in taking over the operation of many of the stations which had been used by both civil and military aircraft. Then there was formed in London an associated Company, International Aeradio Ltd., to provide air-to-ground and point-to-point communications, navigational aids and air traffic control facilities on an international basis throughout the world. Thus the use of radio for which at one time individual pilots were required to pay ten shillings in stamps is now a matter not just of nations and airlines, but of international collaboration.

CHAPTER XVI

CARGOES

Several brace of grouse, pots of Devonshire cream, a consignment of leather and some newspapers—such was the load on the first service across the Channel in 1919. It was not quite what Tennyson had envisaged in 'pilots of the purple twilight, dropping down with costly bales'. It was, if anything, more imaginative. It soon increased in variety, if not in substance. One of the older traffic hands, Frank Blunden, recalls items such as day-old chicks, perfumes from Paris, shock absorbers and telegraphic apparatus among the early cargoes. The first vehicles to be carried were motor cycles which went in 1919 from Britain to Germany, until the German Government imposed heavy import duties in the mid-'twenties.

The possibilities of air freight were quickly, but not alas universally, appreciated by individuals and by firms. In the early days from Hounslow, a lady sent a single loaf of bread to Paris every day over a considerable period. Newsreel companies were among the first customers; among them the Pathé Organization began sending newsreel film to be shown in Paris on the evening of arrival. There was considerable publicity value—as still there is on a much larger scale—in the movement of perishable goods by air. Consignments of mushrooms sent from Paris to London went through the streets of London by pedal-tricycle bearing the legend 'brought by air by Imperial Airways'.

When services were cancelled owing to weather, freight which had arrived at Croydon Airport had to be passed on to East Croydon Railway Station to go by surface transport, and from Le Bourget freight sometimes went to the Gare du Nord. To maintain the prestige of the air, the ever-enthusiastic staff of those days resorted to ingenious but somewhat shady devices to conceal the fact that goods had not been airborne. Customs declarations were required for the consignees which had to indicate the method of shipment and this would have shown that surface transport had been used. An aircraft which had long since crashed carried the registration letters GEBBR; but its rubber stamps had been retained. These were used for consignment notes. Needless to say, it was an unauthorized procedure. If there were any query about a consignment bearing these magic letters, it was a shared secret to the staff on both sides of the Channel that the consignment had travelled by rail and boat.

This was feasible, because any day's goods actually sent by air were not cleared of formalities until the following morning. Goods travelling all night by surface transport, therefore, were able to catch up 'if the job were rushed'. Looking back, even indulgently, over thirty years or so, this undoubtedly emerges as a slightly wicked affair but those who recollect it may well be justified in saying that it was all in a good cause at a time when the air services were fighting for their lives and a reputation for reliability in freight traffic was a matter of life and death to a new industry. With more reliable aeroplanes and weather forecasting, the need for it soon disappeared.

A singular operation of the early 'twenties was the movement of German paper money. It arose from the Allied occupation of the Rhine and the Ruhr and the abnormal financial conditions in Germany. The mark at that time was collapsing and the paper mark notes, gradually amounting to fantastic figures, were printed in Berlin. To reach Cologne, this paper money would have had to pass through French-occupied territory, where it would have been subject to tax. It was therefore flown from Berlin to London, thence to Cologne to avoid the French and Belgian Channel ports, where it was likely to be impounded. On one occasion, an aircraft force-landed at Ostend, and the whole consignment of marks was confiscated. The Instone line was much concerned with this traffic. 'The daily fall in value of the mark in those days,' wrote Alfred Instone, 'gradually decreased the printed value of the mark notes to fantastic figures —in fact, towards the end of the fall, the air transport must have cost more to the German authorities than the intrinsic value of the notes carried. . . .'

The packets of notes in the aircraft—usually a DH 9A—'would be surmounted by a German official armed with a revolver and as the bulk of the marks (and weight) increased, so the carrying capacity of the aeroplane became more and more strained until the question arose whether the German Government would not supply a smaller German official to accompany the notes, so that we could carry more marks.'

From the start, British and French cross-Channel operators found that gold bullion was among the few cargo items in which they could compete easily against surface transport. There followed a price-cutting struggle between the various companies, which meant that this form of freight was not as remunerative to any of them as it might have been. Till 1929 records show that movements were relatively small, consisting mainly of gold for the jewellery and watch trade of France and Switzerland. In that year, however, various import taxes were eased and the gold began to flow more readily over the airlines. Its transport in large quantities, in fact, became a feature of the nineteen-thirties. Bullion often returned over the same routes within a few days of its despatch. There was a notable 'gold rush' in July 1931, when for nearly two weeks the airlines operating from Croydon were heavily laden with bullion consignments. In that period, Imperial Airways carried over seventeen tons. The increase in the size and range of aircraft naturally encouraged this traffic. The rise in the value of the gold itself has also meant that more in value can be carried in terms of less weight. In September 1931, a million pounds would be represented by eight tons of packed gold: today that sum would be represented by only about two and three-quarter tons. Today surface transport cannot compete with the air in the movement of bullion. The great gain in transit time on long hauls is a particularly important factor where a high rate of interest per day is being charged. Moreover it can be shifted at short notice with simplified security arrangements when it goes by air, whereas surface transport means that it has to be re-consigned at every frontier point and conveyed throughout its journey by experienced couriers.

In some stations along the trunk routes, B.O.A.C. officials regard the movement of cases of gold bars with a certain degree of cynical amusement. They sometimes see the same consignments of gold in the same cases passing through their hands up and down the route several times within a month or so. On one occasion at least, these swift, unruffled movements which served to cast the financial balance sheets of the world went wrong. The Suez crisis of 1956 delayed a consignment of gold from London to the Far East for several days. It was then diverted through Istanbul where the aircraft had engine trouble. The consignees became agitated by this delay which was losing them large sums in interest: and a special effort had to be made to keep the gold moving.

A faster aircraft was due to pass through Istanbul and instructions were sent to place the precious cargo aboard and thus expedite its journey. For security reasons these instructions had to be sent tactfully to the local agents in Istanbul. It was thought safer to substitute the word 'metal' for 'gold' in the signal. The agents in Istanbul delved deeper into confusion by interpreting the word 'metal' as meaning 'steel'.

But there was no steel in the delayed plane—only a performing seal, which happened also to be consigned to the Far East. This was obviously what had been meant. A reassuring cable was despatched to the impatient consignee saying that all was well and that the 'metal' would be on board the fast aircraft out of Istanbul. With all eagerness, the performing seal was then despatched while the gold dallied on. Granted a priority passage to a climate in which it could hardly have felt at ease, the seal was still the least uncomfortable of those well-intentioned people who took part in this particular movement.

The safeguarding of gold, diamonds and other valuable freight at London Airport and thoughout the whole of the routes operated by B.O.A.C. is a great responsibility. This was recognized when the Corporation, in 1945, appointed as their Chief Security Officer Mr. Donald Fish, who began life as a London constable and graduated to his present post by way of Scotland Yard and M.I.5. Though based in London, Fish's security organization spreads throughout the whole B.O.A.C. network and maintains close and vital communications with police and Customs authorities in Britain, the Commonwealth, and foreign countries. The need for such an organization has increased with the years, as it has become obvious to the world's criminals that not only gold, but every kind of valuable material that is not bulky moves by air and the airlines are now so extended that they may be expected to be more vulnerable than they were a couple of decades ago.

B.O.A.C. was the first international airline to set up the sort of security service which is organized by Fish. Its need is indicated by the crime sheet during the last decade. A tin box containing £2,000 worth of diamonds disappeared in 1947 between London and Singapore. In 1951, part of a gold consignment to South Africa disappeared. Though it was under lock and key in a safe during the time it was at London Airport and also aboard the aircraft, one box of gold was found to contain half a builder's brick on arrival. Diamonds worth £1,000 were missed from the cargo on a Constellation between London and Bangkok. In 1954, gold bars worth £3,000 were stolen between the Gold Coast and London Airport. £3,000 worth of diamonds vanished within six minutes of a Britannia touching down at London Airport after flying from Singapore in 1957.

Taken individually, these may be serious losses in themselves: but they do not suggest any laxity in the treatment of freight by B.O.A.C. When they are considered against the background of the world-wide network of operations, the percentage of losses is, in fact, slight when compared with figures quoted for other transport services. Cargoes carried by B.O.A.C. in any year are worth many million pounds. They pass through dozens of hands, loaders and unloaders, checkers and guards. The constant vigilance of the Security Section has been so effective that over the past ten years with freight always increasing in amount and value, the losses have never exceeded £50,000 in any one year.

Donald Fish and his men have a world-wide beat and control an intricate security routine: but it is a routine which can lead to adventure, as it did in July 1948, when one of the employees of B.O.A.C.'s precious cargo warehouse at London Airport reported to Fish that he had been approached by a gang. The informer was a loader on the warehouse staff with ambitions to enter the security organization. During the Second World War, when he had been a prisoner of war in Germany, among his fellow prisoners he had met a member of the gang which now was planning to raid the warehouse on the night of July 29. They knew that an aircraft was expected carrying £250,000 worth of gold, which would be placed in the bonded warehouse, where there were already consignments of precious metal and diamonds worth something like £20,000. The intelligence service of the gang was not very far wide of the mark, and Fish told his employee that he was to collaborate to the full with the raiders and give them all the information they needed, while he himself got in touch with Scotland Yard to work out a plan not only to thwart the raid, but to trap the criminals.

On obtaining full details of the working of the warehouse, the raiders planned to supply the informer with a drug with which he was to dope the tea which was normally served to the security staff towards midnight. As soon as the dope worked, the informer was to signal a nearby café where the gang was keeping a twenty-four hour watch on the warehouse.

The scheme worked out by B.O.A.C. and Scotland Yard was to substitute police and security staff for the men on duty in the warehouse. These were to feign the effects of the doped tea. They, and hidden reinforcements smuggled into the building, were to spring upon the gang as soon as the informer had given them the all-clear signal and lured them into the warehouse. It was difficult to make advance arrangements without arousing the suspicions of the watchers in the café. Fish overcame this by loading his strong-arm squad into the B.O.A.C. freight cars, which were driven up to the bond during the afternoon and backed in as if they were unloading goods. It was only when this force arrived properly dressed in working clothes, that the genuine staff was let into the secret of the substitution and ushered into a safe place. At various points about the airport, hidden from view, were a number of police cars with reinforcements ready to go into action as soon as they received a code message transmitted by telephone from the warehouse. Probably the toughest assignment that night fell to the men substituted for the security guards. They had to act as if they had been doped, even when members of the gang arrived and began kicking them to see if they were doped enough, and then tied them up. As far as it is known, there were eight members of the gang who backed up to the warehouse in their lorry on receiving the appropriate signal from the informer. Only when they were inside, had taken the safe keys from the 'doped' and bound security guards and had started to turn them in the locks did the police announce themselves and demand surrender. The gang was in no mood for this. Some of them were armed with iron bars. Others clutched bottles and spanners. They went into action against the police, who were armed only with truncheons, and for a few moments it seemed as if they might win. The struggle, which went on for some time and was known as the 'Battle of London Airport', was every bit as ferocious as any of the highwaymen's affrays which took place in that neighbourhood by Hounslow Heath in the bad old days. Overpowered, charged and tried, the eight raiders shared between them prison sentences totalling seventy-one years. The gold consignment, which was their main prize, did not arrive on that particular night. Delayed by fog in transit, it was unloaded in the battered and bloodstained warehouse the following day.

Though this was the most violent, it was but one of many episodes in which the security staff of B.O.A.C. have been involved in catching thieves or smugglers not only in London, but in such places as Bangkok, Tokyo, New York and Hong Kong. But Fish maintains that the emphasis of their work is upon prevention.

The B.O.A.C. bonded stores at London Airport are treasure houses of the curious as well as the precious. Every imaginable sample, from tobacco to silk, every kind of luxury from tropical cut flowers to caviare, every kind of human achievement from primitive carvings to French impressionist paintings are to be found there. Almost everything that has been taken by rail or sea has now been carried by air. There are still some surprising items such as the eighteen tons of Pepsi-Cola concentrate and colouring that suddenly had to be shipped from Britain to Egypt. Or the three tons of metal caps for oil drums shipped from London to Lagos where there were thousands of drums which could not be sealed. Much more comprehensible is the carriage of newspapers all over the world which brings the B.O.A.C. a revenue of £120,000 in a single year.

The Berlin airlift of 1948/49 proved that if expense were no object, the most unlikely cargoes can take to the air. B.O.A.C. participated by sending a group of twin-engined aircraft under the command of Captain Nigel Pelly, who had piloted Neville Chamberlain to Munich in 1938. When at length he returned after many hectic weeks, Pelly was no longer dressed as a Senior Captain in B.O.A.C. He was wearing a boiler suit and neckscarf, a suitable garb for cargo loads which included flour, fish, dehydrated potatoes and coal. No passengers were carried by B.O.A.C. during the airlift. It was for them entirely a freight operation.

The performing seal that was misrepresented as bullion was one of the countless creatures which today travel by B.O.A.C. services. Almost every living creature, except a giraffe, has been carried by the Corporation, from sea lions and panthers to fleas and silkworms. The creatures' travelling habits, now the subject of careful study, are sometimes more consistent than those of the people who send them. A large consignment of silkworms went by B.O.A.C. from Tokyo to Rome. When notified of the safe arrival of this cargo in Italy, the shipper rushed into the B.O.A.C. Tokyo office and registered his gratitude by embracing a member of the staff. Then he himself flew off to Rome—by another airline.

The business of moving livestock has become of such importance that the Corporation has prepared a printed booklet advising staff and potential shippers about living cargo, including instructions for feeding, watering, exercising—and recapture in case of escape. For instance, there is the need to talk to travelling orang-outangs, which suffer from loneliness which makes them restless. They can be calmed by human company. Mammals, we learn, are best carried in semi-darkness but birds must be stowed facing the light as they will not eat in the dark. Hints on the carriage of dogs includes 'a little fuss from crew and ground staff'. Nothing is overlooked. 'A dog is always more responsive if called by its pet name, and this should always be shown on its documents.' Crocodiles and porpoises, on the other hand, desire nothing more than to be left alone, though they appreciate a daily watering with a hose.

Great emphasis is laid upon correct and adequate crating—for every animal must, of course, be confined when travelling by air, even if it be a domestic pet travelling on the same aircraft as its master. Through the R.S.P.C.A., international standardization of packaging for livestock is being attempted. Recommendations for feeding and watering are detailed. Three meals a day of bread and butter with jam and honey, together with fruit and greens, are recommended for orang-outangs, gorillas and chimpanzees, who also appreciate lumps of sugar and pieces of cake between meals. Beasts of prey, such as lions, tigers and panthers prefer to be fed but once a day; if possible late in the afternoon. Their intake is calculated at 1½ kilos of raw meat for every 30 kilos of live weight.

When large numbers of animals are travelling in a B.O.A.C. freighter, a member of the Corporation's security force travels in the aircraft throughout the journey, mingling roughly the duties of keeper and steward. He feeds and waters the animals while they are airborne and looks after them at stopping places, exercising some and making sure that others are not suffering from changes of temperature.

One of the biggest livestock operations was when the Corporation undertook to fly twenty young elephants from Bangkok to various points in Europe. Numerous flights were arranged. Five of the elephants took off for England, making the 7,000-mile journey to Billy Smart's circus.

'Each one weighed nearly half a ton and stood shoulder high [wrote Mr. T. Ivan Pyle, a B.O.A.C. official who travelled with them]. All five were female—female elephants are used for circus work as they are more amenable to training.

'Special stalls of teak wood were constructed in the aircraft at Bangkok and a wooden floor was laid over the normal metal floor. Over half a ton of hay, a generous supply of sugar cane, and several gallons of water were also loaded on to the aircraft before take-off . . . .

'As we began to move along the runway, we gave them each a few sticks of sugar cane—which they consider to be a great delicacy. This occupied their attention as we became airborne. They were then given a good supply of hay and soon settled down in their new surroundings. It was necessary, however, to keep a watchful eye on their inquisitive trunks as they examined the details of the aircraft's construction!

'We left Bangkok just before sunset and, in what seemed no time at all, the lights of Rangoon were twinkling merrily away to port. As we headed along the coast of Burma, the moon sent a broad swathe of shimmering gold across the Bay of Bengal. Inside the aircraft the atmosphere was charged with mutual cogitation. The elephants stared at their human companions with a cool, steady, appraising gaze. We responded with the calm, knowledgeable demeanour of people who had been handling elephants all their lives. Neither side spoke. It was thus on terms of polite, but somewhat frigid, amiability that we arrived at Calcutta.

'The next morning we set off for Karachi. During the flight

of over seven hours, the initial reserve rapidly dispersed and it was not long before conversation flourished. Admittedly, it was somewhat one-sided conversation. When an elephant bellows a hearty remark about six inches from one's right ear, the only response of which one is capable for some moments is a stunned and rather inane silence. However, the elephants obviously felt that the time had come to "let their hair down", and, ignoring our conversational inadequacy, proceeded to demonstrate one or two of their party tricks.

'One rollicking little game comprised sucking up a trunk-full of the sawdust with which the stalls were strewn and then giving a most impressive imitation of a jet engine running at full power. . . .'

It is admitted by the experts that the tens of thousands of animals that travel by air every month are better off than those which make the much slower and rougher journey by cargo boat. There are certain types of livestock which could not, in any case, travel other than by air, and B.O.A.C. has pioneered methods for transporting such creatures which have limited travelling time. Examples are tropical fish and day-old chicks, for both of which completely new markets have been opened in various parts of the world as a result of new air freight methods. After much experiment, B.O.A.C. has discovered that an ideal way of transporting tropical fish is in oxygen-filled plastic bags set in insulated cardboard containers.

Day-old chicks, which can perhaps claim to be at once the pioneer and the most constant livestock freight, can travel for 72 hours without requiring attention. Allowing for the time spent in surface travel to and from airports, B.O.A.C. gives its maximum of 36 hours for chicks to be airborne. This means that the extent of the market for chicks is limited only by the distance in which an airliner can fly in a day and a half.

B.O.A.C. traffic in livestock has in recent years been greatly assisted by the R.S.P.C.A. Air Hostel for Animals, which is an ingeniously constructed building on the outskirts of London Airport within easy reach of all points of arrival and departure. This is the first hostel of its kind in the world. At the time of writing, a special American mission has been studying its workings in order that the same sort of thing may be opened in Idlewild. The hostel, which is a receiving and holding point for livestock of all kinds coming to London, by far the busiest air junction for livestock traffic, opened in the autumn of 1952. By August 1958, two million living creatures had passed through the hands of the Manager and his highly trained staff. The largest single consignment of living creatures which they have been called upon to handle numbered 40,000. Of these 30,000 were tiny brilliantly coloured Indian finches in rows of bamboo cages. . . . 'But amusement soon turned to dismay when on closer inspection we found them to be artificially dyed.' The remaining 10,000 in this particular shipment are impossible to list in full, but included orang-outangs, cheetahs, tigers, leopards, bears, pandas, gibbons, monkeys, civet cats, flying foxes, cobras, pythons, mongoose, otters, wallabies, parrots, cranes, hornbills, peafowl, slow loris and tropical fish. All these creatures had to be housed, fed, cleaned and examined for sickness or injury. Two hundred different diets had to be fed to them, and on that occasion the staff worked for more than eighteen hours non-stop.

There was an alarming incident when the crew of an incoming B.O.A.C. aircraft signalled that a number of poisonous snakes were loose in the hold. The signal was passed on to the Manager, who was requested to meet the aircraft on arrival and deal with the situation.

> 'No one had any idea what type of snakes they were or how many, and the thought of creeping on my stomach in such a confined space, moving other freight in search of the escapees, did not appeal to me in the least. However, the job had to be done and inside I went head first, tightly clutching a canvas bag in which to put the snakes I hoped to recapture. Some time later I emerged unharmed with sixty-one venomous reptiles, including an eight-foot Diamond-back Rattler, in my bag, but with my nerves in shreds. The snakes were taken back to my premises, sorted and re-packed and were on their way again that same evening.'

The extent to which B.O.A.C. is involved in the ever-increasing traffic of live freight is shown by the recent yearly average of one million living creatures, animals, birds, fish and reptiles (nobody seems to count the insects) carried on the world network. It has in fact been claimed, somewhat irreverently, for B.O.A.C. that every third passenger is a four-footed one.

CHAPTER XVII

AIR TRAVELLERS

At the first airport at Hounslow, and later in a hut at Croydon, wall space was reserved for an assortment of leather flying clothing, helmets and goggles of all shapes and sizes—for the use of passengers who elected to travel in an open cockpit or had no option. We have had it on his own authority that the solitary passenger returning from the first scheduled service in 1919 was sick into his hat, which, of course, he carried in his hand in order to be suitably attired on arrival. The thrill and beauty of flight was compensation enough even if the fare between London and Paris was £21 each way.

His was a solitary and expensive adventure. Yet within his lifetime, only a little more than three decades after his flight, a B.O.A.C. Argonaut pilot was putting up an unacclaimed record in flying an entire family of twenty-four migrants from the Persian Gulf to Israel. His passengers were all closely related and included four generations. 'The great-grandmother, Mrs. K. B. Salen, was 105 years old,' reported Captain Gerald Austin. 'It was the first time she had ever flown in her life, and she behaved just like a veteran. We had to help her on and off the aircraft of course, but otherwise she was like any other passenger, and was not in the least upset by this first experience and, in fact, was obviously quite thrilled.'

What adventure and achievement lies between the centenarian who was 'quite thrilled' by flying from the Persian Gulf to the Promised Land and the ecstatic first passenger out of England, looking for the Eiffel Tower! In surveying the first months of passenger-carrying, Holt Thomas wrote of 'the temporary charms of novelty' and this was indeed a telling element in the early passenger lists. For those who could afford such charms there was sometimes adventure to be had. There was Captain Jerry Shaw, for instance, flying a DH 4A in October 1919, bound from Paris to London with a solitary passenger, an unserviceable compass, little visibility and strong headwinds.

After an hour above the sea without sighting the English coast, Shaw had to admit that he had no idea whether they had drifted into the North Sea or the Bay of Biscay:

> '. . . The only thing to do was to try to get through the clouds and check on the sun—remember that the only navigational instrument other than the compass was then the "bubble". Well, somehow we got up to 11,000 feet but still in solid cloud and then suddenly and inevitably we went into a spin. Realizing the futility of any further effort, I eased back the throttle, centralized the controls and came out of the spin at 3,000 feet, still in cloud from which we emerged in a gentle glide not too far above the waves, which were now pretty big. We were now completely lost, and my fuel running mighty low, but at extreme visibility of half a mile I spotted a vessel bobbing up and down. . . . With the throttle well back, to conserve my remaining gas, we flew round and round the vessel in ever-increasing circles in the hope of seeing land, for she was only a small tramp steamer. No success, and with the light beginning to fade, we went down and closed-in on the vessel. Circling her at deck-level several times, not a soul appeared aboard, but I read "*Harlech London*", under her stern. I then hoped that she might head for land. I dived twice under her bow. That rather desperate manœuvre was effective, but not in the way of my hopes; she swung round, hove to. This created a patch of comparatively calm water on her leeward side at a moment when my engines spluttered. . . . I switched off the engine and, holding her just above stalling speed, landed on the crest of a wave right alongside. Miraculously, and to my utter astonishment, and greater relief, nothing broke and we floated.'

It spoke highly of the workmanship of the relatively flimsy DH 4A that the aircraft stood up so well to this treatment. It was still unreasonable to expect that it would remain afloat for long in such a gale and Shaw's first thought was for his passenger. He jumped up from his own seat in the open cockpit ready to raise the lid of the enclosed passenger cockpit behind him.

The lid was already open. 'There stood my passenger dressed only in his trousers, a thin cotton vest and his bowler hat. In a later well-reasoned explanation of his action, my passenger said that, having been in the U.S. Air Force, he realized we were going into the "drink". He had therefore clamped his bowler hard down ready for the crash, and removed everything else to the limits of decency in case he still had a chance to swim.'

Shaw told his passenger to dress. While *Harlech* was lowering her only boat, the two men made their way with luggage and mail to the tailplane where they clung until they were picked up 'not even wet, but very cold'.

The skipper of the *Harlech* was a Captain Williams. He carried no radio. Over mugs of hot tea (his was a dry ship) he explained to pilot and passenger that Cardiff was his next port of call. Since the rescue had taken place only eleven miles off Beachy Head, it seemed likely that with the gale then raging, the *Harlech* might take several days to reach her destination. At first Captain Williams could not be persuaded to put in elsewhere, then Shaw remembered

> 'we were carrying and still retained H.M. mails, which, as I pointed out, he had now put himself under an obligation not to delay unnecessarily. That idea weakened him, and at dawn next morning we were off Weymouth, where he signalled for a pilot to take us ashore. . . .
>
> 'After putting through a local call box a telegram to Headquarters, announcing our safe landing at Weymouth and advising time of arrival at Waterloo, we got the first train to town. Somewhere along the route we bought the morning papers and read of our disappearance in the Channel. . . .'

Nothing further appears to have been heard of Shaw's self-possessed passenger after the rescue. From the comment he made at the time, it seems that he was American—one of the many transatlantic customers who supported the first British airlines so enthusiastically. It was American passengers who first took children on these flights. Alfred Instone recalled an American father taking a somewhat precocious little boy from London to Paris in the very early days. On being invited to offer his comments on arrival at Le Bourget, the son, using one of the expressions then in vogue, said: 'Gee pop, it's a game.'

American enthusiasm was such that even in the early 'twenties bookings were made in New York for passengers crossing the Atlantic by the big liners and wishing to start their European travels with a flight from England to France. Some of these chose to ride in an open cockpit, among them Charlie Chaplin. When he made his first flight from London to Paris, he sat beside the pilot in a Handley Page 0/400. They met bad weather. Three hours out from Croydon they had only reached Abbeville and the great little man, muffled in his passenger issue of flying kit, became restive. When the pilot shouted over the noise of the engines that they were being held back by headwinds, he was horrified to see his passenger endeavouring to stand up to test the wind for himself. Chaplin was nearly blown overboard. 'Yes, the wind is strong today, isn't it?' he shouted cheerfully as he resumed his seat.

This was by no means the only occasion when passengers had to be restrained from doing mischief to themselves or indeed falling out of a machine. On the first Armistice anniversary 1919, a Handley Page Transport airliner, converted from war use, was making the return trip to London from Brussels. Two of the passengers had elected to sit in the open seats in front of the pilot's cockpit left when the front gun turret had been removed. At 11 a.m. the pilot pulled back the throttle to observe the two minutes' silence while flying at about 2,000 feet over the English Channel.

One of the outside passengers, a Belgian, had inquired eagerly at Brussels whether the two minutes' silence would be observed and was therefore ready for the event. When the machine went into a glide to observe the silence, this passenger tried to rise to his feet, hanging on to the machine with one hand and saluting with the other. Wind pressure and turbulence kept throwing him back into his seat.

> 'We were afraid of losing him over the side . . . [wrote Lloyd C. Ifould who, as flight engineer, was seated with the pilot immediately behind this passenger] we signalled to him to sit down. He eventually caught on and resumed his seat, still saluting, but as we approached the English Coast, another wave of enthusiasm rolled over him. He caught sight of the cliffs of Dover, and as we purred towards the coastline, he leaped to his feet, saluting England's shore. This time, the inevitable happened—a downward bump, and our Belgian

was hanging over the side of the machine. With great effort, he struggled back, falling in a heap on the floor. He now realized the danger and the significance of our urgent signals, but his exuberance was not to be defeated thus easily. Removing his helmet and goggles, he bowed as he passed over the coast. Hitherto, we had only been afraid of losing him overboard. Now, we were afraid that the goggles and helmet would be blown from his grip into the wooden propellers. Then anything could happen! The pilot wrote him a hasty and somewhat profane note, which had the desired effect. The Belgian sat still for the rest of the journey. After this episode, passengers occupying the front seat were not only given a lecture before taking off but we took pains to choose them carefully.'

Even with the universal adoption of cabins, passengers sometimes got themselves into trouble. The earliest cross-Channel passengers were issued with inflatable life-jackets. From nerves, or misplaced eagerness to do the right thing, the four passengers on one trip decided to inflate their life-jackets as soon as they found themselves crossing water. As a result, on their arrival the ground staff at Le Bourget had the greatest difficulty in removing them, blown out to huge proportions, from their confined quarters.

Stunt flying demonstrations had made their mark upon at least one of the passengers flown by the late Captain Gordon Olley in a twin-engined passenger aircraft from Paris to London. Olley and his engineer in their cockpit were separated from the passengers' saloon by a sliding door. There were some half a dozen passengers on a pleasant summer evening. They were running to schedule, and were still over France when Olley, glancing back, saw that one of the passengers was trying to climb out of the cabin window just over the lower wing of the biplane. He immediately alerted his engineer who opened the bulkhead and pushed his way back to the cabin. There he found a number of passengers clinging to the man, who had already succeeded in getting an arm and a leg through the window. The engineer was hefty and immediately flung himself into the struggle while Olley looked for somewhere to land. By the time the machine was safely down at a French airport, the passenger had been overpowered and was offering profuse apologies for his behaviour. He explained that he had had a sudden impulse to walk out on to the wing of the machine, having seen photographs of stunt aviators doing this. Not unreasonably, Captain Olley refused to take him any further. He was off-loaded to continue his journey by boat and train.

Though going was so tough compared with present standards, there was no lack of early feminine travellers. The first woman to fly on the cross-Channel service was Lady Muriel Paget, who travelled from Le Bourget to Hounslow in a DH 4A two days after the service started. The first woman passenger from Britain to France was Miss L. Aldridge who went two days later in a DH 16.

Routes were pioneered and records broken by women aviators, but it was the wife of a British Cabinet Minister who pioneered long-range flight as a passenger. When Lady Maud Hoare took off in December 1926, from London bound for India, no woman had made a long-distance flight of that kind either as a pilot or as a passenger. She was envied by her more venturesome friends. Indeed a woman pilot offered to travel as maid if she could be included in the party.

Apart from the known problems of aviation at that time, there were personal problems for a pioneer woman passenger travelling such a distance with so many stops at which she had to make official appearances as the Air Minister's wife. No one had ever thought of lightweight aviation luggage for instance. Lady Maud had great difficulty in finding a soft leather substitute for the heavy dressing-case which was normal equipment for every lady of the period. The pioneering of lightweight luggage in itself became a matter of some ingenuity.

> 'I blessed the inventors of aluminium and stockinette. My ordinary dressing-case weighed eleven pounds empty, so one with unstiffened top and bottom was eventually found which, with its equipment of Erinoid brushes and combs, weighed only five and a half pounds. Then glass bottles and china pots being heavy as well as breakable, there began a great hunt for lighter fittings, and aluminium solved the difficulty. But when catering for air travel becomes a business proposition, I hope manufacturers will realize that an unfair handicap is placed on would-be purchasers when requests for aluminium bottles produce either an infant's feeding-bottle or a Thermos flask. . . .

18

'My actual wardrobe consisted of a stockinette coat and skirt, with crêpe-de-chine jumper worn most days and a woollen jumper and tweed skirt as a change. Then, in layers according to temperature, woollen cardigan, leather coat and fur coat. The felt hat matched the coat and skirt, and gum boots were occasionally most useful on wet aerodromes. A black lace evening dress for formal dinner parties—one night we met the Emir Abdullah at Amman, and the next night King Feisal at Baghdad—and a demi-toilette completed the visible list; but my most cherished possession was a Shetland dressing-gown, light, warm and uncrushable. This met all requirements of comfort, and, I hope, of suitability too. For, on arrival at Delhi, when we went straight into luncheon at Viceregal Lodge without unpacking, an old friend greeted me with: "But, of course, you have changed out of your travelling clothes." He appeared amazed when I told him that, as he saw me, so had I left London.'

Before many years, however, the click of knitting needles—if they could have been heard above the din—was a welcoming reassurance to passengers venturing upon the Empire air routes. The American journalist, Webb Miller, rushed off at a moment's notice from London to Karachi in May 1930 to interview Gandhi. Once aboard the 'huge six-ton biplane as big as a house', he settled down to survey—with an eye for colour—his fellow travellers.

'Of the six passengers, only two had booked through to India. Lady Leighton, snowy-haired and sixty-three, was hurrying to Basra on the Persian Gulf to the bedside of a critically ill niece. Barry Lawther, hard-bitten chief of the Intelligence Service and deputy inspector of British police of the North-West Frontier Province, who spoke Hindu, Pashto, and Persian, veteran of many tribal skirmishes during twenty years of the Afghan frontier, his face the colour of an old saddle, was rushing back to Peshawar because the Afridis had gone on the warpath and interrupted his two years leave. Quin-Harkin, a blond giant who survived the terrible anti-Bolshevist campaign in the winter of 1918, with the British Forces in Northern Russia [now with I.A.T.A.], Fleming, a rosy-cheeked Glasgow shipbuilder on his first aeroplane flight, and nervous about it, was going to Athens to sell ships to the

Greek Government. Finally there was an American business man *en route* to Vienna, and myself.

'We settled in our seats and stuffed cotton wadding in our ears to deaden the thunderous roar of the engines. Lady Leighton began knitting a half-finished "jumper", picking it up where she had left off when she decided to fly to the Persian Gulf.'

By the mid-'thirties, the comfortable click of airborne knitting needles symbolized a new pattern of life for many people stationed overseas. The late Captain J. H. Lock, in charge of a flying-boat homeward bound from Karachi to Alexandria, observed that three of the passengers he took on at Karachi were expectant mothers.

'This was no unusual occurrence, and I took no particular notice of it until arriving at Bahrein, where we picked up yet two more expectant mothers. I did think that it was overdoing it somewhat, but imagine my amazement when, on departure from Basra, we picked up two more! One was in an obviously advanced stage.

'It was amusing when going below on my morning rounds to hear the click of knitting-needles, and to see balls of wool being woven into warm woolly garments to keep the darling daughter or son safe from the rigours of an English winter.

'During the course of the day the Indian officer's wife asked me: "What is this aeroplane, Captain? A travelling maternity home?" '

Lock subsequently discovered that one of the passengers had actually been refused passage by a shipping company owing to the advanced state of her pregnancy. In after years, regulations were drafted to cover such delicate matters. So long as expectant mothers are in good health, they may travel by B.O.A.C. up to the end of the thirty-second week of pregnancy in pressurized and non-pressurized aircraft where oxygen is available. The Corporation has medical advisers on hand along every route. Staff are briefed on these and other problems. There is, for instance, a printed manual of rules for dealing with sufferers from arthritis, asthma, mental deficiency and with elderly passengers and blind people.

The beginnings of the traffic in children flying between schools in the United Kingdom and homes abroad are now lost in airline history. The practice no doubt began as a luxury excursion to be made only once during the years of school. Before the Second World War, a limited number of children used Imperial Airways for annual visits to parents. In the post-war years the traffic has grown prodigiously. It is not unknown for children to make three return journeys a year, in each of the school holidays, to points as far distant as Singapore. For these veteran passengers, B.O.A.C. started a Junior Jet Club in 1957, issuing log books in which Club Members can record their air mileage, obtaining the signature of the Captain for each flight they make. The badge, a pair of gilt wings with a blue shield, had been issued by the summer of 1958 to twenty-nine thousand Jet Club members. Apart from those who commute between school and home, there are many children who fly unaccompanied. They can be accepted as passengers from the age of seven. For junior passengers of all ages, there are special amenities, toys, cots, magazines, books, games aboard B.O.A.C. airliners and elaborate facilities on the ground in many stopping places.

It is a curious fact that some of the first young people to fly were actually engaged as aircrew. In April 1922, Daimler Airways took on three cabin boys for their DH 34s. They were all very small, about fourteen years of age, and were recruited from the families of the Daimler hire drivers. They were trained at the Savoy Hotel: and were dressed similarly to hotel page boys in 'buttons' and tight trousers. They were carried in a small seat at the rear of the DH 34 aircraft which the Daimler line was then running. No food nor drinks were served on board. The cabin boys travelled more for decoration than for any real service. It is a sad fact that one of these child pioneers was killed on duty. Another left the service: and the third remained with the airline—but not as a cabin boy, as Daimler dispensed with them when they changed their route in the autumn of that year. This light-weight crew was the first step to the provision of a cabin staff to look after the comfort of passengers. It was the Imperial Airways who first employed a steward similar in his status to that of a ship's steward, to look after the well-being of passengers who might be taken ill (and there were very many more of these in the early days than there are now), to provide rugs against cold and offer the first simple airborne refreshments of coffee and biscuits, packed sandwiches and drinks.

The first stewards, G. H. Steer, F. Jefcoate and G. A. Watts, appeared in 1927 on the Argosy services between Croydon and Le Bourget. Their equipment was contained in a wooden chest which they carried aboard. Mr. G. H. Steer, still with B.O.A.C., recalls:

'It was in 1927 that we started giving lunch to passengers in Argosies. It wasn't really lunch though; we had hot soup in Thermos jars and used to serve this to the passengers in cups. There were snacks afterwards—sandwiches, biscuits and cheese, coffee, tea and Bovril; not large, you know, just enough to keep the passengers interested; oh yes—then there was a small bar containing whisky, gin, beer and mineral waters. We used to charge a lot for drinks and when we gave the passengers their bills we used to hurry away because you didn't know how they would take it. Passengers could have drinks at any time from "three miles out". . . .

'Then with the Hannibals we started something first-class; we went right through the menu then. That is when we went full ahead—a choice of soup or hors-d'oeuvre. There was salmon mayonnaise, or something like that, then we gave the passengers a choice of something hot or cold in winter; then there was sweet, cheese, fresh fruit and coffee—a seven-course in all. Sweets were jellies, stewed fruit and cream, small apple tarts with custard or cream. All the hot things were kept in Thermos jars and they were very successful.

'The teas were very fine, especially coming out of Paris, when we had on board a first-class variety of sandwiches and French pastries.

'We carried on the same method of service later on the Frobishers and Ensigns just before the last war.

'A lot of well-known people flew with me—Field Marshal Smuts, the Prince of Wales, Chaliapin, King Alfonso, stage and film stars. Winston Churchill was always a very good passenger, who meant a pound note every time. Then Mr. Gulbenkian—he was a nuisance because he always brought his own food with him. . . .'

In spite of those who insisted on carrying their own provisions, the food on board the big and comfortable Hannibals soon brought great popularity to Imperial Airways. Only, alas, in fair weather conditions. These sturdy machines were limited in operational height and were thus forced to plough through much bad weather, when the service of meals became as much a matter of hit and miss as those aboard any Channel steamer. Nevertheless, the early flights had their devotees—in one case at least devoted to the death. A former engineer of Imperial Airways still serving with B.O.A.C. recalls two feminine passengers who were regulars in the early 'thirties. They occupied wicker chairs near the buffet, did themselves well and 'were most generous for any service that the crews gave'. When one of these loyal ladies died, her will disclosed her wish that her ashes should be strewn from an aircraft flying over the Channel and that the crew who carried out the last rites should be those who had been known to her. In obedience to these wishes, a charter flight was made.

> 'Our two passengers were an undertaker and the executor of her will. We had a talk of the plan to scatter the ashes from the urn and reaching the point of Dungeness I lay on the floor tummy down near the door and the executor opened the door slightly. The undertaker passed the urn and I deposited the ashes; but, as one knows, the indraught when a door is opened in an aircraft is terrific. Needless to say, I was smothered in grey ash and the small cabin needed dusting. Well, the will being well and truly satisfied, back to Croydon and another satisfied customer.'

One of the recognized advantages of air travel is the lack of tipping and it has long been established that cabin staff serving passengers on B.O.A.C. airliners do not expect any remuneration of that kind. Nevertheless, the *pourboire* impulse of passengers goes back to the earliest days. Wars create heroes and the pilots who flew in the First World War carried a halo of heroism quite unwittingly into civil aviation. When the first old ladies took to the air, they delighted to seek out the brave pilot who had flown them in order to press half a crown into his hand. The early American passengers, too, were particularly generous, refusing to take 'no' for an answer and insisting that the pilot should pass a proffered tip to an air charity if he were unwilling to accept it for himself. The status of pilots and crew in the airliners of B.O.A.C. is such that the possibility of their being offered any form of gratuity by passengers might seem out of the question. Yet it can still happen: and the high degree of tactfulness which must be worn every day with the uniform must find the right words which give no offence.

Travellers on Imperial Airways and B.O.A.C. have in the past become attached to an individual or a certain class of airliner—as in the case of the Empire flying-boats. *Heracles*, the aircraft which bore the name of the famous class serving the European routes of Imperial Airways, was another example. In the course of its seven years of service, in which 95,000 passengers were carried, this machine sometimes received birthday telegrams at Croydon sent by admirers who had travelled aboard. Perhaps because of the greater size of contemporary machines and of the less leisurely patterns of travel, sentimental expressions of this kind are on the wane.

Relationships between passengers, crews and machines have often been closest where aircraft have been specially chartered. From the earliest days, charter business has been an integral part of all airline operation. Newspapers were among the first to appreciate the possibilities of charter, for air photography and the quick movement of reporters. Film companies were also early patrons. In 1920 the late Claude Friese-Green, son of the inventor, took moving pictures of spots in the British Isles from the open cockpit of an Airco 9. The massive airliners of today are still chartered by film companies—but for transportation. Since the war, B.O.A.C. has flown on charter whole film units between the United Kingdom and Ceylon, East Africa and various locations in the British West Indies.

While the airliner was still a novelty, there were countless publicity stunts involving special flights. An example of this was an airborne dancing party organized in 1925 aboard the largest airliner Imperial Airways could provide on charter. The pilot's instructions were to take his party up to 4,000 feet and there to fly level and smoothly 'while we dance the Charleston'. It was a 'first time' occasion and the pilot, not a dancing man, did not see the humorous side of this exploit. He faithfully carried out his orders, however, and gave vent to his feelings only at the end of the party when he was asked to pose for photographs with the dance band leader and the Charleston experts when he made a very sullen picture.

During the 'twenties when dance bands and their leaders were making their first noisy impact upon Britain, they were frequently carried from place to place in chartered aircraft. The publicity was good—for the airline as well as for them—and in those days of struggle to attract passengers, every bit of publicity was needed.

With the greater size of the contemporary airliner and the abundant regular services all over the world, charter by an individual of an aircraft in the fleet of B.O.A.C. is rare—though the late Aga Khan chartered B.O.A.C. airliners to fly to Nice from Delhi and from Cairo. The demands of governments and commercial undertakings have increased with the years: but it is unlikely that these times will witness again such an individual charterer as Captain Alfred Loewenstein. This fabulous Belgian financier of the boom years after the First World War observed that other millionaires owned yachts, ran special trains and kept fleets of motor-cars. He was airminded—to the extent ultimately of meeting his death by disappearing from an aeroplane in mid-Channel. To impress and out-distance his rivals, he took on charter from Imperial Airways a fleet of eight landplanes and one amphibious craft. The late Captain Gordon P. Olley was seconded to manage the fleet, which at least on one occasion, between Biarritz and Barcelona, flew in formation.

Travel agencies were closely associated with commercial aviation from its beginning, and even in the early days promoted ambitious schemes. In August 1934, the Polytechnic Tourist Association sponsored the 'first escorted air cruise of the capitals of Europe in the largest passenger airliner in the world' to be flown in a Heracles chartered from Imperial Airways. This tour was to have taken passengers 2,829 miles in fourteen days through Holland, Germany, Czechoslovakia, Austria, Hungary, Italy and France. Though the fare, to include all expenses, hotel accommodation and food was only 75 guineas and the project received the widest advance publicity, there was so little support that it never took place. Today the travel agencies play an important part in the promotion of charter flights. Through these and through direct approach, B.O.A.C. carry out charter missions of great variety. British Olympic teams were carried to New Zealand and to Finland. The Amateur Athletic Association was taken on a tour of Europe. The Royal Opera Ballet, the Old Vic Company, D'Oyly Carte, the New York City Ballet, and the Scots Guards Band were carried on charter flights between Britain, Canada, the West Indies, the Far East and East Africa. There is a large traffic in immigrants and in groups of students and teachers. During the last four years there has also been an increasing business in the exchange of ships' crews, between the United Kingdom and distant points such as Australia and Japan and also between such points as Rio de Janeiro and Tokyo.

Such air operations as these derive simply from commercial expediency. Political and social needs must also be served. The Berlin airlift, already mentioned in these pages, was a freight operation for B.O.A.C. and other operators. An example of an airlift of supreme humanitarian and political importance was the dual operation, in 1947, exchanging populations between the newly formed states of India and Pakistan. The passengers carried were people who were flying not for business or pleasure but because their lives were in danger.

In August 1947, R.A.F. Headquarters in New Delhi signalled London asking for the help of B.O.A.C. and charter companies in flying seven thousand Pakistan Government servants from Delhi to Karachi. The airlift was to include complete households, with wives, children and dependents. Brackley flew out to Karachi to organize Operation Pakistan on behalf of the Corporation. The twenty-three aircraft at his disposal were Dakotas, apart from two Yorks and one Lancastrian. B.O.A.C. provided twelve of the Dakotas; the rest came from Scottish Airways, Silver City Airways and Westminster Airways. During the course of September 1947, the operation was stepped up until an average of six hundred passengers a day were being moved. A day's operations went on till midnight. Another day's began at 2.30 a.m. covering the 670 miles between Delhi and Karachi. Up to eighty passengers were sometimes carried in airliners with a normal capacity of fifty-seven. Towards the end of the operation when the refugee stream reached panic proportions, permission was granted for seats to be removed to increase the passenger capacity. Aircraft were sometimes turned round after forty minutes at Delhi or Karachi. By the time this Operation Pakistan ended on September 15, 1947, the aircraft involved had flown more than 330,000 miles. Those who flew them saw plenty of evidence for the necessity of the airlift in burning villages, refugee-lined roads and the vultures that hovered overhead awaiting the victims. Indeed Captain V. G. Parker of B.O.A.C., flying a York, collided with a vulture, smashing the safety glass of his windscreen.

Operation India followed soon afterwards, in October 1947 when it became apparent that thousands of Indians in Pakistan were in danger of their lives. This was the greatest civil air operation which has ever been attempted. It began with three aircraft and built up to twenty-one. From October 20 to November 30, 1947, these aircraft lifted thirty-five thousand people and covered 875,000 miles. Most of these people were trying to take with them everything they possessed. While they were individually limited to 44 lb. of baggage, the load greatly exceeded that amount. The airlift was a B.O.A.C. responsibility and once again Brackley was in charge with Commander B. W. Galpin, the Corporation's permanent representative at Delhi, maintaining contact with the Indian Government. When the Corporation undertook the airlift, it did so with the provision that none of its normal services would be affected by Operation India. For that reason, a number of private enterprise charter firms were brought in to help. Before dawn on October 16, 1947, the first aircraft of the fleet left the United Kingdom for India. All along the line they used B.O.A.C. Stations. At Palam airport, New Delhi, the Operations Room was reminiscent of any war-time airfield.

> 'On a huge blackboard covering one wall of the "Ops Shop" were the numbers of the aircraft, the names of the captains, the destination. The aeroplanes went as far afield as Peshawar, Rawalpindi, Quetta, Amritsar and Lahore as well as to small, almost unknown airstrips, remote and almost forgotten since the R.A.F. left India. Loaded with their human cargo, they left each morning from five till eight at fifteen-minute intervals. On the return journey they dropped most of their passengers at Ambala, which became one of the largest and most incredible camps of all time. It was impossible for Delhi to accommodate all the Hindus wanting to come into India, and, therefore, they were put in Ambala until homes or occupations could be found for them'.

Brackley received some strange messages. One Captain, grounded by the authorities at Quetta, for lack of landing permit, signalled: '*Impounded No Fuel No Heat No Money No Hope*.'

'The refugees were no ordinary air passengers. Most of them were terror stricken—in fear of their lives [wrote an eye-witness]. Many of them reached security and the unknown without money, without food, without a home or an address to go to, and in a number of cases, without the complete family with which they had started out.

'It was a case of the survival of the fittest. A small child could be seen running down the strip after an aircraft which was taxiing to take-off; she was crying bitterly and being blown back by the slipstream. The parents had got themselves on board, the child had been lost in the crowd.

'Who is to name the things that a man values most? If you are allowed 44 lb. of baggage, what will you take out of everything you own—knowing that you will never see again the things you leave behind? Not an easy problem, and some of the choices made seemed strange to Western eyes. A small and rather battered child's cane chair; a moth-eaten-looking parrot; a large and cumbersome radio, built obviously about the time Marconi thought them up, a larger and even more cumbersome box of batteries. A length of fine suit material worn round the shoulders like a shawl and trailing in the dust . . . a tea urn. Each pathetic little group had, in addition, the inevitable bed-roll, something of sentimental value, some thing chosen from past poverty to give comfort in a new and greater poverty in the future.

'Day after day the captains and the crews of the mercy aircraft dealt with these people, with their pleas, and their misery. At the beginning of the operation many of the crews came back silent and thoughtful after a day's trip; they had seen too much that was distressing.

'Sometimes the gratitude shown to the crews was pathetic and overwhelming, sometimes the pleas to take the extra two or three kilos were too pathetic to ignore. Human nature came down to very near the bone on "Operation India"; many of the men flying the planes found themselves having to make decisions which they knew might make the difference between life and death for those concerned.

'One captain had to decide which were the thirty-five most deserving cases out of a crowd of over two thousand.

'Hundreds of solemn dark-eyed children were carried during this operation. Even the tiniest of them seemed to have an air of responsibility, weighed down by small bundles and wrapped in far too many nondescript clothes, summer suits or winter suits, or what served for them, it didn't matter so long as they were worn somehow and so saved precious space for household equipment.'

Such was Operation India—in which 35,000 people had been moved between India, Pakistan and Baluchistan with one and a half million pounds of personal baggage and belongings.

In our time an air passage has sometimes become a matter of life and death and the personal drama of such a situation was never more evident than in the case of Mrs. Petrov, who was booked on a regular B.O.A.C. service leaving Sydney for the United Kingdom in April 1954.

'A surging crowd was gathered round the aircraft [wrote Captain Jack Davys, who commanded the B.O.A.C. airliner carrying this very significant passenger] yelling and shouting and in the middle an eddy slowly advancing towards the aircraft steps which was Mrs. Petrov, her escort and airport security officials. They slowly got to the aircraft steps where almost a free fight went on and my two stewards ran down the steps to help her up and on board, while the rest held the crowd back who then started booing and throwing things at the aircraft so the airport officials called up the fire tender and threatened to use it if the crowd did not keep back. Ten minutes later, having completed formalities, I went on board to the sound of "boos" and the door was shut.

'Although we had had no official word at all we had by now gathered what was going on and were in rather a difficult position as these were our passengers and had to be treated as such. I spoke to Mr. Kislitsin, the Second Secretary [of the Soviet Embassy] who was in charge of the party and apologized for his rough handling. He introduced me to Mrs. Petrov who was a bit dishevelled and distraught and in tears which could easily be accounted for by her recent ordeal and as for the two so-called "gunmen" from Moscow, they were old friends whom I recognized at once, Mr. Jarkov and Mr. Karpinsky who were the Russian diplomatic couriers who always travelled with us—model passengers and always good for a shy "good morning".

'I had a talk with the Chief Steward, Mr. Muir, and it was decided that as passengers they must be treated with every courtesy but that if Mrs. Petrov wished to talk to anyone, he or one of his staff would always be available near the ladies' powder room—and so we left Sydney.

'An hour or so later Mrs. Petrov went back to the powder room where the stewardess helped her to tidy herself and they had a short talk but nothing more, but later when she went back the Chief Steward was there and he had a long conversation with her, which he reported to me and was to the effect that she couldn't believe what had happened to her husband but thought he was dead. When assured that he was safe in Australia, she said she wanted to stay but what could she do? The Chief Steward pointed out that she could get off at Darwin but she said the two couriers were armed. He reassured her on this point and there the matter rested.

'I was pondering on the wording of a signal to warn the authorities at Darwin and had decided to wait till I was in short range radio range rather than broadcast it to the whole world, when the Radio Officer handed me a signal, from Cloncurry which were we just passing. Apparently the Prime Minister had heard of the affair at Sydney Airport and had directed his Chief Security Official to take action—they also did not want it broadcast to the world and so the signals were short and to the point.'

Signals from the ground inquired about Mrs. Petrov's condition, whether she showed any sign of fear and whether she had indicated in any way that she wished to remain in Australia. In his final signal to Sydney, the Captain said that Mrs. Petrov was 'scared of her armed guards'. The signals went on throughout the night as the airliner traversed the continent of Australia.

At Darwin the Captain hurried away from his aircraft and

'found everything in full swing—the two couriers being disarmed by very large and very tough North West Police—Mr. Kislitsin protesting violently to the Security Officials who surrounded him but did not touch him, and Mr. Leydin, the Governor's representative, talking to Mrs. Petrov. They seemed to have the situation well in hand so I saw the rest of the crew and the passengers off for breakfast except the Chief Steward who remained to help if possible.

'Mrs. Petrov was by this time quite distraught and didn't know what to believe, her firm conviction still being that her husband was dead. Mr. Leydin talked to her quietly then Mr.

Muir had a go at soothing her down—Mr. Kislitsin protested, the couriers looked sulky and so on round and round and getting nowhere, so I told the Station Manager I would delay the service until someone made up their minds.

'At last someone hit on the bright idea of getting her husband on the telephone, so the line to Canberra was requisitioned and we all crowded into a little office big enough for about six people but now containing the four Russians, Security Guards, Mr. Leydin, reporters, myself and anyone else who could get in. The call was put in and the phone handed to Mrs. Petrov. None of us could understand the conversation which followed, though she seemed to keep saying "no, no". At last she put down the receiver and turned to us and shook her head and at the same time made a little sign to Mr. Leydin with her hand dangling by her side where the Russians could not see it. Mr. Leydin immediately led her alone into the next room amid much protesting where she said to him "It was my husband, I want to stay" so he took her out the back way, popped her in his car and drove off.'

After this, the revolver ammunition was impounded by the authorities and Captain Davys was handed two revolvers in a sealed package. He apologized to Kislitsin for the manhandling of his men which was a matter outside B.O.A.C. control and asked him whether he would like to stay on board at Jakarta. The Russians did this and at the next stop, Singapore, they were smuggled out of the airport and given a suite of rooms at Raffles Hotel. They travelled on to Calcutta and eventually left the flight at Beirut. On parting company, they were proffered the sealed package containing the revolvers, but denied all knowledge of them—evidently being determined to continue their journey unarmed.

CHAPTER XVIII

'AS LORDS EXPECTED'

MRS. PETROV did not set out as a V.I.P. though she certainly finished as one. To the dismay of many people in air travel business and outside it, the initials V.I.P. have taken root in the English language both as an adjective and as a noun. Their use derives from the R.A.F. in the Second World War when it was found necessary for security reasons to camouflage the movements of Very Important Persons. The noun was convenient at the time. Its use was soon extended adjectivally to 'V.I.P. treatment'. As such it sometimes took on a derisive flavour and at one time it seemed as if it would lose its force like so many other war-time phrases. Yet it lingered on and prospered to such an extent that it might be applied as readily to a comedian as to a king and it is now widely in use throughout the airports of the world and, because of that, we must use it somewhat reluctantly in this chapter devoted mainly to special passengers.

The earliest cross-Channel passengers during the First World War were all V.I.P.s—though they were unaware of the label, of course, because it had not been invented. Winston Churchill and Bonar Law were among the first prominent British statesmen to use air travel. When Major J. R. McCrindle was still commanding a Communications Squadron of the R.A.F. in the spring of 1919 he was requested to fly Lord Hardinge of Penshurst, the head of the British Air Delegation, from Paris to London. In no circumstances was he to take any risk. If the Head of the Delegation were killed flying it might be a great setback for the civil aviation which Britain hoped soon to start. Therefore he was instructed to do the flying himself 'under the erroneous belief that a Squadron Commander must be the best pilot in the Squadron'.

'We set off and had to fly above the cloud with, of course, no radio. After flying for an hour or so, I could see no break and so turned back. Lord Hardinge did not know that we had turned back until he saw the Eiffel Tower. On landing he was very annoyed and when I told him of my instructions said he was not frightened if I wasn't. So, annoyed in turn, I filled up and went off. Eventually I saw a break in the clouds and came down over the Kent coast. I had not enough petrol to get to London, but just managed to get down on an emergency strip on his Penshurst estate. He was delighted and became a firm supporter of Air Transport which, as one item on the Conference Agenda was the Paris Air Convention, was extremely useful.'

Though statesmen sometimes flew on their official missions during the 'thirties, and were given special treatment where necessary, there were no flights made in that era to compare in their dramatic impact with those which brought it to a close when the British Prime Minister, Neville Chamberlain, visited Adolf Hitler. Until that time, British Prime Ministers had not readily taken to the air, nor indeed indulged in sudden missions such as these that attempted to save the peace of the world.

McCrindle, as it happened, was involved also in this episode, no longer as a pilot, but as a director of British Airways. The first intimation of Chamberlain's intentions—at least to anybody in aviation—came when the telephone rang at Pooks Farm, a lonely medieval cottage in Sussex which was McCrindle's country seat. Chamberlain's personal private secretary was telephoning on the evening of September 14, 1938, to ask whether the Prime Minister could be flown to Germany by special plane the following morning.

'I said yes, and asked where to. He replied that he could not tell me on the telephone where the Prime Minister was going, but when I explained that the pilot would require maps and would have to work out a flight plan, etc., he said "Do you know where the Nazis have their Headquarters?"—to which I could not help replying that if anyone were listening they probably knew too!

'I gave the necessary instructions and informed Clive Pearson, our Chairman, who rang up Claridges and ordered a magnificent luncheon to be put on the aircraft. However, we were later informed that the Prime Minister (who was making his first flight) only wanted tea. So I lent him our tea basket which we had at the farm which was duly returned and which I still use.'

The flight was made from Heston Airport in a British Airways Lockheed Electra commanded by Captain C. N. Pelly who reported: 'The Prime Minister was asked several times how he was feeling and on each occasion he replied—"Very well indeed". He appeared to enjoy the journey, and his one worry seemed to be as to whether London was cognizant of our position from time to time: we reassured him on that point.'

Having returned from this flight, Chamberlain used a British Airways aircraft again to fly to Germany on September 29, 1938, for the signing of the Munich Pact, returning from which he waved his famous scrap of paper and spoke of peace 'in our time'. This second flight caused questions in the House. W. D. R. Perkins asked the Air Minister whether he was aware that the flight had been made in an American-made machine and whether 'he can give an assurance that, when, in future, any Minister flies to any foreign country in an official capacity, a British-made aeroplane will be available'.

The Ministerial reply confirmed that the aircraft was indeed American and went on to say: 'The selection for any particular charter flight must necessarily depend on what suitable aircraft are available at the time. When the new civil aircraft now under construction have been delivered, I hope that similar demands for charter facilities will be able to be met with British-built equipment.'

The coming of the Second World War, the departure of Chamberlain and the Prime Ministership of Churchill, signalled a new outlook towards the use of air travel by the heads of Governments and States.

'If a plane comes down in the sea, which way should survivors swim?' Churchill once asked a B.O.A.C. steward.

'Follow the others,' the steward replied.

Churchill then inquired what he should do if he were the only one left, and the steward at this point counted himself lucky that he could make a quick exit before the theme developed.

This incident occurred on board the B.O.A.C. Stratocruiser *Canopus* on a flight to Washington in the post-war years. The great man's jest would have had more of an edge to it back in 1942 when the first Churchillian Atlantic flight was made. In January of that year it was well known to enemies as well as friends that he had been visiting the White House for consultations with Roosevelt. It was assumed that he would return, as he had come, by sea. When the new British battleship *Duke of York* suddenly disappeared from Chesapeake Bay, it was naturally assumed that the Prime Minister was on board. In fact the Prime Minister went aboard the B.O.A.C. Boeing flying-boat *Berwick*, one of the three purchased from America earlier in the war. In command was Captain J. C. Kelly Rogers, who had been called to the British Embassy in Washington to prepare for a special flight from Norfolk, Virginia, to Bermuda. Kelly Rogers himself and his crew had gone through the normal procedure of Customs and Immigration at Baltimore Base before taking *Berwick* to the harbour at Norfolk to pick up the Prime Minister's party. To all outward appearances, they had 'done the drill' for a routine Atlantic crossing. The idea was to fly Churchill under cover of secrecy to pick up the *Duke of York* with its naval escorts at Bermuda, thus curtailing the journey by sea and confusing the enemy who were known to be alert for what to them would have been the greatest prize of the war.

Churchill was much taken by the flying-boat. He also struck up a friendship with the Captain.

> 'I took the controls for a bit, to feel this ponderous machine of thirty or more tons in the air. I got more and more attached to the flying-boat. Presently I asked the Captain, "What about flying from Bermuda to England? Can she carry enough petrol?" Under his solid exterior he became visibly excited. "Of course we can do it. The present weather forecast would give a forty mile an hour wind behind us. We could do it in twenty hours." I asked how far it was, and he said, "About three thousand five hundred miles." At this I became thoughtful.'

Churchill was, in fact, making up his mind that the flight could and should be done: and soon after arrival in Bermuda he called a conference to debate the matter. Kelly Rogers himself was lunching quietly on board the *Berwick* in the harbour when a launch came alongside to take him immediately to Government House. There in the drawing-room of the Governor, Lord

Knollys, afterwards Chairman of B.O.A.C., one of the most momentous cross-examinations of any B.O.A.C. captain in history took place. Round the table were such figures as Air Chief Marshal Sir Charles (now Viscount) Portal, Chief of Air Staff, Sir Dudley Pound, First Sea Lord, Commander Thompson, always described by Churchill as his 'Flag Commander', Captain Gordon Store of B.O.A.C. and others. Through the open windows, there was a good view of H.M.S. *Duke of York* riding at anchor, 'waiting to take me to England, which I can reach in seven to nine days,' stated Churchill, as he opened the conference.

' "During that time I have ears to hear but no lips with which to speak. On the other hand, Captain Kelly Rogers assures me that in the aeroplane in which we have flown to Bermuda today, we can fly to England tomorrow in not more than twenty-two hours. This is many days saved, and during that time many things can happen. Two important battles may be fought, and one major decision." He paused and then added: "Such a flight cannot be regarded as a war necessity but it is a war convenience." '

In his own memoirs, Winston Churchill recalls the reluctance at first expressed by his two chiefs of staff. It occurred to him that both these officers thought he meant to fly by himself, leaving them to return in the *Duke of York*. When he pointed out that there would be room for them, Lord Beaverbrook and several others, 'they both visibly changed countenance'.

The cross-examination of Kelly Rogers took a more favourable turn to such an extent that Churchill was able to bring the conference to an end with the remark: 'He seems to have all the answers, doesn't he?'

It was then agreed that as long as the weather held, the flight would be made. The passenger list was to be restricted to seven and the Churchill Memoirs record that the most desperately disappointed man of the day was Commander Thompson. 'I reminded him of his devotion to the naval service, and of the pleasures to a hardy sailor of a life on the ocean wave.' Nevertheless the gallant commander had ideas of his own and very soon he had persuaded one of *Berwick*'s stewards to let him take his place, even if it meant doing the washing up. By the time he mentioned this amiable plot to Churchill, he had even gone to the trouble of ascertaining that he weighed less than the steward. His Chief shrugged off all responsibility for this as he went to bed. In the morning, when he came to go aboard the *Berwick*, Churchill found his Flag Commander standing disconsolately among those who were seeing him off. 'The Captain had brushed his projects aside in a way that captains have. The steward was a trained member of the crew; he could not take one single person more; every tank was filled with petrol.' This first transatlantic flight by a British Prime Minister was relaxed and smooth. The Captain was invited to join the passengers for coffee after luncheon. He found the Prime Minister full of fun, gaily imagining the surprise of his Cabinet colleagues in England at finding him returning five days before he was expected, for it must be remembered that this flight was carried out under conditions of complete radio silence, with no forewarning to the United Kingdom of *Berwick*'s mission. After what he described as an 'agreeable' afternoon, and a 'merry' dinner, Churchill took Beaverbrook with him to the flight deck before retiring.

> 'Darkness had fallen and all the reports were good. We were now flying through dense mist at about seven thousand feet. One could see the leading edge of the wings, with their great flaming exhausts pouring back over the wing surfaces. In these machines at this time a large rubber tube which expanded and contracted at intervals was used to prevent icing. The Captain explained to me how it worked, and we saw from time to time the ice splintering off as it expanded. I went to bed and slept soundly for several hours [He woke just before dawn and mounted once more to the flight deck]. After sitting an hour or so in the co-pilot's seat I sensed a feeling of anxiety around me. We were supposed to be approaching England from the south-west and we ought already to have passed the Scilly Islands, but they had not been seen through any of the gaps in the cloud floor. As we had flown for more than ten hours through mist and had had only one sight of a star in that time, we might well be slightly off our course. Wireless communication was, of course, limited by the normal war-time rules. It was evident from the discussions that were going on that we did not know where we were. Presently Portal, who had been studying the position, had a word with the Captain and then said to me, "We are going to turn north at once." This was

done and, after another half-hour in and out of the clouds we sighted England, and soon arrived over Plymouth, where, avoiding the balloons, which were all shining, we landed comfortably.'

Probably the great man was the least worried of those aboard the *Berwick* that morning. He learnt afterwards that if they had not changed course, they might well have been over the German batteries at Brest within minutes. As it was, *Berwick* was at one time reported in Britain as a hostile bomber coming in from the French coast and six Hurricanes from Fighter Command were ordered out to intercept her. 'However, they failed in their mission,' Churchill said uncomplainingly afterwards. As for Kelly Rogers, he admitted to having felt a little too naked for comfort in the clear early morning sky at a time when his distinguished passenger was asking him casually what he would do if enemy aircraft were sighted, and he made evasive replies. Even the day after arrival when he was invited to Downing Street for a reunion luncheon with the Churchill family, he kept these thoughts to himself.

Churchill himself felt such confidence in B.O.A.C. that he flew the Atlantic both ways a few months later, in June 1942. At least one concession he made to the hazards of such a flight under war-time conditions was a letter addressed on the eve of his departure to King George VI, naming his successor in case of disaster.

On the way out, he slept soundly again in the bridal suite, enjoyed two luncheons with a six hours' interval and, after a non-stop flight of twenty-seven hours, approached Washington in the evening.

> 'As we gradually descended towards the Potomac River, I noticed that the top of the Washington Monument, which is over five hundred and fifty feet high, was about our level, and I impressed upon Captain Kelly Rogers that it would be particularly unfortunate if we brought our story to an end by hitting this of all other objects in the world. He assured me he would take special care to miss it.'

On June 26, he started the return journey from Botwood after a meal of fresh lobsters. Once again he spent much time in the second pilot's seat and was there when they alighted on the Clyde just after dawn.

On doctor's advice, he went on his third war-time Washington conference by sea, but he made the return crossing in May 1943 in the B.O.A.C. flying-boat *Bristol* from Botwood direct to Gibraltar. During this trip, he was awakened from a long comfortable sleep by a sudden shock and bump. He put on his zip suit and went up to the flight deck to sit beside the pilot, Captain Gordon Store, who explained with somewhat forced casualness that the flying-boat had been struck by lightning. With this he went back to sleep but just before dawn he was active once more:

> 'I went forward again, as I love to see the daylight come. When you are flying east at 160 miles an hour you meet the sun very early and he rises quickly. I adhered to my rule in these long flights that meals should be regulated by stomach-time. When one wakes after daylight, one should breakfast; five hours after that, luncheon. Six hours after luncheon, dinner. Thus one becomes independent of the sun, which otherwise meddles too much in one's affairs and upsets the routine of work.'

After alighting at Gibraltar, the Prime Minister continued his journey to North Africa. His presence in those parts was no secret to the enemy. To shoot him down on his return flight would have been a major triumph to them. That the Luftwaffe was particularly on the alert had disastrous consequences for a number of civilian passengers who joined one of the routine flights from Lisbon to Bristol, in June 1943. Among them was Arthur Chenhalls, a brilliant accountant, a massive man of Churchillian proportions who had recently injured a leg and was therefore making use of a Churchillian walking stick. He was fond of the good things of life and liked a cigar. He was a man of commanding presence and character. He had gone to Lisbon with the film actor Leslie Howard who was himself on a propaganda mission. At a cursory glance, from behind, he might well have passed for Churchill.

The unarmed airliner in which he set out for Bristol with other passengers broke silence to say first that it was being pursued, then that it was being attacked. It vanished without trace. The service on which it was operating between Bristol and Lisbon (later extended to Gibraltar) was inaugurated during the war years by K.L.M. on charter for B.O.A.C. Queen Wilhelmina of the Netherlands, wearing tennis shoes, was one of the passengers who made use of this security-curtained 'back door' connecting blacked-out war-time Britain with the bright lights of one of the few neutral corners of Europe. B.O.A.C. pilots and machines shared the services with the Dutch and, apart from the regular exchanges of newspapers between the belligerent powers, which was facilitated by this service, there were many interesting passengers—and no other casualties than the particular flight on which Chenhalls travelled.

From her war-time retreat at Badminton, Queen Mary drove to Whitchurch to see the workings of this terminus where passengers came and went with such a high degree of secrecy. Though she had somewhat wistfully followed the growth of civilian aviation, she, like her husband, King George V, never made use of air travel. Her son George VI, as a prince, qualified as a pilot. He and his brother Edward VIII made cross-Channel flights, in Handley Page 0/400 bombers in the First World War. Though they both flew far and wide in later years, they neither of them as monarchs made official use of the British Merchant Air Service.

After the First World War, the heir to the throne, the then Prince of Wales, used an airliner for the first time for an international journey during the General Strike of 1926. He had been recuperating from an illness in Biarritz and he had reached Paris by the time the British railways came to a standstill. It was decided that he should continue his journey in a Handley Page W 10 fourteen-passenger airliner of Imperial Airways with Captain O. P. Jones in command. When the Prince arrived at Le Bourget, there was considerable argument about the weather. Officials from the Paris Embassy thought the reports—rain and low clouds over Northern France and Biggin Hill—constituted a danger, though they were not unusual for the time of year. After conferring with Jones, the Prince waved aside these protests and took off, his machine being closely followed by a Vickers Vulcan to pick him up in the event of a forced landing. Travelling in the open cockpit with Captain O. P. Jones was Engineer L. C. Ifould. After they left the French coast, Jones requested Ifould to go back into the cabin and ask the Prince if he would care to spend a little time in the cockpit. The Prince was delighted with the idea, changed places and went forward wearing the engineer's helmet and goggles.

In the cabin of the W 10 a brass plaque was afterwards installed commemorating this first flight by a member of the reigning House in one of the regular cross-Channel airliners. This distinction had such passenger appeal that it became quite a nuisance. Prospective travellers would upset existing bookings in order to travel in the machine that had carried the Prince of Wales, sometimes postponing their journeys for several days in order to have the honour of doing so.

Appropriately, it was Captain O. P. Jones who commanded the first civil aircraft in which the heiress to the throne, Princess Elizabeth with the Duke of Edinburgh flew the Atlantic in 1951. They used a B.O.A.C. Stratocruiser from London to Montreal, to start their tour of Canada, the Duke sitting beside the pilot as they circled before landing at Dorval Airport.

Royal arrivals must be very exactly timed and the Stratocruiser was due at 12 noon. Arriving over their destination early, Captain Jones took his royal party on a wide circuit of the surrounding district and after landing taxied the aircraft to the disembarking point as slowly as possible. 'At noon precisely the door of the aircraft opened and as the Princess stepped out there was a crash of cannon. It was a most impressive moment,' he said afterwards.

The most poignant and momentous of all royal journeys began on January 31, 1952 with a happy scene at London Airport, when King George VI, making a first appearance after an illness, together with many other members of the Royal Family and Ministers of the Crown, bade farewell to the then Princess Elizabeth and her husband on their departure on another Royal tour. They were flying in the B.O.A.C. Argonaut *Atalanta* to Nairobi on the first stage of their proposed tour of Australia and New Zealand. As the world now knows, the present Queen was seeing her father for the last time as he stood waving at London Airport. Her reign began in Kenya on the King's death and it was aboard *Atalanta* that she took off from Entebbe in Uganda on February 6, 1952, to fly back to ascend the throne. At London Airport on February 7, in marked contrast to the joyful departure a week earlier, a silent gathering headed by Winston Churchill watched the new monarch slowly descend from the Argonaut to set foot on English soil for the first time as Queen.

Later that year Queen Elizabeth, the Queen Mother, accompanied by Princess Margaret, went for a four-hour flight in a new B.O.A.C. Comet 1. Without touching down on foreign soil, they made a wide circuit of two thousand miles over France, the Alps, Italy and the Mediterranean. The Queen Mother herself took the controls of the aircraft for a short while during the trip. In August that year, the Duke of Edinburgh also flew in a Comet on an official visit to Helsinki for the opening of the Olympic Games.

With the opening of the reign of Queen Elizabeth II, the use of air travel for the monarch herself, for the Royal Family and for Ministers of the Crown on official business was firmly established. From the time she took off as Queen from Uganda in 1952, till her return from New York direct to London in October 1957, the Queen travelled 26,438 miles on B.O.A.C. aircraft. The Queen Mother, who never flew while her husband was on the throne, has logged 36,688 miles with B.O.A.C. at the time of writing.

The flights of royalty and statesmen on official duty and ceremonial occasions are made in conventional passenger airliners when the cabins have been suitably modified. The machines must be refitted to meet the special circumstances and during the nineteen-fifties B.O.A.C. had great experience of this. The necessary modifications can now be made at short notice to any aircraft in the Corporation's fleets. The first requirement is privacy for the royal passenger, who must travel with numerous entourage. To achieve this, it has been found possible to use either the aft or forward cabin exclusively for the royal passenger, leaving the other cabin for members of the Household. A sleeping cabin is made by the erection of a false bulkhead and the fitting of two divans in the place of four chairs on either side of the gangway. These by day are used as seats and at night can be converted into beds.

In addition to the sleeping cabin, there is a dining compartment which usually consists of two specially fitted dining tables on either side of the gangway with four aircraft chairs to each table. There is also a bar/lounge unit where cocktails can be served. Although this suite of three cabins, with toilets, is designed for the exclusive use of the royal passenger, their amenities are usually extended to members of the Household during the day. The Queen, for instance, frequently invites flight companions to join her for meals.

The general aim of those who have gained experience in arranging these matters is to provide the privacy of a home. A member of the staff of B.O.A.C., who has frequently travelled in the same aircraft with the Queen and the Duke of Edinburgh states: 'From personal observation, I know that once the aircraft door closes, all concerned are able to relax completely and a very jolly and happy atmosphere prevails. By virtue of having a Royal Compartment at their disposal which is broken up into two or three cabins, it allows the royal couple to have varying degrees of privacy entirely on their own or, in the dining-room and lounge with members of their Household, and they spend their time either in reading or "doing homework" which entails "swotting up" on the places and the people they are going to meet.'

Landings are frequently ceremonial occasions. The hour before arrival is therefore somewhat hectic for these very special passengers. Not only do the royal travellers have to turn out in full regalia but so do the members of the Household, particularly equerries and gentlemen-in-waiting who have to be adorned in full regalia with decorations and swords. In fact many of them have to be literally booted and spurred, which is not particularly easy even in a spacious modern airliner which may be descending through turbulent air towards a royal rendezvous which must be carried through with unruffled dignity.

Royal flights are worked out in great detail beforehand. The channel for arranging them is usually from the royal Household to the Captain of the Queen's Flight who in turn approaches the B.O.A.C. Chief of Flight Operations. Details of general administration are handled by a special committee.

The meals to be taken aboard are the responsibility of the B.O.A.C. Cabin Services Manager, who submits his menus to Buckingham Palace well in advance of the royal departure. He also looks after feeding arrangements aboard a royal flight from any distant point inwards to the United Kingdom.

For Prime Ministers and other statesmen a similar procedure is followed. These, like the royal flights, are formally based on charter arrangements paid for by public funds. Usually the British Government takes full financial responsibility for the flight out and back. Travel in any particular territory is usually the responsibility of the Government concerned.

In the course of the forty years covered in these pages, B.O.A.C. and its predecessors have carried nearly four and a half million passengers through the seven skies. During the whole of that period the relationship between the airline and the passenger has been personal to a degree hitherto unknown in any other field of travel. The relationship has come to be more flexible and more intimate with the years as air travel has become more popular. The individual touch continues to be of paramount importance with passengers of all races and ages. It is not necessary to be a royal personage to obtain individual attention. A passenger need only state in advance what he is, a Jew, a Moslem, a Hindu, a Buddhist, or a non-sectarian vegetarian to be served in flight with the appropriate food. Passengers in this age have become knowledgeable and discerning. An airline such as B.O.A.C. covering the world is constantly on the alert to changing needs and tastes. Seventy-five per cent of the Corporation revenue derives directly from passengers. The most important single route is that across the Atlantic; and it was in this field, in 1952, that one of the greatest post-war developments took place.

The internal airlines of America had been building up a great network of tourist or 'coach' services with cheap fares. Such services were based upon all-round lower standards. Flight schedules were slower, with more stopping places along the route. Cabins were rearranged to carry more people with less space for each. There were less elaborate meals. All frills were cut out.

The response inside America was staggering. The average American realized that he could afford to fly and could choose airways in preference to railways. Moreover, the popularity of these new tourist services had no adverse effect on the first class bookings. On May 1, 1952, the various airlines flying the Atlantic by common agreement inaugurated transatlantic tourist class flights. B.O.A.C. converted Constellations into 68-seaters, and on these tourist flights between London and New York return fares were reduced from £254 to £173. These services have flourished throughout the nineteen-fifties. The principle of two classes has been extended to B.O.A.C. services throughout the world. Some long-range airliners carry two classes aboard—some have one class only.

Reduced rate 'economy' fares were introduced on the Atlantic run in 1958. They were 20 per cent cheaper than the tourist rates, and were immediately popular. Simple, but wholesome meals were provided free aboard Britannia and DC 7C airliners. Many who used these services also took advantage of the ticket instalment plan by means of which a passenger could fly from London to New York, and back, after making an initial payment of only £16 4s. od., the balance of payment being spread over twenty-one months. All classes of travel throughout the whole B.O.A.C. network became available on the instalment plan. The deposit on any fare would be as little as 10 per cent of the total cost for an immediate flight. A seasonal family plan was also started in 1958. Under this system, a man and wife making the return journey between London and New York at economy fares, combined with the family plan and ticket instalment facilities would pay a total deposit of £27 8s. od.

Superficially it might seem that the dividing-up of a once classless air travel is against the democratic trends of the century. On the contrary, it seems to be an indication of mass aspiration towards air travel. To the man in the street, at long last an aeroplane is no longer necessarily regarded as a weapon of destruction or as a luxury vehicle for the rich and privileged. With this new acceptance of universal air travel has come the realization that speed is but one of several qualities which appeal to those who go by air. Directness, certainty of a place (and no standing!), palatable food, personal attention, lack of luggage problems, are all practical attractions which have been fostered during the long years that B.O.A.C. and its forerunners have been in the business. In the act of flight itself, there will always be cause for debate—by those who find a thrill and aesthetic pleasure in the skyscapes of the air and those who declare air travel to be the most tedious device of man.

Let the poet Coleridge, then, speaking out of his time at the turn of the eighteenth century, provide the epilogue. . . . '*everywhere the blue sky belongs to them and is their appointed rest and their native country and their own natural homes, which they enter announced, as lords that are certainly expected and yet there is a silent joy at their arrival. . . .*'

APPENDIX

Table of Aircraft

prepared by Captain William Armstrong, A.F.C.

This table is offered as a supplement to Chapter XV for those who might like to know something more about the aircraft which were used during the forty years of this narrative. The dates of most of the early aircraft are those of construction, from 1940 of acquisition by B.O.A.C.

While some of the data are claimed as accurate, much are unavoidably approximate, e.g. tare (or empty) weights, and consequently payload capacities which are subject to change throughout the life of an aircraft, as are horse-power and thrust—and consequently speed and range. Range—the distance an aircraft can fly—is subject to many variables, e.g. the manner of operation, the load carried, whether calculated in 'still air' or with full operational reserves. For these reasons, payload capacity has been left out and passenger capacities only shown, while range has also been omitted.

Speeds, being dependent upon operational factors, vary widely. While, generally, those covering the pre-war period can be accepted as 'average operational cruising', those of the remainder are manufacturers' figures, taken for the most part from Jane's *All the World's Aircraft*.

Data for the last three aircraft in the table are given with reserve. At the time of completion of this table only the Comet 4 had been delivered and some changes can be anticipated over the next few years, covering all three.

The list of aircraft, while comprehensive, does not include those of lesser significance (for the purposes of this Appendix), while others, which played an important part during the war, though only on loan to the Corporation have been included.

Date	*Contractor's Name*	*Type*	*Span*	*Length*	*Max. Weight*	*Passenger Capacity*
1919	H.P. 0/400	biplane	100′ 0″	63′ 0″	6 tons	10
	D.H. 9C	,,	42′ 5″	30′ 6″	3,560 lb.	2
	,, 16	,,	46′ 6″	31′ 10½″	4,380 lb.	4
	,, 4A	,,	42′ 4½″	29′ 6″	3,722 lb.	2
	Vickers Vimy	,,	68′ 0″	42′ 8″	5 tons	10
1920	D.H. 18	,,	51′ 2¾″	39′ 0″	7,000 lb.	8
1922	D.H. 34	,,	51′ 4″	39′ 0″	7,200 lb.	8
1923	Vickers Vulcan	,,	49′ 0″	38′ 0″	5,900 lb.	8
1922/6	H.P. W 8 B	,,	75′ 0″	60′ 1″	5½ tons	14
	,, W 8 F	,,	75′ 0″	60′ 1½″	5½ ,,	12
	,, W 9	,,	79′ 0″	60′ 4″	6½ ,,	14
	D.H. 50	,,	42′ 11″	30′ 5″	4,200 lb.	4
	Sea Eagle	flying-boat	46′ 0″	37′ 4″	5,800 lb.	6
1926	H.P. W 10	biplane	75′ 0″	60′ 4″	6 tons	14
	A.W. Argosy Mk. I	,,	90′ 5″	66′ 7″	8 ,,	20
	D.H. Hercules	,,	79′ 6″	55′ 6″	7 ,,	8
1928	Short Calcutta	flying-boat	93′ 0″	66′ 0″	9 ,,	15
1930/31	,, Scipio	,,	113′ 0″	78′ 6″	14 ,,	15
1931	H.P. 42 Hannibal (Eastern)	biplane	130′ 0″	86′ 6″	13 ,,	18/24
	H.P. Heracles (Western)	,,	130′ 0″	86′ 6″	13 ,,	38
	Avro (10) Achilles	monoplane	71′ 2″	47′ 6″	4½ ,,	8

Abbreviations: D.H. de Havilland: H.P. Handley Page: R.R. Rolls-Royce: P.W. Pratt & Whitney: Cons. Consolidated.

Crew and Stewards	Engines	Total H.P.	Average Cruising Speed in M.P.H.	Remarks
3	2 R.R. Eagle v	710	75	wood/fabric construction
1	1 A.S. Puma	230	95	,, ,,
1	1 R.R Eagle viii	350	90	,, ,,
	1 Napier Lion	450	110	,, ,,
1	1 R.R. Eagle vi	320	100	,, ,,
1:2	2 R.R. Eagle viii	710	95/100	,, ,,
1	1 Napier Lion	450	103	,, ,,
2+c.b.	1 ,, ,,	450	102	,, ,, (c.b.—cabin boy)
1	1 ,, ,,	450	103	wood/fabric construction
2	2 R.R. Eagle viii	710	85	,, ,,
2	1 R.R. Eagle 2 A.S. Puma	845	85	,, ,,
2	3 x A.S. Jaguar	1,125	100	,, ,,
	3 x Br. Jupiter	1,125	100	,, ,,
1	1 A.S. Puma	240	95	used later for charter work
1	1 R.R. Eagle ix	375	84	wood/fabric construction
2	2 x Napier Lion	900	90	,, ,,
2+1	3 x A.S. Jaguar	1,260	95	steel longeron and tubular wing bracing
2	3 x Br. Jupiter vi	1,260	95	,, ,,
3+1	3 x ,, xi F	1,455	80	mostly of metal construction
3+1	4 x ,, x FBM	2,220	100	,, ,,
3+1	4 x ,, xi F	1,960	90/95	Aluminium alloy and steel construction fabric covered wings and tail
3+2	4 x ,, X FBM	2,220	90/95	
2	3 x A.S. Lynx iv C	645	95	

A.S. Armstrong Siddeley: A.W. Armstrong Whitworth: Br. Bristol Aeroplane Co.:

Date	*Contractors' Name*	*Type*	*Span*	*Length*	*Max. Weight*	*Passenger Capacity*
1932/3	A.W. Atalanta	monoplane	90′ 0″	71′ 11″	9½ tons	10
1933	Westland Wessex	,,	57′ 6″	37′ 6″	6,300 lb.	4
1934/6	D.H. (86) Diana	biplane	64′ 6″	46′ 1″	4½ tons	10/14
	Short Scylla		113′ 0″	83′ 10″	14½ ,,	39
1935	Avro (652) Avalon	monoplane	56′ 6″	42′ 3″	3½ ,,	6
1936	Short 'C' Empire	flying-boat	114′ 0″	88′ 0″	20 ,,	24/17
1937	Short Mayo Composite (upper component)	seaplane	73′ 0″	50′ 11½″	9 tons	1,000 lb. (mail)
1938/9	Short 'C' S.33	flying-boat	114′ 0″	88′ 6″	23½ ,,	20
	Lockheed 10A		55′ 0″	38′ 7″	4½ ,,	10
	Lockheed 14		65′ 6″	44′ 2″	8 ,,	14
	A.W. Ensign		123′ 0″	114′ 0″	23 ,,	27/40
	D.H. Frobisher		105′	71′ 6″	13 ,,	22
1940	Short 'G'	flying-boat	134′ 3″	103′ 2″	33 ,,	40
	Lockheed Lodestar		65′ 6″	49′ 10″	9 ,,	11/14
1941	D.H. Flamingo		70′ 0″	50′ 7″	7¾ ,,	20
1941/2	Boeing 314A	flying-boat	152′ 0″	106′ 0″	38 ,,	40
	Cons. Liberator		110′	66′ 0″	22/25 ,,	11/16
	Cons. Catalina	flying-boat	104′	65′ 1″	14 ,,	6
1942/3	Douglas Dakota		95′ 0″	64′ 5½″	11/12½ ,,	13/21
1943	Short Hythe	flying-boat	112′ 9½″	84′ 6″	25 ,,	22

Abbreviations: D.H. de Havilland: H.P. Handley Page: R.R. Rolls-Royce: P.W. Pratt & Whitney: Cons. Consolidated.

Crew and Stewards	Engines	Total H.P.	Average Cruising Speed in M.P.H.	Remarks
2	4 x A.S. Double Mongoose (later Serval)	1,520	120	Cantilever monoplane
2	3 x A.S. Genet Major I C	420	100	used for charter work
2	4 x D.H. Gipsy vi	800	141	
3+2	4 x Br. Jup. x FBM	2,220	90	
2	2 x A.S. Cheetah ix	680	165	Subsequent aircraft were monoplanes
3+2	4 x Br. Pegasus X C	3,680	164/200 max.	All metal except for flying control surfaces
2	4 x Napier Rapier	1,300	182/212	All metal except for flying control surfaces
3+2	4 x Br. Perseus xii C	3,600	164	
2	2 x P.W. Wasp. Jun.	800	176/186	
2/3	2 x P.W. Hornet	1,500	201/223	
3+2	(*a*) 4 x A.S. Tiger ix	3,700	170/205	
	(*b*) 4 x Wright Cyclone	4,400	160/210	
2+1	4 x D.H. Gipsy xii	2,100	193	All wood
5+2	4 x Bristol Hercules iv	5,400	180/213	
2	2 x P.W. Twin Wasp	2,400	250/277	Similar to L.14—slightly greater length
3	2 x Bristol Perseus xii C	1,780	174/239	
8+3	4 x Wright Cyclone	6,000	188/210	
4/5	4 x P. & W. Twin Wasp	4,800	180/212	
3	2 x P. & W. Twin Wasp	2,400	135/max. 190	
3/4+1	2 x P. & W. Twin Wasp	2,400	207/230	
5+1	4 x Bristol Pegasus	4,200	156/213	

A .S. Armstrong Siddeley: A.W. Armstrong Whitworth: Br. Bristol Aeroplane Co.:

Date	*Contractor's Name*	*Type*	*Span*	*Length*	*Max. Weight*	*Passenger Capacity*
1944	Avro York		102′	78′	30 tons	19/24
1945	Avro Lancastrian		102′	76′ 10″	29 ,,	6/8 (13 BSAA)
1946	H.P. Halton		103′ 8″	73′ 7″	29 ,,	9/13
	Short Plymouth	flying-boat	112′ 9½″	86′ 3″	26 ,,	22
1947/8	Lockheed/Constellation 049		123′	95′ 1″	44 ,,	43/60
	,, ,, 749		123′	95′ 3″	48 ,,	30/60
1949	Short Solent 2	flying-boat	118′	88′ 6″	35 ,,	34/39
1949/50	Canadair Argonaut		117′ 6″	93′ 7½″	36½ ,,	40/54
	Boeing Stratocruiser		141′ 3″	110′ 4″	65 ,,	40/81
1950/52	H.P. Hermes 4		113′	96′ 10″	38½ ,,	40/54
1952/3	D.H. Comet 1		115′	93′	48 ,,	36
1954/5	Vickers Viscount		93′ 8½″	81′ 10″	28 ,,	40/48
1955/6	Bristol Britannia 312		142′ 3½″	124′ 3″	80 ,,	48/111
	,, ,, 102		142′ 3½″	114′	69 ,,	40/92
1957	Douglas DC 7C		127′ 6″	112′ 3″	64 ,,	72/81
1958	D.H. Comet 4		114′ 9″	111′ 6″	69½ ,,	40/81
	Boeing 707		142′ 5″	152′ 11″	132 ,,	66/180
	Vickers VC. 10		140′	158′	133½ ,,	52/146

Abbreviations: D.H. de Havilland: H.P. Handley Page: R.R. Rolls-Royce: P.W. Pratt & Whitney: Cons. Consolidated.

Crew and Stewards	*Engines*	*Total H.P.*	*Average Cruising Speed in M.P.H.*	*Remarks*
4	4 x R.R. Merlin	5,040	200 (max. 290)	
4+1	4 x R.R. Merlin	5,040	265/310	
5+1	4 x Bristol Hercules Mk. 100	6,700	210/320	
5+2	4 x P.W. Twin Wasp	4,800	175/238	
5+2	4 x Wright Cyclone BA	8,800	300/340	
4+3	4 x ,, ,, BDI	10,000	328/350	
5+3	4 x Bristol Hercules	6,700	260/282	
4+3	4 x R.R. Merlin 626	7,040	276/302	
6+4	4 x P.W. R. 4360	14,000	340/375	
5+2	4 x Bristol Hercules 763	8,400	300/357	
5+2	4 x D.H. Ghost	20,000 lbs. thrust	490	Turbo-jet
2+2	4 x R.R. Dart	6,960	311/331	Turbo-prop.
5+4	4 x Bristol Proteus 755	16,352	390 normal high speed cruise	,, ,,
4+4	4 x Bristol Proteus 705	15,200	361 ,, ,,	,, ,,
5+3	4 x Wright 3350	13,600	346/406	
4+2	4 x R.R. Avon 29	42,000 lbs. thrust	514	Turbo-jet
4+4/6	4 x R.R. Conway	64,000 lbs. thrust	525/570	,, ,,
4+4/6	4 x R.R. Conway	64,000 lbs. thrust	525/577	,, ,,

A.S. Armstrong Siddeley: A.W. Armstrong Whiteworth: Br. Bristol Aeroplane Co.:

A SHORT BIBLIOGRAPHY

A Million Miles in the Air by Captain Gordon P. Olley (Hodder & Stoughton 1934)

Sefton Brancker by Norman MacMillan (Heinemann 1935)

Pioneer Pilot by William Armstrong (Blandford Press 1952)

Immortal Era by Lloyd C. Ifould (Adanac Press, Montreal, Canada, 1948)

Early Birds by Alfred Instone (Western Mail & Echo 1938)

Empire of the Air by Viscount Templewood (Sir Samuel Hoare) (Collins 1957)

India by Air by Sir Samuel Hoare (Longmans, Green 1927)

A Flying Visit to the Middle East by Sir Samuel Hoare (Cambridge University Press 1925)

Brackles by Frida H. Brackley (Putnam 1952)

Australia and Back by Sir Alan Cobham (Black 1926)

Twenty Thousand Miles in a Flying Boat by Sir Alan Cobham (Harrap 1930)

Skyways by Sir Alan Cobham (Nisbett 1925)

Aircraft of the Royal Air Force by Owen Thetford (Putnam 1957)

The Log of a Merchant Airman by Capt. John Lock and John Creasy (Stanley Paul)

Nationalisation in Practice by John Longhurst (Temple Press 1949)

Aerial Transport by G. Holt Thomas (Hodder & Stoughton 1920)

A History of Flying by C. H. Gibbs-Smith (Batsford 1953)

Into the Wind by J. C. W. Reith (Hodder & Stoughton 1949)

Passengers, Parcels and Panthers by John W. R. Taylor (Dobson)

Wings for Tomorrow by J. W. R. Taylor and M. F. Allward (Ian Allan)

The Poetry of Flight by Stella Wolfe Murray (Heath Cranton 1925)

Unsung Heroes of the Air by A. H. Narracott (Muller 1943)

Second World War III and IV by Winston Churchill (Cassell 1950)

The War in the Air by Walter Raleigh (Clarendon Press 1922)

British Air Mails by N. C. Baldwin (Francis J. Field)

Merchant Airmen (H.M. Stationery Office)

Qantas Aeriana by E. A. Crome (Francis J. Field)

INDEX

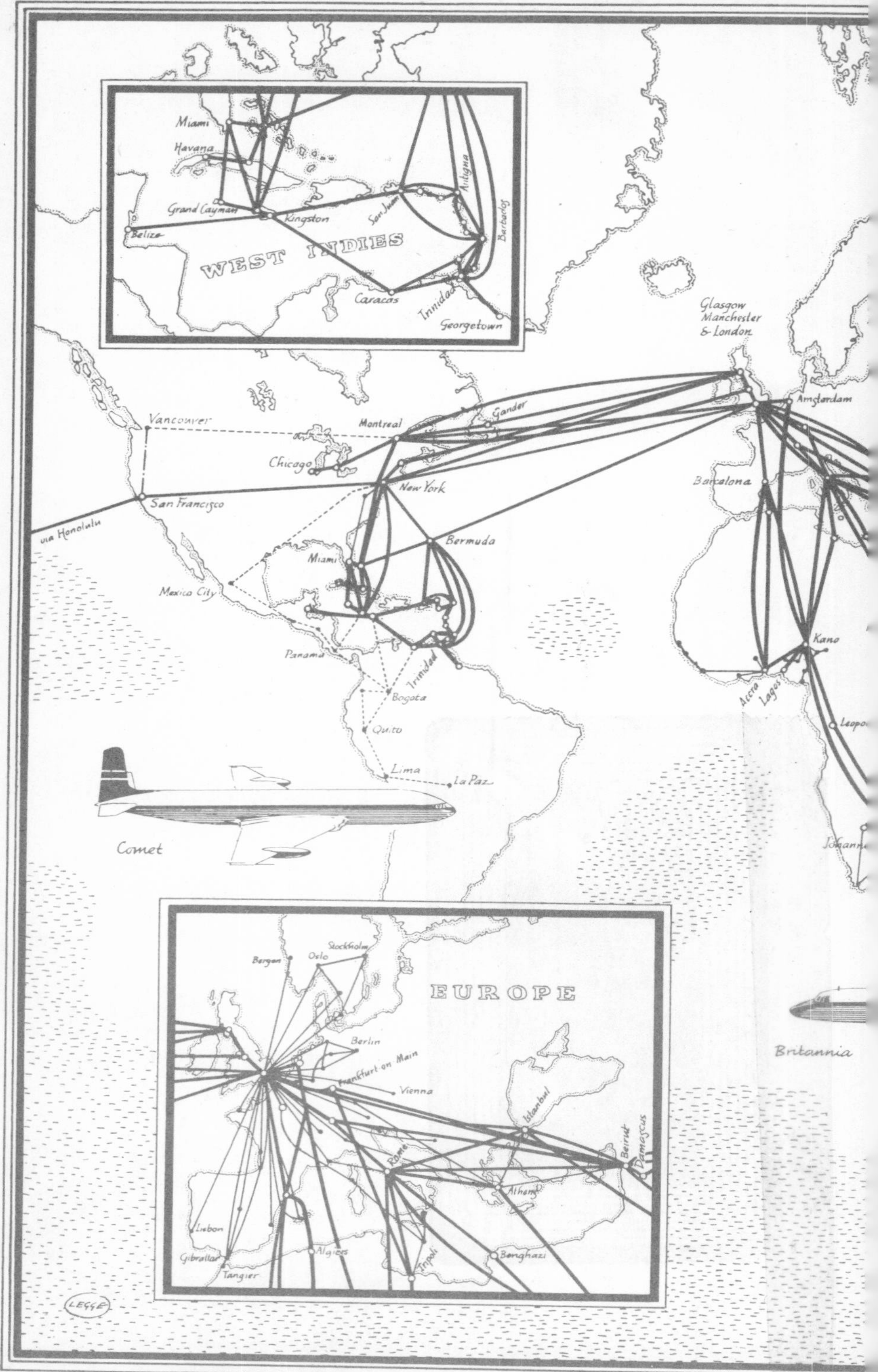

Miami
Havana
Grand Cayman
Kingston
San Juan
Antigua
Barbados
Belize
WEST INDIES
Caracas
Trinidad
Georgetown
Glasgow
Manchester
& London
Amsterdam
Gander
Vancouver
Montreal
Chicago
New York
Barcelona
San Francisco
via Honolulu
Bermuda
Miami
Mexico City
Kano
Panama
Trinidad
Bogota
Accra
Lagos
Quito
Lima
La Paz
Comet
EUROPE
Bergen
Oslo
Stockholm
Berlin
Frankfurt on Main
Vienna
Istanbul
Beirut
Damascus
Rome
Athens
Lisbon
Gibraltar
Tangier
Algiers
Tripoli
Benghazi
Britannia
LEGGE